CLEVELAND

A Metropolitan Reader

CLEVELAND

A Metropolitan Reader

Edited by W. Dennis Keating,

Norman Krumholz, and David C. Perry

THE KENT STATE UNIVERSITY PRESS

Kent, Ohio, & London, England

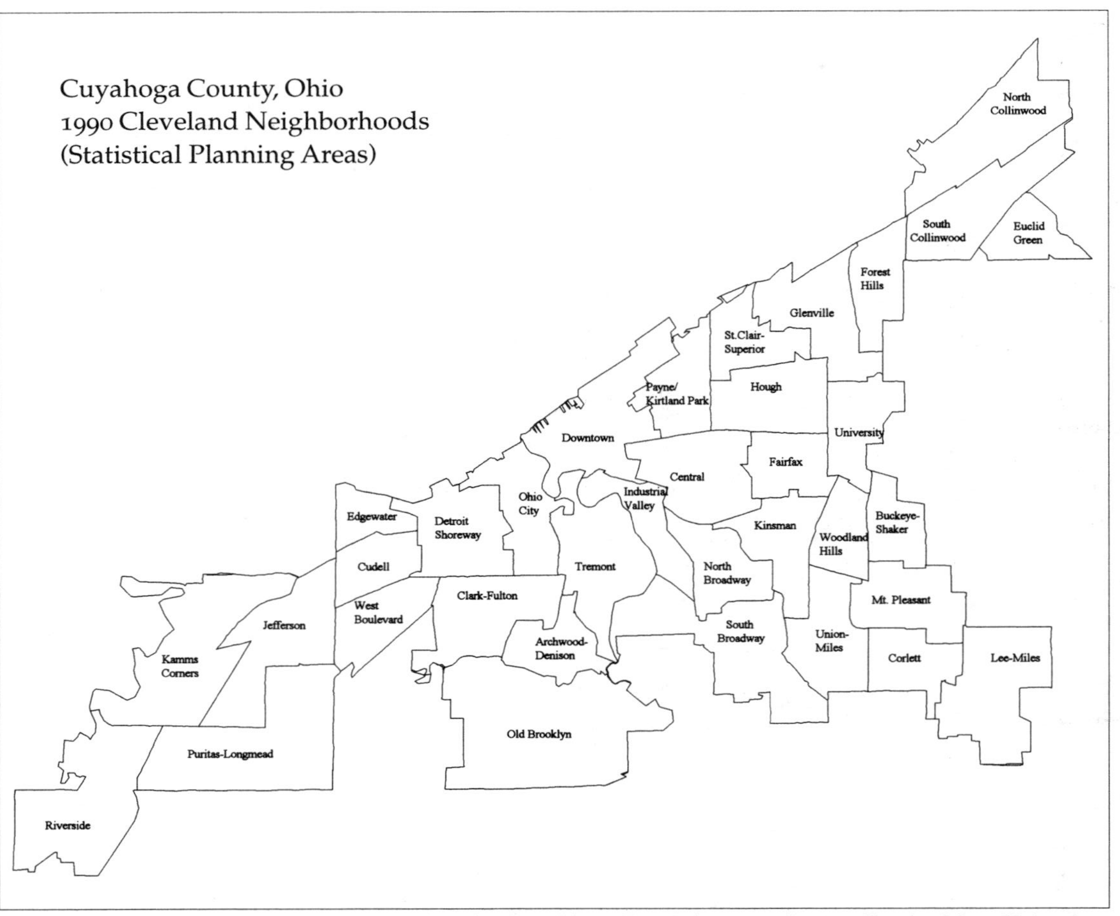

Source: 1990 TIGER/Line Census Files. Prepared by Northern Ohio & Data Information Service, Cleveland State University.

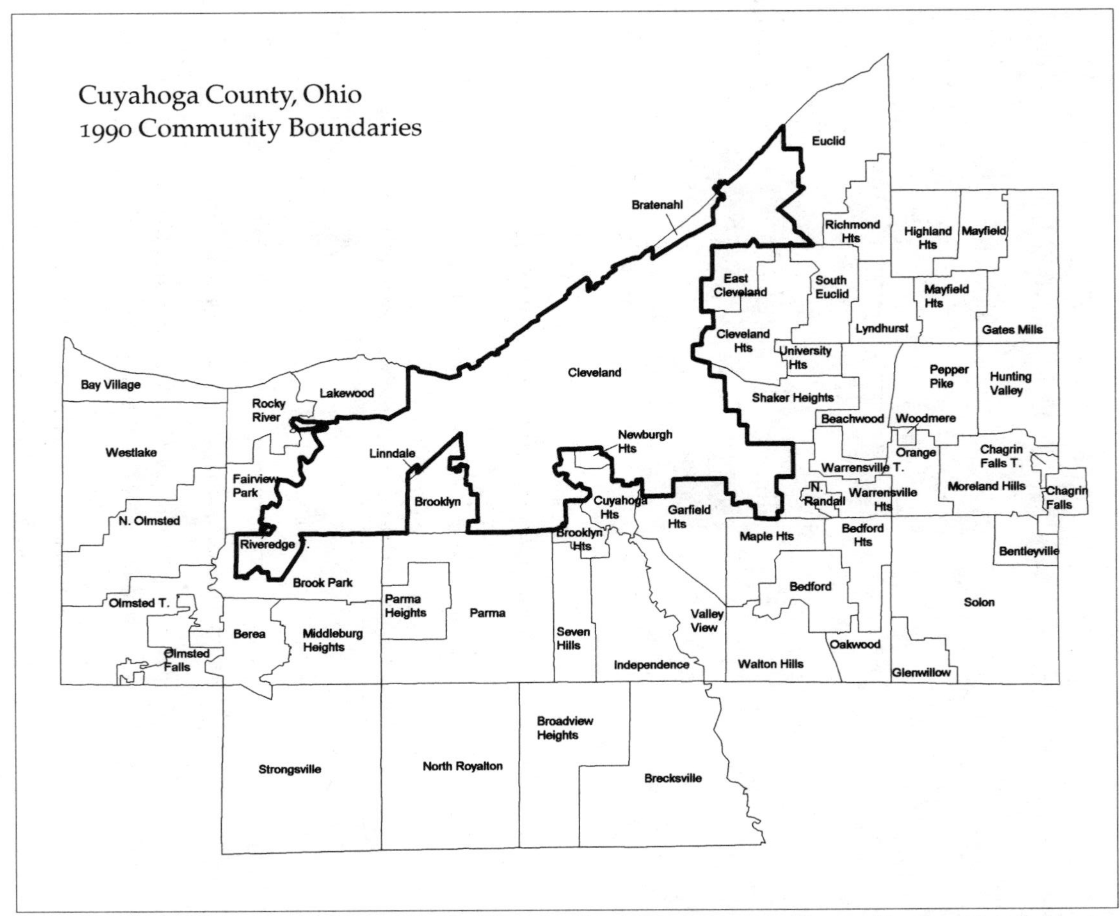

Source: 1990 TIGER/Line Census Files. Prepared by Northern Ohio & Data Information Service, Cleveland State University.

Library of Congress Catalog Card Number 95-5535
ISBN 0-87338-492-X
Manufactured in the United States of America

10 09 08 07 06 6 5 4 3

Library of Congress Cataloging-in-Publication Data

Cleveland : a metropolitan reader / edited by W. Dennis Keating,
Norman Krumholz, and David C. Perry.
p. cm.
Includes bibliographical references and index.
ISBN 0-87338-492-X (pbk.) ∞
1. Cleveland (Ohio)—Social conditions. 2. Cleveland (Ohio)—Economic conditions.
3. Cleveland (Ohio)—Politics and Government.
I. Keating, W. Dennis (William Dennis). II. Krumholz, Norman.
III. Perry, David C.
HN80.C6C57 1995 95-5535
306'.09771'32—dc 20

British Library Cataloging-in-Publication data are available.

Contents

Acknowledgments

With its comprehensive emphasis on the political economy, social development, and history of Cleveland, this book represents an important part of the academic mission of its editors and the college in which we teach. The Maxine Goodman College of Urban Affairs is dedicated to the teaching, as well as the research, of materials that enhance our understanding of the issues and conditions that comprise the future and the past of Cleveland. We certainly owe a debt of gratitude to the college and its dean, David Sweet, for providing generous support and the overall collegial atmosphere in which to develop and ultimately produce a project like this. A substantial portion of our work was conducted under the auspices of the Albert A. Levin Chair of Urban Studies and Public Service, and we thank Maxine Levin and the members of the Levin Chair Committee for their dedicated support of research on Cleveland.

This book is intended as an introductory text on Cleveland. Its inspiration in part has been the interest of our students at Cleveland State University and the lack of a comprehensive reader like this. We wish to thank the many Clevelanders who agreed to be interviewed, including the late Paul A. Walter, Esq., and former mayors Carl B. Stokes, Ralph J. Perk, and Dennis J. Kucinich. Most importantly, we want to acknowledge our wonderful relationship. Editing a book, under the best of circumstances, is a complex and difficult process. In this case, the difficulties have been minimized through a truly unique and comfortable process of learning and working together. At various stages in its development, the book has benefited greatly from the assistance of Kathleen Mooney, John Shannon, Martin Sokolich, and Karen Malec. Word processing assistance was ably provided by Ellen Baumgardner and Jeanie Stearns. All of this has been significantly augmented by the efficient and thoughtful editorial guidance of the staff at The Kent State University Press, including John T. Hubbell, Director; Julia J. Morton, Senior Editor; and Linda Cuckovich, Assistant Editor.

W. Dennis Keating
Norman Krumholz
David C. Perry

Introduction: Lessons From Cleveland

David C. Perry

IN PART this book is an outgrowth of a series of the Albert A. Levin Lectures in Urban Studies and Public Service held at Cleveland State University in 1990 and 1991. Over these two years we, at the Maxine Goodman Levin College of Urban Affairs of Cleveland State University, invited urban scholars from around the nation to come to the Levin College of Urban Affairs and lecture on the contemporary state of the American city. One set of lectures in particular grabbed the interest and imagination of the university community and the public at large: titled "Changing Urban Practice: Lessons from Cleveland," the lectures all recounted special practices in planning, policy, and economic development which had changed the city for the better and had instructive value for urban practice in other cities as well.

Each of these lectures implied a broader theme—namely, that the city, at all stages of its formation, its successful eras and its times of decline, represents the process of American urbanization in general. To study a mature city like Cleveland, located in the geographic midwest of the country and founded about the temporal "center" of the nation's Euro-history, was also to study a city at the "center" of the urban experience itself—with all the economic, political, and racial/cultural change this centrality implies.[1]

The process of urban change or the urban experience in Cleveland, therefore, provides us with lessons. It is this theme of "lessons from Cleveland" that forms the structure and the rationale for selecting each of the articles in this book. From Cleveland, one of the oldest major cities in the United States, we have much to learn about the particulars of its formation, about the political, economic, and social relations that determine the practices of its leaders and its people.

While our authors will often refer to Cleveland as the "city," the readings included here will just as likely be directed at the entire region—the city and its suburbs. The book is therefore subtitled "A Metropolitan Reader." The introductory section of the book fleshes out this notion of "lessons"; if, as the first chapter in part one suggests, the United States is a nation of cities, then Cleveland is a clear and instructive example of this urban characterization.

While not inclusive, privatism, economic restructuring, and ethnicity and race are characteristics of social formation that represent well the American urban political economy. The first section of this book isolates these features of American life and discusses their development in Cleveland, suggesting that the ways they have been played out there tell us as much about America as they do about the city and its surrounding metropolitan area.

The second section of the book, History: Growth to Decline, builds upon these themes, reinforcing some and adding others. Cleveland has a history of constantly making and remaking itself. Its history is not an inexorably linear traverse across time; rather, it is a dynamic, sometimes fitful, sometimes transcendent adventure of urban change and development. What was made, for example, into a mercantile outpost and Great Lakes port was not so much "unmade" in later years as it was remade as a new industrial center, the productive efficiencies of which literally transcended the old economic order, giving the private city a new and more complex economic character.

The history of Cleveland is also the history of what one turn-of-the-century observer called "the city of immigrants."[2] Cleveland, we learn, is a city—indeed a region—that, by the mid-1880s, was already a destination place for large numbers of European immigrants. The city soon segregated into ethnic neighborhoods which served, and continue to do so, as geographic signposts of the city. The suburbs are among the oldest and most storied in the United States. Historians Carol Poh Miller and Robert A. Wheeler paint a picture of Cleveland, city and suburbs, that clearly mirrors the social and economic transformation of American cities in general.

The third section, Economy: Roots to Restructuring, provides a more detailed discussion of the economic relations of American urban life. The approach taken here is that the structure of the urban economy is defined and redefined by shifts in the dominant means of production—the mercantile, manufacturing, and service sectors of the economy. As a mature midwestern city, the economic *re*structuring of Cleveland is a continuous process directed by the marketplace and influenced by local political, economic, and sociocultural interests. While this section does address the early economic history of Cleveland, most is dedicated to describing, in some detail, the last century of economic change. During the early years of the twentieth century, Cleveland emerged as one of the national centers of manufacturing activity, attracting hundreds of thousands of new residents; on the eve of the Great Depression, the city was the sixth largest urban center in the United States. While the manufacturing base of the region carried Cleveland through the Depression and the rapidly changing economic era after World War II, social transformations of the 1960s and 1970s were quickly matched in the late seventies by a dramatic and irreversible restructuring of the Cleveland area's economic base. The region suffered a precipitous loss of manufacturing jobs, and, today, the service sector is a dominant new means of production, redefining the structure of the regional economy.

The fourth section of the book is titled Politics: Conflict and Reform, and the readings suggest an urban politics filled with conflict and characterized by reform. At the heart of the conflict in most American cities have been battles either for economic control of urban resources or between the races. The history of politics in Cleveland is no exception. It is apparent that, while Cleveland politics is filled with economic and racial conflict, it has also exhibited exemplary reform tendencies. These tendencies are most evident in the career of, arguably, Cleveland's first political reformer, Mayor Tom Johnson. In his essay on Johnson, Frederic Howe offers a primer on the Progressive practices of Johnson, suggesting that during his tenure as mayor (1901–9) Johnson was the epitome of urban reform politics.

An essay by Todd Swanstrom discusses the politics of fiscal crisis in Cleveland in the late 1970s where, in a monumental power struggle, the banks of Cleveland foreclosed on the city's unpaid municipal bonds, forcing the city into default. We learn that the default was caused by more than economic pressures. Swanstrom makes the case for reassessing this period in light of the political struggle between the bankers and the new mayor, a self-styled "populist" and reformer.

A second reading by Christopher Wye, with a postscript by Norman Krumholz, chronicles the rise of race politics in Cleveland, suggesting that early on Cleveland was a center of integrationist reform politics. As the twentieth century unfolded, however, racial harmony broke down and, with it, progressive racial politics. With the terrifying race riots in Hough and Glenville in the mid-1960s came the election of the first black mayor in any major American city, Carl Stokes.

The readings in the fifth section of the book, collected under the heading of Governance: Public and Private, build upon the patterns discussed in the previous section. Here the authors suggest that there is a close, often conflictual, relationship between the agencies of public governance and the private sector. In one essay, longtime political observer Roldo Bartimole traces the history of this relationship through his discussion of the successive political regimes of Cleveland mayors, beginning with Ralph Locher in the early 1960s. In Bartimole's essay it becomes evident that one cannot understand executive political power in Cleveland without understanding the influence of the region's large corporations.

A second reading in this section, written by Myron Magnet of *Fortune* magazine, seems to be the proof of Bartimole's analytic pudding, as Magnet recounts how the leaders of the largest corporations in Cleveland banded together to form a private sector organization called Cleveland Tomorrow, which in turn was used to amass large amounts of capital for important development projects. Cleveland Tomorrow's leadership also directly intervened in the political world by selecting, financing, and electing its own mayoral candidate. Such activities by this self-styled "conspiracy" are evidence, in Magnet's view, of how the private sector has turned the city around.

Keating, Krumholz, and Perry describe another example of conflict over urban governance: the century-long struggle of the private utility to take control of the city's public-owned electric utility company. In their essay the authors describe example after example of unrelenting pressure by the private sector to force the city to give up its electric utility, Muny Light, which stood as a lasting legacy of the Progressive politics of Tom Johnson.

In 1916 Herbert Miller introduced his book *Schools and the Immigrant* by suggesting that Cleveland had become a "city of immigrants," because only five other cities in the United States had more than one hundred thousand in population registering a higher percentage of foreign-born residents than Cleveland. These ethnic groups, coming from literally scores of countries, according to Edward Miggins in his article "Between Spires and Stacks: The People and Neighborhoods of Cleveland," settled in a geographic plethora of ethnically defined neighborhoods. The city was less a melting pot than a mosaic with clearly delineated neighborhoods surrounded by more ethnically mixed and materially affluent suburbs.[3]

In the section Neighborhoods: City and Suburbs, the authors trace and redefine this historic spatialization of race, ethnicity, and class in the American city. Edward Miggins discusses the migration of ethnics and then African Americans into the neighborhoods of Cleveland. He traces the deterioration of these neighborhoods and the post–World War II suburbanization that cut the city's population literally in half. Claudia Coulton and Julian Chow pick up where Miggins leaves off and look more closely at the conditions of neighborhood decline in light of the profile of poverty that has come to characterize much of Cleveland.

As poverty has become more pervasive and persistent, the problems of housing for this population have also become more complex. Mittie Olion Chandler discusses the politics and policy problems facing public housing in Cleveland and claims that the politics of public housing is being played out in a climate of increased fear and a growing sense of failure—fear and racism over the apparent increasing intractability of the structurally impoverished and failure and futility over the plight of the homeless and other disadvantaged urbanites. All this occurs against a backdrop of decline of the city's housing in general, writes Thomas E. Bier in "Housing Dynamics of the Cleveland Area, 1950–2000." He paints a grim picture of problems in federally subsidized housing, insurance redlining, and deliberate destruction of neighborhoods through highway location. He goes on to explain how such policies and suburbanization have combined to vitiate the housing stock in some parts of Cleveland.

The articles presented in the Neighborhoods section all serve as an important introduction to the next section of the book, Race and Discrimination. As almost every previous article in this book suggests, race and racial conflict have played an important role in Cleveland's history. In fact, it can be argued that, if privatism is the dominant ideology of the American city, race is the central feature of political struggle. The three articles in this section trace some of the key patterns of this struggle. Kenneth Kusmer outlines the early settlement pattern of African American Clevelanders, leading to the construction of the first major black ghetto in the early twentieth century. William Nelson discusses black politics in Cleveland as a new practice led by new leaders of what we call "liberal" politics. He identifies individuals as part of a "new breed" of black liberal Democratic politicians, all of whom appear to be substantially different from each other. This analysis includes a discussion of Carl Stokes, power broker and former City Council president George Forbes, and new "reform" mayor Michael White.

Kusmer's and Nelson's essays are the building blocks for Dennis Keating's piece on the pervasive patterns of residential racial segregation. "Open Housing in Metropolitan Cleveland" describes the racial dynamics of the housing market in the city, leaving the reader with a better understanding of how these patterns of segregation are the tragic legacy of the trends discussed by Kusmer and the unresolved problems of the reform policies of black political leaders discussed by Nelson.

The policy agenda for Cleveland is addressed more generally in the last section of the book, Urban Redevelopment: Policy, Planning, and Prospects. Political leaders, whether they are African American or white, have a broad range of problems facing them and just as broad a range of alternative policy approaches from which to choose when attacking these problems. It is these policy "lessons from Cleveland" that occupy the attention of the authors in this section.

In keeping with its history as a center of reform—both political reform and private sector intervention—present-day Cleveland continues to offer examples of success and innovation. First, in planning, Norman Krumholz, former planning director of Cleveland (1969–79), offers a model of "equity planning." During his tenure as planning director, Krumholz led an initiative that put urban planning on the side of the poor and working class with the objective of providing the residents of Cleveland's declining neighborhoods with more choices for positive change.

Richard A. Shatten, former executive director of Cleveland Tomorrow, offers a "blueprint" for organizing corporate urban capital to intervene on a long-term and highly integrated basis in the problem-solving process in a city. And Christopher Warren, a former community organizer and director of a neighborhood-based housing development organization, describes the process whereby poor and working-class residents took control of the housing development process in their neighborhoods and undertook the complex and financially difficult process of reclaiming abandoned buildings for home ownership.

Keating, Krumholz, and Metzger analyze the pluses and minuses of such public-private partnerships in Cleveland and are far less sanguine than most over the balance of benefits that accrue to the public in the operation of such development partnerships. Their essay provides a telling comparative analysis of the partnership approach.

In the final essay on redevelopment, Phillip Clay discusses the changes in Cleveland as part of what he calls "transformation," or the new urban dynamic. Indirectly, his discussion serves as a summary of the previous readings in this section, suggesting that all of those approaches have something to offer the city and that, together, what they describe are all parts of this new urban dynamic—the affirmative "transformation" of American cities. But, says Clay, Cleveland is far less likely to be transformed than are other, more economically secure, less racially troubled cities.

The underlying assumption of all the readings, whether directly asserted or implied, is that the patterns of change, the transformations in Cleveland from 1796 to the present, are evidence of urban change in America generally. Each of these readings is not only a lesson about Cleveland but is also a lesson *from* Cleveland about us—all of us who live in urban America.

Notes

1. Carol Poh Miller and Robert Wheeler, *Cleveland: A Concise History, 1796–1990* (Bloomington: Indiana University Press, 1990), 1–3.

2. Herbert Miller, *Schools and the Immigrant* (Philadelphia: William F. Fell, 1916).

3. Edward Miggins and Mary Morgenthaler, "The Ethnic Mosaic: The Settlement of Cleveland by the New Immigrants and Migrants," in *The Birth of Modern Cleveland, 1865–1930*, ed. Thomas Campbell and Edward Miggins (Cleveland: Western Reserve Historical Society and the Cleveland Public Library, 1988).

Part 1

CLEVELAND

Composite American Urbanism

Introduction

FOR THE EDITORS of this book, Cleveland is not an object of temporal curiosity or a select or special urban phenomenon. Rather, we view Cleveland as more general than select, a community with a history so representative of urban life in America as to be a heuristic, teaching all of us not only about the city of Cleveland and its environs but also about ourselves and the particular city or community we come from. Historians Carol Poh Miller and Robert Wheeler suggest that Cleveland "is a composite of the issues and movements that generally constitute American urban history."[1] This part of the book embraces the Miller and Wheeler thesis, providing an overview of the history and some of the key characteristics of urban social formation that serve as a signature of the American city in general and of Cleveland in particular.

Central among these characteristics are privatism, economic restructuring, and ethnicity and race. The following chapter traces the practices of privatism[2] in Cleveland from the arrival of Moses Cleaveland, who as an investor and representative of the Connecticut Land Company established the first settlement as part of a land speculation strategy, to the present-day practices of property speculation most dramatically portrayed in the array of new high-rise office buildings lining the streets of the downtown core. Cleveland was and remains a good example of the importance of property to the urban development process in America.

The chapter is also concerned with the long term patterns of economic restructuring found in Cleveland. The economic transformation of the region over the past two centuries is just as instructive as the city's privatistic history of land speculation and entrepreneurship. Indeed, structural changes in Cleveland's economy, as it moved from mercantile to industrial and, now, to struggling "post-industrial" economy, have served as bellwether conditions of American urbanism. Cleveland is a clear example of the ways in which American cities have been both beneficiaries and victims of global, as well as national, changes in capitalism.

The remainder of the chapter introduces the reader to the long and storied history of Cleveland's ethnic and racial diversity: a city that quickly became an "ethnic mosaic" during the nineteenth century has turned into a place of racial segregation in the twentieth century. The notion that the American city can be a "melting pot" has been tried and challenged in Cleveland.

Notes

1. Carol Poh Miller and Robert Wheeler, *Cleveland: A Concise History, 1796–1990* (Bloomington: Indiana University Press, 1990), 1.

2. For a more detailed introduction to the notion of privatism, see Stephen Elkin, *City and Regime in the American Republic* (Chicago: University of Chicago Press, 1987), chap. 1; Sam Bass Warner, *The Private City: Philadelphia in Three Periods of Growth* (Philadelphia: University of Pennsylvania Press, 1968), chap. 1.

Cleveland: Journey to Maturity

David C. Perry

In early March 1982, the staff in Mayor George Voinovich's office was delighted: for the second time in recent years Cleveland had been declared an All America City. National recognition of this sort so soon after the city's 1978 bankruptcy and the long-term economic decline that had prompted pundits to dub the city "the mistake by the lake" was welcome news to Voinovich—the hand-picked candidate of a reinvigorated civic elite. But what did the National League of Cities mean by declaring Cleveland an "All America City"? The proclamation cited the city for its "enactment of major government reform, streamlining City Council and implementation of a comprehensive fiscal recovery strategy, and restoration of a downtown performing arts and entertainment complex."[1] The mayor interpreted this award as recognition of a process in which "public and private sectors continue to work together to solve [the city's] problems."[2] Other observers had long viewed Cleveland as a city representative of much, if not all, of America and the nation's history of urban change. The purpose of this introduction is not to provide the city with another boosterish accolade—whether Cleveland is an All America City is not as interesting as the notion that the city is representative of the full panoply of experiences comprising American urban change. As one of the nation's oldest middle-size cities, Cleveland's early existence is rooted in its emergence as a postcolonial outpost of economic extraction and land investment—a new version of what historian Sam Bass Warner has called the "private city."[3] In the nineteenth century, Cleveland was at the forefront of national development, as break-bulk cities such as Cleveland exhibited structural entrepreneurship in the shift from a mercantile to an industrial economic base. This shift attracted legions of ethnic immigrants, as well as new migrants, both African American and Appalachian white, from the South. Twentieth-century Cleveland has been no less instructive as an example of urban change: the city has evidenced a long and storied period of racial and ethnic unrest and economic decline and restructuring.

Thus, although the notion of Cleveland as the All America City may be excessively hyperbolic, viewing Cleveland as a highly representative example of the dominant features of American urbanism is reasonable. A more general version of this thesis has been put forth by historians Carol Poh Miller and Robert Wheeler, who suggest that "Cleveland . . . is a composite of the issues and movements that generally constitute American urban history."[4] In joining Miller and Wheeler I do not want to leave the impression that "it all happened" in Cleveland, but I will try to show that certain salient features of American urbanism are key to the city's development. Among them are, first, the American city as first and foremost a product of profit making[5] or urbanism as the communal representative of the national ideology of privatism;[6] second, the city as the spatial center of the structuring and restructuring of the national economy;[7] and third, the city as contentious, not always a melting pot of races and ethnicities.[8]

The urban political economy of the United States, though not reducible to these characteristics of social formation—privatism, restructuring, ethnicity, and race—is certainly well represented by such features. The particular way each is found in the history of Cleveland tells us much about the development of cities in the nation, as well as about Cleveland.

The Propertied Roots of Privatism: The Case of the Western Reserve and Early Cleveland

THE PRIVATE CITY

After describing, with some emotional effect, the twentieth-century city as a "picture of endlessly repeated failures," historian Sam Bass Warner, in his classic urban treatise *The Private City*, goes on to suggest: "The twentieth century failure of urban America to create a humane environment is the story of an enduring tradition of privatism in a changing world. The story is a complicated one. It doesn't separate itself nicely into good and evil, times of victory and times of defeat; rather it is the story of ordinary men and commonplace events that have accumulated over time to produce the great wealth and great failure of twentieth-century American cities. Moreover the story is a long one, reaching back to the eighteenth century, when our tradition first was set in its modern form."[9]

This tradition of privatism, ingrained in the American fabric of development from the beginning, encapsulates the ideology and experience of the earliest European immigrants. In the main, immigration to the New World was not a spiritual journey but a material one. The new lands of America represented a potential that Europe could not supply—access to property and material wealth. The journey to America was, from the beginning, a search for "streets paved with gold." As Warner puts it, "The first purpose of the citizen is the private search for wealth; the goal of a city is to be a community of private money makers."[10]

From the colonial beginnings, the streets of the American city and the property and buildings abutting them were commodified—placing property rights at the center of urban life and politics. Such a trend was so important that it moved historian Howard Chudacoff to observe: "Americans have always considered the management and disposal of land and buildings as sacred civil rights."[11]

Often the practices of privatism and its embodiment in the property exchanges created a politics of urban development that presaged the highly innovative speculative practices of urban development. The early frontier towns were an extension of the property-righteous development of the colonial era. They came into existence as an enterprise of the process leading to "the private ownership of property, but with a difference: Most of the new towns were not developed by settlers coming to untitled and previously unowned land (unowned, that is, by Europeans). They came, instead, to land that was owned by land-development companies. These land-development companies were, in effect, wholesalers of land. That the western lands should be settled was national policy, and Congress sold these lands in great blocks to privately owned land companies with an understanding that the companies, in turn, would re-sell to small buyers."[12]

The "wholesaling" of land was a principal practice of early privatistic urban development, and it was extremely profitable.[13] More particularly, this practice meant that Congress sold great tracts of the western wilderness to private land companies, which in turn platted the land, packaged it as "cities," and resold it to individual buyers. As a result, both the government and the land companies made money off the "city land" often before a shovel had been turned or a full-time resident had arrived. From the very beginning, therefore, frontier development set in motion the politics of speculative urban development, characterized by boosterism, land transfers, and the psychology of risk and "quick profits."[14] As one newspaper advertisement put it: "Would you make money? (asked an advertisement luring settlers to Columbus, Nebraska). . . . Find then the site of a city and buy the farm that it is to be built on. How many regret the non-purchase of that lot in New York, that block in Buffalo, that quarter section in Omaha? Once these properties could be bought for a song . . . fortunes (are to be made) that way."[15]

THE WESTERN RESERVE

There is perhaps no better example of the speculative practice of early urban development than the first frontier activity in the Western Reserve that resulted in the siting and early settlement of what was to become the city of Cleveland. The Western Reserve was a piece of land of over 2.5 million acres, stretching 120 miles west into the state of Ohio from the Pennsylvania border and 80 miles south from Lake Erie. The Reserve was originally part of the lands claimed as part of the colony of Connecticut. After the revolutionary war, Connecticut, in an agreement with Congress, joined other former colonies in giving up its claim to noncontiguous frontier properties, with the exception of the Western Reserve. For a long time the Reserve had been known as "New Connecticut," but soon it was called the "Western Reserve" of Connecticut.

FRONTIER AS LAND SPECULATION

During the early 1790s Connecticut sought unsuccessfully to arrive at some plan for the Reserve. But by the middle of the decade the land remained unplanned, "untitled and (especially) unprofitable."[16] In 1795, the General Assembly of Connecticut joined most other states in a move to add quick monies to the state treasury by placing the millions of Reserve acres on the market. The land was purchased within weeks by a newly formed company called the Connecticut Land Company for the promised sum of $1.2 million. One of the members of the board organized to manage the company was Moses Cleaveland, a veteran of the revolutionary war who had continued to dabble in the state militia after the war, eventually rising to the rank of general. Cleaveland also earned a law degree and began to practice both law and politics.

Cleaveland had not only signed on to help manage the land deal, he had also invested over $30,000 toward its purchase and, in early 1796, agreed to lead the first survey party. While the tasks of the forty-plus members of the Connecticut Land Company party were multiple, the overall purpose was quite simple: to prepare the land as quickly as possible for resale. Settlement and commercial development of the area were not high on the list of priorities of land company representatives.

In the span of just over two months the survey party journeyed to the site where Cleveland is today. During this period, Cleaveland and his aides secured an agreement with the Indians declaring that the land was "owned" by the company. In exchange, the Indians were deeded a rectangular tract running west from the Cuyahoga River some sixty miles and extending south about forty miles.

Moses Cleaveland and his party arrived on the Reserve on July 4, 1796, and, working within a directive requiring that "the principal town was to be laid out as quickly as possible,"[17] Cleaveland determined by July 22 that the mouth of the Cuyahoga "will be the place." He judged that the town "must command the greatest *communication* either by land or water of any river on the purchase or in any ceded lands from the head of the Mohawk to the western extend or I am no prophet."[18] It should be emphasized that Cleaveland's notion of *"communication,"* the siting of the capital town of the purchase, later to be known as Cleveland, had little to do with urban development, or *community,* and much to do with the *"communication"* process involved in making the land attractive to potential land buyers from other parts of the new nation—especially Connecticut.[19]

The next goal of Cleaveland, now that he had an agreement with the Indians and a site for the capital of the Reserve, was to use the river to transport men, food, and the awkward survey instruments quickly to the interior to continue the survey. "Fortunately," observe Carol Miller and Robert Wheeler, "it was possible to go up river 25 miles in a small boat. Had that been his only purpose he could have established a temporary camp at the mouth of the Cuyahoga, but he laid out the capital there because he saw the commercial prospects of the river, which was navigable for lake sloops for 5 miles and for smaller vessels 10 miles farther if the river was cleared of debris. That was a large 'if' because little support for improvements to the river and harbor was forthcoming until the 1820s."[20]

Little attention was given to the actual plan for the city itself. In fact, like many other survey teams of this era, the land company surveyors simply drew up a physical map of a "capital" that looked like the ones back home—the agricultural New England village, replete with a ten-acre public square ringed with individual plots, ready for sale in 1797.[21]

The Connecticut Land Company, however, did not exactly encourage settlement of this new city, now called Cleveland (named after Moses Cleaveland, its new spelling the result, it is reported, of an error by the surveyors when recording the name of the new town on the first maps). This policy was best evidenced by the activities of Moses Cleaveland himself. Within a few weeks of first setting foot in the Western Reserve, he returned to Connecticut, never to journey to the Reserve again. It appears that his intent and that of the other members of the board was to design a process that would allow them to capture a fast return on their investment.

To do this they set in motion a policy that actually mitigated against rational communal settlement of the lands, much less the new "New England style" town of Cleveland. "As soon as the final surveys of the Reserve were completed in January 1798, the tracts in the reserve were offered for sale in land lottery. The lottery system itself made settlement haphazard since investors picked land of varying quality from separate lottery boxes, which prevented them from owning contiguous tracts." This policy made the settlement of the Reserve even less orderly, and the lack of such order made the "town" of Cleveland even more isolated.[22]

Even what could be construed as a deliberate settlement policy for Cleveland was confusing. Although the Connecticut Land Company gave away some downtown lots in an effort to attract early settlers, it spent virtually no money on improvements in the tract. For example, it built only one rough road cut from Pennsylvania to Cleveland. Once settlers did arrive in Cleveland to take up residence on their free plots, the conditions that Moses Cleaveland found ripe for "communication" were far from ideal for long-term settlement. Much of the land in the new "town" and immediately surrounding the Cuyahoga River was filled with stagnant water and marshes that bred malaria, fever, and other diseases at such a rapid pace as to slow almost all development.[23]

By the turn of the century, the U.S. census reported fifteen hundred residents in the entire Reserve, but the only full-time resident of Cleveland was a man named Lorenzo Carter. Carter, a member of the first survey party, stayed on to build a large log cabin in the area now known as the Flats. According to one early settler, Samuel Huntington, in a letter written to Moses Cleaveland in February 1802, Carter's economic practices could be counted on to drive away most prospective settlers. Carter, it was said, told all newcomers that the mouth of the river would never be opened as a port and "that nothing can be made by trade . . . at the same time he is clearing $1,000 per annum by his Indian trade."[24]

It is not clear whether Moses Cleaveland ever answered Samuel Huntington, but it does appear that Cleaveland turned a profit on his $32,000 investment, that his survey team partner Lorenzo Carter was every bit as emblematic of early frontier economic practices as Samuel Huntington, and that the siting of Cleveland was dictated first and foremost by the speculative demands of the land company and not the settlement of the town. Cleveland is a clear-cut case of how frontier towns were often the product of a very particular form of the practice of the private ownership of property. They were the enterprise, not of settlers come to live in platted new versions of European-style villages, but of land companies that designed and sited them within the dictates of colonial and postcolonial land speculation.

Restructuring: The City as Bellwether of Nineteenth-Century American Economy

FROM SPECULATION ECONOMY TO MERCANTILE CITY

Soon the village took hold, and by the 1830s, with the Erie Canal to the east and roadways being built to the west, Cleveland had become a center of frontier commerce. By 1840, ships filled the harbor that Lorenzo Carter had bleakly predicted to early settlers would never become a commercial port.[25] In 1851, when the population topped seventeen thousand, the first railroad joined Cleveland to the South—finally making the commercial economy a twelve-month venture.

At the same time, iron ore was being mined in Ohio and refined in Cleveland. This limited activity expanded greatly with the opening of the Soo Canal between Lakes Michigan and Superior, where large amounts of high-grade ore had been discovered. Therefore, as the nation moved toward the Civil War, the city of Cleveland was positioned to play an important role as a new center of industry. It was the home of six banks, it was serviced by six railroads, and it was the center of production and distribution of iron, hardware, and a vast array of consumer goods.[26]

THE NEW INDUSTRIAL CITY

By the end of the Civil War, Cleveland's economy was positioned for a pattern of growth that inspired one recent historian to suggest that it had become "a mirror of the American Industrial Revolution": "Fueled initially in the 1860's by the Civil War, sustained in the latter decades of the century by the construction of a national transportation system, the growth of an internal market and technological innovation, voracious growth continued into the first three decades of the 20th century on the crest of a wave of corporate consolidation, World War I, and a new industrial orientation toward consumer production. Highly sensitive to changes in the national economy, Cleveland made an economic transition from the commercial center of the Civil War era to the nation's 5th largest city by the middle of the prosperity decade [the 1920s]."[27]

The city of Cleveland was not only a mirror of national economic change, it was at the geographic center of this change, its economic and political leaders, in many respects, at the helm of the industrial revolution. The city where, in the fall of 1800, Lorenzo Carter was the only permanent resident, was quite a different place on the evening of October 16, 1879, when John Hay, journalist and former secretary to President Abraham Lincoln, invited a few friends to dinner at his home on Euclid Avenue. The dinner party was composed of some of the most powerful political, economic, and intellectual leaders in the nation—and many of them were from Cleveland and the Western Reserve: president of the United States and Ohioan Rutherford B. Hayes, future president James A. Garfield from Mentor, Ohio, congressional leader R. C. Parsons, and nationally prominent economic leaders Amasa Stone, Samuel L. Mather, Henry Payne, and W. J. Boardman. Hayes had asked these influential neighbors and friends to dinner to honor another native of the Western Reserve, his old teacher and now editor of the *Atlantic Monthly* William Dean Howells.[28]

The list of the dinner guests alone stood as evidence of how far Cleveland had come in the years since Moses Cleaveland had first stood on the banks of the Cuyahoga evaluating the placement of the town from the point of view of land-speculation strategy. Ninety years later, Edmund Kirke of *Harper's New Monthly Magazine* stood at what he assumed to be the same spot as Moses Cleaveland and wrote about the results of a very different economic strategy: "If we stand on the precise spot where General Cleaveland landed on that summer day in 1796, and look about us for a moment, we shall be able to form some idea of the great wealth and immense activity of this teeming hive of industry. . . . Here ten thousand machines move night and day in ceaseless hum, sending away, upon the numerous rail tracks which everywhere interlace the district, iron in its various forms." Within Kirke's immediate view, report historians Harry F. Lupold and Gladys Haddad, could be seen hundreds of acres "covered by ships and lumber yards, planing and flour mills, iron foundries and factories, oil and chemical works."[29] Some of the leading fortunes of the world were being made in these industrial flats as factories emblazoned with names such as Chisholm, Otis, Hanna, and Rockefeller churned out a substantial share of the nation's iron, steel, hardware, and refined oil.

On December 15, 1978, ninety-nine years after the glittering dinner party around John Hay's dining room table on Euclid Avenue, the young mayor of Cleveland, Dennis Kucinich, sat at another table with a similar group of Cleveland business and political elites: Maurice Saltzman, the garment manufacturer; Brock Weir, chairman of Cleveland Trust; and George Forbes, president of City Council. But the leaders at this meeting were a far cry from those assembled by Hay: they were not the successful representatives of new economic activities in a growing city and national economy but a battered and beleaguered set of profoundly conflicted local leaders of a now declining city. "The subject of discussion was the pressing need of the city of Cleveland to rollover (extend time) $14 million in short term notes due that day to area banks." According to the mayor, the bankers were attempting to blackmail the city into selling the city-owned electrical utility to the area's private utility. According to Weir, the banker, they were just trying to regain some sense of fiscal sanity in a city that had long been hurtling politically and economically out of control. "We had been kicked in the teeth for six months. On December 15, we decided to kick back," said Weir.[30]

In any case, at midnight on December 15, 1978, Cleveland, the city once described as the "mirror of the American industrial revolution," became the first major city since the Great Depression to go into default. In many ways the default served as a form of political economic denouement: Cleveland, once the urban leader of national economic growth, now appeared as the urban symbol of very different national patterns—deindustrialization and political bankruptcy. These new conditions, both literally and figuratively, were case lessons in the failure of the American city as a successful center of privatism.

In the 1920s, at the height of Cleveland's industrial prowess,[31] a substantial share of the labor force was employed in manufacturing, representing the basic industries of the city's economic structure. The city in the 1920s had experienced what economist Edward Hill described as a five-decade period of "unrivaled industrial entrepreneurism." The early development of iron ore, coal, oil, and shipping industries had matured into an internationally competitive durable goods economy "that included automotive production, lighting, electrical motors, and chemicals, paints, and coatings."[32]

In the two decades preceding the mayor's default announcement, this industrial structure changed dramatically. The manufacturing economy, long the mainstay of the city's economic base, had come apart in the postwar era, losing eighty thousand jobs or almost 30 percent of its manufacturing work force between 1963 and 1987. Steel and heavy metals production was radically diminished and oil refinement had declined substantially, leaving Cleveland as a new mirror of national economic development—this time reflecting deindustrialization, unemployment, and disinvestment.

For all this, Cleveland remains, somewhat ironically, "a command and control center of modern manufacturing capital . . . the largest complex of manufacturing employment in the region is composed of the Big Three automakers and their suppliers." Decisions in the auto-related manufacturing sector are made outside the region, while manufacturing decisions made inside the region are often made for factories outside the region. This complex geography of regional manufacturing labor and capital has led to a second irony: "As local durable goods manufacturing employment is more dependent on automobile production, locally headquartered firms are less dependent on supplying the automotive industry. They used automotive technology and retained earnings from supplying assemblers in the 1950's and 1960's to diversify into electronics and aircraft parts production."[33]

As a result of these complex relations of economic restructuring, the economy of the city and its surrounding area is substantially different today from what it was at the beginning of the century: the lion's share of the employment base of Cleveland is now found in the service economy. The riverside from where *Harper's Magazine* writer Edmund Kirke had once viewed ten thousand humming machines of the industrial revolution is now filled with young, affluent white suburbanites who come downtown for a night of bar hopping in the Flats. The neighborhood of John Hay is no longer filled with mansions. For vast stretches, Euclid Avenue is not even filled with buildings. Rather, there are long blocks of vacant buildings, storefronts, abandoned factories, and empty lots supporting nothing but weeds and broken glass. Although the central business district has been "reborn," as in many old industrial cities, with new offices filling new tall buildings dwarfing the old cityscape, most of the new jobs and new houses are found in the suburbs of Cuyahoga County.

Cleveland has become a clear example of the reversal of Gurney Breckenfeld's old doughnut theory of development.[34] Urban change in Cleveland, as in most cities, was once characterized by a decline of development at the core and increased neighborhood and economic development at the outer rings of the city proper. Today, Cleveland is redeveloping at the center of the business district, declining rapidly in much of the remainder of the city, and sending most of its affluent residents and jobs to the suburbs beyond the city rim.

Ethnicity, Race, and the Unmeltable City

THE UNMELTABLE CITY

Just as Cleveland is a classic example of economic transformation of urban America and the practices of privatism, so too, it is a good example of the American city as the center of not-so-meltable ethnicities and races. The notion held for so long that the American city was a "melting pot"—the place where an "intense and unprecedented mixture of ethnic and religious groups in American life would soon blend into a homogeneous end product"[35]—was a less than credible shibboleth used to explain dramatic and often violent experiences of social control and social acceptance. At the same time, the melting pot thesis was legitimated by the very difference of social formation found in the ethnic-racial polyglot of America cities when compared to European cities. It is often pointed out that, though both European and American cities were places of ethnic and cultural diversity, the "melting of cultures" was an elite experience in Europe—a "cosmopolitan" one, if you will—whereas it was the order of the day for *everyone* in the United States. Hence the allusion to the city as America's melting pot.

But as Nathan Glazer and Daniel Patrick Moynihan argued in their study of New York almost thirty years ago, "The point about the melting pot . . . is that it did not happen. At least not in New York and, *mutatis mutandis*, in those parts of America which resemble New York."[36] My point here is not that Cleveland is like New York but rather that Cleveland, along with New York, represents the American cultural experience—at once intense and unprecedented in its historic long-term mixture of ethnicities, races, and beliefs at all class levels.

THE CITY OF MATERIAL DREAMS

The private city, as Sam Warner has informed us, was not the city of our souls but the city of our pocketbooks. Immigrants from around the world came to the United States for material reasons—not out of ethnic solidarity and rarely, except for the first rounds of European Protestants, for religious reasons. Cleveland, a "shining" example of the private city, was, almost from its beginning, a city of immigrants. One Italian immigrant described his experience and that of many Clevelanders:

> America, as it is believed to be even today in every country is a mirage. If one does not come here in person to see for himself, he believes he will find gold nuggets on the sidewalk. Actually if one does not work hard and without stopping for even one day, one cannot, will not, live. The dollar is made of sweat and endless sacrifices. But for those who came as we did, not knowing the language, and in the era in which we came, life was cruel. Other immigrants who had been fortunate to live in countries where English was spoken treated the tongue-tied newcomers like beasts. I called to mind all the talk I had heard on the ship. Someone had said, "I shall stay in America for a few years. I shall make stern sacrifices, but, then I shall return home, buy a mule and a cart, and no longer have to till the soil." Someone else added that his wife had encouraged him to emigrate because they needed some kind of dowries with which to marry their four daughters. One after another, they all were out to seek their fortunes, many to send their sons to school to become doctors, lawyers, or engineers, to fill the professional void in their little villages. Poor immigrants, how many dreams they had, dreams that vanished all too quickly when they came into contact with harsh reality.[37]

AMERICAN ETHNICS

As the dreams of returning to Europe vanished, the immigrants became reconciled to the "harsh realities" of the American city, building new forms of communal and geographic representations of their ethnicities: as the American city assimilated many cultures within one boundary, it also segregated them into different neighborhoods. As a result, "one of the most remarkable characteristics of modern American cities is the congeries of segregated neighborhoods in which urban dwellers live out their lives."[38]

Ethnic groups were as much bound together as they were separated by their differences, and, as the generations proceeded, they changed under the influences of American society. The ghetto neighborhoods were "partly a reconstitution of [an Old World] village and partly an accommodation to the fragmented social order of the metropolis."[39] As the neighborhoods changed, the residents changed and yet maintained an ethnic identity—no longer Italian but Italian-American, for example. This meant that "the ethnic group in American society became not a survival from the age of mass immigration but a new social form . . . . Ethnic groups, then, even after distinctive language, customs, and cultures are lost, as they largely were in the second generation, and even more fully in the third generation, are continually recreated by new experiences in America."[40] Even today, the vestiges of the early policies that brought millions of immigrants to America continue, and the immigrants continue to arrive. They arrive in cities that can still be defined spatially and culturally as segregated, variated ethnic polyglots. Cleveland, it is said, is such a city—a city of immigrants—the unmeltable city.[41]

CLEVELAND: CITY OF IMMIGRANTS

The population of the city did not grow substantially as a result of foreign-born arrivals until after 1830. Indeed, there were just more than seven thousand people living in Cleveland in 1840. This changed almost at once with the expansion of the canal network; there were eleven thousand residents in Cleveland by 1845, and, with the opening of the railroad, another eight thousand people were added between 1850 and 1853. By 1860, the population had increased by over five times, standing at forty-four thousand. Of these residents, less than 30 percent were "native" or original-settler households. The remaining households in Cleveland were headed by a foreign-born ethnic, the largest ethnic populations being Germans (33 percent of all households) and the Irish (22 percent of all households).[42]

By 1880, the ethnic population of the city (59,409) was more than one and one-third times the *total* population of Cleveland just two decades earlier. The lion's share of these foreign-born ethnics still came from northern Europe, although there were some central and southern Europeans (especially Czechs).

A decade later, the foreign-born population of the city had jumped by another 40,000 to 97,095 and almost one out of five immigrants came from Slavic and central European countries. By 1890, the total foreign stock of the city had more than doubled with almost 60 percent represented by new arrivals (now with new groups of Italians emigrating from the *calabria desolata* of peasant life in the Italian countryside).[43]

Events of this period moved some observers to describe Cleveland as an "ethnic mosaic"—a crazy quilt of cultural differences spreading across the urban landscape. To speak to a Clevelander at the turn of the century was not only to speak to a city dweller but more often than not to speak to a resident of "the Cabbage Patch," or "Warszawa," or "Dutch Hill," or "Little Italy," or "Cuba," or "Vinegar Hill," or

"Whiskey Island," or "The Angle," or "Goosetown," or "Chicken Village," to name a few of the ethnic ghettos of the city.[44] In sum, as one study pointed out early in the new century, "Cleveland is one of the most foreign cities in the United States. Of the fifty cities having a population of over 100,000 inhabitants . . . only seven . . . contained a larger population of foreign inhabitants. Cleveland's foreign population would constitute by itself a city larger than any other in the state of Ohio except Cincinnati, and equalled or surpassed in size by only 28 other cities in the entire country."[45]

Before the Civil War, African Americans also increased in numbers but never represented more than 2 percent of the population. Contrary to the experience of white immigrants, most blacks did not reside in ghettos but lived throughout the city. Moreover, Cleveland was different from many other cities in that "blacks in nineteenth-century Cleveland achieved near-equality in access to public facilities . . . they also found the door of economic opportunity open wider in the Forest City than most other communities." One newspaper, the *Cleveland Leader* (May 11, 1859), reported that the city's African American community contained many "old intelligent, industrious, and respectable citizens, who own property, pay taxes, vote at elections, educate their children in public schools, and contribute to build up the institutions and to the advancement of the prosperity of the city."[46] It appears that Cleveland's long-standing abolitionist history and the longtime residency of African Americans placed many of the city's blacks more in the category of "natives" or early settlers and other English-speaking Anglo-Saxons than that of white foreign-born ethnics.

CLEVELAND: FROM CITY OF IMMIGRANTS TO SEGREGATED CITY

All this started to change in the 1870s, and by the turn of the century, the ghettoization of African Americans in Cleveland had begun, mirroring the formative years of black ghetto development in the rest of urban America. One historian observed that because of the ghettoization of blacks, the "city of immigrants" had by 1920 become "the segregated city."[47] This segregation of blacks in Cleveland was, according to Kenneth L. Kusmer, "part of a general urban phenomenon [in which] these . . . communities were not homogeneous, but they did occupy fairly distinct sections of the city; relatively few of the new immigrants lived outside these areas."[48]

For the rest of the twentieth century, the history of African Americans would be one of increasing social, economic, and geographic segregation. The segregation of African Americans was never more apparent than in the city's Hough neighborhood. It has been argued that the history of Hough and its African American residents is typical of the black experience in other cities as well as Cleveland. Further, it is an example of the general pattern of urban decline that is most evident in the decline of the urban neighborhood.

Hough, a historic neighborhood in Cleveland, bounded by the major streets of Superior and Euclid, just beyond Millionaires' Row and ending at East 105th, was a middle-class and working-class neighborhood before World War II. In 1950, it was still the home of a largely white population, but many of the larger homes were being subdivided, housing code violations were going unattended, and run-down houses, crime, and blockbusting were becoming common. When urban renewal displaced African Americans from other parts of the city, they moved into Hough so that by 1960 almost three-quarters of the population of Hough was non-white.[49] The physical decay was more than matched by failures in the economy—welfare as a way of life in the black community was increasing and 25 percent of all welfare cases could be found in Hough. Political promises to rehabilitate fourteen hundred homes in Hough were not honored, private housing deteriorated further, and cases of arson proliferated.

The community failed its new residents at every level, and the frustration over the failures erupted in the summer of 1966, when, on July 18, race riots broke out in Hough. After the smoke had cleared and the National Guard had backed off, four residents were dead and millions of dollars of property had been destroyed.[50] The Hough riots seemed like a dramatic signal of the ongoing decline of the city once known as the mirror of industrial progress. For almost twenty years, city services and budgets were vitiated, the industrial economy went into eclipse, and the affluent residents deserted the city.

Journey to Maturity

Today, the population of the city suggests that urban America has entered a new era in which the majority of city residents are nonwhite. In 1990 there were 500,526 residents of Cleveland, of whom 252,766, or 50.5 percent, were nonwhite. Over 92 percent or 233,245 members of this group were black. If these trends continue, by the year 2000, African Americans will make up a majority of the population. The "City of Immigrants" will become the "City of African Americans." It will be a poorer, more fragmented, and less economically resilient city than it has been in the past.

It will also be a city with an entirely new downtown business district. Rising above streets that little more than a decade ago had been written off as poor investments are fourteen new buildings and thirteen renovated buildings, hotels, and banks, accounting for almost ten million square feet of "Class A" office space and a new stadium-sports complex. It is projected that this development will generate over one hundred thousand jobs downtown by the turn of the century, and it is estimated that at least $5 billion of construction will be completed in the 1990s.[51] All this will occur on land that, until recently, was as unattractive to investors as the stagnant land by the Cuyahoga once overseen by Lorenzo Carter was to early settlers.

The city of the late twentieth century is a highly conflicted one containing a dual economy: as neighborhoods have declined in economic viability, at the same time becoming more and more the homes of nonwhites, the city has practiced a political economy of central business district development that is not unlike the speculative traditions of the old Connecticut Land Company. Instead of land give-aways downtown there are tax abatements, and instead of empty plots of land there are empty offices. Thus, although very few residents will actually live in the downtown business district, the property has been turned into building space that investors hope someday will turn a profit. The psychology of risk and profit that characterized development of the Western Reserve is part and parcel of central business district development in the postindustrial city of Cleveland.

The emerging African American city with its shiny new business district is the city of the future with a new racial structure and a new version of the speculative politics of privatism initiated by its first settlers.[52] In the past, Cleveland was a mirror of both the success and the failure of urban America. Whether in the future it will reflect renewal and hope, despite the harsh realities of the moment, cannot be divined. The city will continue to change, it has the historical capacity to renew itself, and its journey to maturity is not at an end.

Notes

This paper benefits greatly from the comments and camaraderie of Dennis Keating and Norman Krumholz, the assistance of Kathleen Mooney, John Shannon, Richard Guarino, Gilbert Chin, and Karen Malec, the observations of Helen Liggett, and the early inspiration of Seymour Sacks. I owe a particular intellectual debt to the work of Carol Poh Miller, Robert Wheeler, Edward Miggins, and Sam Bass Warner. Finally, the support of the Albert A. Levin Chair of Urban Studies and Public Service is gratefully acknowledged.

1. Citizens League of Greater Cleveland, "Cleveland Named All-America City by National Municipal League" (Cleveland: News Bureau of Cleveland, 1982), 1.

2. Ibid.

3. See Sam Bass Warner's classic study of privatism, *The Private City: Philadelphia in Three Periods of Its Growth* (Philadelphia: University of Pennsylvania Press, 1968).

4. Carol Poh Miller and Robert Wheeler, *Cleveland: A Concise History* (Bloomington: Indiana University Press, 1990).

5. See, for example, William Angel and David Perry, "The Politics of Efficiency: A Paper on the Political Economy of the American City" (Austin, Tex.: Unpublished, 1978); David C. Perry and Alfred Watkins, "People, Profit and the Rise of the Sunbelt Cities," in *The Rise of the Sunbelt Cities,* ed. David C. Perry and Alfred J. Watkins (Beverly Hills: Sage, 1977), and David Perry and Lawrence Keller, "Toward a Theory of Local Public Administration," in Richard Bingham et al., *Managing Local Government: Public Administration in Practice* (Newbury Park, Calif.: Sage, 1991).

6. For various treatments of the notion of privatism see Warner, *Private City;* Stephen L. Elkin, *City and Regime in the American Republic* (Chicago: University of Chicago Press, 1987); John Mollenkopf, *The Contested City* (Princeton: Princeton University Press, 1983); and Paul Peterson, *City Limits* (Chicago: University of Chicago Press, 1981).

7. A growing literature on the spatialization of the urban political economy includes such works as Edward Soja, *Postmodern Geographies: The Reassertion of Space in Critical Social Theory* (London: Verso,

1989); Michael Dear and Allen J. Scott, eds., *Urbanization and Planning in a Capitalist Society* (New York: Methuen, 1981); Michael Storper and Richard Walker, *The Capitalist Imperative: Territory, Technology and Industrial Growth* (Oxford: Basil Blackwell, 1989); and Robert A. Beauregard, ed., *Economic Restructuring and Political Response* (Newbury Park, Calif.: Sage, 1989).

8. See, among others, Nathan Glazer and Daniel Patrick Moynihan, *Beyond the Melting Pot: The Negroes, Puerto Ricans, Jews, Italians, and Irish of New York City* (Cambridge, Mass.: MIT Press, 1976); Kenneth L. Kusmer, *A Ghetto Takes Shape: Black Cleveland, 1870–1930* (Urbana: University of Illinois Press, 1976); Robert Mier, Joan Fitzgerald, and Randolph A. Lewis, *African-American Elected Officials and the Future of Progressive Political Movements* (Chicago: School of Urban Planning and Policy Center for Urban Economic Development,University of Illinois at Chicago, 1991); Henry Taylor, "Social Transformation Theory, African Americans, and the Rise of Buffalo's Post-Industrial City," *Buffalo Law Review* 39 (Spring 1991): 569–606; and William J. Wilson, *The Truly Disadvantaged: The Inner City, The Underclass, and Public Policy* (Chicago: University of Chicago Press, 1987).

9. Warner, *Private City*, xi.

10. Ibid., 10.

11. Howard P. Chudacoff, *The Evolution of American Urban Society* (Englewood Cliffs, N.J.: Prentice-Hall, 1975), 102.

12. Lawrence J. R. Herson and John M. Bolland, *The Urban Web: Politics, Policy, and Theory* (Chicago: Nelson-Hall, 1990), 50.

13. Ibid., 51.

14. See Herson and Bolland, *Urban Web;* Chudacoff, *Evolution of American Urban Society;* Charles N. Glabb and A. Theodore Brown, *A History of Urban America* (New York: Macmillan, 1976); and Constance McLaughlin Green, *American Cities in the Growth of the Nation* (New York: J. DeGraff, 1957).

15. From Glabb and Brown, *History of Urban America*, 108, as quoted in Herson and Bolland, *Urban Web*, 51.

16. Harlan Hatcher and Frank Durham, *Giant from the Wilderness: The Story of a City and Its Industries* (Cleveland: World, 1955), 11.

17. Miller and Wheeler, *Cleveland: A Concise History*, 9.

18. As quoted in the editors' introduction to David D. Van Tassel and John J. Grabowski, eds., *The Encyclopedia of Cleveland History* (Bloomington: Indiana University Press, 1987), xvii.

19. See Miller and Wheeler, *Cleveland: A Concise History;* Van Tassel and Grabowski, *Encyclopedia;* Harry F. Lupold and Gladys Haddad, eds., *Ohio's Western Reserve: A Regional Reader* (Kent, Ohio: Kent State University Press, 1988); and Thomas F. Campbell and Edward M. Miggins, *The Birth of Modern Cleveland, 1865–1930* (Cleveland: Western Reserve Historical Society and the Cleveland Public Library, 1988).

20. Miller and Wheeler, *Cleveland: A Concise History*, 9.

21. As found in the Original Plan of the Town and Village of Cleveland, Ohio, October 1, 1796 in the archive of the Western Reserve Historical Society, Cleveland, Ohio.

22. See Miller and Wheeler, *Cleveland: A Concise History*, 10.

23. Described by Van Tassel and Grabowski (1987) in the introductory essay to their historical encyclopedia on Cleveland.

24. Quoted in Miller and Wheeler, *Cleveland: A Concise History*, 17.

25. Glabb and Brown, *History of Urban America*, 38.

26. Ibid.

27. Ronald Weiner, "The New Industrial Metropolis: 1860–1929," in Van Tassel and Grabowski, *Encyclopedia*, xxix–xxx.

28. Lupold and Haddad, *Ohio's Western Reserve*, 196.

29. Ibid.

30. Todd Swanstrom, *The Crisis of Growth Politics: Cleveland, Kucinich, and the Challenge of Urban Populism* (Philadelphia: Temple University Press, 1985), 154.

31. George E. Condon, *Cleveland: The Best Kept Secret* (Cleveland: J. T. Zubal and P. D. Dole, a Division of John T. Zubal, 1981), 114–24.

32. Edward Hill, "Cleveland, Ohio Manufacturing Matters, Services Are Strengthened but Earnings Erode," in Richard D. Bingham and Randall W. Eberts, eds., *Economic Restructuring of the American Midwest* (Boston: Kluwer, 1990), 103.

33. Ibid., 105–6.

34. Gurney Breckenfeld, "Refilling the Metropolitan Doughnut," in Perry and Watkins, *Rise of the Sunbelt Cities.*

35. Glazer and Moynihan, *Melting Pot,* xcvii.

36. Ibid.

37. Frank Alesci, *It Is Never Too Late: A True Life Story of an Immigrant* (Cleveland: St. Francis Publishing House, 1963), 9–10. See also Charles D. Ferroni, *The Italians in Cleveland: A Study of Assimilation* (New York: Arno Press, 1980), 2.

38. Josef J. Barton, *Peasants and Strangers: Italians, Rumanians, and Slovaks in an American City, 1890–1950* (Cambridge, Mass.: Harvard University Press, 1975), 16.

39. Barton, *Peasants and Strangers,* 172.

40. Glazer and Moynihan, *Melting Pot,* 16–17.

41. Edward Miggins and Mary Morgenthaler, "The Ethnic Mosaic: The Settlement of Cleveland by the New Immigrants and Migrants," in Thomas Campbell and Edward Miggins, eds., *The Birth of Modern Cleveland, 1865–1930* (Cleveland: Western Reserve Historical Society and the Cleveland Public Library, 1988), 104. Also see Glazer and Moynihan, *Melting Pot.*

42. Miller and Wheeler, *Cleveland: A Concise History,* 52–55.

43. Miggins and Morgenthaler, "Ethnic Mosaic," 104–5.

44. Ibid., 104–41. See also Barton, *Peasants and Strangers,* 173, and Lloyd P. Gartner, *History of the Jews of Cleveland* (Cleveland: Western Reserve Historical Society and the Jewish Theological Seminary of America, 1987), 3–29.

45. Herbert A. Miller, *The School and the Immigrant* (Philadelphia: William F. Fell, 1916), 11.

46. As quoted in Kusmer, *Ghetto Takes Shape,* 17.

47. Ibid., 35.

48. Ibid., 44.

49. Miller and Wheeler, *Cleveland: A Concise History,* 166–67.

50. See Carl B. Stokes, *Promises of Power: A Political Autobiography* (New York: Simon and Schuster, 1973), and David Rogers, *The Management of Big Cities: Interest Groups and Social Change Strategies* (Beverly Hills: Sage, 1971).

51. These estimates are from verbal and written reports supplied by Patricia Gallagher of the Cleveland Growth Association and Karen Malec, director of marketing research for Grubb and Ellis Real Estate Service, on October 14, 1991.

52. Timothy Barnekov, Robin Boyle, and Rich Daniel, *Privatism and Urban Policy in Britain and the United States* (Oxford: Oxford University Press, 1989), vii.

Part 2

HISTORY
Growth to Decline

Introduction

Carol Poh Miller and Robert A. Wheeler provide the historical framework for the sections that follow. The remainder of the book is organized by six general topics. The essays within those sections refer to historical periods and specific issues and events that have shaped metropolitan Cleveland.

Miller and Wheeler give the reader a concise yet colorful portrait of the city from its earliest growth to its more contemporary decline. Their summary history is organized in chronological fashion, beginning with the settlement of Cleveland and its transformation from a small village to a commercial city. They focus on transportation networks—especially the Erie Canal and the Ohio Canal and the development of railroads—which fostered trade. They explain the factors, beginning with the Civil War, that led to the rise of Cleveland as an industrial city: technological advances, geographic location, entrepreneurial leadership, and mass European immigration providing cheap labor for manufacturers. Miller and Wheeler note the early appearance of industrial pollution and labor unrest and the emergence of ethnic villages that created a multinational mosaic of people and neighborhoods.

They trace Cleveland's transcendence, in the early twentieth century, as an industrial and commercial power and, finally, its decline from a prosperous blue-collar manufacturing center to a troubled city undergoing massive economic and social upheaval. They note the city's declining population, growing poverty rate, economic restructuring, and commitment of resources to redevelopment of the downtown core as a regional entertainment and business center. These issues are analyzed in detail throughout the book.

Cleveland: The Making and Remaking of an American City, 1796–1993

Carol Poh Miller & Robert A. Wheeler

Cleveland owed its rise to prominence in the nineteenth century to its location on Lake Erie at the mouth of the Cuyahoga River, which gave the city potential both as the northern terminus of a water connection between the lake and the Ohio River and as a Great Lakes port. Such strategic placement helped a sleepy and miasmic village develop, first, into a thriving mercantile center, then into one of the world's great manufacturing cities. In the process, Cleveland attracted successive waves of optimistic traders, farmers, craftsmen, merchants, entrepreneurs, and, finally, foreign immigrants, who filled its streets and determined its character as a big, busy, multiethnic industrial city.

Until the Ohio and Erie Canal arrived in the late 1820s, Cleveland struggled. With no harbor, relatively poor farmland, and a location far from populous eastern states, its attractions were few. Speculators—members of the Connecticut Land Company—had bought the site, part of a large tract called the Western Reserve, from the state of Connecticut in 1795. The following year, they sent a surveying party to lay out townships and a "capital town." The head of the expedition, Moses Cleaveland, explored locations along the shore of Lake Erie and chose the east bluff overlooking the mouth of the Cuyahoga River because "it must command the greatest communication either by land or water of any River on the purchase. . . ."[1] To facilitate quick sale, surveyors laid out a village of two-acre lots, with a ten-acre Public Square bisected by wide streets.

Settlers trickled in, but few found reason to stay. In 1800, the first and only permanent resident, tavern-owner and trader Lorenzo Carter, discouraged other settlers for fear they would interfere with his trade monopoly. Other would-be inhabitants moved on when they became sick from the stagnant water in the river flats. When John Melish visited Cleveland in 1811, he found sixteen houses, several taverns and stores, an economy limited to "a little salt . . . a little flour, pork, and whiskey," and a "putrid" smelling, sandbar-obstructed river.[2] Lake traffic increased after 1810, and some soldiers arrived during the War of 1812, when Cleveland served as a storage depot and the site of a fort. After the war, with the British and Indian threat diminished, a series of poor harvests in the East propelled people west.

In 1809, Cleveland was chosen as the county seat of the newly created Cuyahoga County. By 1815, it was a village, with its own president, trustees, and other officers. Formation of the Commercial Bank of Lake Erie in 1816, discussions in the Ohio legislature of the feasibility of a canal connecting Lake Erie to the Ohio River in 1817, and publication of the first newspaper, the *Cleaveland Gazette and Commercial Register* a year later, were all harbingers of the city's commercial potential. The first steamboat on Lake Erie, the *Walk-in-the-Water,* visited Cleveland in 1818. The same year, the *Gazette* announced that "the tide of emigration continues to course in [this] direction with unabated strength; and trade and commerce are increasing in the same ratio as population."[3] Despite the physical obstacles, shipping increased gradually so that, by the early 1820s, more than fifty ships regularly traded at the village of two hundred people, including the first steamboat of local manufacture, the *Enterprise,* completed in 1824. Incoming goods were offloaded onto lighter boats for the trip up the Cuyahoga, then stored in the warehouses that now lined the east side of the river flats.

With a growing population, signs of a more formal civic life appeared. After 1815, several schools and churches provided eastern cultural connections. Village leaders attempted to control frontier tendencies by outlawing horse racing, the discharging of weapons, and the discarding of animal carcasses on the streets. They were proud of the many "genteel private dwellings" being built in the first residential neighborhood, north and west of Public Square.[4]

The protracted debate over the location of the northern terminus of the Ohio and Erie Canal ended in 1825 when Sandusky was rejected in favor of Cleveland. In some respects, the eight-year wait had been beneficial, for in the meantime the Erie Canal, connecting Buffalo with Albany, was completed. The new water route allowed Ohio products to travel via lake, canal, and the Hudson River to New York City. In addition to the vast new market opened by the canal, contractors and laborers whose work in New York was finished simply moved on to Cleveland and began work on the Ohio Canal. On July 4, 1827, the first segment, connecting Akron with Cleveland, opened with much fanfare. The same year, the federal government financed the improvement of the harbor; the flow of the river was first blocked and then released, cutting a straight path to the lake. The largest boats now enjoyed direct access to the river. More important, the now free-flowing river dramatically reduced the incidence of sickness caused by the formerly stagnant waters.

For the next twenty years, the village of Cleveland served as a major transshipment point, gathering agricultural products from the interior for shipment east and manufactured goods from the East for shipment south. Even before the canal was finished in 1833, the volume of trade grew tremendously. Forwarding and commission agents saw the amount of merchandise passing through Cleveland increase from half a million pounds in 1827 to three million in 1830 to a peak of nineteen million in 1838. Cleveland became a major port for flour, 461,000 barrels crossing its docks in 1841. Lake shipping kept pace, with the number of vessels entering the harbor topping a thousand annually by 1838 and exceeding sixteen hundred by 1844. "The Lake is white with canvass [*sic*]," a newspaper observed in 1833.[5]

Prosperity produced rapid change in the village. Barter, once common, became outmoded as agents such as M'Curdy and Dow advertised that they would "pay cash for any quantity of wheat."[6] By 1830, there were just over a thousand residents; most new arrivals either worked on the docks or else helped build housing, which was in constant demand. Cleveland was one of the fastest-growing areas in the country, a place of optimism and promise.

Despite a national depression in 1837, which dampened growth, Cleveland reached six thousand residents by 1840. This figure did not include the sixteen hundred people living on the west side of the river in the rival "City of Ohio," which for eighteen years threatened to eclipse Cleveland in size. The west bank of the Cuyahoga had remained part of American Indian territory until 1806. Thereafter, its population increased gradually so that by 1835 the unification of both sides of the river was a frequent topic of discussion. Cleveland so jealously guarded its superior position, however, that the village to the west decided union was impossible and applied for incorporation as a city in 1836, beating Cleveland to the distinction by two days. The two rivals bickered over trade, and the construction of a bridge connecting Columbus Street with the Wooster and Medina turnpike south of Ohio City, which Ohio City residents viewed as an attempt to divert trade away from their city, resulted in a skirmish in 1836. The two cities continued to posture over control of the river until 1854, when they were finally united.

The canal not only drew Cleveland into the national economic sphere, it also improved the city's ties with national cultural and political currents. Cleveland became a stop on the national lecture circuit and home to branches of many eastern charitable and religious organizations. In 1826 a chapter of the American Colonization Society was formed to help former slaves return to Africa. By the 1830s, antislavery groups and temperance societies appeared. According to the first city directory, published in 1837, there were eight Christian churches in Cleveland—including one for German Protestants, the first of literally hundreds of ethnic congregations that would appear—and four newspapers. Interestingly, the education-minded New England settlers who accounted for most of Cleveland's population did not establish a public school system until 1837. Before then, various private academies opened and closed with regularity. Explosive growth, meanwhile, kept the village scrambling to provide services. Volunteers staffed four firehouses by the mid-1830s, while police protection was provided by a marshal and companies of watchmen, who canvassed the streets and wharves.

Local society gradually separated into distinct, but not widely dispersed, groups. The crowded area "under the hill," in the river flats, provided the least expensive accommodations, attracting many transients. The cholera that ravaged the Great Lakes in the 1830s hit this area hardest; some inhabitants were so destitute that a meager system of poor relief was begun. The middle portion of Cleveland society—laborers, craftsmen, and small-business owners—sought housing near their work.

Many lived in the growing retail district located north and west of Public Square. The top of local society, meanwhile, began to build imposing homes around the square that mirrored eastern styles and demonstrated the social stature of their owners, who attended numerous cotillion balls and celebrated the Fourth of July with elaborate ceremony.

In 1840, with just over six thousand residents, Cleveland was the largest city in northeast Ohio. (Its closest rival, Warren, had a population of 1,996.) Its status was confirmed when a medical college in Willoughby, twenty miles to the east, moved to Cleveland because the majority of the physicians in the Western Reserve "regard Cleveland as the only place in Northern Ohio whose size, situation, and commercial importance render it a fit location for a . . . medical school."[7] Additional links by canal—to Pittsburgh and Marietta, for example—added to Cleveland's status as a regional hub. The canals now funneled coal from the Mahoning Valley to Cleveland and carried dairy products, especially cheese, from the counties of the Western Reserve to distant markets. Lumber and wheat imports soared.

Throughout the 1840s, commerce dominated the Cleveland economy. What little manufacturing existed employed a rising but still small portion of the labor force. The first heavy industry in the county, the Cuyahoga Steam Furnace Company, founded in 1830 in Ohio City, expanded in the 1840s to include the manufacture of locomotive engines and steam boilers for lake vessels. It was soon joined by several other ironworks and an active shipbuilding industry. Financial institutions also sprang up, six new banks appearing between 1845 and 1850.

The impressive canal and lake traffic attracted more and more people—seventeen thousand by mid-century—until the city ranked thirty-seventh in size in the nation. The economic expansion of the preceding decade had attracted many Germans and Irish to Cleveland. Germans were more likely to hold stable jobs such as those in building trades or meat processing, which required some skill. In contrast, half the Irish heads of household in 1850 were day laborers with no steady work and were employed only half the year. Both groups were scattered throughout the city, but concentrated pockets of Germans and Irish appeared that would grow larger with time. To preserve their traditions and enhance their social lives, Germans founded a newspaper in 1846 and several singing, hunting, and military groups, while Irish residents formed self-help organizations such as the Irish Naturalization Society and attended the growing number of Roman Catholic churches.

Blacks, who never made up more than 2 percent of the population before the Civil War, were not isolated residentially but were scattered throughout the city. Most were employed as semiskilled or skilled workers. As early as the 1830s, Cleveland's black community supported a school, a library, and a lecture series. In 1850, money raised through fairs enabled the African Methodist Episcopal congregation to dedicate a new church building.

As early as the mid-1840s, newspapers warned Clevelanders of the need to support railroad development and to nurture manufacturing or else be left behind by rival cities. The warnings brought prompt action; investors saw railroads as an opportunity to build on the economic advantages gained by canal trade. An 1853 city directory characterized the town before the rail era: "Our year was but eight months long; Lake and Canal were ice-bound during the entire winter, and with the first hard frost, the business of the city went into a state of hybernation [*sic*]."[8] Funding schemes, which multiplied in the late 1840s, succeeded by 1851 when the first railroad, the Cleveland, Columbus & Cincinnati, entered the city. Two years later, rails linked Cleveland to Pittsburgh, New York, Chicago, and St. Louis, and by 1860 the city was a national rail center. The advent of railroads brought a precipitous decline in canal traffic. Pork shipments alone fell from seventy-five hundred tons in 1854 to one hundred tons in 1860, while in 1856, twenty-five thousand tons of pork and bacon were shipped through Cleveland by rail. Similar losses in wheat and corn signaled the shift to railroads, which now kept Cleveland busy year-round.

The discovery of huge iron-ore deposits in the Lake Superior region in the 1850s, together with the completion of a canal at Sault Ste. Marie, which opened a water route to the lower lakes, made Cleveland the most important port on the Great Lakes and irrevocably changed the city's economy. Cleveland's position as the meeting place of iron ore from the upper lakes and coal from Pennsylvania and Ohio would usher it into the industrial age. The discovery of oil in nearby Pennsylvania in 1859, meanwhile, hinted at the city's eventual role as an important refining center. But much of this expansion still lay ahead. Before the Civil War, the vast majority of manufacturing establishments in Cleveland made furniture, clothing, woodenware, and farm implements; even by 1860, fewer than one-tenth of local workers were employed in factories.

Railroads brought more and more people to the city, and by 1860 it had grown to nearly forty-four thousand. Part of this growth was the result of the annexation of Ohio City in 1854. Cleveland voters in the early 1850s had rejected several proposals to unite but finally agreed when the benefits of a broader tax base and access to the West Side's advanced freshwater delivery system and substantial heavy industry overwhelmed the detractors of unification. The annexation of Ohio City added seven thousand people to Cleveland's total population and put it on track to become a modern, consolidated city.

As foreign immigration increased, the number of native-born heads of households declined so that by 1860 they made up only one-third of all Cleveland households. German-born residents, products of the recent revolutions in Germany, made up a similar percentage, while Irish household heads constituted another one-fifth of the total. German neighborhoods emerged on the West Side, south of Bridge Avenue, while Irish neighborhoods developed on the west bank of the river and on the hillside at the foot of Franklin Boulevard, the West Side's most prestigious street. The most prominent Clevelanders migrated east on Euclid Avenue, building a succession of stately mansions that would win fame nationwide as Millionaires' Row.

Urban problems multiplied with the population. Complaints of "prostitutes, blacklegs, shoulder strikers, and loafers" appeared regularly in newspapers.[9] Several orphan asylums, the Ragged School for poor children, and the first hospitals were established to minister to those in need, as were many charitable societies formed by the women of the city's thirty-four Protestant, eight Catholic, and two Jewish congregations. Cricket clubs, gymnasiums, and boat clubs were organized as an antidote to the anonymity of city life.

By the 1850s, gas lights, paved streets, a horse-powered street railway, and elevated sidewalks had reached Cleveland. The Cleveland Board of Education was organized in 1853 and built the city's first high school three years later. Health problems aggravated by poor sanitation prompted the appointment of a public health officer and board of health in 1856. Twelve fire companies, still staffed by volunteers, and a paid police department with forty patrolmen served the city by 1860. Such services suggest that on the eve of the Civil War, Cleveland was a fully developed city participating in national trends and poised to benefit from the spreading industrial revolution.

Sufficiently isolated from the battlegrounds of the Civil War yet connected with the rest of the North by rail, Cleveland emerged as a significant production center for war material. Because the Mississippi River was closed to commerce, the war also stimulated trade on the Great Lakes. Moreover, higher taxes on imported raw materials encouraged the rapid development of the Lake Superior iron-ore industry and, with it, Cleveland. In 1860, five hundred men worked in the city's nascent iron industry; by 1866, three thousand did so. In addition to railroad iron and hardware, Cleveland businesses supplied knitted goods, uniforms, and meat and produce to the war effort.

Clevelanders supported the Union cause not only with goods but also with volunteers. From the first call issued by President Lincoln in 1861, residents filled quotas quickly, mustering at seven area camps. Of the ten thousand sent from Cuyahoga County, seventeen hundred died and two thousand were wounded. Many of those who did not go to war gathered supplies needed by the army or helped soldiers and returning veterans through such groups as the Soldiers' Aid Society of Northern Ohio. Seemingly all Clevelanders joined the nation in mourning the death of Abraham Lincoln when his funeral train, en route to Springfield, Illinois, stopped in the city on April 28, 1865.

After the war, the process of annexation begun with Ohio City continued as portions of Brooklyn and Newburgh townships, East Cleveland, West Cleveland, and parts of Glenville were all gradually added to the mother city. Six railroads were now operating in and out of Cleveland, and the Flats teemed with roundhouses, warehouses, oil tanks, and factories. The intensive development co-opted the lake shore for industrial use and forced many businesses out of the Flats. The onetime residential neighborhood north and west of Public Square was rapidly transformed into a commercial district as wholesalers of hardware, furniture, groceries, and clothing built new, more substantial structures. The fate of Millionaires'

Row was sealed when it was bisected by railroad tracks at Willson (East 55th) Street and, later, invaded by commerce.

While contributing to the city's economic vitality, industrialization also had negative consequences. By the 1870s, the waters of the Cuyahoga were seriously polluted by industrial wastes and the runoff from sewers, which emptied untreated into the river. Parts of the city had become badly blighted. A newspaper, in sensational style, described one of the worst areas, the hill leading out of the Flats on the West Side, with its "straggling half-whitewashed houses, filthy rags, dirty-faced, half-naked, white-headed children, poorly clad women, the hundreds of cats and dogs, and the millions of flies." Some visitors, like this one in 1883, glorified the industrial scene: "Since 1860 the city has rapidly developed in the direction of manufacturing industries . . . old pasture grounds of the cows of 1850 are now completely occupied by oil refineries and manufacturing establishments . . . [including] copper smelting, iron rolling and iron manufacturing works, lumber yards, paper mills, breweries, flour mills. . . . The scene at night . . . [is] lit up with a thousand points of light from factories, foundries and steamboats, which . . . are reflected in the waters of the Cuyahoga, which looks like a silver ribbon flowing through the blackness." By day, however, this romanticized scene looked quite different. A recent immigrant described his first impressions of the Cuyahoga River in 1889: "The water was yellowish, thick, full of clay, stinking of oil and sewage. The water heaped rotting wood on both banks of the river; everything was dirty and neglected." Still, the *Cleveland Leader* typified the prevailing attitude toward industrial pollution when it warned that Cleveland would be ridiculed by rival cities if it "indicts her rolling mills because they smoke, and prohibits coal oil refineries because they smell badly."[10]

A befouled city did not stop more and more people from coming to Cleveland. The city in 1870 had more than ninety-two thousand residents and ranked fifteenth in population in the nation. It had become one of the nation's important iron-manufacturing centers, with some fourteen rolling mills producing four hundred tons of finished iron daily. Plants supplied sulfuric acid, hydrochloric acid, soda ash, and other chemicals to a rapidly growing petroleum industry. In 1870, the city processed two million barrels of petroleum, making it the premier refining capital of the country, and with completion of a pipeline linking Cleveland to the Pennsylvania oil fields, the oil tanks of John D. Rockefeller's Standard Oil Company and dozens of other refiners mushroomed across the Flats. Other leading industries included lumber and woodworking, railroad machinery and repair, wire, clothing, cooperage, cigars, engines and boilers, paper, and shipbuilding. Manufacturing now employed over 30 percent of Cleveland's work force.

Even though the West Side had been promised a high-level bridge at the time of annexation, the promise was not kept. Some complained that the city's West Side was "a mere suburb" to the East Side, while others objected to the traffic jams created by many who had no business in the Flats but were forced to cross the river there. Finally, in 1878, the Superior Viaduct was opened. The stone-and-iron engineering marvel, rivaling the recently opened Brooklyn Bridge in New York, permitted through traffic to cross high above the Flats. Over three thousand feet long, the bridge accommodated streetcars, horse-drawn carriages, and pedestrians, and a center swing section pivoted to allow tall ships to pass in the river below.

In 1880, with 160,000 residents, Cleveland ranked twelfth in population in the nation. In new patents, however, it ranked fourth, suggesting the city was fertile ground for innovation. Among the most important new inventions were Alexander Brown's mechanical hoist for unloading iron ore from ships, which dramatically reduced both manual labor and unloading time; Charles Brush's electric lighting, electric motors, and storage batteries, which led to the establishment of a large and vital new industry; and Francis Drury and Henry Crowell's oil-burning stoves, which soon replaced wood- and coal-burners. By the close of 1883, there were 136 establishments in Cleveland devoted to the manufacture of iron and steel and their products: railway equipment, sewing machines, electrical apparatus, hardware, stoves and furnaces, foundries, machinery, and nuts and bolts. Shipbuilding also expanded rapidly in the 1880s. Cleveland was the major producer of ore boats and, by the early 1890s, was the second leading shipbuilding city in the nation after Philadelphia. Slaughtering and meat packing, the men's clothing industry, flour and grist mills, malt liquor production, and paint manufacture all employed large numbers of Clevelanders.

As elsewhere in late nineteenth-century industrial America, Cleveland factory workers worked long hours at low wages under dangerous conditions. Periodic depressions resulted in drastic wage cuts and were often accompanied by strikes and the subsequent importation of foreign strikebreakers. The year 1877, for example, saw numerous strikes: railway workers at the Collinwood Yards, barrel makers at Standard Oil, steelworkers at the Cleveland Rolling Mill. In general, mill owners refused to accede to workers' demands and labor unrest continued unabated. The one hundred local unions in the city by 1900 continued to press their demands for better pay and working conditions.

The vast number of new arrivals in the city, many of whom came with little or no financial cushion, required assistance that soon outstripped the disorganized efforts of local voluntarism. While churches continued to work among the city's poor and various groups targeted the special needs of orphans, alcoholics, and the elderly, the Bethel Associated Charities, organized in 1884, coordinated fund-raising and attempted to ensure that only the "deserving poor" received charity. Settlement houses, beginning with Hiram House in 1896, were established to help immigrants adjust to life in their new surroundings. As the economic depressions of 1877 and 1893 demonstrated, more Clevelanders lived on the edge of poverty than ever before.

City government was hardly prepared to cope with booming growth and the massive social changes that accompanied it. Still operating under its 1852 charter, with a figurehead mayor and a handful of permanent administrative committees, the city dealt with each new need as best it could, usually by creating special commissions. Finally, in 1891, a plan modeled after the federal government was adopted, creating separate departments of police, fire, accounts, public works, and charities and correction, with the mayor serving as chief executive. Unfortunately, the new structure was quickly co-opted by politicians, who blunted efforts to increase efficiency in favor of continuing to build their fiefdoms.

Indeed, solutions to most municipal needs came slowly. The city water supply, for example, needed constant updating. Not until 1896 did construction begin on a new intake tunnel designed to avoid pollutants by collecting water four miles out into the lake. Sewage treatment would wait until the twentieth century; in the 1890s, fifty million gallons of raw sewage were discharged into Lake Erie each day. And though public parks were sorely needed, an extensive park system assembled in the mid-1890s with the help of various benefactors was not within easy reach of the working classes who might most benefit from it. Just as the park system served some residents better than others, a system of parochial and private schools—including Hathaway Brown, University, and Laurel schools—emerged to provide better education for the children of Cleveland's elite.

In 1890 manufacturing employed fifty-three thousand Clevelanders and led all sectors of the local economy. The city was now a national ore-processing center, and it confirmed that position by widening the river channel to accommodate larger ore carriers and extending the breakwater. Though Cleveland's role as a leading petroleum refiner waned as production in the Pennsylvania oil fields declined, the city ended the century with the formation in 1899 of the American Shipbuilding Company, which united ship construction in Cleveland, Milwaukee, Chicago, Detroit, and Superior, Wisconsin, and by 1900 owned every shipbuilding facility on the Great Lakes save one.

Downtown saw an unprecedented building boom, including construction of the city's first tall buildings—among them, the Arcade, Society for Savings, Western Reserve, and Cuyahoga buildings—and the architecturally resplendent Hollenden Hotel and Sheriff Street Market. The advent of electric streetcars (the first line opened in 1893) widened the possibilities for leisure. In the 1890s, Euclid Beach and Puritas Springs amusement parks opened, as did League Park, home of the major-league Cleveland Spiders baseball team. At the Euclid Avenue Opera House on Sheriff (East 4th) Street, touring companies of the first rank played to large audiences.

Fully three-fourths of Clevelanders were now either foreign-born or the children of foreign-born parents. Since the 1880s, most new immigrants had come from southern and eastern Europe—Italians, Greeks, Hungarians, Slovaks, Serbs, Croats, Czechs, Poles, and Russian Jews. Many were "birds of passage," sojourners who came for jobs and not to become permanent residents and who returned to their homelands with the money they earned. The city's neighborhoods, with their foreign-language churches, social clubs, and cafes, helped many immigrants feel at home. When Czech immigrant Frank Vlcek woke on his first morning in Cleveland, he "heard Czech being spoken on every side. Even a street merchant . . . cried his wares in Czech."[11] It is likely that other new arrivals had similar first impressions of Big and Little Italy, Birdtown, Kouba, Warszawa, and a dozen other foreign enclaves.

In 1896 Cleveland concluded its first century, having become one of the nation's great industrial and commercial centers. But there was a dark side to this success; for many, the city was bleak and inhospitable. The Women's Department of the city's centennial commission acknowledged the contrast in a time capsule deposited at the historical society, which read in part: "We bequeath to you a city of a century, prosperous and beautiful, and yet far from our ideal. . . . Many of the people are poor, and some are vainly seeking work at living wages. . . . Some of our children are robbed of their childhood. Vice parades our streets and disease lurks in many places that men and women call their homes."[12] Much remained to be done.

By 1900, Cleveland was one of the world's preeminent manufacturing centers. Iron and steel mills, foundries and machine shops, meatpacking plants, and automobile, clothing, and paint and varnish factories gave substance to a growing population that, in a single decade, almost doubled—from 381,768 in 1900 to 560,663 in 1910. Immigration, especially from Italy, Poland, and Hungary, accounted for much of the increase. Cleveland grew in territory, too, with the annexation of Glenville and South Brooklyn in 1905 and Collinwood in 1910. The flourishing economy left its imprint. Tall buildings multiplied downtown, while in the city's expanding neighborhoods, two-story frame houses and brick apartment buildings clustered around multistory business blocks. By 1898, a network of street railways reached as far west as Rocky River and Rockport (Kamm's Corners) and as far east as Euclid Beach Park, Five Points (Collinwood) and what would later become Cleveland Heights. With improved transit, residential development spread farther and farther from Public Square, with new speculative allotments enticing buyers "into the pure air" and away from the "smoke and grime of closely built up city streets."[13] The most affluent Clevelanders, meanwhile, retreated along the lake shore and into the Appalachian foothills, building mansions in Clifton Park (Lakewood), Bratenahl, and Amber Heights (later Cleveland Heights).

According to journalist Lincoln Steffens, Cleveland during this period was "the best governed city in the United States."[14] During his four terms as mayor, industrialist-turned-reformer Tom L. Johnson presided over a decade of progressive reform. Johnson built neighborhood playgrounds and public bathhouses in the poorest neighborhoods, professionalized city departments, and adopted a comprehensive building code. An important legacy of Johnson's tenure as mayor was the adoption of the Group Plan in 1903. The plan proposed the clearance of a large area of squalor northeast of Public Square and the formal grouping of the city's major public buildings around a broad mall, or promenade, reaching toward Lake Erie. Over the next three decades, a classically styled courthouse, city hall, public auditorium, main library, and school administration building all rose in conformance with architect Daniel Burnham's vision. An ardent champion of public ownership of utilities, Johnson proposed building a municipal electric light plant, a project that came to fruition with the opening of the largest municipally owned central station in the country in Cleveland in 1914. His quest for municipal control of the street railways, however, pitted him against the private Cleveland Electric Railway Company and other powerful business interests in a bitter and protracted contest that eventually led to Johnson's defeat at the polls.

Cleveland in the first decades of the twentieth century was a buoyant and prosperous city. A remarkable collection of vaudeville and motion picture palaces at Playhouse Square downtown vied for business with a lively "Uptown" district at Euclid and East 105th. The new Detroit-Superior Bridge, with its lower streetcar deck, opened in 1917, providing the city's first truly high-level connection across the industrial Flats. It was a bountiful era of cultural philanthropy during which the city's leading families endowed the Cleveland Orchestra, the Cleveland Museum of Art, the Cleveland Play House, the Cleveland Institute of Music, and a host of other institutions. The Cleveland Metropolitan Park District, formed in 1917, preserved some of the county's most scenic real estate for public enjoyment and established the foundation for an "emerald necklace," or greenbelt of parks, encircling the county.

World War I emptied the city of its young men and put an end to large-scale European immigration. To replenish the supply of manual labor, southern blacks were recruited to come to Cleveland and other industrial cities in the North, setting off the "Great Migration." In a single decade, between 1910 and 1920, the city's black population increased 308 percent—from 8,448 to 34,451. Most new arrivals settled in the Central Avenue district, home to the largest number of Cleveland blacks before the war and later the site of the city's black ghetto.

Early in the century, two reclusive brothers, O. P. and M. J. Van Sweringen, had bought land in the old Shaker community on high ground east of the city. They now embarked on an ambitious plan to build the model suburban community of Shaker Heights. Well-to-do Clevelanders already had begun to look for new luxury housing outside the city. To attract them to their development, the Van Sweringens built a rapid-transit line connecting the new suburb with downtown Cleveland, though automobile ownership already was growing rapidly. In 1916, there were 61,000 automobiles in Cuyahoga County; ten years later, there were 211,000. An expanding pool of mobile Clevelanders prompted the large-scale development of new middle-class housing in Lakewood, Cleveland Heights, Garfield Heights, and Parma. Suburban voters, "content in their municipal independence and the charm of their residential sections" (as Cleveland advertising executive William Ganson Rose would later put it),[15] began rejecting bids for annexation, and by 1932 Cleveland was territorially arrested at seventy-six square miles.

By 1930, statistics show, there were great differences between the city and its suburbs—differences in race, nativity, literacy, employment, and wealth. Population was increasing on the periphery of the metropolitan area and decreasing at the center. The city's ethnic groups were dispersing, while the black community was becoming ever more concentrated in a ghetto bounded by Euclid and Woodland avenues and East 14th and East 105th streets. The metropolitan region's highest economic areas, as defined by statistician Howard Whipple Green, were located outside of Cleveland. There, Green wrote in 1931, "the picture is quite different than in the low economic areas. Homes are owned, families have radios, family heads are native white of native parentage, illiteracy is low, unemployment is uncommon, population is spread out over ample areas, the juvenile delinquency rate is low, likewise the infant mortality rate and the general death-rate are low." Cleveland, Green reported in 1933, was "decaying at the core."[16]

Downtown Cleveland nevertheless remained the strong economic heart of an expanding metropolitan region. In 1923 ground was broken for the largest building project in the city's history: the $150-million Cleveland Union Terminal complex. The "city within a city" developed by the Van Sweringen brothers at the southwest corner of Public Square had as its centerpiece the fifty-two-story Terminal Tower—the tallest building between New York and Chicago—with a new rail passenger station below grade. The project eradicated most of the old Haymarket district, restored Public Square to prominence as the center of commercial and civic life, and created a new visual symbol for the city. The celebrating, however, was short-lived.

The year 1930 marked a watershed in the city's fortunes—an end to prosperity from which, it might be argued, Cleveland has never fully recovered. Following the great stock market crash of October 29, 1929, the city's economic preeminence rapidly shifted to a fight for survival. An estimated forty-one thousand jobless in Cleveland in April 1930 swelled to one hundred thousand by the following January. The city had to cope with rapidly shrinking tax revenues and escalating demands for food, clothing, and shelter. The federal government, under the leadership of President Franklin D. Roosevelt, stepped in to carry most of the relief burden. Large public works projects kept many Clevelanders employed; the first public housing projects in the nation, the sprawling Main Avenue Bridge, and Cleveland Municipal Stadium were built, and the metropolitan parks were substantially developed with federal aid. Nevertheless, expenditures for direct and work relief in Cuyahoga County during the Depression represented just one-sixth of the loss of normal wage and salary payments.

Cleveland rebounded when America entered World War II. The city's factories turned out planes, tanks, trucks, artillery, bombs, binoculars, and telescopes. But the city enjoyed a diversified industrial base as a producer of machine tools, electrical goods, and metal products. A large supply of trained workers, abundant low-cost power and water, and its location at the natural meeting place of raw materials and within five hundred miles of half the population of the United States gave credence to the claim, first made in 1944, that Cleveland was "the best location in the nation."[17]

Industrial workers, including large numbers of Appalachian whites and southern blacks, swelled Cleveland's wartime population. To meet the demand for housing, single-family homes were subdivided into several units, beginning a pattern of overuse and overcrowding and laying the groundwork for future deterioration. At war's end, the housing shortage worsened with the return of servicemen eager to start new families. Pent-up demand was met with large new housing projects in Brooklyn, Lyndhurst, Mayfield Heights, Maple Heights, and South Euclid. A Cleveland Chamber of Commerce report published in 1941 acknowledged the phenomenon of decentralization, stating: "It is evident that most people who live in Cleveland are anxious to move to the suburbs. . . . Experience has shown that if their economic status permits, the majority of Clevelanders prefer to live outside of the central area."[18]

By the early 1950s, Cleveland stood at a crossroads. Its central business district and its neighborhoods were deteriorating, crime was worsening, and thousands of city residents were leaving for new homes in the suburbs. The 1960 census would show a loss, for the decade, of almost 39,000 residents (from 914,808 to 876,050). Civic and business leaders struggled to define the problem, but answers remained elusive. Meanwhile, the implementation of two federal programs—urban renewal and construction of the interstate highway system—dramatically and permanently changed the face of the city.

Until 1950, Cleveland had relied on the construction of public housing to fight blight. Now, using its power of eminent domain, the city would purchase property in specific project areas legislatively determined as blighted, clear and improve it for redevelopment, and sell it to private developers at a reduced cost, with the federal government paying two-thirds of the bill. The urban renewal program in Cleveland, encompassing just over 6,000 acres and seven inner-city areas, all on the East Side, was the largest in the nation. But only Erieview, embracing some 160 acres between East 6th and East 17th streets and between Chester Avenue and the lakefront, was successful in attracting substantial new private investment. Elsewhere, the program succeeded only in dispersing large numbers of the city's poorest residents into adjacent neighborhoods. By 1958, City Council members were voicing their concerns about the effects of displaced slum dwellers in Hough, Glenville, Mount Pleasant, and upper Central. The construction of a network of interstate highways, meanwhile, displaced thousands more Clevelanders—an estimated nineteen thousand by 1975—resulting in significant losses of both income and property taxes.

In August 1964 the "Parade of Progress" opened in the city's new underground Convention Center, showing off the best of the city's industry and technology, science, arts, and education. Nearby, construction at Erieview was giving Cleveland a new physical image and Clevelanders a sense of pride and success some thought no longer possible. Such signs of well-being were illusory, however, for as civic and business leaders focused on the revitalization of downtown Cleveland, the city's neighborhoods were in disarray.

Nowhere was this more apparent than in Hough, a changing neighborhood bounded by Superior and Euclid avenues and East 55th and East 105th streets. Beginning in the 1940s, Hough had changed from a middle- to a working-class neighborhood. In 1950 it was home to sixty-six thousand Clevelanders, 95 percent of whom were white. Many of the neighborhood's large houses had been subdivided into multiple units by landlords who routinely ignored housing code violations. In the 1950s, blacks displaced by urban renewal began moving to Hough, and by 1960 the neighborhood was 74 percent black; four years later, it housed a quarter of the city's welfare cases. In a series of articles in 1965, the *Cleveland Press* warned of a "crisis in Hough" and described the area's widespread suffering from poverty, overcrowding, vandalism, and arson. The following summer, frustration erupted into violence. Four days of rioting resulted in the deaths of four blacks and millions of dollars in property damage. With the jeeps of the National Guard lining the major arteries, Mayor Ralph S. Locher called the East Side rioting a "tragic day in the life of our city."[19]

Cleveland, once one of the most progressive and attractive of cities, now faced staggering losses on all sides. It was losing people and jobs. Formerly sound neighborhoods were becoming provinces of the poor, and on streets where people had once lived and shopped, only empty, gutted buildings remained. As the city's neighborhoods declined, so did its much vaunted public schools. Longtime businesses—including the William Taylor, Bailey's, and Sterling-Lindner department stores—were closing; so were the theaters at Playhouse Square. City parks had become dumping grounds, while the downtown, offering little to attract people, was virtually dead at night. To outsiders, Cleveland was the "mistake-on-the-lake"—an aging city where nothing seemed to go right, where even the river caught fire.

In 1967, in the aftermath of the Hough riots, many looked to Carl B. Stokes, the first black to be elected mayor of a major U.S. city, as "insurance" against further racial disorder. However, the following summer Cleveland police and black militants clashed in Glenville, leaving ten dead and dozens wounded. The subsequent revelation that corporate donations to Cleveland Now, a Stokes initiative that channeled money into myriad improvement projects, had been traced to a central figure in the Glenville shootout ended much of the mayor's support.

Though Cleveland had been losing population since 1950, the exodus accelerated dramatically after 1960. Between 1960 and 1970, the city lost more than 125,000 residents, its population dropping from 876,050 to 750,879. By the early 1970s, some 20,000 people were leaving the city each year. Economic activity, meanwhile, was moving to the periphery or else out of the region altogether. Between 1958 and 1977, Cleveland lost an estimated 130,000 jobs, while the suburbs of Cuyahoga County gained almost 210,000 jobs. Heavy industry, however, was leaving the region, choosing to relocate to the Sun Belt or abroad, where wages were lower. In 1972 Richard B. Tullis, president of Harris-Intertype Corporation, told the *Cleveland*

Press that the city would have to face up to the inevitable trend of major industries leaving and light manufacturing and service industries taking their place.[20]

Though three-term mayor Ralph J. Perk had built a successful political career by articulating the grievances of his largely ethnic, working-class constituency, the mood of the city was changing. In 1977 mayoral candidate Dennis J. Kucinich successfully targeted three issues: stopping the proposed sale of the Municipal Electric Light Plant to the Cleveland Electric Illuminating Company, ending tax abatement as a means of luring developers downtown, and concentrating the city's increasingly scant resources in the neighborhoods rather than downtown. But the young populist mayor who modeled himself after Tom L. Johnson alienated business leaders and community groups alike with his confrontational style. Kucinich narrowly survived a bitter recall election in 1978 but was swept out of office a year later.

In 1976, in a lawsuit brought by the Cleveland chapter of the National Association for the Advancement of Colored People (NAACP), U.S. District Judge Frank Battisti ruled that the Cleveland and state boards of education were responsible for the racial segregation of Cleveland's schools and must desegregate them. The historical problem of segregation in the schools was in large part the consequence of segregation in the city's housing patterns. Since at least the 1930s, however, school construction and decisions about school boundaries and teacher assignments had elicited protests from the black community. A major school-building program undertaken in the 1960s was perceived as a further attempt to strengthen de facto segregation. The court-ordered remedy—crosstown busing—accelerated the movement from the city to those who could afford suburban homes, blacks as well as whites, and resentment of busing helped defeat a succession of school levies.

Perhaps Cleveland's darkest moment came on December 15, 1978. Unable to repay $14 million in short-term notes that came due, it became the first city in the nation to default on its debts since the Depression. The default was the product of the dramatic loss of jobs and people, with a consequent shrinkage of the tax base. The roots of the fiscal crisis reached back to the early 1970s, when voters defeated two proposals to increase the city's income tax. At the end of Carl Stokes's second term as mayor, the city had a $13 million budget deficit. To cover revenue shortfalls, Stokes's successor, Ralph J. Perk, borrowed heavily and tapped bond funds to cover operating expenses and sold or leased a number of valuable city assets. Expenditures continued to mount, while revenues continued to shrink. When Dennis J. Kucinich took office in 1978, he faced a critical financial situation. In December 1978, when local banks refused to roll over the short-term notes, default became a bleak reality.

George V. Voinovich handily defeated Kucinich in the mayoral election of 1979 and guided the city back to financial health. He patched up relations with the business community, persuaded local banks to refinance the city's defaulted notes, and cut and consolidated public services. In 1981 Cleveland voters approved an income tax increase from 1.5 percent to 2.0 percent, earmarking half the proceeds for debt repayment and capital improvements. Later that year, they voted to reduce the City Council from thirty-three to twenty-one members and changed the term of office for both council members and the mayor from two to four years. Cleveland reentered the bond market in 1983, and in 1987, the last of its debts repaid, the Financial Planning and Supervision Commission appointed to oversee the city's financial recovery was disbanded.

Along with other cities in the nation's industrial crescent, Cleveland continued to struggle with wrenching economic change. Since the 1960s, the city had watched its heavy industries decline in the face of foreign competition. In the early 1980s, a nationwide recession further eroded Cleveland's traditional economic base as companies cut back and restructured, leaving thousands of Clevelanders without jobs. Between 1970 and 1985, the Cleveland metropolitan area lost more than eighty-six thousand manufacturing jobs; over the same period, service employment—especially in the areas of law, health care, and business—climbed by almost seventy-seven thousand jobs. Whereas in 1970, manufacturing had accounted for 47 percent of all jobs in Greater Cleveland, by 1987 manufacturing provided just 27 percent of jobs in Greater Cleveland. Cleveland's traditional blue-collar work force was largely left behind by the emerging service economy, and the service jobs that former factory workers did fill generally paid less than their old jobs.

In the late 1980s an improved national economy, local development initiatives, and growth in the service sector helped stabilize area employment, but poverty continued to tighten its grip on the city. According to a 1989 report by the Council for Economic Opportunities in Greater Cleveland, three-quarters of the county's poor (about 215,700 people) lived in Cleveland. City neighborhoods, plagued by drugs and drug-related crime, continued to erode, and more than seventeen thousand Clevelanders were living in what one federal official described as "the second-worst public housing" in the nation.[21]

Between 1970 and 1980, the city's population had dropped a precipitous 23 percent, from 750,879 to 573,822. In the 1980s the rate of loss slowed but showed no sign of abating. Despite an infusion of new immigrants—Chinese, Vietnamese, Cambodians, Latinos, and Poles—Cleveland lost more than 18,000 households. Most of those were middle-income families, black and white, relocating to inner-ring suburbs where there was a glut of housing. Many left to escape a school system plagued by political infighting, patronage, declining enrollment, and a dropout rate of almost 50 percent.

Despite these problems, Cleveland in the 1980s witnessed a remarkable building boom downtown and the palpable return of civic pride. Standard Oil Company (acquired by British Petroleum and renamed BP America in 1987), Ohio Bell, and Eaton Corporation each built large new headquarters buildings, while shopping-mall developers Richard and David Jacobs built the glass-roofed Galleria at Erieview, with two levels of stylish shops, and the heroic Society Center, at fifty-six stories the state's tallest building. Forest City Enterprises, meanwhile, reconfigured the historic Cleveland Union Terminal as part of a $400 million mixed-use project encompassing a shopping mall, offices, a rebuilt rapid-transit station, and a luxury hotel.

At Playhouse Square, the ambitious theater restoration project launched by Ray K. Shepardson in 1975 was substantially completed; the restored Ohio, State, and Palace theaters were now home to the Great Lakes Theater Festival, the Cleveland Ballet, and an array of popular entertainment. In the city's historic Warehouse District, nineteenth-century commercial buildings were turned into offices, loft apartments, and new shops and restaurants. Nearby, the Flats was similarly transformed; the site of the city's earliest industries was now a popular entertainment district, with restaurants, shops, and nightclubs. Meanwhile, following the Baltimore and Boston models of economic development, public and private interests combined to build the North Coast Harbor, a protected basin and waterside promenade at the foot of East 9th Street. Opened in 1988, the harbor was expected to attract new private development.

After a record ten years as mayor, George Voinovich decided to seek the governor's office. His successor, Michael R. White, appealed to a broad coalition of Cleveland voters by urging racial unity and pledging to build affordable housing and improve city schools. White helped persuade a majority of county voters to approve a tax on alcohol and tobacco to help finance a new professional baseball stadium and basketball arena (although all but one city ward rejected the measure). By 1990, a large swath of land in the old Central Market district had been cleared for construction of the $350 million Gateway sports complex, which White called the "linchpin project" for the city's future.[22]

In 1993, as the Gateway complex took shape on the southern rim of the downtown, there were other large-scale projects under way or on the drawing board: the Rock and Roll Hall of Fame and Museum, a Great Lakes science museum, an aquarium, and a downtown subway with a rail link connecting downtown Cleveland with University Circle. To win the Rock and Roll Hall of Fame, the city agreed to raise most of its $84 million price tag. Part of that money would be raised by diverting property taxes from the deficit-ridden city school district; lost tax revenue, advocates of the project claimed, would be offset by new economic development spurred by an expected seven-hundred-thousand visitors a year. Increasingly, civic leaders looked to tourism rather than to industry to create jobs and provide economic stability.

Cleveland in 1993 was far different from the city that, only six decades earlier, had celebrated the opening of the Union Terminal with such pride. Once the nation's sixth largest city, it was now twenty-fourth in size; once home to 75 percent of Cuyahoga County residents, it was now home to only 36 percent. As early as 1930, statistics showed, there were two Clevelands; the core of poverty and ring of affluence facilitated by the streetcar and accelerated by the automobile and the highway were, in 1993, even more pronounced. Despite robust development downtown, the city's neighborhoods continued to decline. Cleveland was home to the county's poorest residents, while the economically well-off lived in suburbs that now reached deep into adjacent, formerly rural counties. "The New Cleveland is corporate headquarters, service and professional jobs, downtown construction, recreational and cultural amenities," a reporter for the *Washington Post* observed in 1986. "The Old Cleveland is neighborhoods struggling against decay, double-digit unemployment, racial tension, factory closings, poverty, and long-suffering schools."[23] That dichotomy, it seemed all but certain, would persist long into the future.

Notes

1. Moses Cleaveland to Oliver Phelps and the Directors of the Connecticut Land Company, August 5, 1796, Moses Cleaveland Papers, Western Reserve Historical Society.

2. John Melish, *Travels in the United States of America, in the Years 1806 & 1807, and 1809, 1810, & 1811* (Philadelphia, 1812), 2:265, 267.

3. *Cleaveland Gazette and Commercial Register,* August 11, 1818.

4. *Cleaveland Herald,* June 6, 1822.

5. Ibid., September 21, 1833.

6. Ibid., September 2, 1830.

7. Ibid., November 14, 1843.

8. *Knight and Parson's Business Directory of the City of Cleveland* (Cleveland, 1853), 30–31.

9. *Cleveland Leader,* October 14, 1854.

10. Ibid., July 14, 1873; Willard Glazier, *Peculiarities of American Cities* (Philadelphia: Hubbard Brothers, 1883), 148–49; František J. Vlček, *Povídka Mého Života* (Cleveland: Privately printed, 1928), 129–30 (translation courtesy of Donald Tipka); *Cleveland Leader,* March 5, 1861.

11. Vlček, *Povídka Mého Života,* 119.

12. Elroy McKendree Avery, *A History of Cleveland and Its Environs* (Chicago: Lewis Publishing, 1918), 1:307–8.

13. *Cleveland Plain Dealer,* April 2, 1910.

14. Lincoln Steffens, *The Struggle for Self-Government* (New York: McClure, Phillips, 1906), 161.

15. William Ganson Rose, *Cleveland: The Making of a City* (1950; reprint, Kent, Ohio: Kent State University Press, 1990), 965.

16. Howard Whipple Green, *Population Characteristics by Census Tracts, Cleveland, Ohio, 1930* (Cleveland: Plain Dealer Publishing Company, 1931), 72; *Real Property Inventory of the Cleveland Metropolitan District,* Report No. 1 (Cleveland: Committee on Real Property Inventory, 1933), 6.

17. Rose, *Cleveland,* 1023.

18. L. S. Robbins, *Decentralization: A Problem in Cleveland's Future* (Cleveland: Cleveland Chamber of Commerce, 1941), 13.

19. *Cleveland Press,* February 10–13, 15–18, 1965; *Cleveland Plain Dealer,* July 20, 1966.

20. *Cleveland Press,* September 5, 1972.

21. Gertrude Jordan, Midwest regional director, U.S. Department of Housing and Urban Development, as quoted in the *Cleveland Plain Dealer,* May 21, 1989.

22. *Cleveland Plain Dealer,* July 28, 1991.

23. Keith Sinzinger, "Cleveland: The Simultaneous Rise and Fall of an American City," *Washington Post,* August 19, 1986.

Part 3

ECONOMY

Roots to Restructuring

Introduction

ONE OF THE MOST common ways of organizing our understanding of cities is to view them as markets—places where our relations are influenced by exchanges of goods and services. It is this version of the city—the market city—that is the subject of this section. Political scientist Dennis Judd observes that "in nineteenth century America, cities were regarded almost purely as economic entities. The constant process of territorial expansion which lasted until the 1880s put new towns at the leading face of economic exploitation and territorial claims."[1]

Cleveland, as we learned in the first two sections of this book, is a definitive example of the early economic relations of American urban life. At the very beginning landholders exhibited classic patterns of the speculative practices of frontier land development. As the town matured, it quickly became a dominant mercantile center because of its strategic location at the mouth of the Cuyahoga River.[2] For the entire nineteenth century, Cleveland served as an important transfer point for primary agriculture and mining goods.

The accumulation of profits and the increased volume of unrefined goods arriving in Cleveland soon combined to provide the city with the potential to be a center of manufacturing in the Midwest. Having passed through two successive eras of economic restructuring—speculative land economics and mercantile development—in just over one half-century, Cleveland, at the close of the Civil War, was ready to assume the mantle of manufacturing prominence.

Edward Hill's essay in this section really begins at about 1870, charting, in some detail, the last 120 years of regional economic change. His thesis is that economic restructuring in a mature city like Cleveland is a continuous process directed by the marketplace yet influenced by local political, economic, and sociocultural interests. Hill traces Cleveland's last century of economic development through four periods. First, from 1870 to the late 1920s the city experienced a long period of industrial entrepreneurism. Riding the crest of the industrial revolution, Cleveland became an early center of iron-ore and oil refinement as well as machine tools manufacture, transforming the economic base into one of heavy manufacturing. This rapidly changing economic structure brought to Cleveland hundreds of thousands of new immigrants who became the heart of a large labor force specializing in the production of industrial and consumer durable products.

Unlike many other frontier break-bulk cities turned into production centers, Cleveland retained a great deal of local ownership over the new manufacturing sectors. As a result, Cleveland has remained a "headquarter city." At the beginning of the Depression, Cleveland was the sixth largest city in the United States, its economic structure was deeply rooted in heavy manufacture of durable goods, and its productive investment, like that of many urban centers, was heavily overextended. The city's economy stagnated during this, the second stage of economic restructuring in the twentieth century.

The region's manufacturing economy rebounded during the third period of the economy discussed in this essay—a period in which growth was triggered by World War II and which lasted almost thirty-five years. All this came to an end in 1979. The final stage of economic change, from 1979 to the present, is treated with more detail than the previous stages. Hill traces the change in the regional economic structure from the "old order" industrial base to what he calls the "new order" economy of restructured Cleveland.

This latest stage of development, according to Hill, began with the recession of 1979, which unleashed a spate of international competitive forces that have eroded many of the region's traditional manufacturing-based competitive advantages. The old economic order passed away from 1979 to 1983, replaced by the new order, with its reconfigured manufacturing base and large and expanding service sector. This restructuring has had serious effects on the daily lives of the people of Cleveland. Hill ends his essay with a discussion of some of these impacts on the poor and on housing, providing a comprehensive and sensitive treatment of the city as market.

Notes

1. Dennis R. Judd, *The Politics of American Cities: Private Power and Public Policy* (Boston: Little, Brown, 1979), 2.

2. George Condon, *Cleveland: The Best Kept Secret* (Cleveland: J. T. Zubal and P. D. Dole, 1981), 3.

The Cleveland Economy: A Case Study of Economic Restructuring

Edward W. Hill

IN 1978 everything seemed to come apart in Cleveland: politically, the mayor survived a voter recall by 236 votes; fiscally, Cleveland was the first city to suffer a bond default since the Great Depression; and ecologically, Lake Erie was declared dead. Coterminous with these disasters, the economy of Greater Cleveland experienced an irreparable secular erosion of its durable goods base, starting in the third quarter of 1979 and continuing until the first quarter of 1983, signaling the end of the old economic order.

This essay discusses Cleveland's shift from the old to a new order economy. A brief description of the emergence of the industrial old order economy is followed by an analysis of the new economic structure. This analysis suggests that the new economic structure involves more than the numbers of jobs lost or changed. It is also evident in changes in the incidence of poverty, the relative costs of housing, and the occupational characteristics of the residential labor force.

After 1979: A Summary, "By the Numbers"

Employment in the four-county Cleveland Primary Metropolitan Statistical Area (PMSA) peaked in the third quarter of 1979 at nearly 903,000 and then began a slide that did not stop until the first quarter of 1983 (see Figure 1).[1] The region lost 30 percent of total employment and 14 percent of its annualized earnings over this time period, amounting to $2.4 billion per year in 1982–84 dollars.[2]

A gradual recovery began in 1983, but it ended when the national recession hit the region in the summer of 1991. In 1990 total employment in the PMSA stood at 950,200, and 909,100 of the residents held jobs. The recovery from this second recession set in quickly, but it was gradual—nationally it became popularly known as a "jobless" recovery. Sure signs of a pickup in employment did not reappear in Greater Cleveland until mid-1993.

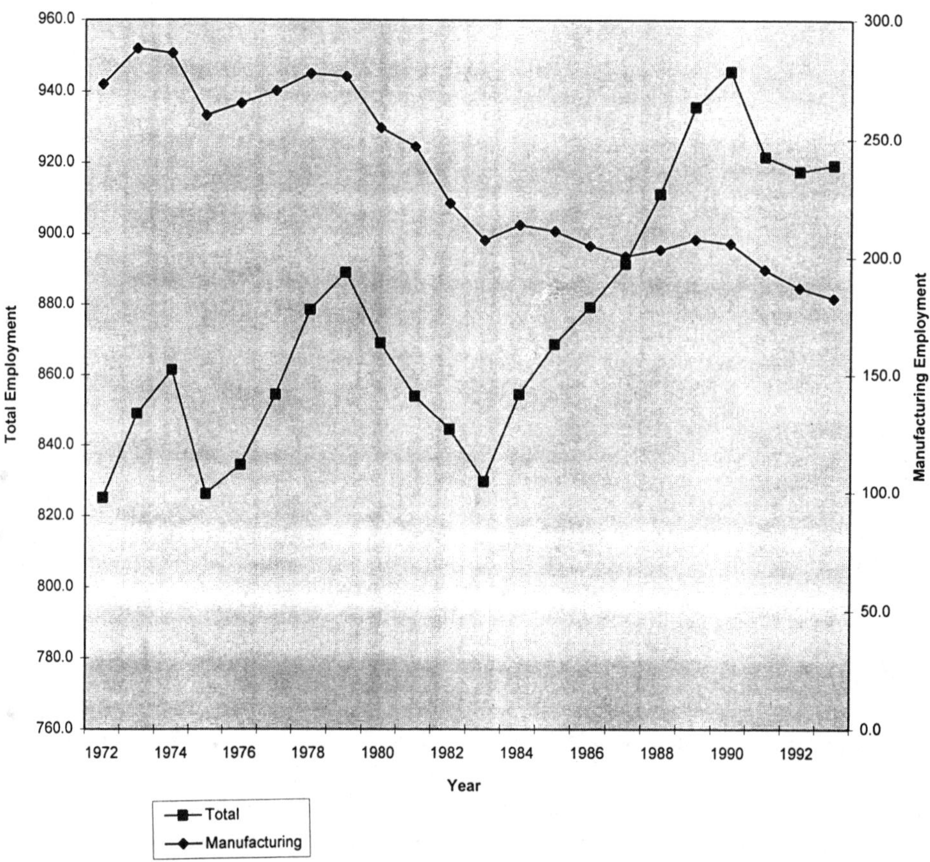

Year	Employment Total	Employment Manufacturing	Year	Employment Total	Employment Manufacturing
1972	825.2	273.0	1983	829.8	207.3
1973	849.0	288.0	1984	854.5	213.8
1974	861.4	286.1	1985	868.7	211.2
1975	826.3	260.0	1986	879.2	204.9
1976	834.4	265.1	1987	891.6	200.6
1977	854.4	270.3	1988	911.3	203.3
1978	878.5	277.5	1989	935.8	207.6
1979	889.1	276.3	1990	945.6	205.9
1980	869.1	254.9	1991	921.8	194.9
1981	854.0	246.8	1992	917.6	187.0
1982	844.6	223.0	1993	919.5	182.6

Figure 1
Cleveland PMSA—Employment

The composition of employment is very different from what it was in 1979. The direction of the change was similar to that of other Rust Belt metropolitan areas. One-quarter (68,442) of all manufacturing jobs present in 1979 disappeared by 1983; another 5,000 were lost between 1983 and 1987. Manufacturing employment increased from 1987 until the recession began to be felt in late 1990. It then began to slide once again, reaching 182,600 jobs in 1993. Manufacturing employment accounted for 30.3 percent of total employment in 1979, but in 1993 it was 19.9 percent. Three sectors increased their shares of local employment over this time period: services from 18.6 to 29.2 percent; retail trade from 16.2 to 16.8 percent; and finance, insurance, and real estate from 5.2 to 6.6 percent.

Structural shifts and cyclical fluctuations in the economy were matched by population losses in both the city of Cleveland and the PMSA. Between 1970 and 1980, the PMSA lost 8 percent of its population, or 165,000 people. The city of Cleveland lost 23.6 percent of its population from 1970 to 1980. Out-migration continued; the 1990 population of the city was 505,616, a loss of 11.9 percent from 1980.

The simple loss of population is less troubling than the apparent selective nature of the out-migration. The remaining population is increasingly poor. Even though the reported unemployment rate dropped from 1983 to 1990, the number of poor in the city and surrounding county increased.[3] Nearly 40 percent of the city's population was below the poverty line in 1987, up from 27 percent in 1980.[4]

The Greater Cleveland region is composed of two economies: the city of Cleveland and the rest of the region. Work by Ziona Austrian and Richard Bingham showed that through the first year of the recent recovery the performance of the Greater Cleveland region mirrored that of the nation, while employment in the city of Cleveland dropped dramatically.[5] The city lost almost 12,000 jobs during this recovery, while the rest of the region gained nearly 3,500 jobs.[6]

Victor S. Voinovich echoed Austrian and Bingham in his survey of the commercial office rental market in Cuyahoga County. Voinovich said that "we're a tale of two cities."[7] The *Plain Dealer* reported that suburban office space is filling at the expense of space downtown. Voinovich interprets the vacancy rates as meaning that there is a "shakeout of the service business." The highest demand is for buildings that combine office space and warehousing, which is a product that is located in the suburbs near the highway system.

Austrian and Bingham feel that the city of Cleveland is not without its bright spots: legal services, educational institutions, and medical services. They conclude that "it is difficult to be enthusiastic about two economies in the Cleveland metropolitan area—a growing suburban economy and a declining City economy. For the city, it is just as important to stem the flow of jobs . . . as it is to stem the flow of residents. For the suburbs it is important to think regionally."[8]

In 1979 an era, or economic long wave, of development ended, and in 1985 a new economic order was clearly in place. To understand how and why this transition came about, we must look at the region's economic history.

The Industrial Base of Old Order Cleveland

The foundation for old order Cleveland was laid from 1870 to the late 1920s. This period witnessed unprecedented industrial entrepreneurism, which took advantage of natural resource endowments and transportation cost advantages to build a city that was the sixth largest in the United States in 1930.[9] The economy went into a prolonged hiatus during the Great Depression, but the region became an industrial giant during World War II. Cleveland was a city of big industries and big labor, devoted to the production of industrial and consumer durable products. Cleveland differed from other Great Lakes cities in one respect: many of its manufacturing plants were locally owned; they were not branch plants. This gave the city corporate headquarters employment, which is the basis of much of its current development efforts.

In the late 1800s, railroads running from New York to Chicago, another running from southern Ohio north, and lake freighters all met in Cleveland. The city was a classic break-in-bulk point. The steel industry was fed by boats bringing ore from the Upper Peninsula of Michigan, later from Minnesota's Mesabi Range, and coal hauled by rail car from southern Ohio and West Virginia. Cleveland became the largest Great Lakes iron-ore and coal port. Transportation was also vital in the development of the oil industry. Crude oil was shipped by rail to Cleveland, processed into kerosene, and shipped by boat to Buffalo, Chicago, and Canadian cities. By 1870 there were more than twenty oil refineries in a section of the Cuyahoga River valley called the Flats, processing crude from Pennsylvania, West Virginia, and Ohio. The Flats was home to the largest refining complex in the world. John D. Rockefeller organized Cleveland's oil industry as the foundation of one of the nation's largest industrial monopolies. Production of lake freighters boomed, and turn-of-the-century Cleveland became one of the largest shipbuilding centers in the United States.

Each of these activities formed the basis of a major industrial complex. The steel industry produced wire and rails for the development of the West. Flat-rolled steel was produced and used by the appliance and automotive industries. The combination of steel and shipbuilding led to the production of machine tools, fasteners, industrial fittings, and, later, automobiles and automobile parts. The oil industry, coupled with low-cost transportation of minerals from the states bordering the Great Lakes, was the foundation of a large industrial complex in chemicals, paints, and coatings. Each of these industries was devoted to industrial or consumer durable goods production.

One major manufacturing complex in this region—the lighting industry—was more dependent on inventive genius than on transportation cost advantage. The arc light was invented by Charles Brush in 1878. His company was absorbed by General Electric in 1891 and later became its lamp division. Westinghouse was founded in Cleveland in 1886 and in 1890 began producing castings for power transmitting equipment in a lakeside factory. During the 1930s, Westinghouse began to use this plant for its lighting division. Cleveland also specialized in the production of electrical motors, which led to the development of several machine tool companies. Firms such as Lincoln Electric, founded in 1895, produced motors and later developed arc welding equipment, and Reliance Electric, established in 1905, manufactured variable speed motors.

Samuel P. Orth summarized the economic history of the region from 1819 to 1910: "Two decades of hand industry, two decades of primitive manufacture, preparing the products of the farm for the market, followed by two decades of the development of iron and steel, which development is continued to the present day. The decade of 1870 was the decade of oil; the decade of 1890 that of clothing and paints; and the decade of 1900 has been the decade of the automobile."[10] There were 1,617 factories in Cleveland in 1905, employing nearly 71,000 people and supporting a population of 450,000. Iron and steel accounted for nearly half of the value of production. The iron and steel industry supported 11 bridge-building steel plants, 134 foundries, 10 wire plants, and innumerable machine shops. This industrial complex was followed in importance by the apparel and slaughtering businesses.

The major change in the economy from 1905 to the end of World War II was the rise of automobile and truck manufacturing, concomitant with the demise of apparel and slaughtering. By 1930 Cleveland's automotive industry was well established. The region had become a supplier of automotive parts and accessories, providing a major source of employment in the region and forming the basis for Cleveland's gradual emergence into the electronics, aircraft parts, and defense industries.

In the 1950s and 60s steel and automotive production flourished, but this prosperity was short-lived. Factory workers began to lose jobs with the end of the Vietnam War and the beginning of the recession of the mid-1970s. Major local corporations such as TRW and Eaton also began to adjust their business strategies, moving out of cyclically sensitive durable goods production into other product lines.

TRW was founded in 1900 as Cleveland Cap Screw, producing connectors and fittings for automobiles and light machinery. The firm became a leading supplier of automobile valves and during World War I began to make valves for airplanes. In 1926 the name was changed to Thompson Products, with two major divisions, automotive and aircraft parts. Following World War II the company increasingly specialized in aerospace and defense work. Its center for production employment shifted to Los Angeles, although the headquarters remained in Cleveland. This movement was accentuated by the firm's aggressive closure of Cleveland-area automotive parts facilities from the mid-1970s through the 1979 recession. The 1994 *Ohio Industrial Directory* indicates that TRW has two manufacturing plants in the Cleveland PMSA: its Valve Division employed 1,400, down from 1,950 in 1978—and its Piston Division employed 80. TRW sold its PC Airfoils division to Precision Castparts Corp., of Portland, Oregon, and production moved from Cleveland to Wickliffe, Ohio. Its metals division closed between 1978 and 1989.

Eaton Corporation has a similar history. The firm was founded in 1911 to manufacture truck axles and moved into the production of other automotive components and springs. Eaton became a leading engineer and producer of power steering and air conditioners during the 1950s and 1960s. During the 1970s the corporation made a strategic decision to diversify into more recession-resistant industries. In 1978 it purchased the Cutler-Hammer Company of Milwaukee and entered the electronics and electric controls business. By 1980 Eaton was moving out of its traditional base. The company sold its Cleveland-based industrial drive division, and in 1983, 1,100 Clevelanders lost their jobs when the axle plant closed. Eaton's remaining Brooklyn factory employed 225 people and manufactures air-actuated industrial clutches and brakes. Eaton maintains a small fasteners operation in Cleveland, employing 41. More than half of Eaton's sales are in electronics. The firm is headquartered in Cleveland, but its electronics plants are located elsewhere.

The list of closures from 1978 to 1983 is striking. Westinghouse, founded in Cleveland but now headquartered in Pittsburgh, had used its lakeside manufacturing plant since 1890. The plant was closed in 1979, and the company stopped all manufacturing of lighting products in the region in 1982. Westinghouse did keep a large concentration of sales and service employees in the region, and its Oceanic Division manufactures torpedoes and various underwater equipment in its one remaining Cleveland factory. But this too was threatened with defense cutbacks in the early 1990s. The company is developing new products in attempt to stave off its closing, one being an electric motor scooter. General Electric kept its lamp division headquarters and engineering facility in East Cleveland but closed six factories that manufactured bulbs and components and shifted mainly to offshore suppliers. Midland-Ross Company was founded in 1884 and grew by producing auto frames. By 1969 the firm had nineteen divisions and operated fifty-seven plants, but in 1986 the company was sold, and the headquarters closed in early 1987. Harris Corporation ended an eighty-five-year association with the region in 1978 when it moved its headquarters to Melbourne, Florida, to be near its integrated circuit plant. This move completed the firm's shift from its Cleveland heritage, making printing presses and information processing equipment, to electronic communications, integrated circuit production, and defense work.

These brief corporate histories capsulate the economic history of the region. Growth in demand for durable products peaked in 1968. These products became susceptible to offshore competition, in part because of the high cost of manufacturing labor and shortsighted investment strategies of management. As major local employers shifted out of durable goods manufacturing, often into electronics, they built plants where concentrations of specialized labor existed. In many cases, the headquarters employment remained. Cleveland still has a strong manufacturing base, but one that is smaller, more competitive, and more reliant on locational advantages than on market power. This is especially true of the remaining steel and automotive plants.

The economic restructuring of Cleveland is paradoxical. Cleveland is a command and control center of modern manufacturing capital. The Big Three automakers and their suppliers are the largest manufacturing employers in the region, but decisions regarding this complex are not made locally. The durable goods industry is much less diversified than it was before the economy was restructured. Before 1979 this sector was evenly balanced among automobiles, steel, and machine tools, accompanied by significant employment in paints, chemicals, and oil. The economy as a whole has become more diversified, but the durable goods sector is much more dependent on the fortunes of the automotive industry than it was before 1979. Ironically, as local durable goods manufacturing employment is more dependent on automobile production, locally headquartered manufacturers are less dependent on supplying the automotive industry. They used automotive technology and retained earnings from supplying automobile assemblers in the 1950s and 1960s to diversify into electronics and aircraft parts production.

Is There a New Order Cleveland?

Did a new economic base emerge in Greater Cleveland during the 1979–91 business cycle? The region clearly remains a manufacturing center. Even though manufacturing's share of local employment dropped, it remains substantially above the national average. Cleveland retained a strong specialization in durable goods manufacturing, even though nearly sixty-two thousand jobs were lost in this industrial division.[11] At the same time, services have strengthened to the point that the division's proportion of employment is above the national average. Social services and wholesale and retail trade are now part of the region's economic base; they were not in 1979. Specific major groups of employment in producer services are also basic to the region's economy. The largest proportional changes in producer services are in electric, gas, and sanitary services, business services, and legal services.

MANUFACTURING

The Cleveland region led the nation in losses in manufacturing employment during the first part of the 1979–83 business cycle and lagged in gains during the recovery, from 1983 to 1991. Data on regional manufacturing employment are shown in Figure 1. Manufacturing employment rebounded slightly from 1983 to 1984, but erosion set in and employment stability was not reached until 1988. This period of relative stability was short-lived, however; employment declined with the beginning of the 1991 recession. The rate of decline in manufacturing employment indicates that restructuring was largely completed from 1983 to 1984.

The relative strength of manufacturing rests on a few major groups in durable goods production. Even though employment decreased markedly in some of these groups, it did so at a slower rate than in the same industries nationally. A good example is primary metals. The industry lost nearly seventy-five hundred jobs from 1979 to 1986, and in 1993 it employed about sixteen thousand workers. Forty-eight percent of the employment that remains in this group is in the blast furnace and steel mill industry, Standard Industrial Classification (SIC) 3312, and another third is in the gray iron foundry industry (SIC 3321). The primary metals industry has lost employment nationally and locally, but the large integrated mills are concentrating their production in the Chicago-Gary region and in northeastern Ohio. A key to the continued health of this industry is continuing its relentless drive to improve product quality and labor productivity. In 1980 it took ten hours of labor to make a ton of steel; now it takes three hours.[12] A second critical variable in the industry's future is the price of iron ore relative to steel scrap. If ore is expensive compared to scrap, mini-mills have a cost advantage; if scrap is expensive compared to ore, integrated mills have the advantage.

USX closed its Cleveland plant and sold part of its ownership interest in its pipe and bar mill in Lorain to Japan's Kobe Steel. LTV cut back employment drastically, but its two factories continued to run with bankruptcy court protection (which it gave up in 1993), give-backs by its employees, and newfound concern for product quality. LTV's Cleveland complex is the nation's largest integrated flat-rolled production facility and opened a galvanized steel mill in partnership with Sumitomo Metals. The mill's customers are concentrated in the automobile industry. American Steel and Wire is a new firm, which reopened the old U.S. Steel wire plant in July 1986.

The region has also benefited from the evolution of the instruments industry, which is becoming part of the economic base, even though it is a relatively small employer. Two components of this industry are part of the region's industrial base. These are measuring and controlling devices (SIC 382) and medical instruments (SIC 384). The 1994 *Ohio Industrial Directory* lists 168 establishments in the four county PMSA that manufacture instruments. The region contains about 30 percent of the state's establishments and 27 percent of its employment in this industrial grouping. Cleveland has developed a specialization in the process control instrument industry (SIC 3823) and in an industry the SIC calls "instruments, measuring, testing electrical and electronic signals" (SIC 3825). Examples of firms active in these industrial segments include: Solon's Keithley Instruments, which manufactures electronic test instruments for laboratories and production lines; Victoreen, which manufactures instruments for the nuclear industry; and Cleveland's Parker Hannafin Corporation which manufactures motion control systems in part of its plant.

Four major groups of manufacturers of nondurable goods were also part of the region's economic base in 1986: printing and publishing (especially greeting card manufacturing and periodical publishing), chemicals and allied products (here the largest areas of specialization are paints, miscellaneous chemical products, industrial chemicals, and plastics), rubber and miscellaneous products (where tires have been replaced by fabricated rubber products and miscellaneous plastic products in importance), and petroleum and coal. All with the exception of printing are closely connected to national headquarters activity of the direct line of business. For example, British Petroleum (BP) absorbed Sohio and moved BP's North American headquarters from New York into Sohio's corporate headquarters. In addition, major coal operators are headquartered in Cleveland and employment is relatively high because of the presence of the steel mills. Relative to employment changes in the nation as a whole, the weakest performing of these industries was printing and publishing.

Chemical and allied products are well represented in Cleveland but are concentrated in the paint and coating segments of the industry. Chemical factories in Cleveland are very different from those located near Niagara Falls. Cleveland's plants are not intensive users of electricity. Instead, PPG's automotive finishes division is headquartered in a factory complex in Lakewood, bordering Cleveland. Sherwin Williams's national headquarters and research development laboratories are at the edge of Cleveland's Public Square. Glidden is headquartered near the Public Square, and its industrial coatings division is based in the region. Ferro Corporation recently moved into new corporate headquarters and employs eight hundred people in the region. Its coatings, color, and refractories divisions are located in the city of Cleveland, and the Bedford chemicals division has a plant in the suburbs.

The rubber and miscellaneous products group in Greater Cleveland was restructured completely from 1979. Aggregate data for this major group hide the dynamic nature of the region's firms. They have experienced substantial declines in the rubber business—many corporations divested their tire and rubber operations—and grown in plastics and polymer production and fabrication. In the late 1980s the Small Business Administration identified 140 fast-growing manufacturing establishments in the Cleveland region. Eighteen polymer manufacturers form the largest cluster on the list. Nearly all of the polymer firms that responded to a 1989 survey conducted by the Greater Cleveland Growth Association indicated that transportation access to their customers provided the Cleveland region with a competitive advantage over other potential sites.[13]

Interviews conducted with economic development professionals reveal a concern about the polymer industry in Northeast Ohio. The region is rich in research and development, but production is taking place elsewhere. Several reasons are offered. The concentration of research makes the region one where large firms need a presence to keep an eye on new developments in materials, but production takes place elsewhere because of regional cost disadvantages. Plastics production is capital intensive and is sensitive to state and local taxes, as well as differences in the cost of workmen's compensation insurance. Other differences cited are the cost of transporting feed stocks to make the raw material and the cost of shipping raw materials to factories. These are just speculations however. Definitive research on the locational determinants in this important industry has not yet been conducted.

Little Tikes, a division of Rubbermaid headquartered in Hudson, Ohio, pioneered rotational modeling of plastics to manufacture extremely durable children's toys. In the late 1980s, the firm employed eleven hundred in the region. Evenflo Products, manufacturers of infant care products, employed two hundred people in Ravenna. Glastic Company, purchased by Japan's Kobe Steel, employed more than two hundred in the city of Cleveland and produces insulators, fiber optic rods, and various injected molded plastic parts.

The M. A. Hanna Company restructured its holdings in reaction to shifts in the regional and national economies. The company is an old-line Cleveland firm that helped to open Michigan's iron pits and the Mesabi range. Until recently Hanna invested heavily in iron-ore and coal properties. By 1986 the scope of its restructuring was evident. The firm sold its Minnesota and Michigan iron mines and in 1995 divested its remaining iron-ore and coal properties. The company has largely moved out of the metals business, selling Hanna Silicon in the process. The bulk of the proceeds from these sales were used to move Hanna solidly into polymer production businesses. Many of these new subsidiaries are located in the Cleveland-Akron metropolitan complex.

The fabricated metals major group has held its position relative to the nation despite massive regional employment losses. It is difficult to find anything optimistic to say about the performance of fabricated metals in Cleveland. Only two small industries did not decline from 1979 to 1983. These are the metal cans business (SIC 3411), which employed 375 people in 1986, and hardware not elsewhere classified (SIC 3429), which employed 861. The latter industry lost a significant number of jobs from 1983 to 1986. Those parts of the fabricated metals industry which lost at least a thousand positions are screw machine products (SIC 3451); bolts, nuts, rivets, and washers (SIC 3452); and automotive stampings (SIC 3465). Metal stamping not elsewhere classified (SIC 3469) gained 548 employees; and metal services, plating, and polishing (SIC 3471) gained 534 jobs. Overall, employment in this major industrial group increased by 1,500 in the second part of the business cycle.

Nonelectrical machinery remains a basic employer despite losing nearly twenty thousand jobs from 1979 to 1983. The two segments of the machine tools industry (SIC 3541 and 3542) declined by more than two-thirds. Industrial trucks and tractors (SIC 3537) lost over 90 percent of its 1979 employment base, and construction machinery (SIC 3531) declined by more than 80 percent. These employment losses are memorialized on Cleveland's East Side, where the former White Motors Truck plant is partially filled as an industrial incubator, and in the former sites of heavy construction machine factories in Euclid and Hudson.

The electrical and electronic machinery business nearly disappeared. Almost half of the jobs lost in the electrical equipment industry were in electric lighting and wiring (SIC 364). The largest share of the loss was generated by the electric lighting fixtures industry (SIC 3645), because of General Electric's closing of its production facilities. Two components of the electrical equipment industry—radio and television communications equipment (SIC 3662) and electrical engine equipment (SIC 3694)—disappeared for all practical purposes during the 1979 downturn in the business cycle.

The story of the transportation equipment business is complicated. Its share of employment has dropped, but it remains a dominant force in Cleveland's Consolidated Metropolitan Statistical Area, which consists of the Cleveland, Akron, and Lorain PMSAs. The apparent loss of comparative advantage in the PMSA is largely attributable to the closure of General Motors' Coit Road factory on the East Side of the city of Cleveland and the decrease in employment in parts plants throughout the region. Yet Ford and Nissan Motors erected a new minivan plant in Avon Lake, near Lorain, and Ford Motor Company made large investments in Brook Park to build a new generation of six- and eight-cylinder engines. Nearly half of the remaining employment in the transportation equipment major group is in the motor vehicle parts and accessories industry (SIC 3714), which employed seventy-six hundred people in 1987.

THE CYCLICAL SENSITIVITY OF CLEVELAND'S MANUFACTURING BASE

Has restructuring lessened the region's traditional exposure to cyclically caused unemployment? Approximately 40 percent of Cleveland's manufacturing employment is in major industrial groups that are sensitive to business cycle fluctuations (Table 1). Unfortunately, 68 percent of manufacturing employment is in industries that have experienced a steady decline through the past business cycle; 30 percent of total manufacturing employment is in the intersection of these two sets—declining and cyclically sensitive industries.

Those major industrial groups that were classified as being stable through the cycle are part of the region's economic base employing 35,218 people, or 18 percent of manufacturing employment. The instruments group was the only part of the base that was a growing employer.

Clearly, a large portion of Cleveland's manufacturing economic base is dependent on the success of the American automobile industry and the local steel industry. Half of the employment in the transportation equipment group, most of the workers in primary metals, and a large fraction of the chemical business are part of the automotive industrial complex. These jobs are vulnerable to both business cycles and offshore competition. Cleveland's automotive suppliers have not made large inroads in supplying Japanese-owned automotive factories located in the United States.[14]

A distinction is made in Table 1 between major industrial groups that experienced decline throughout the cycle and those that experienced steep decline. Unfortunately, electrical and electronic machinery fell into the latter category but remains one of the largest manufacturing employers in the region. This industry, along with fabricated metal and nonelectrical equipment, will be at risk to major

Table 1
Classification of Manufacturing Industries:
Employment and Average Quarterly Earnings, First Quarter, 1987

Category	*SIC*	*Name*	*Employment*	*Average Earnings*
Stable Noncyclical	27	Printing and publishing	15,905	5,754
	29	Petroleum and coal	4,416	11,254
	39	Miscellaneous industries	3,080	5,139
Stable Cyclical	30	Rubber and plastics	11,817	5,273
Declining	20	Food and kindred	6,806	6,505
	25	Furniture and fixtures	2,094	6,163
	28	Chemicals	14,212	8,652
	35	Machinery except electrical	29,092	6,520
	37	Transportation equipment	19,557	10,141
Steep Decline	22	Textile mill products	727	4,021
	23	Apparel	4,078	3,945
	36	Electrical & electronic equipment	18,205	7,167
Cyclical Growing	24	Wood and lumber products	1,768	6,379
	38	Instruments and related	6,878	7,591
Cyclical, Declining, Strong Rebound	32	Stone, clay, and glass	3,748	6,933
	33	Primary metal[a]	23,301	
Weak Rebound	34	Fabricated metal	31,627	6,656

Source: ES-202, U.S. Department of Labor.
[a]Data for SIC 33, primary metal, is from *County Business Patterns* 1986:1.

employment losses in any future recession. Indeed, research by Richard Bingham and Ziona Austrian documented such losses in the 1991 downturn. Together these three groups accounted for 78,924 jobs in the first quarter of 1987.

A note of caution must be made about predictions based solely on employment trends. In this essay I do not examine causal relationships. The data do not indicate what caused the loss of employment over the business cycle. These losses may have been caused by any of a large number of problems: an irreversible loss of comparative advantage, high wages, outmoded capital, adversarial labor-management relations, poor product quality, the collapse of traditional sources of demand, or poor strategic decisions on the part of management. All of these factors have been blamed for the collapse of the manufacturing sector in the Cleveland region. No doubt all came into play at some time during the 1980s, and all have been the subject of public and private initiatives. The stabilization of employment in these major industrial groups depends on the success of those efforts.

The restructuring of the region's manufacturing base has had striking results. The region is less diversified within durable goods manufacturing than it was in 1979, but it appears to be more competitive. Two new major industrial groups have been added to the economic base—polymers and instruments. Employment in transportation equipment and primary metals is more dependent on demand for domestic automobiles than ever before. The jobs of tens of thousands employed in fabricated metals and electrical and non-electrical machinery industries remain exposed to the vagaries of the business cycle. Their continued presence appears to be tied to the health of local steel and automobile production.

SERVICES

During the first part of the business cycle, from 1979 to 1983, employment in the service sector fell from 450,673 to 430,835 (Table 2). Most of the drop was in retail trade, followed by wholesale trade and transportation services. The loss in employment occurred because retail sales plummeted as blue-collar incomes declined and employment in the transportation and durable goods wholesale groups declined along with the region's manufacturing base. All five components of the service sector grew during the recovery, accounting for 90 percent of private sector job growth during that period. Nearly one-quarter of the increase was in wholesale trade, and retail trade accounted for 16 percent.

Social services and some major industrial groups within producer services became part of the region's economic base between 1979 and 1986. The absolute number of persons employed in social services increased from 1979 to 1983 because employment increased in the region's hospitals. Employment in producer services dropped slightly during the first part of the cycle, but its relative share within the service sector increased. Business services were the dynamic force within producer services.

In 1979, transportation and wholesale and retail trade constituted 40.5 percent of the service economy. This segment reached 37 percent in 1987. In 1994, there were at least four steel service centers in the region with employment of more than one hundred workers, and there are major wholesalers of industrial machinery. The continued strength of wholesale trade may be the result of wholesalers of foreign-made goods replacing some domestic manufacturers in the national economy.

Nondurable goods supplanted durable goods as the primary wholesale employer during the recovery. Retail trade was also a substantial employer, gaining 10,407 jobs from 1983 to 1986. The dynamic characteristics of these two industries may be linked, but additional data must be collected to verify that suspicion.

Table 2
Employment in the service sectors, Cleveland PMSA, 1979, 1983, 1986

Sector	*SIC*	*1979*	*1983*	*1986*
Employment for services		450,673	430,835	495,162
Transportation	40–42, 44–47	24,211	18,254	19,806
Wholesale and retail trade		158,582	140,848	166,710
Wholesale	50–51	63,356	56,881	72,336
Retail	52–57, 59	95,226	83,967	94,374
Producer services		119,473	118,174	136,858
Communications	48–49	21,444	21,337	20,500
Banking	60–62	20,275	21,514	21,717
Insurance	63–64	17,717	14,235	16,751
Real estate	65–66	11,278	11,795	12,681
Engineering and architecture	891	4,008	4,429	5,670
Accounting	893	4,542	4,127	5,516
Miscellaneous business services	67, 73, 899	35,139	34,821	46,787
Legal services	81	5,070	5,916	7,236
Social services		79,015	89,399	100,390
Medical services	801–805, 807–808	19,921	25,070	31,302
Hospitals	806	34,704	38,403	40,154
Education	82	13,518	15,019	13,370
Welfare	832	0	0	0
Nonprofit	86	4,248	9,240	13,462
Postal services	43	NA	NA	NA
Government	91–99	NA	NA	NA
Miscellaneous	833–839	1,624	1,667	2,102
Personal services		69,392	64,160	71,671
Domestic	88	0	0	0
Hotels	70	8,828	6,583	7,611
Eating and drinking	58	42,734	40,885	46,900
Repair	725	0	0	0
Laundry	721	3,870	3,104	2,909
Barber and beauty shop	723–724	3,594	3,624	4,087
Entertainment	78–79	8,194	7,658	7,597
Miscellaneous	725–729	2,172	2,253	2,567

NA = Not available.
Source: County Business Patterns: 1979, 1983, 1986.

Producer services generated nearly nineteen thousand new jobs during the recovery, most in miscellaneous business services, which are composed of holding and other investment offices (SIC 67), business services (SIC 73), and services not elsewhere classified (SIC 889). This sector generated nearly twelve thousand net new jobs during the recovery. The Cleveland region has developed a competitive advantage in this services group. Four of the components of producer services grew throughout the cycle: engineering and architecture (SIC 891), legal services (SIC 81), real estate (SIC 65 and 66), and finance (SIC 60, 61, and 62).

Browning and Singlemann placed the health care industries in the social service category.[15] Health care was the leading generator of employment from 1979 to 1983. Two-thirds of employment growth in hospitals took place during this phase, but the contribution of hospitals to the recovery of the local economy was dwarfed by that of medical services (SIC 801–805, 807, and 808), which produced twice as many jobs from 1979 to 1986. Hospital employment fell during the recovery phase of the cycle, from 1983 to 1986, in concert with the federal government's change in the way hospitals are reimbursed for Medicaid and Medicare coverage.

The employment pattern within the major employment groups that compose the four service sectors varied. *County Business Patterns* had employment data on twenty-six industries within the service sector. Three were in a state of continuous decline, nine were cyclical, ten grew continuously, and one was countercyclical from 1979 to 1987. Employment data for three of the component industries were not available.

Summary

The economy of Greater Cleveland is more diversified today than it was before 1979, but the region's economy still rests on manufacturing for its health and survival. Durable goods manufacturing remains the center of the region's competitive advantage. In 1991 more than one job in four in Greater Cleveland was a manufacturing job; in the nation as a whole it was one out of five. The Greater Cleveland region is also unusually dependent on durable goods manufacturing; 18 percent of the work force is employed in this sector of the economy.

Durable goods had very high rates of productivity growth during the 1980s and low rates of employment growth—in fact, employment declined. During the late 1980s business services were the key to generating new jobs in the region. The vitality of this industry results from a combination of growth in the number of regional offices; from manufacturers moving into distribution and marketing; and from manufacturing having higher indirect multipliers than in previous decades. In short, growth in business service employment rested on providing services to a broad manufacturing belt in northern Ohio.

The region's economy is built upon a foundation of steel, automobiles, paints, and chemicals. Development in the region depends not just on entrepreneurs but on the economic vitality of these central activities and the relationship of other industries to this core. There are two other components of the region's industrial core: The first is industries that have either corporate or divisional headquarters in

Table 3
19 Highly Specialized and Competitive Industries

Standard Industrial Classification		*Location Quotients*		*Shift Share*	*Percentage Change Employment*		*Competitive*	
SIC	*Name*	*1983*	*1991*	*Competitive Effect*	*Cleveland*	*U.S.*	*Score*	*Rank*
277	Greeting cards	4.56	13.28	2,510	318.5	46.9	6.64	2
291	Petroleum refining	0.04	3.19	4,089	8363.3	18.0	3.59	3
354	Metalworking machinery	3.44	4.26	2,493	52.8	25.9	2.97	4
494	Water supply	0.46	5.25	1,321	1267.9	21.9	2.60	6
289	Misc. chemical products	2.51	4.14	1,639	90.7	17.9	2.36	7
331	Blast furnaces & basic steel products	4.17	4.70	1,214	-5.8	-14.5	2.31	9
343	Plumbing and heating, except plastic	3.33	4.90	893	77.5	23.2	2.18	10
345	Screw machine products, bolts, etc.	5.64	5.91	137	8.2	5.5	2.09	11
496	Steam & air-conditioning supply	1.99	5.60	80	63.6	-40.5	1.93	13
364	Electric lighting & wiring equipment	1.71	2.65	1,681	69.4	11.8	1.78	14
334	Secondary nonferrous metals	3.40	4.80	254	23.1	-10.9	1.72	16
495	Sanitary services	1.03	2.38	1,708	366.4	105.6	1.69	17
285	Paints & allied products	3.65	4.31	353	25.2	8.4	1.59	19
295	Asphalt paving & roofing materials	1.80	3.29	403	82.8	2.2	1.20	24
601	Central reserve depository	2.81	3.53	191	35.9	10.5	1.16	25
347	Metal services, nec.*	1.88	2.44	642	60.3	25.9	1.02	34
349	Misc. fabricated metal products	2.23	2.50	531	-2.6	-11.1	0.97	35
544	Candy, nut & confectionery stores	1.90	2.63	224	67.1	23.3	0.82	43
393	Musical instruments	1.21	2.57	174	45.0	-30.2	0.76	48

Source: Edward W. Hill, "The Economy, Jobs, and Training," Report 94-1 (Cleveland: The Urban Center, Cleveland State University, April 1994).
* not elsewhere classified

the region coupled with production activities. This is true of greeting cards, petroleum refining, blast furnaces and basic steel products, electric lighting and wiring, paints and allied products, nonplastic plumbing and heating products, drug stores and proprietary stores, and automobile parking. Metal-working industries, the second component, are well represented in the core, which can be explained by the presence of competitive integrated steel mills as sources of supply and durable goods manufacturers as customers. Table 3 lists nineteen industries in which the region is both competitive and highly specialized in 1991.

Close connection to metal working is not a sure recipe for success. Some of the most troubled industries in the region are also connected to metal working (Table 4). The Greater Cleveland economy is highly specialized in ten industries that did not fare well during the period studied; eight are manufacturing industries. Losses

Table 4
10 Highly Specialized and Uncompetitive Industries

Standard Industrial Classification		Location Quotients		Shift Share	Percent Change Employment		Competitive	
SIC	*Name*	*1983*	*1991*	*Competitive Effect*	*Cleveland*	*U.S.*	*Score*	*Rank*
443	Freight transport. on Great Lakes	55.43	36.83	(476)	103.4	212.9	14.24	1
346	Metal forgings & stampings	4.69	4.77	(56)	-8.9	-8.4	1.50	20
339	Misc. primary metal products	4.41	3.98	(148)	-1.9	11.0	1.12	28
336	Nonferrous foundries (castings)	3.99	3.85	(194)	4.5	10.8	1.04	33
231	Men's and boys' suits & coats	3.17	3.16	(38)	-32.9	-31.3	0.86	41
299	Misc. petroleum & coal products	3.49	3.01	(72)	-22.8	-8.5	0.78	46
505	Metals & materials, x-petroleum*	2.72	2.60	(259)	-3.9	2.9	0.49	60
359	Industrial machinery, nec.	2.34	2.32	(238)	25.1	29.0	0.39	67
332	Iron & steel foundries	5.01	3.08	(2,704)	-43.8	-6.6	(0.92)	261
362	Electrical industrial apparatus	5.06	2.54	(4,502)	-55.1	-8.8	(2.32)	275

Source: Edward W. Hill. "The Economy, Jobs, and Training," Report 94-1 (Cleveland: The Urban Center, Cleveland State University, April 1994).
*x = except

in metal forgings and stampings (SIC 346) were near the national rate of loss. In 1991 the industry employed 10,704 in the region. Miscellaneous primary metal products (SIC 339) lost employment in Greater Cleveland. Nonferrous foundries and castings (SIC 336) gained employment in the region, but the nation gained at a faster rate. All of these industries have registered relatively small employment losses attributed to weak regional competitive factors. What is worrisome? They could be poised for larger declines. Of greatest concern is the performance of iron and steel foundries (SIC 332), which saw employment drop from 7,256 to 4,075 from 1983 to 1991, and electrical industrial apparatus (SIC 362), where employment plummeted from 9,711 to 4,357 over the same time period. Both are highly concentrated in Greater Cleveland, and both let go nearly half of their workers from 1983 to 1991. These may be lost industries.

Austrian and Bingham determined that the area remained dependent on industries that are declining in terms of employment nationally. In 1991 these industries included primary metals (SIC 33), with 23,981 employees, fabricated metal products (SIC 34), with 37,252 workers, industrial machinery and equipment (SIC 35), with 36,358 jobs, and transportation equipment (SIC 37), with 22,451 employees. These industries provided 12.5 percent of all jobs in the region at the start of the 1990 recession and 12.0 percent at the end of the first quarter of 1992. Austrian and Bingham state that the 8.4 percent employment loss is "significant but not massive."[16]

The fabricated metals industry and industrial machinery industries are the largest durable goods producers in the city of Cleveland. Each of these industries lost nearly 1,000 jobs during the recession, and declines continued during the early stages of the recovery. Durable goods manufacturing in the city as a whole lost 3,900 jobs during the recession and another 3,300 jobs during the early stages of the recovery. The declines in both stages were led by fabricated metals and industrial machinery.

Austrian and Bingham noted very different employment trends in the city of Cleveland and its suburbs.[17] In percentage terms, the city of Cleveland lost more jobs than the suburban ring during the recession in both durable and nondurable goods manufacturing, transportation services, producer services, and personal services. The suburban ring's employment in nondurable goods manufacturing increased during the recession while it declined in the city. Social services employment increased in both the city and the suburbs, growing by 2.2 percent and 0.3 percent, respectively. The major contributors were medical services and education. During the first year of the recovery the suburban ring followed the national trend and the city remained mired in recession.

During 1992, the first year of the recovery, manufacturing employment continued to decline in both areas, but the decline was steeper in the city. An exception is the instruments and related products industry (SIC 38), which saw employment growth in both the city and the suburbs. The number of jobs in this industry increased from 7,542 in 1983 to 8,692 in 1991. In the service industries the city and its suburbs parted ways. The suburbs gained 4,700 service-producing jobs, or 1.3 percent, while the city lost 5,500 positions, or -2.4 percent. Employment in transportation and producer services increased in the suburban ring and declined in the city. In the suburbs employment in wholesale and retail trade and personal services declined a bit (-1.5 percent and -0.1 percent); the same industries declined significantly in the city (-3.0 percent and -4.6 percent). Even suburban social services gained relative to the city during the recovery, indicating that medical services jobs are suburbanizing to be closer to growing areas of population that have both health insurance and money.

There are two ways to consider earnings in the service sector: (1) What are the average earnings in each of its four constituent sectors? (2) Can earnings in this sector compensate, or offset, the effects of earnings losses in the manufacturing sector? The service sector generates lower earnings than the average for the PMSA, despite the relatively high earnings in the distribution sector (excepting retail sales), producer services (excepting real estate), and the health care industry. Large employment gains have been made in low-wage service industries, especially in retail sales and the entire spectrum of personal services.

The service sector has a bimodal distribution of earnings whereas manufacturing employment is tightly grouped around the middle of the earnings distribution. Barry Bluestone, Bennett Harrison, and Katherine L. Bradbury have presented the hypothesis that deindustrialization, or the structural change, of the economy has resulted in a shift in the distribution of earnings.[18] They argue that the distribution has become more bimodal, which implies that there are proportionately more jobs at the upper and lower ends of the wage scale and fewer in the middle. The service sector is adding jobs at the extremes of the earnings distribution while the number of jobs in the middle declines. Empirical work to date has used national data.[19] If the declining-middle hypothesis holds, it should be most evident in a local labor market such as Greater Cleveland, which has historically relied on unionized manufacturing employment.

The Impact of Restructuring on Earnings

A direct test of the hypothesis that the distribution of earnings has changed over time requires inspecting individual and family data, which, unfortunately, are not available. Instead, quarterly average earnings data at the two-digit level of the SIC from the Bureau of Labor Statistics ES-202 records were used to create a "synthetic" earnings distribution.[20]

An important transition in the relationship between different measures of earnings occurred near the 1983 trough. Low-wage employment appears to have become more prevalent in Cleveland's regional economy after the 1983 business cycle trough was reached. A concise picture of change in the earnings distribution is provided by plotting the Gini coefficient (Figure 2).[21] The Gini coefficient measures the spread of the distribution; larger Gini scores indicate wider distributions. The result is unmistakable. Gini scores have been on an unremitting upward climb since the recovery from the 1975 recession.

The rate of increase in the Gini coefficient was a leading indicator of the structural change in the regional economy. A gradual shift in the distribution of earnings throughout the 1976 to 1979 recovery preceded the widely recognized structural change in this particular part of the Rust Belt economy. The rate at which inequality is increasing diminished since 1981 and showed signs of marginal reversal from 1985 to 1987. This means that the economy is generating a fairly stable distribution of earnings—not a more equal distribution.

The earnings distribution has become less tight over time. This by itself tells little about the direction of inequality in earnings. Knowing, however, that the modal wage has shifted from higher to lower quarterly earnings and that, at the same time, the Gini coefficient has increased substantially indicates that the middle of the earnings distribution has deteriorated both in absolute and relative terms.

Economic restructuring may also affect Cleveland's labor market by making the economy less sensitive to swings in the business cycle. People may be willing to trade off earnings at one point in time for higher expected lifetime earnings. This prospect was examined by classifying all two-digit industries according to their

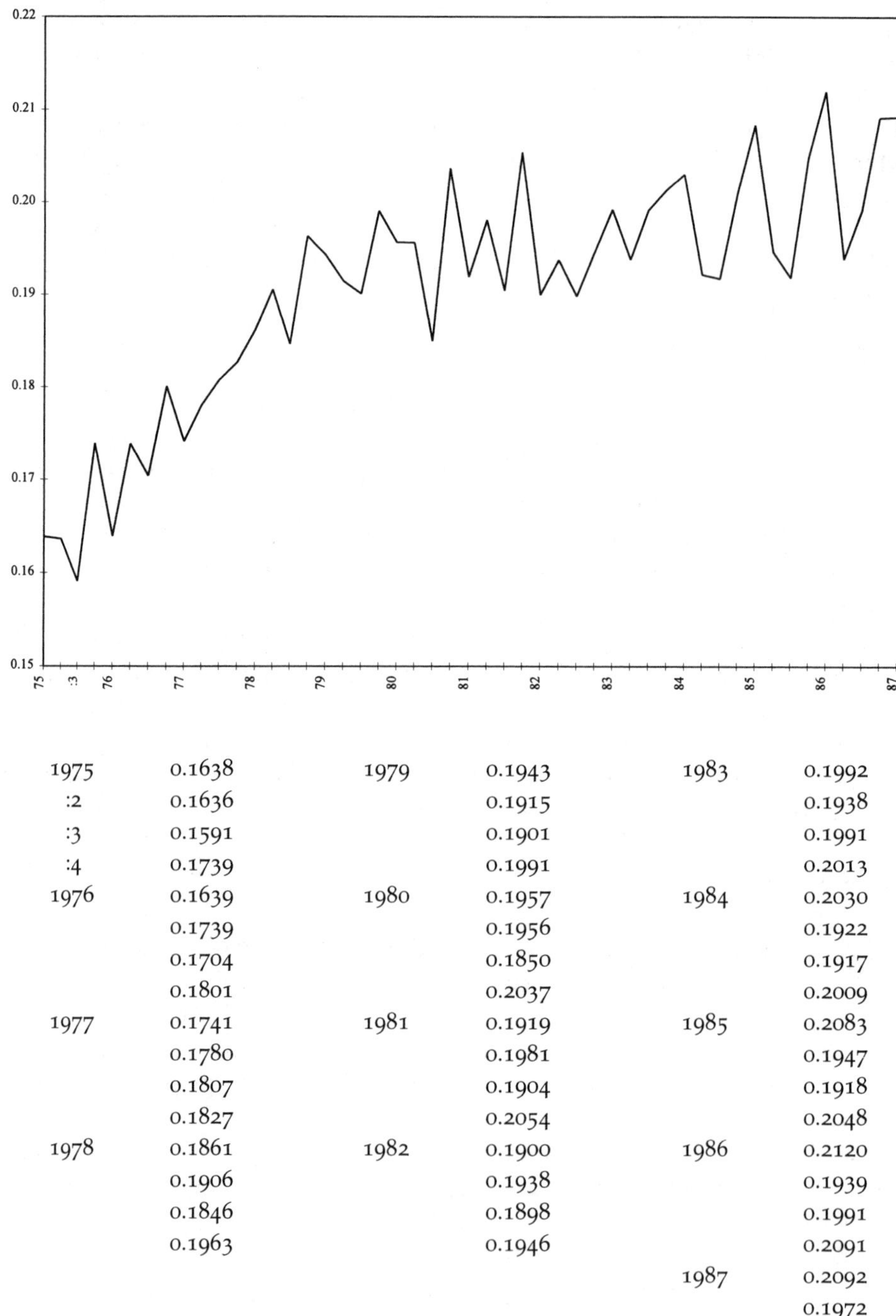

1975	0.1638	1979	0.1943	1983	0.1992
:2	0.1636		0.1915		0.1938
:3	0.1591		0.1901		0.1991
:4	0.1739		0.1991		0.2013
1976	0.1639	1980	0.1957	1984	0.2030
	0.1739		0.1956		0.1922
	0.1704		0.1850		0.1917
	0.1801		0.2037		0.2009
1977	0.1741	1981	0.1919	1985	0.2083
	0.1780		0.1981		0.1947
	0.1807		0.1904		0.1918
	0.1827		0.2054		0.2048
1978	0.1861	1982	0.1900	1986	0.2120
	0.1906		0.1938		0.1939
	0.1846		0.1898		0.1991
	0.1963		0.1946		0.2091
				1987	0.2092
					0.1972

Figure 2
Synthetic Gini Coefficient for Greater Cleveland:
First Quarter 1975 to Second Quarter 1987

Table 5
Seven Components of the Regional Economy, Cleveland PMSA, 1987:1

Employment change, 1979–87	*Cyclical behavior*	*Percent of private employment*	*Average quarterly earnings*
Decline	Noncyclical	17	$7,518
Decline	Cyclical, weak rebound	14	$6,103
Decline	Cyclical, strong rebound	3	$5,952
Stable	Cyclical	12	$4,201
Stable	Noncyclical	13	$5,317
Growing	Cyclical	4	$4,150
Growing	Noncyclical	38	$4,855

Source: ES-202, U.S. Department of Labor

variation in employment over both parts of the 1979 to 1986 cycle. Table 5 lists the level of employment in the seven sets of industries and their average quarterly earnings in the first quarter of 1987.

Nearly 42 percent of private employment in the Cleveland region is in industries that grew during the business cycle, but the average quarterly earnings for these industries were under $5,000. In contrast, over one-third of all private workers were in declining industries, which provide the highest average earnings in the region. One-quarter of private employment is with stable employers. Cyclically sensitive stable employers tend to provide low earnings, $4,150 in the first quarter of 1987, while noncyclical stable industries provided $5,317 in average quarterly earnings.

About one-third of private employment in the Cleveland region is exposed to cyclical fluctuations and 51 percent work in stable or growing noncyclical industries. The remaining workers are in industries that have been in a steady state of decline (most of these are manufacturing industries whose rate of decline can be expected to accelerate in future recessions). The cyclical sensitivity of employment in the region has lessened because of economic restructuring, but it is not inconsequential. Between one-third and one-half of the work force is employed in industries that may feel the effects of the business cycle. Lower earnings and an increased role of services in Cleveland's economy will not insulate the region from the negative effects of future business cycles.

How does the decline in earnings and the spread in the earnings distribution affect the social fabric of Cleveland? I examine this question in the remainder of the essay by looking at the spatial distribution of occupations, poverty, and housing values—all indicators of the strength or weakness of neighborhoods. The assumption is that these changes reflect the shift in the distribution of earnings and the decline in the average purchasing power of real earnings. There should be declines in those parts of the metropolitan area where the blue-collar middle class and those who aspired to join its ranks lived before the downturn in the regional economy took place in 1979. I do not attempt to associate these indicators directly with changes in the earnings distribution because inferential statistics cannot be used. The conclusions must be considered to be suggestive and somewhat speculative.

Attention will now focus on Cuyahoga County, not the PMSA, because poverty and housing data do not exist for the other three counties in the PMSA.

Distribution of Skills in 1980

Regional economic change is transmitted to neighborhoods through the residence patterns of those who benefit or lose from restructuring. Neighborhoods in American metropolitan areas tend to be fairly homogeneous in the social and economic status of their residents. In the case of Cleveland's economic change from 1979 to 1987, we would expect that census tracts with high concentrations of operators, fabricators, and laborers, occupations that depend on manufacturing-based economy for work, would be hard hit. Those tracts that will benefit from new order Cleveland will be those which attract managers and other professionals. It is expected that those areas contiguous to the tracts housing the managerial class will also benefit as new housing is constructed to satisfy the demands of this expanding class. The abutting tracts will be on the periphery of the county.

In this section the residential pattern of old order Cleveland is described, as depicted in the 1980 census. The census serves as the baseline against which to measure changes in the two indicator variables of neighborhood health: the growth in poverty and changes in housing values. Map 1 shows the percentage employed as operators, fabricators, and laborers.[22] Neighborhoods that should benefit the least from restructuring, along with areas with large poverty populations in 1980, are concentrated in tracts emphasized in Map 1. Cleveland's city boundary is outlined with a heavy black line on the map.

The city of Cleveland has very few census tracts with large concentrations of managerial or professional workers. The highest concentrations are along the western suburban lakeshore, in the cities of Rocky River and Westlake, and in the high-status eastern suburbs, Shaker Heights and those areas that are in a direct eastern corridor from Shaker Heights. Lower, but still significant, concentrations exist in the outer suburban ring. Operators, fabricators, and laborers have a completely different residential pattern. The highest concentrations are in the city of Cleveland. In no census tract outside of the city was more than 35 percent of the residential work force in these occupations in 1980. It is expected that residents in these

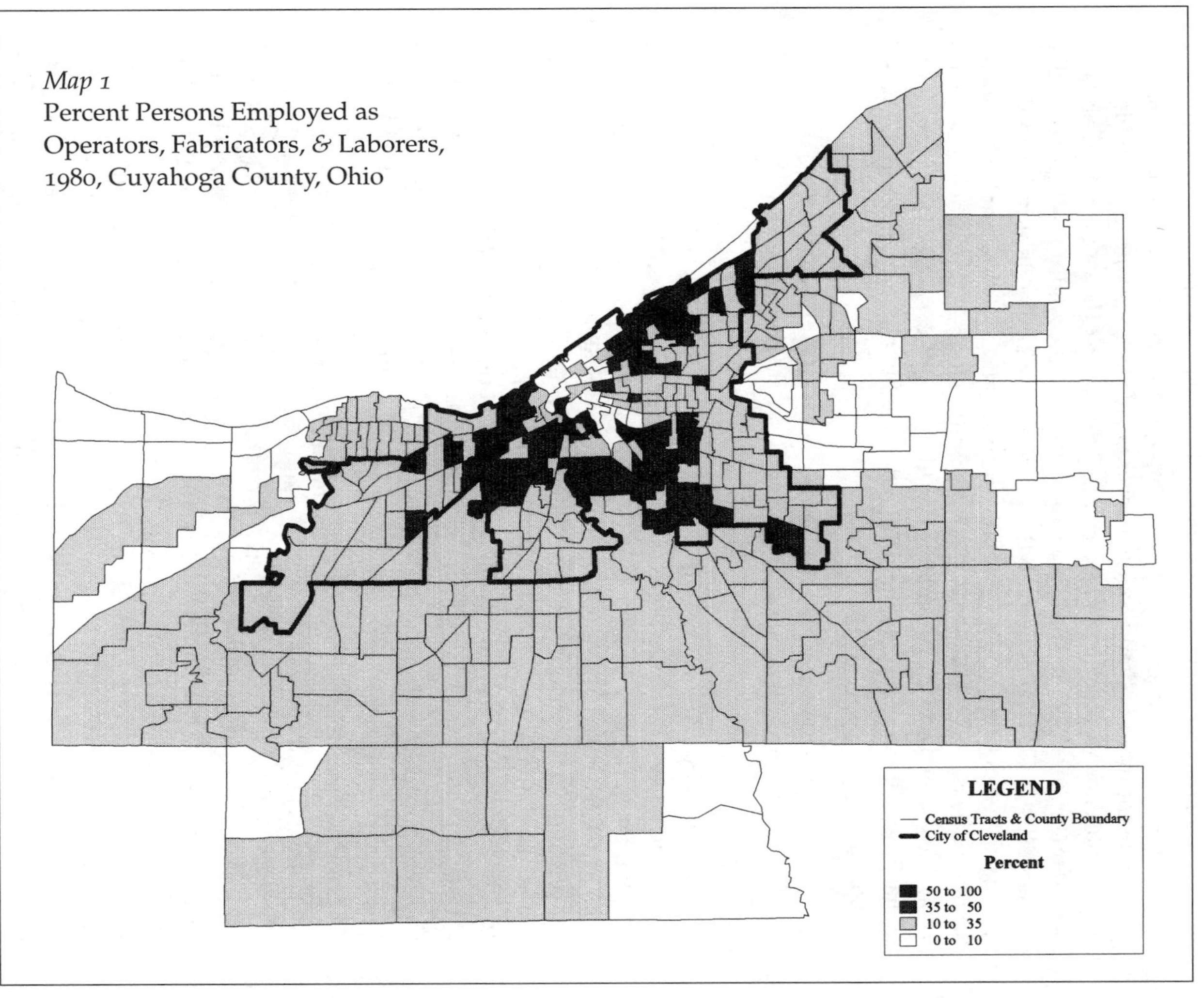

Map 1
Percent Persons Employed as Operators, Fabricators, & Laborers, 1980, Cuyahoga County, Ohio

Source: 1980 Census of Population and Housing. Prepared by Northern Ohio Data & Information Service, Cleveland State University.

areas will experience the greatest losses from the transition of the regional economy.

These locational expectations are conditioned upon two facts. First, the overall level of economic activity remains stagnant. The new sectors of the economy are not generating enough jobs to create a temporary shortage in the housing market. More vibrant metropolitan economies were confronted by the twin problems of rapid household formation and job creation that raised the value of land and created demand for upgraded used housing. These two preconditions to gentrification do not exist in Cleveland. Second, there are no major geographical constraints to the expansion of Cleveland's metropolitan area. There is still vacant land available in the southern and western parts of the county within a commuting time of less than thirty minutes to the central business district and suburban nodes of employment. This will retard the adaptation of older neighborhoods to meet the demands of increased professional employment.

Impact on Poverty

The poverty population was tightly concentrated around the core of the city of Cleveland when the 1980 census was taken. Poverty existed on the West Side of the city, but the bulk of the poverty tracts were on its East Side. Tracts in which more than half of the population is classified as poor are located both in Cleveland and in the predominantly African American suburb of East Cleveland. The poverty population grew rapidly from 1979 to 1987. Nearly half of the population in the city's traditionally black East Side neighborhoods is poor, and the poverty rate on the West Side reached 25 percent. What is confusing is that the growth in the numbers of poor has increased while the unemployment rate has decreased. The unemployment rate in Cuyahoga County was 5.6 percent in 1980 and the poverty rate was 13.6 percent. Unemployment peaked in 1983 at 12.0 percent, when the poverty rate was 16.1 percent. In 1988 the unemployment rate dropped to 5.8 percent, yet the estimated poverty rate rose to 18.6 percent.[23]

The 1987 poverty estimates derived by the Council of Economic Opportunity for the county indicate that there was a huge expansion in the number of tracts in which a majority of the population lived in poverty (Map 2). The entire East Side of the city is dominated by poor residents, as are sections of several suburban municipalities. The growth of poverty on the West Side of the city and in one of its western suburbs, Lakewood, is also noticeable.

Ordinary least squares were used to correlate the incidence of poverty in the county's census tracts in 1980 with its incidence in 1987 and the occupational characteristics of each tract's residents in 1980.[24] There was a strong positive association between a tract's poverty rate in 1980 and its rate in 1987. Essentially, the rate of poverty grew by 50 percent from 1980 to 1987. Additionally, tracts that housed blue-collar workers in 1980 experienced extremely large increases in the percentage of their resident population who were poor in 1987. If a third of the workers

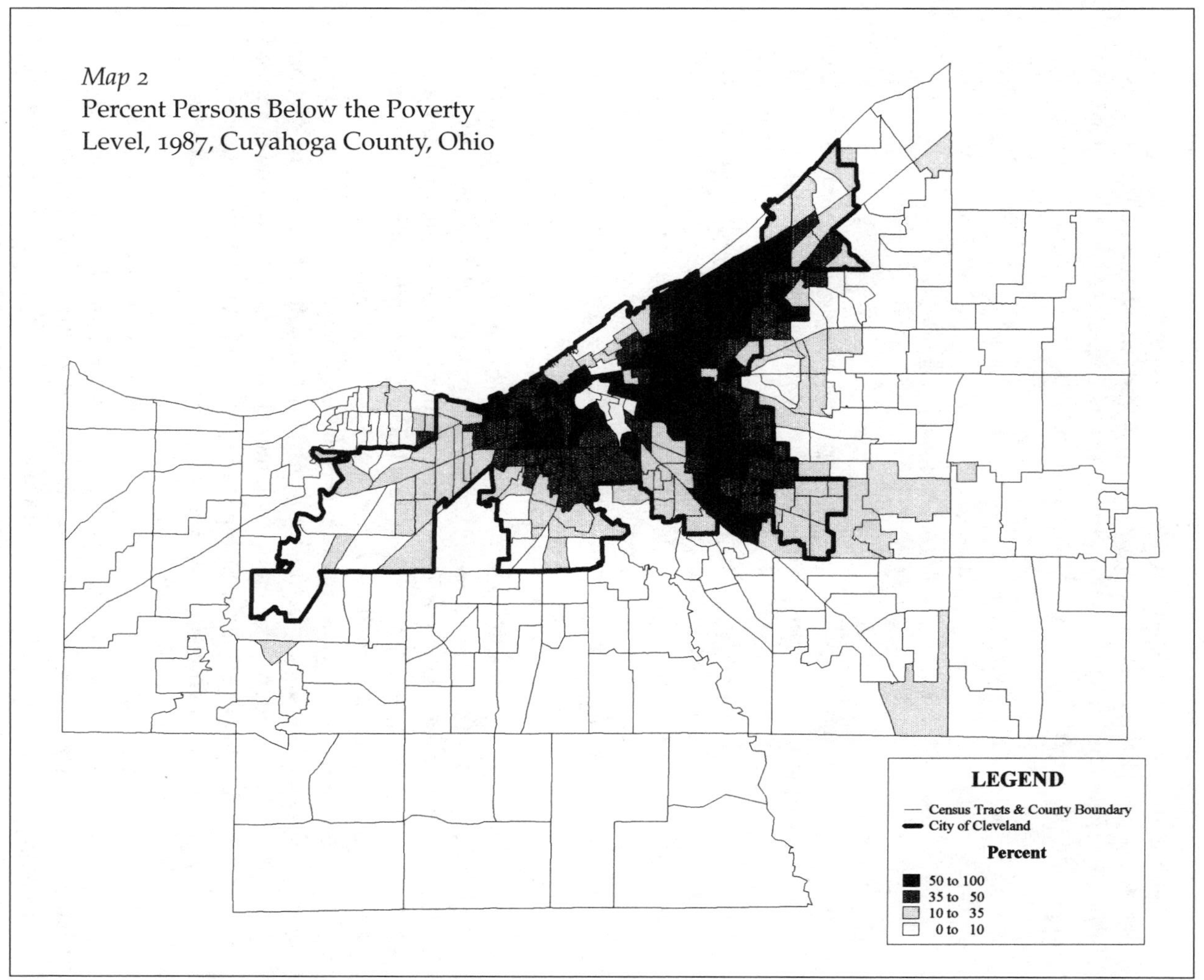

Source: Council for Economic Opportunities in Greater Cleveland. Prepared by Northern Ohio Data & Information Service, Cleveland State University.

living in a tract in 1980 were operators, fabricators, or laborers, the tract's 1987 poverty rate would be 9.6 percentage points above the county's average rate.

Poverty increased in tracts dominated by the poor in 1980. Areas in which large portions of the work force were employed in lower-skilled occupations associated with factory work were spawning grounds for poverty at the end of the 1980s. This strongly suggests that change in the structure of the regional economy had a direct impact on the neighborhoods of the city and on sections of its close-in suburbs.

Impact on Neighborhood Housing

Between 1950 and 1986, 1.5 housing units were built (most of them in the suburbs) for every additional household living in the region. Expansion of the suburban supply at a rate greater than the household growth enabled a steady stream of population to move outward. As the population shifted into more preferred housing and locations, the least preferred were abandoned. In the 1970s, the city of Cleveland lost thirty thousand households; the suburban portion of the metropolitan area gained seventy-four thousand. A lost household resulted in an abandoned housing unit; Cleveland lost 21 percent of its households and 30 percent of its housing units.

The price of houses in Cleveland is low compared with its suburbs. Cleveland's median value in 1987 was in the $30,000 range, whereas houses in the suburbs were valued in the $60,000 range. Also, the county contained a very large supply of homes priced between $20,000 and $80,000—about 75 percent of all units fall into this range. Finally, there were relatively few high-priced units. Only 12 percent of the stock was valued at more than $100,000.[25]

This profile of housing, nearly all built before 1979, was largely a product of the Cleveland area's economy before the recession of 1979. It reflects the interaction of supply and demand in an economy dominated by blue-collar earnings and the relatively small number of higher-income households that lived in the region in the past. The distribution of housing values complements the tight distribution of earnings that existed in old order Cleveland.

The housing industry built products in response to the expressed demands and incomes of an economy dominated by manufacturing workers. The economic changes that began in the 1970s and accelerated in 1979 effectively removed a significant portion of demand for working-class housing. The departing jobs left behind not only empty factories and plants but also mid-priced homes with fewer potential buyers. At the same time, economic change created demand for higher-status (and higher-priced) homes. The old order housing profile is not compatible with the new order economy.

Change, 1979–1987

The impact of economic change on housing values was intense and is evident in the data in Figure 3. The graph represents the sale prices of median single-family homes in the city of Cleveland and the suburban portion of Cuyahoga County relative to changes in the Consumer Price Index (CPI); 1967 is the base year. If sales price appreciation keeps pace with the CPI, the percentage difference will be 0.0; if home prices rise faster than inflation there will be positive appreciation; if they rise less than inflation the gains will be negative.

Between 1967 and 1978, sales prices in the suburbs greatly outpaced inflation. Initially, prices in Cleveland declined relative to inflation, but they began to recover in 1970 and had nearly regained their 1967 real values in 1978. The Gini coefficient provides a possible explanation of the divergence in appreciation. The earnings distribution was widening at an accelerating pace from 1975 to 1978. Those who were at the upper end of the distribution, or gaining access to the upper end, may have been moving to the suburbs. The partial recovery of the inner-city portion of the market could be attributable to first-time home buyers and those with declining real incomes who were searching for relative housing bargains.

In 1979 both the city and suburban markets went into precipitous decline. People who owned homes in 1978 took substantial capital losses on their investments.[26] Prices in the city of Cleveland hit bottom in 1982. The suburbs did not bottom out until 1985, when the recovery had been under way for nearly two years. Between 1984 and 1985, the city's housing values gained marginally relative to both the CPI and suburban values, but in 1986 and 1987 the suburbs began to gain relative to the city.

Losses in median sales prices over time differ among census tracts. The impact of decline resulting from economic restructuring must be sorted out from the loss in value resulting from the overall decline that Cleveland has experienced since 1979. The average price in the county, expressed in real terms using 1983 dollars, declined from $63,269 in 1979 to $43,360 in 1987, a $20,000 loss. There was an $808 rebound in the value between the 1983 trough and 1987.

The loss in average value was not evenly distributed throughout the county. A statistical model indicated that the presence of managers and professionals in a census tract in 1980 was associated with a relative increase in housing values and a large portion of residents employed in blue-collar occupations appeared to discount sales prices.[27] The value of the coefficients across time is fairly constant. The markup (in real terms) owing to the presence of professionals and managers was $1,402 in 1979, $1,292 in 1983, and $1,438 in 1987, always positive with a slightly higher value at the end of the time period than at the beginning. The discount for operators, fabricators, and laborers was $1,374 in 1979, $920 in 1983, and $1,014 in 1987. The data are biased, however, in minimizing the negative impact of the blue-collar variable. In all, 5 percent of the tracts could not be used in the 1983 and 1987

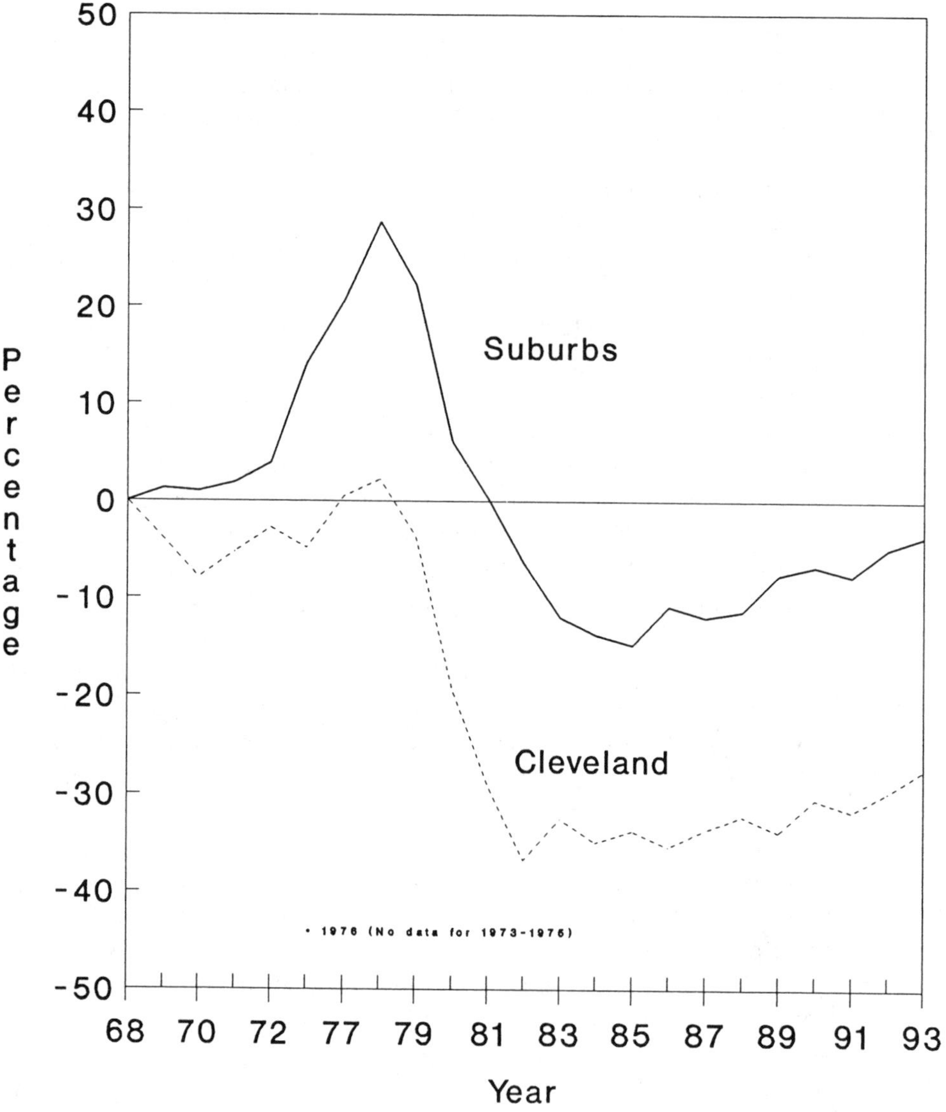

Figure 3
Price Relative to Inflation, Single Family Sales

estimating equations because they had sales in 1979 and no sales in 1983 or 1987. The housing market ceased to exist in these tracts, and a large share of their residents were operators, fabricators, or laborers in 1980.

The best way to compare the distributional impact of occupation on housing values in each of the years is to calculate the value of the markup and discount as a percentage of the average sales price for the year the equation was estimated.[28] The percentage markup resulting from the presence of managers and professionals increased in each of the years, from 2.2 percent in 1979 to 3.3 percent in 1987. This means that a percentage point difference in the portion of managers living in a census tract accounts for a 3.3 percentage increase in the value of housing. The discount associated with blue-collar residents increased over the time period, a sure sign of restructuring and of the loss of economic status in the neighborhoods where the blue-collar labor force lived in 1980. The impact of these differences is large and increased over the time period studied. In 1979 the total differential, adding the blue-collar and white-collar coefficients, between white- and blue-collar census tracts was 4.4 percent of the average house price in the county; it was 5.8 percent in 1987.

In Cleveland's inner-city neighborhoods, where the lowest-priced housing in the county is located (under $20,000 in 1987 dollars) and where the city's poorest residents live, sales prices have deteriorated the most in real terms. By 1987, nearly all of Cleveland's innermost neighborhoods had lost one-half, and some two-thirds, of their real 1967 sales value. These losses were aggravated by the switch in the economy's base in 1979. The outer neighborhoods of the city, those closest to the suburbs, fared the best, but even there real prices fell 20 to 30 percent.

Suburbs within the county with median sales prices over $100,000 in 1987 dominate the group of communities with the highest sales price appreciation. The $100,000-plus communities are the only ones where the current value of housing exceeds the inflation-adjusted 1967 value. And those high-priced communities are where most of the new residential construction is occurring. Buyers and residents in those communities are linked by their occupations to the economic activity that represents the growing and best-paying component of the changed Cleveland economy.

Substantial gains were experienced in the outermost suburbs and those sections of the county where professionals and managers lived before the 1979 recession took hold. The other areas of the county showed losses or little appreciation. These observations are consistent with changes in the earnings distribution. Those areas of the county populated primarily by the blue-collar middle class have felt the effects of earnings losses; those that house the professional and managerial classes have done somewhat better. Gains made in service sector employment or income have not been large enough to produce strength in the portion of the housing market that once depended on the wages of the middle of the earnings distribution.

Conclusion

The lesson to be learned from Cleveland's experience is that the effects of economic restructuring are widespread but uneven. The changes that took place in terms of employment, poverty, and housing values were not spread evenly across the metropolitan area. They took place in specific neighborhoods. The distributional impact of Cleveland's restructuring is evident through the marked growth in poverty and uneven changes in home sales prices. The occupation of workers and the socioeconomic status of their neighborhoods provide the link between the world of work and the residential world.

This research also indicates that the existing stock of housing will not be upgraded by market mechanisms without tremendous economic expansion, accompanied by high rates of household formation. These twin forces create pressure to upgrade the incumbent housing stock because of increased land values. But if the expansion in the regional economy is unbalanced, a pattern will develop of winning and losing neighborhoods and residents. The filtering process will be accelerated in regions that have seen erosion in the middle of their earnings distribution. In fact, the poor may become better off as the value of low- to moderate-quality housing becomes discounted. But they must move to take advantage of the depreciated stock. The city will experience continued population losses, and those who remain behind will be the poorest of the poor—people who cannot move.

In Cleveland, where the recovery has been uneven, the real losers will be those who own middle-valued housing and the neighborhoods in which they are located. Their property values have been reduced, and their capital losses will make it hard for them to move. I suspect that this conclusion holds for many metropolitan regions in the heartland of the United States. Strong demand for older neighborhoods with less than elite status, therefore, requires either reduced suburban construction or areawide job growth that outpaces suburban development.

The true impact of economic restructuring is felt by more than just those who either lose or change jobs. Because restructuring does not affect a random group of workers spread evenly throughout a metropolis, it generates spillover effects that reach into neighborhoods. Economic restructuring affects classes of workers and their families based on the occupation of the worker. In the case of Cleveland, the spatial effects of restructuring resulted in changes in the vitality and prospects of neighborhoods and their residents.

Notes

1. Cleveland's PMSA changed in 1993. Before that year the PMSA was made up of Cuyahoga, Geauga, Medina, and Lake counties. Ashtabula and Lorain counties were added to the original four-county PMSA in 1993. All data, with the exception of Tables 3 and 4, refer to the old definition of PMSA.

2. For a more complete discussion of the data see Edward W. Hill and Thomas Bier, "Economic Restructuring: Earnings, Occupations, and Housing Values in Cleveland," *Economic Development Quarterly* 3 (May 1989): 123–44.

3. There is a controversy as to the accuracy of the unemployment rate that is reported by the Ohio Bureau of Employment Services. It appears to understate unemployment in the Greater Cleveland region. The undercount is especially troubling in the city of Cleveland. See Edward W. Hill, "Greater Cleveland's Economy: Challenges and Prospects in the Mid-1990s," Report 94-2 (Cleveland: The Urban

Center, Cleveland State University, March 1994).

4. The data on poverty in Cleveland and Cuyahoga County were developed by George C. Zeller and published in *Poverty Indicators, Trends: 1970–1988, Cuyahoga County, Ohio* (Cleveland: Council for Economic Opportunities, 1988); also see the chapter by Claudia Coulton and Julian Chow in this book.

5. Ziona Austrian and Richard Bingham, "The Cleveland Area Economy and the Recession of 1990" (Cleveland: The Urban Center, Cleveland State University, February 1, 1994).

6. Austrian and Bingham, "Cleveland Area Economy," Table 6.

7. *Cleveland Plain Dealer,* March 10, 1994.

8. Austrian and Bingham, "Cleveland Area Economy," 31.

9. This section was distilled from several sources, including *Common Bonds, Divergent Paths: An Economic Perspective of Four Cities* (Cleveland: Federal Reserve Bank of Cleveland, 1986); Aaron S. Gurwitz and G. Thomas Kingsley, *The Cleveland Metropolitan Economy* (Santa Monica, Calif.: Rand Corporation, 1982); Ohio Writers' Project, *The Ohio Guide* (Washington, D.C.: Works Progress Administration, 1940), 15–37, 56–63, 216–45; Samuel P. Orth, *A History of Cleveland, Ohio* (Chicago: S. J. Clarke, 1910), 629–40; and David D. Van Tassel and John J. Grabowski, eds., *The Encyclopedia of Cleveland History* (Bloomington: Indiana University Press, 1987), xvii–lv and 361–64.

10. Orth, *History of Cleveland,* 638.

11. Extensive data on the relative strength of Cleveland's economy can be found in Edward W. Hill, "Cleveland, Ohio: Manufacturing Matters, Services are Strengthened, but Earnings Erode," in *Economic Restructuring of the American Midwest,* ed. Richard D. Bingham and Randall W. Eberts (Boston: Kluwer, 1990), and Hill, "Greater Cleveland's Economy."

12. Nell Ann Shelley and Edward W. Hill, "Identifying the Steel Industrial Complex in Northeast Ohio: Executive Summary" (Cleveland: United Labor Agency, 1990).

13. Sharon A. Flynn, "The Greater Cleveland Polymer Survey" (Cleveland: Greater Cleveland Growth Association, 1989).

14. Richard Florida, Martin Kenedy, and Andres Mair, "The Transplant Phenomenon," *Economic Development Commentary* 12 (Winter 1988): 3–9; Donald T. Iannone, "Policy Implications of Foreign Business Recruitment Strategy: The Case of Japanese Automotive Company Investment in the United States," *Economic Development Review* 6 (Fall 1988): 25–39.

15. Harley L. Browning and Joachim Singlemann, "The Transformation of the U.S. Labor Force: The Interaction of Industry and Occupation," *Politics and Society* (1978): 481–509.

16. Austrian and Bingham, "Cleveland Area Economy," 28–29.

17. Ibid., 26–27.

18. Barry Bluestone and Bennett Harrison, *The Deindustrialization of America* (New York: Basic Books, 1982); Katherine L. Bradbury, "The Shrinking Middle Class," *New England Economic Review* (September–October 1986): 41–55; Bennett Harrison and Barry Bluestone, *The Great U-Turn* (New York: Basic Books, 1988).

19. Michael W. Horrigan and Steven E. Haugen, "The Declining Middle-Class Thesis: A Sensitivity Analysis," *Monthly Labor Review* 111 (May 1988): 3–13.

20. See Hill and Bier, "Economic Restructuring," and Hill, "Cleveland, Ohio: Manufacturing Matters," for a more detailed explanation.

21. The Gini coefficient is a summary measure of inequality of income or earnings distributions. The coefficient varies from 0 to 1, where 0 means complete income equality and 1 complete inequality. Therefore, greater inequality is associated with higher Gini scores. Because these Gini coefficients come from synthetic distributions the absolute Gini score cannot be compared to Gini coefficients that are calculated from national data on individuals. The slope of the line that is plotted is what is important here. See William C. Apgar and H. James Brown, *Microeconomics and Public Policy* (Glenview, Ill.: Scott, Foresman, 1987), 211–13.

22. Zeller, *Poverty Indicators, Trends,* 68; see also Edward W. Hill and Rosalyn Allison, *Barriers to African-American Male Employment: Local Manifestations of a National Problem* (Cleveland: Urban League of Greater Cleveland, 1992).

23. The results are reported in Hill and Bier, "Economic Restructuring." For a discussion about the problems with the calculation of local unemployment rates see Hill, "Greater Cleveland's Economy," 3–7.

24. For more detail see Hill and Bier, "Economic Restructuring," and Hill, "Cleveland, Ohio: Manu-

facturing Matters."

25. The volume of sales activity in the county was also affected by the business cycle. In 1979, 16,040 single-family homes were sold. This number declined by 26.3 percent in 1983 to 12,019. Activity accelerated to 14,464 in 1987 but was still 9.8 percent below the 1979 level. Another indicator of the impact of restructuring and of the expansion of the metropolis is the increase in the number of tracts in which there were no sales over a period of time. In twenty-seven tracts there were no home sales in 1979, 1983, and 1987; in sixteen tracts there were sales in 1979 but not in the other two years; in twenty-eight tracts there were more than five sales in 1979 but between one and four in 1983 and 1987. The market for single-family homes is weak to nonexistent in nearly 20 percent of the county's census tracts.

26. See Hill and Bier, "Economic Restructuring."

27. Ibid.

28. This is done by calculating the markup, or discount, as a percentage of the intercept of each estimating equation.

Part 4

POLITICS

Conflict and Reform

Introduction

IN THIS SECTION, articles by Frederic C. Howe, Todd Swanstrom, and Christopher Wye and Norman Krumholz give the reader a sense of Cleveland as a crucible for political conflict and reform.

Howe provides in the first article a stirring portrait of the vision and struggles of Tom L. Johnson, mayor of Cleveland from 1901 to 1909 and a leading Progressive. Johnson was the epitome of the great Progressive reform spirit that shook American society in the two decades before America's entry into World War I. Although Johnson and other Progressives might agree on little else, they shared the view that the social order could and must be improved and that such change must not await God's will or the laws of the marketplace. Progressives meant to speed up social progress by attacking poverty, privilege, graft, and other evils by facing them squarely and resolving them with the energy characteristic of industrial society. Johnson's ten-year fight against privilege and for "A City on a Hill" was a moving moral crusade, rarely seen in American politics. Howe was a Progressive urban reformer who worked with Mayor Johnson and remained politically active from the Progressive Era into the New Deal.

Swanstrom provides a less emotional and more analytic account of a struggle seventy years later against many of the same forces engaged by Tom L. Johnson. Swanstrom outlines the politics of crisis that led Cleveland to default on its fiscal obligations in 1978. Contrary to the popular belief that the default was caused by economic pressures alone, Swanstrom persuasively argues that default was caused by the political power and discretion of the bankers who held the city's debt during a crucial period. Key to their actions was their disdain for the urban populism espoused by Mayor Dennis J. Kucinich and the threat he posed to the dominance of business values in Cleveland city government. The fate of Muny Light, a legacy of Tom L. Johnson, which is discussed in several places in this book, also figures as a major cause of the default.

Wye and Krumholz offer a history of black civil rights in Cleveland from the early years of the nineteenth century to the present. In the fifty years following the

Civil War, Cleveland's black population grew very slowly to about eighty-five hundred in 1910. At that time, conditions were considered to be better for blacks in Cleveland than almost anywhere else in the nation. Then, from 1910 to 1920, blacks streamed into the city from the South, seeking a less hostile social environment and better job opportunities. In 1920, Cleveland's black population stood at thirty-five thousand, and was concentrated in an East Side ghetto. Racial discrimination became overt and pervasive. Black leaders in Cleveland reflected a national pattern of black thought, some emphasizing an integrationist approach and others an accommodationist view. The Depression of the 1930s set back civil rights but produced new black organizations with greater assertiveness and a sharper focus on economic matters. Economic gains in World War II were followed by the Hough and Glenville riots and the 1967 election of Mayor Carl B. Stokes. In 1989, with the election of a second black mayor, Michael R. White, and a black-white population split equally, Cleveland's political liberalism related to racial issues remained an uncertain question.

A Ten Years' War

Frederic C. Howe

Mr. Johnson called his ten years' fight against privilege a war for "A City on a Hill." To the young men in the movement, and to tens of thousands of the poor who gave it their support, it was a moral crusade rarely paralleled in American politics. The struggle involved the banks, the press, the Chamber of Commerce, the clubs, and the social life of the city. It divided families and destroyed friendships. You were either for Tom Johnson or against him. If for him, you were a disturber of business, a Socialist, to some an anarchist. Had the term "Red" been in vogue, you would have been called a communist in the pay of Soviet Russia. Every other political issue and almost every topic of conversation was subordinated to the struggle.

The possibility of a free, orderly, and beautiful city became to me an absorbing passion. Here were all of the elements necessary to a great experiment in democracy. Here was a rapidly growing city with great natural advantages and with few mistakes to correct. Here was a wonderful hinterland for the building of homes, a ten-mile waterfront that could be developed for lake commerce, a population that had showed itself willing to follow an ideal, and, most important of all, a great leader.

I had an architectonic vision of what a city might be. I saw it as a picture. It was not economy, efficiency, and business methods that interested me so much as a city planned, built, and conducted as a community enterprise. I *saw* the city as an architect sees a skyscraper, as a commission of experts plans a world's fair exposition. It was a unit, a thing with a mind, with a conscious purpose, seeing far in advance of the present and taking precautions for the future. I had this picture of Cleveland long before the advent of city planning proposals; it was just as instinctive as any mechanical talent. I saw cities in this way from the first lectures of Dr. Albert Shaw at Johns Hopkins; I went to Germany in the summers, especially to Munich, drawn there by orderliness, by the beauty of streets, concern for architecture, provision for parks, for gardens and museums, for the rich popular life of the people. And I studied cities as one might study art; I was interested in curbs, in sewers, in sky-lines. I wrote about cities—in articles and books. I dreamed about them. The city was the enthusiasm of my life. And I saw cities as social agencies that would make life easier for people, full of pleasure, beauty, and opportunity. It could be done so easily and at such slight individual expense. Especially in a city like Cleveland that had few mistakes to correct, that was flanked on one side by a lake front that could be developed with breakwaters into parks and lagoons, and with natural park-ways extending about it far back into the country.

I have never gotten over this enthusiasm. I never grow tired of city building, of city enthusiasms, city ideals. And with all of its crudities and failures I have never lost faith that the American city will become a thing of beauty and an agency of social service as yet unplumbed.

The mad king of Bavaria dreamed no more ambitious dreams of city building than did I of Cleveland. Here democracy would show its possibilities; the city would become our hope instead of our despair, and in a few years' time all America would respond to the movement. The crusade of my youth, the greatest adventure of my life, as great a training school as a man could pass through—this the decade of struggle in Cleveland from 1901 to 1910 was to me.

The immediate struggle revolved about two main issues: the public ownership of utilities, especially the street railways and electric lighting service, and the reduction of street railway fares to three cents. Neither of them seemed adequate to explain the bitterness of the conflict and the power which reaction was able to organize to obstruct the movement. These issues mobilized the conservative forces of the city—banks, the Chamber of Commerce, lawyers, doctors, clubs, and churches. The press was partly owned by Mark Hanna, while advertisers were organized to bring pressure on editors and owners. Instinct held the propertied classes together no matter how detached they might be from the interests that were directly menaced. Before the expiration of the first two years of Mr. Johnson's term of mayoralty the city was divided into two camps along clearly defined economic lines. There was bitterness, hatred, abuse, social ostracism, and business boycott. The press was unscrupulous in its attacks. On the one side were men of property and influence; on the other the politicians, immigrants, workers, and persons of small means. This line of cleavage continued to the end.

And I was not on the side I would have chosen to be on. The struggle brought me into conflict with friends, clients, my class. I preferred to be with them, I liked wealth and the things that went with wealth; I enjoyed dining out, dances, the lighter things of life. I suffered from the gibes of men with whom I had once been intimate and fancied slights that did not in fact occur. I could not see why men would not treat political differences as natural; why my opinions on municipal ownership should make me any less desirable socially than I had been while living at the settlement engaged in uplift work.

Now, too, I was part of a political machine, was part of the spoils system, was apparently approving of things I had once thought to be the supreme evils in our politics; I was counseling with ward leaders, many of whom were saloon keepers, none of whom were of my class or had any interest in politics beyond jobs, political power, and such distinction as came through the party organization.

This departure from former ideals did not disturb me as did the loss of old friends. I wanted to live with my class, to enjoy its approval, to exhibit the things I had learned at the university among people who lived in fine houses, who made the social and club life of the city.

Still, I was happy in the fight. It was always dramatic, and I had a passion for the things we were fighting for. I saw that the city must own its transportation system before it could begin to plan anything else; it ought to own its electricity supply; most important of all, it must end class war, which I was beginning to see was caused by the fight for franchise rights of great value involving most of the prominent men in the city. My passion for the city was also a passion for Tom Johnson. And I had come to love him as fervently as I loved the things he promised to achieve.

Street railway franchises in Ohio were for twenty-five years. Many of them were expiring in Cleveland and the companies had been trying for years to secure their renewal. Mayor Robert E. McKisson's opposition to Mark Hanna and the efforts of the Municipal Association had helped to balk the granting of the new franchises. Finally Mr. Johnson had been elected by a large majority on a perfectly clear issue of municipal ownership and immediate three-cent fares.

To me it seemed that his program was one easy of achievement. He and the people were united. Democracy had spoken; it had chosen a natural leader, a businessman known by every businessman in the city to be a man of extraordinary talent and experience. "A million dollar mayor that Cleveland has gotten for five thousand dollars," was Albert Johnson's comment on his brother's election. "I would gladly give Tom a million dollars a year to work for my street railways," he added.

But the city had no legal right to own and operate the street railways. This prevented a direct attack on the situation.There were two alternatives, both almost impossible of execution. One was to negotiate with the companies and induce them to accept a new grant providing for a three-cent fare, with the right reserved to the city to buy the lines at their actual reproduction value. This Mr. Johnson said was impossible, because there were twenty millions of watered securities in the properties, much of it issued by the promoters to themselves. These securities would be wiped out under the mayor's plan. The second alternative was to find someone who would agree to build new lines on the city's terms, with a straight three-cent fare, and provision for the easy purchase of the lines by the city at their investment value. This seemed still more difficult of realization. Self-interest and herd interest would keep bankers and railway promoters out of such an enterprise.

Mr. Johnson chose, however, the latter line of action. Endless efforts were made to secure new lines of street railways on streets that had not been occupied by the existing companies. Routes were laid out on unoccupied streets and bids invited. The old company put in dummy bids at a low rate of fare, with no intention of building. These dummy bids had to be thrown out. New routes were planned and new bids secured. Finally a grant was made to Mr. Ermon du Pont, of Delaware, a friend of Mr. Johnson's. To get even so far had taken the greater part of two years.

When the grant was made to Mr. du Pont, I thought we had won the war. I supposed that the companies would negotiate, that they would not be able to stand the competition of three-cent fares. Moreover, some of the franchises had expired and they had no right in the streets. Mr. Johnson knew better. He said we had won only a skirmish. He knew the laws of the state and the skill with which they had been drawn to prevent competition by newcomers in the field. He knew that the grant to a new company simply meant a long legal battle.

He was quite right. The ordinance to the low-fare company was immediately attacked by an injunction issued by one of the Republican judges. The case had to be fought through the common pleas court, then through the circuit court, then through the supreme court of Ohio, which was partisan, having been carefully hand-picked for such contingencies. After the supreme court of the state had disposed of the case, there was a further delay on appeal to the Supreme Court of the United States.

All this meant long delay. It meant that Mr. Johnson would have to stand for a second election on unfulfilled pledges. The companies planned to wear out the public as they had done for years until they should secure a pliant administration that would give them a franchise. In the meantime, they were continuing to collect five-cent fares.

Nobody knew where the money to finance the low-fare company came from. Mr. Johnson did not confide the secret even to his intimate friends. Years later, when I went with him one day in New York to call on August Lewis, I learned who the good angel was. The two had long been friends, brought together by a common affection for Henry George. Outside on the street, after we had left, Mr. Johnson said:

"August Lewis is the finest Jew since Christ. You know it was he who put up the money to build the first three-cent-fare line and to carry on the legal fight. We could have done nothing without his help. He never fully expected to get his money back, and he only half expects it now."

As time went on, the war widened. Men were selected for office, from city council to the supreme bench, about this issue. President Roosevelt lent his aid to defeat the enterprise by urging Congressman Theodore Burton to run for mayor. Tom Johnson, he said, must be defeated, otherwise he might become a national figure. But the fight was carried on for the most part in the courts, upon which the opposition relied. All told, over fifty injunctions were granted against the city, in its efforts to use its own streets as it saw fit, to provide people with cheaper fares, and to build a municipal electric lighting plant. To defeat the will of the community the flimsiest of legal objections proved sufficient. The sovereignty of a great city was far less important to the courts than that of the most insignificant property owner who urged some damage to himself or some failure by the city to observe an obscure provision of the laws.

Almost all of the best-known lawyers of the city were retained by the companies. When the city sought to employ outside legal assistance, the only prominent lawyer who would accept its brief was Mr. D. C. Westenhaver, then an associate of mine in the law and later appointed United States district judge.

Mr. Johnson knew as much about the courts as did his opponents. He had been a street railway operator and a shrewd monopolist, and he had no illusions about the blindfolded Goddess of Justice. He took such means as he could to get his cases tried before friendly judges. He nominated for the bench men in whom he had confidence, and in almost every instance he was able to say in advance what the outcome of the litigation would be; it depended on the judge who heard it.

"When I was in business," he said to me once, "and wanted my lawyers to both decide and write the decision of a case in the federal courts, I employed the firm of ———. They represent most of the big corporations, and the federal judge is indebted to them for many favors, not the least of which is his nomination to the bench. When I wanted a fair and square fight in which the best man should win, I employed E. J. Blandin; for a rough-and-tumble fight and someone to roughhouse a hostile judge, I chose L. A. Russell.

"Judges act like other men," he concluded. "If it is unpopular to side with me on a political issue, they will decide against me. They watch the election returns; they know who decides the nominations. They decide for their party and their class with their eyes open."

The long fight was featured by the press. Mr. Johnson had the support of the *Cleveland Plain Dealer,* the most influential morning paper, and the *Cleveland Press,* a very powerful evening paper. The *Leader* and the *News,* papers owned by Senator Hanna and his associates, were bitter in their attacks, and especially in their innuendos of personal dishonesty. Homer Davenport, the cartoonist of the Hearst papers, was brought on from New York by the *Leader,* while the Associated Press carried cruelly unfair stories for the opposition. Mr. Johnson was charged with almost every conceivable political crime, the most widely accepted one being that he was trying to get possession of the street railways for himself.

One of the mayor's difficulties was to keep the members of his own party in line, as defections were always occurring in the council. It was necessary to hold ward meetings, to bring pressure on councilmen who were weakening. The traction interests spent money lavishly, and from long control of the city they knew how to reach men through relatives, contracts, bank influence, and other means.

Year by year some gain was made, some construction work completed. But the low-fare lines could not get to the center of the city. The central part of the city was free territory; that is, existing tracks could be used by any company on the payment of rental, and this free territory was our objective. One day the mayor called into his office men on whom he could rely. Teamsters were engaged; rails and ties were assembled. One night on the stroke of twelve the entire outfit was set in motion. The plans worked perfectly. Rails were laid along Superior Avenue on the top of the pavement to the Public Square. Barrels filled with cement were placed along the curbstones and in them supporting poles were erected to carry the electric current. Wires were strung and connections were made with the tracks of the low-fare company on the West Side. The aim was to have the cars running to the Public Square by morning and in that way escape another injunction. It would then be possible to extend the lines out into the East Side of the city. But the old company routed a complacent judge out of bed, who issued a blanket injunction against the operation of the cars. In the morning they were still halted on the farthermost side of the square.

Year after year passed, with the controversy still unsettled. Mr. Johnson had to face the people in three separate elections. His methods of campaigning were spectacular. He purchased and equipped two big circus tents, capable of seating several thousand people. The tents were set up in vacant lots about the city, and the mayor with a group of supporters would motor from tent to tent, making three or four speeches an evening. Mr. Johnson drove his own car, known as the "Red Devil," with reckless speed. He had little respect for the law, and the police winked at his violations of the speed ordinances. After the meetings we would gather at his home to outline the campaign for the following day.

I had had no training in public speaking, but standing before a crowd of people in the circus tent, many of them hostile and ready to hurl questions at the speaker, taught me something of the art. The opposition hired men to heckle us, and we had to be ready with our answers or lose more than we gained by a speech. There was always a campaign on; there were endless referendum elections on ordinances or bond issues, as well as state campaigns, in which the "Red Devil" and the tents were brought into requisition for tours about the state. The opposition spared no money or effort to block every measure sponsored by the mayor or to thwart him in the legislature and through the courts.

The cost of the long struggle was exhausting and might have worn out a man less resourceful than Tom Johnson. At one time it looked as though the whole enterprise might have to be abandoned for lack of funds. As an experiment, Mr. Johnson appealed to the public to subscribe for stock in the low-fare company. The return on the stock was limited to 6 percent, and at that time such lines as had been laid were buried two feet under the ground, as the courts would not permit the cars to be operated on them. Yet the people were so aroused that money poured in from stock, even though the subscribers questioned whether they would ever get their investment back. The subscriptions came in small sums like savings bank deposits and amounted to several hundred thousand dollars. Most of the subscribers were working people, many of them foreigners. Here was evidence that people believed in democracy, that they would make sacrifices for it, once an issue was presented that appealed to their deeper convictions. The poor loved Tom Johnson for the fight he was making, and his majorities were largest when attacks on him were most virulent.

Our opponents at last, in 1908, put up the white flag. Many of their franchises had expired. Stock that had been sold as high as $115 before 1901 had steadily fallen to less than $70 a share. Finally, after every conceivable lawsuit had been exhausted, and bankers had become frightened over the collapse of securities, a settlement was reached. The old companies agreed to a valuation on their properties far below the capitalized valuation. On this valuation they were to receive a fixed return of 6 percent and no more. The street railway properties were to be leased to an operating company of five men, trustees of the city, selected by the mayor, who bound themselves to pay only operating costs and a 6 percent return on the outstanding capital stock. All earnings in excess of these sums were to be used as the city might direct. The rate of fare was to be on a sliding scale. It was to start at three cents and go up or down as the earnings of the company made it possible.

Mr. Ermon du Pont was made president of the company, I was vice-president and treasurer, and W. B. Colver was secretary.

The war was over, and we were ready to turn to the program of city building which Mr. Johnson had had in mind from the beginning. The "City on the Hill" would now become a reality. Something had already been done in breathing spaces between the fighting. Fred Kohler, Mayor Johnson's brilliant young chief of police, had instituted a Golden Rule policy in his department that had shocked some ministers of Christian churches but had won admiring commendation from President Roosevelt. Harris R. Cooley, a lifelong friend of Mr. Johnson's and his director of charities and corrections, had one morning astounded the city by a wholesale workhouse delivery. "Imprisonment for debt," Mr. Cooley called the detention of men and women in the workhouse because they were unable to pay fines imposed by the police court. A hue and cry was raised against him, opposition papers said the city would be filled with criminals, but Mr. Cooley went on with his policy and in time Cleveland became proud of its official humanity. A new workhouse, situated in a tract of two thousand acres laid out as a park, infirmaries, a boys' farm school, outdoor work for prisoners, and the introduction of the honor system were some of Mr. Cooley's happiest achievements.

With a brilliant executive and community behind us, we would make an experiment in democracy, in municipal ownership, in town planning, and in the taxation of land values. We were free at last to follow our ultimate ideals.

But we leaned too confidently on our success. We assumed that the officers of the old company were glad to see the controversy ended and that the stockholders preferred an assured income from their stock rather than a return to insecurity and speculation. We did not realize the sense of balked power, the latent hatred, or the nationwide hostility on the part of financiers and street railway owners to a three-cent-fare experiment or to any advance toward municipal ownership. Nor did we dream of the things that could be done to make municipal ownership a failure.

A new line of attack was now adopted. The credit of the operating company was to be undermined. If the municipal company could be made to default in the payment of its guaranteed rental the contract would be forfeited and the properties would go back to the old owners, supported by a twenty-five-year franchise. This was one of the securities provided for when the properties were transferred to the municipal company. The industrial depression of 1907 and 1908 played havoc with our earnings. Thousands of men were out of work and did not use the cars. A disagreement arose with the employees. It was not very serious and might have been adjusted, but it offered a further opportunity to embarrass us. A strike was called. There was evidence that officers of the street railway union had been paid large sums of money to bring it about. Certainly they received aid from the reactionary press that had never shown any sympathy for organized labor. Dynamite was used on the tracks. Car riders were terrified, employees assaulted. There were threats that the powerhouses would be blown up. Night after night we toured the city in police automobiles protecting the property or responding to calls from employees who remained loyal to us. Our earnings fell off. Finally word was passed around to the strikers to file referendum petitions against the ordinance upon which the settlement was based. The opposition papers supported the petitioners, and in a short time enough names to require the ordinance to be voted on by the people had been filed with the city clerk. We were in for another election. But for the first time we were on the defensive. We had to explain our failures. The community had stood by us when we were battling against an unpopular corporation, but now we were fighting organized labor. The forces of discontent were now against us. We received little support from the press. Our friends were overconfident and remained away from the polls. The evening of the election we followed the returns at the City Hall with every expectation of victory, but the issue hung in the balance all through the night, and in the morning it was still uncertain. We lost out by a few hundred votes.

The verdict could not be reviewed. There was no appeal to another test. The street railway lines went back to the old companies. Their victory was an empty one, for their dividends were limited to 6 percent and could not exceed a fixed amount, while the rate of fare started at three cents and rose or fell as earnings might determine. But the city had lost. A great movement was ended. The dream of municipal ownership, of a free and sovereign city, was set back indefinitely.

This defeat was Tom Johnson's death blow. For eight years he had given every bit of intelligence, every ounce of energy he possessed to the city. When victory was in his hand, the people turned against him. His health failed, his fortune was dissipated, and when he died, within two years, he questioned not the truth of his great economic vision but the value of his own effort, whether any good had come out of it all.

Urban Populism, Fiscal Crisis, and the New Political Economy

Todd Swanstrom

THE SHIFT away from the purely political explanations of urban politics characteristic of the pluralists and elitists has been a healthy development. The pendulum may have swung too far in the opposite direction, as the shift from internal political factors to external economic factors has created its own conventional wisdom, an abstract economic determinism that requires critical examination.

The basic logic of this new conventional wisdom is simple and elegant: local politicians require a prosperous economy to provide adequate tax revenues for basic services and to retain voter support; the economy will not prosper unless mobile wealth (both capital and residents) is attracted into the city; mobile wealth will not be attracted into the city unless local policies cater to its needs and interests. As a result, local policy making is tightly constrained by the functional need to serve mobile wealth.

My animus here is not a full-fledged theory but rather a tendency within existing theories to emphasize the impact of economic factors, in a particular way, on urban outcomes. The substance of the argument is economic; the form is structural-functional. Policies are not viewed as the result of the intentions of political actors but as the product of the function of the political system in the economy. It does not matter who is in power; in the long run, policy must conform to the needs of the economy. Following David A. Gold et al.,[1] I shall refer to the argument as "economic structuralism." Although it has the logic of a structuralist argument, it should be kept strictly separate from structuralist political theory associated with the French structuralists such as Nicos Poulantzas.

One of the intriguing aspects of economic structuralism is that it is endorsed by writers of both the left and the right. Probably the purest expression of the left-wing version of economic structuralism is Fred Block's "The Ruling Class Does Not Rule," but numerous other scholars, working generally from a left or Marxian tradition, have developed variations on the same theme.[2] The primary characteristic of economic structuralism is that it does not rely on conscious political organization or manipulation by an elite. In the words of Block, the constraining effects of the business climate originate from purely economic decisions: "Conspiracies to destabilize the [left-of-center] regime are basically superfluous, since decisions made by individual capitalists according to their own narrow economic rationality are sufficient to paralyze the regime."[3] Whereas Block pitched his argument at the level of the nation-state, many have observed that, logically, the effect will be greater at the local level than at the state or national level because of the greater ease with which capital can cross highly permeable local political boundaries.[4]

The right-wing version of economic structuralism has its roots in neoclassical economic theory, specifically as it has been applied to government in welfare economics. Local governments are viewed as analogous to firms in a competitive market, an approach first developed by Charles Tiebout.[5] Like analysts on the left, analysts on the right emphasize the objective need for cities to adapt their policies to the imperatives of a mobile capitalist economy.[6] The difference between the left and right is that whereas the former finds the economic pressures on cities to be understandable but regrettable, the latter finds them both understandable and laudable. Right and left tendencies are synthesized in Paul Peterson's *City Limits*. Acknowledging a debt to welfare economics and structural Marxism, Peterson argues that rational local policies must conform to economic constraints, yet in the end he calls for redistributive policies at the national level.[7]

I propose here to engage in what Michael Smith has called "a dialogue between structural logic and historical process."[8] Specifically, I propose to examine the validity of economic structuralism through a detailed study of one city, Cleveland, focusing on that city's fiscal crisis and default that led to the defeat of the populist mayor Dennis Kucinich. Although a single case cannot disprove a broad argument like economic structuralism, it can suggest, I believe, ways of combining economic and political factors that acknowledge the insights of economic structuralism without falling into economic determinism.

Cleveland: The Politics of Fiscal Crisis

When we think of defaults, we think of accountants leaning over calculators adding up long columns of numbers. If the numbers don't add up, if the money isn't there, the city goes into default. In fact, defaults are rarely determined by economic pressures alone; there is almost always room for political discretion. In one of the few historical studies of urban fiscal crisis in the United States, Eric Monkkonen concludes, based on an analysis of 941 municipal defaults between 1850 and 1930, that, with the exception of the Great Depression, "external economic forces alone did not force default on the cities. Instead . . . most important, the dimensions of local political struggle determine[d] who defaulted and when."[9] Essentially, cities chose not to pay back certain debts for political reasons, whether as part of an effort by the mercantile elite to disfranchise propertyless voters (Memphis) or as the result of a victory of local taxpayers over growth-oriented entrepreneurs (Duluth).

Cleveland's default, only the second by a major city since the Great Depression,[10] confirms Monkkonen's findings on the politicalness of municipal defaults. In this case, however, it was the lenders who precipitated default, not the borrowers. Dennis Kucinich, populist mayor of Cleveland from 1977 to 1979, charged that bankers attempted to blackmail the city into selling a valuable asset for the benefit of private interests. Kucinich, who became embroiled in political conflicts with the city's business establishment, described a meeting with Brock Weir (chairman and chief executive officer of Cleveland Trust) the day of default: "At that meeting, Mr. Weir told me that only if I agreed to sell the Municipal Light System to CEI [Cleveland Electric Illuminating Company, the area's private utility] would he agree to roll the notes. He also offered to raise $50 million in city bonds, but only if the Light System was sold."[11] According to Kucinich, the banks were involved in a monumental conflict of interest because they, and financial interests close to them, stood to benefit from the sale of Muny Light. In addition, by forcing Kucinich either to sell Muny Light or to default, the bankers were guaranteeing political damage to a mayor they had an avowed interest in defeating.

The most thorough study of Cleveland's default, a staff study for a subcommittee of the Committee on Banking, Finance, and Urban Affairs of the United States House of Representatives, tentatively concluded that Cleveland's default was politically motivated:

> The interlocking relationship of Cleveland Trust Company and some of the other banks with much of the corporate community and the deep animosities and political crosscurrents in which some bank officers became involved, suggest the strong possibility that factors, other than pure hardnosed credit judgments, entered the picture. At a minimum, it is impossible to conclude that key bankers donned green eyeshades, locked themselves in their board rooms, and made dispassionate decisions based solely on computer runs.[12]

In the next two sections, I will present evidence to demonstrate that Cleveland's default was, indeed, political. This contradicts Block's argument that narrowly economic decision making is sufficient to paralyze left-of-center regimes.

Muny Light and Default

To comprehend Cleveland's default, it is necessary to understand how Muny Light, a small, dilapidated public utility, became the center of a raging political controversy that precipitated the city's default. Born in conflict during the administration of populist mayor Tom Johnson (1901–9), Muny Light successfully overcame CEI's strenuous opposition and established itself as a viable competitor, offering consumers in many parts of the city a choice between competing utilities.[13] Until the

1960s, Muny prospered, growing to serve more than fifty-eight thousand customers and reporting consistent operating profits. In the 1960s, however, Muny began to experience operating problems such as outages, which CEI took advantage of with an aggressive marketing campaign to attract Muny's customers. From 1906 through 1968, Muny reported profits of $31.5 million as well as significant subsidies to the city's general fund; from 1969 through 1977, it lost $31.1 million. The general fund was forced to subsidize Muny.

In 1971, Ralph Perk ran for mayor vowing to save Muny Light. Unable to sell bonds for the ailing plant, however, Perk later reversed his position and in September 1976 announced that an agreement had been reached to sell Muny to CEI. In May 1977, the city council passed an ordinance, eighteen to fifteen, to sell Muny Light.

Kucinich, who had been elected citywide clerk of courts in 1975, became a vocal opponent of the sale. Through challenges in court and before the Federal Power Commission (FPC), Kucinich attempted to block the sale. The Save Muny Light Committee, which he chaired, gathered 29,758 signatures to put the sale before the voters in a referendum. The Election Board, however, ruled the petitions invalid because of improper language. Kucinich appealed that decision in the courts and challenged the Zoning Board's approval of the sale. With a legal cloud hanging over the proceedings, Kucinich was just able to prevent completion of the sale until he became mayor in November 1977. As Mayor, Kucinich had the power to block the sale.

One question hangs over the entire Muny Light controversy: was Muny a drain on the city or was it a public asset? This is not an easy question to answer. Basically, it hinges on whether Muny's huge losses from 1969 to 1977 were the result of mismanagement or were caused by predatory efforts of CEI to eliminate its competitor. If the latter is the case, the losses are turned into an asset because, under the nation's antitrust laws, the city can recover triple damages—which in fact it tried to do in a $150 million lawsuit against CEI, filed in 1975. (The first trial ended in a hung jury; the second ruled in favor of CEI. The city appealed the case. The Sixth Circuit Court of Appeals ruled against the city in 1984.)

Findings issued by the Atomic Safety and Licensing Board of the Nuclear Regulatory Commission (NRC) in 1977 supported the city's case. The most serious finding concerned CEI's refusal to allow Muny, which is surrounded by CEI, to purchase outside electricity. Since Muny began purchasing cheaper outside power through its new interconnection, required by the NRC as a condition for CEI's license to operate nuclear power plants, Muny's steep plunge into the red was halted and the utility has been basically operating in the black ever since. The NRC also called CEI's conditions for Muny's access to the power generated at the nuclear power plants, which included setting Muny's rates, an "outrageous affront" to the nation's antitrust laws. The NRC concluded that CEI had violated the Sherman Antitrust Act, attempting to eliminate its public competitor through unfair and anticompetitive acts.[14]

Cleveland's financial crisis, which culminated in default, was inextricably bound up with the struggle between CEI and Muny Light. Nine days after Kucinich took office in November 1977, CEI filed a certificate of judgment of lien on lands and property of the city to recover disputed debts owed CEI by Muny. Faced with a general fund deficit of $10 million, the Kucinich administration lacked the money to pay the debt. When Cleveland Trust refused to roll over $7.8 million in short-term notes in May 1978, the city was forced to purchase its own notes using funds slated for other purposes. Soon after, Standard and Poor's suspended Cleveland's bond rating and Moody's Investor Service downgraded the city's bond rating for the second time. Cleveland was gradually shut out of the national bond market.

More bad news came in August, when the national accounting firm of Ernst and Ernst reported that $52 million in bond money for capital projects had been misspent for operating expenses (most during the previous Perk administration). For the first time, the Kucinich administration became aware of the perilous financial condition of the city.

In September, $3.34 million in short-term notes came due, and the banks again refused to refinance. Kucinich was forced to dip into the city's meager cash reserves. Having narrowly survived a recall election one month earlier, Kucinich this time took the offensive against the banks with a blistering political attack containing anticapitalist rhetoric generally outside the pale of American politics. Kucinich challenged the banks to come to the aid of Cleveland "even if they can't make the same extraordinary profits as they do elsewhere." He concluded with a political threat: "Unless the banks begin to respond to the needs of Cleveland residents, a tremendous uprising of anger and bitterness will be directed against them. We must bring democracy to the banks as we have to our political life. This administration will be in the forefront of a movement to severely hamper normal business operations of area banks if they do not begin to respond to the needs of the city government and city residents. The banks leave us no choice but to fight back to save our city."[15]

Ignoring Kucinich's attack, the banks again, in October 1978, refused to roll over short-term notes. The notes were refinanced internally with the few remaining city funds. Meanwhile, a time bomb was ticking in the budget: $14 million in short-term notes, held by six local banks, would come due on December 15, 1978. And the city still owed CEI $5.7 million. A federal district court ruled that, unless the CEI debt was paid by the end of the year, Cleveland's $150 million antitrust suit would be thrown out.

In December, everything came to a head. United States marshals began tagging city property for CEI's debts. By December 13, about fifty of Muny's repair trucks were impounded. Kucinich was able to squeeze money from operating expenses to pay CEI and keep the antitrust suit alive, but this meant there were no funds to purchase the $14 million in short-term notes due on December 15. With the City Council supporting a plan to sell Muny Light and Kucinich rejecting that and offering his own plan, the city was unable to agree on what to do to avoid default. When, at midnight on December 15, before packed chambers, the council rejected the mayor's plan on a procedural vote seventeen to sixteen, Cleveland officially went into default.

If default was the dramatic climax, the period that followed was the denouement. One week after default, the council worked out a compromise, passing ordinances that placed before the voters in February both a 50 percent increase in the income tax and the sale of Muny Light. Kucinich led an effective grass-roots campaign that, according to polls, turned around public opinion on Muny Light.[16] The electorate voted to retain Muny Light and increase the municipal income tax—both by almost two-to-one margins. Kucinich began paying off the defaulted notes with the income tax receipts late the next summer, but Cleveland remained technically in default throughout his administration.

The Politicalness of Default

To say that the default was political is to say that factors other than immediate economic interests entered into the decisions leading to default. A 1979 congressional study suggested two factors, "other than pure hardnosed credit judgments," that could have entered into the bankers' decision not to roll over the notes, thus forcing the sale of Cleveland's public utility to CEI and politically crippling the Kucinich administration.[17] By demanding that Muny Light be sold as a condition for rollover, Kucinich was placed on the horns of a dilemma in which either horn (selling Muny or default) would exact severe political damage.

Definite proof of the bankers' intentions would require getting into their heads. Sufficient circumstantial evidence exists, however, including statements by the participants and evidence of their material interests, to prove beyond a reasonable doubt that the bankers had other motives in mind when they refused to roll over the notes beyond simply the ability of the city to repay a loan.

With regard to the sale of Muny Light, there is, first, no doubt that CEI had long desired to eliminate its competitor. That was CEI's first admission in the antitrust suit (though CEI denied using any illegal methods). Second, strong ties existed between CEI and the banks involved in default, especially Cleveland Trust. Altogether, five of the six banks (one provided no information) held almost 1.8 million shares (about 5 percent) of CEI's total outstanding stock. Also, extensive interlocks existed between the banks and the private utility. Of the eleven directors of CEI during 1978, eight were also directors at four of the six banks. Four directors of Cleveland Trust were also directors of CEI. Cleveland Trust managed CEI's pension fund, served as bond trustee and counsel, and was registrar for CEI's stock. Of the Cleveland banks, four had $72 million in lines of credit available for the utility. Indirect links drew the net of common interests tighter. The six banks had seventy-nine director interlocks with twenty other corporations that also shared one or more directors or officers with CEI. Top officials of CEI also had extensive social ties to bank executives through such associations as the elite Union Club and the Growth Association, Cleveland's Chamber of Commerce.

In short, evidence exists of a massive conflict of interest between the banks' loan-making functions and their considerable ties to the private utility, especially their trust holdings. Ever since court rulings, beginning in 1961, it has been contrary to public policy for trust and commercial departments within a single bank to trade material inside information. As a result, banks have constructed what have come to be known as "Chinese Walls" between their trust departments—which are supposed to act solely in the interest of the institutions or persons whose money they manage—and their commercial loan departments, the purpose of which is to make loans purely on the basis of creditworthiness, so as to protect the interests of bank shareholders.[18]

In this case, at least, there is evidence that the wall broke down—that is, the banks' refusal to roll over the city's notes was influenced by the benefits that would accrue to trust department holdings, as well as to the economic and political interests of bank officers. In the case of Cleveland Trust, suspicions are further aroused when one learns that in October 1978, shortly after Kucinich's verbal attacks on the banks, decisions regarding city debt at Cleveland Trust were removed from the commercial bank level to an executive committee at the holding company level. In other words, the decision not to roll over the notes was not made on one side of the wall but by high-level executive officers sitting atop the "Chinese Wall."

A second alleged ulterior motive of the banks in causing the default, besides forcing the sale of Muny Light, was a desire to damage Kucinich politically and prevent him from being reelected. Considerable evidence exists of the bankers' hostility toward Kucinich. At least seventy officers and directors of the six banks involved contributed to the campaign to recall Kucinich, including Brock Weir and seventeen of thirty-two directors of Cleveland Trust. (Very few, if any, lived within the city of Cleveland.) A month before default, Claude Blair, chairman of National City Bank, which Kucinich had attacked for obtaining a tax abatement, was quoted on television news as saying, according to confidential sources, that he would not refinance the notes held by his bank because of the "Kucinich administration's antagonism toward the business community" and that he was "willing to accept the consequence to Cleveland as the price to pay to see Mayor Kucinich defeated in next year's election."[19]

Weir, however, was the most visible leader in the banks' conflict with Kucinich. After default, Weir made statements that indicated his intentions toward the Kucinich administration. Perhaps the most telling is the following statement made less than a month after default: "We had been kicked in the teeth for six months. On December 15 we decided to kick back."[20] In addition, a January 1979 *Boston Globe* article, based on an exclusive interview with Weir, contained the following paragraph: "Although public finances are a mess and virtually all the upper middle class has deserted the city for the suburbs, the business climate remains healthy. Weir said, 'The only problem is the little canker downtown.'"[21]

Not only is there evidence concerning the bankers' motives, there is also evidence that they acted on those motives. Conditioning rollover of the notes on the sale of Muny Light stood to benefit the financial interests attached to CEI as well as put the bankers' adversary, Kucinich, on the horns of a political dilemma: either sell Muny Light or default.

Overwhelming evidence exists that this quid pro quo was communicated to the city. According to Kucinich, Weir made the corrupt offer at the crucial meeting among Kucinich, Weir, Maurice Saltzman (president of Bobbie Brooks), and George Forbes (City Council president) on December 15. This meeting, however, is bathed in controversy; only a tape recording could settle the issue. Unfortunately, no tape exists. Two participants at the meeting originally backed up Kucinich's version of the story. A few days after default, Saltzman was quoted as saying: "Brock [Weir] was nice. He said, 'Look, Dennis, get this [Muny Light] out of the way. Sell the building, we'll roll over the notes, and I personally will help with the $50 million in bonds.'"[22]

It is unnecessary to prove, however, that the bankers communicated the quid pro quo to Kucinich in person, for it was communicated clearly enough through the media; at the time, all the principal actors assumed that the sale of Muny Light was the sticking point in default. Certainly everyone in Cleveland who read the newspapers or watched television knew that it was Kucinich's refusal to sell Muny Light that was the cause of the banks' unwillingness to roll over the notes. The *Cleveland Plain Dealer*, for example, linked the sale of Muny Light to rollover of the loans in front page headlines the day before default.

Significantly, Brock Weir did not deny the widespread stories linking the sale of Muny to rollover until eleven days after default.[23] On December 26, in a letter to Cleveland Trust employees, later reprinted as a newspaper advertisement, Weir denied that Cleveland Trust had any interest in who owned Muny Light.[24] Why Weir did not make his position clear, at considerably less trouble and expense, at the time that it mattered, is inexplicable. It would have been a simple matter to call the newspapers and clear up this monumental misunderstanding. The bankers' inaction implicitly confirmed reports that the sale of Muny Light was a condition for rollover. Together with Cleveland Trust's refusal to go along with Kucinich's plan for avoiding default and the approval, in executive committee, of a rival plan that included the sale of Muny, the only reasonable conclusion is that the banks, and especially Cleveland Trust, wanted the city to know that it must either sell Muny Light or the notes would not be rolled over.

Another way to determine if any political motivations were involved is to examine whether the Kucinich administration was treated differently from other similar administrations or borrowers. First, rollovers are routine in the financial community. Rollover of short-term notes, as in Cleveland's case, is not a decision to lend money but rather a decision to extend in time a line of credit already granted.[25] Rollovers are often granted to private corporations with declining fortunes and are a prime tool used to restore them to financial health.[26]

Questions are also raised concerning Cleveland's default when it is compared to the other major municipal default in the postwar era, that of New York. In an article comparing the defaults in Cleveland and New York, John Beck presents evidence that New York's fiscal crisis was caused by abnormally high expenditures on "marginal" social welfare functions. "Although New York may be described as a high-tax/high-expenditure city, Cleveland did not exhibit extreme behavior in this regard."[27] Cleveland was not overtaxed and still had considerable assets; a 1981 Ernst and Whinney audit appraised the city's net worth, including all of its land and buildings, at slightly more than $1 billion.[28] With the full faith and credit of the city behind the notes, the banks were in little danger of losing their investment. Nevertheless, the banks refused to refinance a relatively small $14 million debt.

By contrast, the New York legislature, with the implicit approval of the bankers, declared a moratorium on the repayment of $2.5 billion of outstanding notes in 1975. Although this was technically the same as default, New York City avoided the stigma, even though it was more overextended and the banks had much more to lose than in Cleveland's case. In 1975, New York's cumulative deficit was about $8 billion; soon after Kucinich left office, Cleveland's was estimated at $111 million. The difference in treatment raises the question of whether it was related to the fact that Cleveland was governed by an angry populist mayor whereas New York was led by politicians who promoted a new growth partnership between government and business.[29]

After comparing default in New York and Cleveland, Beck concludes that the explanation of Cleveland's default lay not in its "distressed circumstances at any point in time but with the *prolonged* mismanagement of its municipal finances" (emphasis added).[30] Mismanagement resulted in a high ratio of short-term debt to own-source revenues. Financial mismanagement, however, actually started during the administration of Republican Ralph Perk (1971–77), or earlier. Perk practiced sloppy bookkeeping, sold capital assets to pay for operating expenses, and relied heavily on short-term borrowing, yet the banks routinely, and without probing questions, rolled over the notes of the Perk administration.

On many issues, Kucinich was a radical, but on fiscal matters he was basically a conservative. It is difficult to argue that Cleveland's finances deteriorated during his administration. Kucinich added almost no new debt during his two years in office; he was able to pay off, out of operating funds, a sizable Muny Light debt that had accumulated during the previous administration as well as millions in short-term debt; the payroll dropped from 11,640 to 9,500 by a process of attrition; and, unlike Perk, Kucinich did not succumb to the dubious practice of selling assets to meet operating expenses. Finally, although the informational demands placed on the Kucinich administration by the banks were not unreasonable, given the city's questionable bookkeeping methods, they were clearly much greater than during the previous administrations.[31]

Objective evidence indicates that the Kucinich administration was discriminated against compared to its predecessor; there is also the testimony of Weir, who admitted that Kucinich was treated differently from the way Perk was and, in explaining why, so much as confessed to a political bias: "We weren't asking the type of questions of them [Perk administration] that we were asking this [Kucinich] administration. There are a couple of reasons why. First, New York happened. That taught us all a lesson about asking questions. The second reason is the *attitude of the Kucinich Administration*. The Perk Administration was not as antagonistic toward the business community and the banking community as to precipitate a showdown" (emphasis added).[32] In short, the banks treated Kucinich differently from Perk for political reasons.

Evidence also exists that the banks treated Kucinich differently from his Republican successor, George Voinovich.[33] Interestingly, Mayor Voinovich, who improved Muny's ability to compete with CEI, eventually came to see the same conspiracy against Muny Light that Kucinich saw.[34] In 1984, the Voinovich administration negotiated with CEI to take over all of Muny's private customers in exchange for, among other things, a promise by CEI not to move its more than a thousand employees to the suburbs, as threatened, but to locate them instead in a major downtown development. Voinovich, perhaps fearing a Kucinich comeback, killed the deal, saying that CEI's decision over where to locate its headquarters should have nothing to do with Muny Light. Indeed, CEI's attempt to link staying in Cleveland with the sale of the municipal utility is another example, like default, of political discretion in investment. Voinovich, who said he never believed the story that the business community offered to prevent default if Kucinich would sell Muny Light, said he was not so sure the story wasn't true after the incident described above.[35]

In summary, there is strong evidence that the bankers had motives for demanding that Cleveland sell Muny Light or go into default; there is incontrovertible evidence that this demand was, in fact, communicated to the city; and finally, there is substantial evidence that Cleveland city government, under Kucinich, was treated differently from other borrowers, other cities, and other administrations. In sum, Cleveland's default was political.

Elite Intervention in a Structural Crisis

The political unity of Cleveland's financial elite in pursuit of its political interests exceeded that which would be predicted by an economic structuralist analysis. Unlike Block's formulation, "decisions made by individual capitalists according to their own narrow economic rationality" were not sufficient, at least in Cleveland's case, to paralyze the regime. In Cleveland, a financial elite had to override narrow economic rationality in order to manipulate the electoral process, using an instrument of power that goes well beyond the legitimate use of lobbying or campaign contributions: the political allocation of credit.[36]

Cleveland's default, then, seems to fit clearly within the tradition of elite theory (at least in the negative sense of an elite using its control over credit to destabilize a left-of-center regime) rather than economic structuralism. Before concluding that this is a pure example of elite instrumental intervention, however, it is necessary to analyze the conditions that made the exercise of this power possible in the first place.

At root, Cleveland's default is an example of one group acquiring a monopoly over a needed commodity, in violation of market theory, and then exercising political discretion in its decision to withhold that commodity. For this monopoly power to operate, four conditions were necessary: (1) The city had to be shut out of the national bond market and forced to depend on local banks. (2) The local banks had to possess extraordinary unity of political purpose and action. (3) Forced to deal with a united phalanx of local banks, the city had to be placed in a highly unique bargaining relationship with the banks. (4) Finally, the political leadership of the city had to be willing to resist the demands of the banks.

Of the four conditions, the second is clearly in the domain of elite power structure research, focusing, as it does, on the intentions and organization of the elite through networks such as interlocking directorates and social clubs. I argue, however, that the first, third, and fourth conditions are rooted in the structures of modern political economy. They result not from the intentional political actions of elites but from the structurally induced decisions of investors motivated by short-term profit.[37]

Power structure research focuses on the second necessary condition listed above, the political cohesion of the economic elite. Little research has been conducted, however, on the organization of economic elites in declining industrial cities like Cleveland. An exception is the work of Richard Ratcliff on St. Louis. Whereas the massive shift of investment out of industrial cities presented obvious problems for the maintenance of elite rule, Ratcliff observes, the metropolitan capitalist class in St. Louis remained highly organized around a core elite. In a study of bank directors in St. Louis, Ratcliff found "a hierarchical system of stratification which separates and makes distinct a core network of capitalists closely bound together by multiple economic and social ties."[38] Much the same result was found for Cleveland.

In Cleveland a financial elite headed by Cleveland Trust led the fight against Kucinich's urban populism and the threat it posed to the dominance of business values in city government. This financial elite showed remarkable political unity throughout the city's fiscal crisis. The six banks that held the notes formed a tacit agreement that all would go forward together or none would; the demanding rule of unanimity was adopted as the principle of political unity. In apparent violation of antitrust laws, Cleveland had the benefit of only one credit judgment, not six.[39]

The political cohesion of the Cleveland banks is not surprising, given the social ties as well as the tight network of interlocking relationships among the banks and between the banks and the private utility. One factor that has not been noted is the economic concentration within the banking community and, within that, the dominance exerted by Cleveland Trust over the entire financial sector. Congressional studies in the late 1960s documented Cleveland's centralized pattern of bank stock ownership and control, calling it "the most alarming of any of the 10 cities under study."

> According to the latest FDIC concentration statistics as of June 30, 1966, the five largest banks in the Cleveland metropolitan area held 91.7 percent of all the commercial bank deposits in the area, one of the highest concentrations in the Nation. . . .
>
> It is clear from the major Cleveland banks' extensive web of stockholder links, more pervasive than in any other city examined thus far, that competition among these banks is bound to be adversely affected.[40]

A year later another congressional study, focusing on trust holdings, found Cleveland to be one of four cities (out of ten examined) where banking was dominated by a few institutions with permanently entrenched managements. "All in all, it is clear from the Subcommittee's survey that not only is Cleveland banking from the point of view of commercial bank operations, dominated by the Cleveland Trust Co., but when the additional factor of trust investments combined with interlocking directorships is considered, the Cleveland Trust Co., along with the other banks surveyed in Cleveland, is probably the single most influential element in the entire economy of the area."[41] The 1979 congressional study of default confirmed the earlier pattern, concluding that Cleveland Trust "remains by far the dominant financial institution in the city."[42]

In short, the near monopoly of the major banks in Cleveland, their strong ties to each other and to most major corporations through investments and interlocking directorates, and the intimate social and political connections between key bank executives created a community of interest among the major bankers in Cleveland. Led by Cleveland Trust, finance capital in Cleveland showed remarkable solidarity throughout the December default crisis. This is important because if only one bank had broken ranks, Kucinich's hand would have been greatly strengthened and the city might have been able to work out a refinancing plan.

The evidence shows, then, that there was a well-organized financial elite in Cleveland that was ready and willing to represent conservative business interests against an insurgent populist mayor. Without three other conditions being in place, however, this elite never could have exercised the power that it did. These other necessary conditions were not primarily the result of political organization but of deep-seated economic trends.

First, Cleveland had to be forced out of the national bond market, requiring it to rely on the local banks for financing. This occurred in the months before default when the two national rating agencies dropped Cleveland's bond ratings below investment grade. The fundamental reason for these low ratings was the city's long-term financial problems stemming from the suburbanization of its middle class and the disinvestment of its industrial base. Yet Cleveland's financial situation under Kucinich was little different from what it had been under the previous mayor, Perk. Undoubtedly, the refusal of local banks to refinance short-term debt beginning in May 1978 and the discovery of the missing bond funds that summer were the major proximate causes of the lowered bond ratings.[43] Regardless of the reason, by December 1978 the national bond market was unavailable to the city. Having exhausted its cash reserves paying the CEI debt and purchasing notes the banks earlier refused to roll over, Cleveland could finance the existing notes in December 1978 only through the local banks that held them.

Forced to deal with a united local banking establishment, the city found itself in a highly uneven bargaining relationship. If default can be thought of as a complex game of chicken, as the *Congressional Study* suggested,[44] then, clearly, the banks were driving the equivalent of a Sherman tank, the city a beat-up Volkswagen. Ironically, the unequal financial situations of the banks and city government resulted, in large part, from the actions of the banks themselves. For years, Cleveland banks had diverted mortgage investment from the city to the suburbs. In 1978, for example, local financial institutions invested over $1 billion in housing in the county; only 16 percent of this money went to Cleveland even though the city contained about 42 percent of the total residential units in the county. A study for the Federal Reserve Bank of Cleveland concluded that area banks redlined black and racially mixed neighborhoods in Cleveland. Cleveland banks continued to invest in downtown office buildings, but they pulled much of their housing and industrial investment out of the city. In 1981, several community organizations challenged Cleveland Trust's application for mergers under the Community Reinvestment Act, claiming that between 1977 and 1979 the bank pulled $156 million in loans out of the Cleveland area, investing the money, among other places, in a $40 million loan to a nonunion southern steel mill.[45]

Able to tap into a national lending market, the banks involved in the city's default had many places to loan their money. The banks were able to exercise political discretion by calling in the notes owed by the city government because these notes represented such an infinitesimal portion of their assets. For example, Cleveland Trust's $5 million share of the notes represented less than 1 percent of its loans to states and political subdivisions ($689 million) and less than one-tenth of 1 percent of its total outstanding loans.[46] Even a complete write-off would have made only a small dent in the total equity of the Cleveland banks.

The banks had many places to lend their money, but the city had only one place to borrow. Moreover, like many cities of the Northeast, Cleveland was in a perpetual fiscal crisis owing to forces beyond its control. In 1978, Cleveland had a desperate need for credit. Having to pay the debt immediately meant curtailing basic services and massive layoffs; not paying meant default, with all of its long-run implications for future access to credit. Clearly, the confrontation between the public and private sectors was dramatically uneven.

One more ingredient was necessary before the banks could exercise political power: a mayor who was willing, even eager, to resist their demands. Urban populism in Cleveland has been interpreted as an expression of a crisis in growth politics.[47] For nearly a century, Cleveland enjoyed phenomenal growth as one of the world's premier industrial cities. Government played a limited role during this boom period, providing minimal services and keeping taxes low. After 1950, however, Cleveland contracted even faster than it had grown, losing more than 40 percent of its population and over 50 percent of its manufacturing jobs. Extreme disparities developed between declining neighborhoods and industry and a burgeoning downtown corporate service sector. In an effort to deal with the growth crisis, Cleveland city government took on an expanded role in economic and community development.

Kucinich's urban populism was fundamentally an expression of the frustration and resentment of inner-city ethnics stuck in a dying industrial economy and with only a marginal place in the emerging service economy. Playing on the suspicions many ethnics felt about the growing collaboration between the public and private sectors brought on by the growth crisis, Kucinich based his appeal on confrontation politics, attacking big banks and corporations.

Default would never have occurred if Cleveland's mayor had refrained from attacking the banks and had been willing to sell Muny Light. Kucinich may have even desired a confrontation with the banks; more important, however, because he had staked so much of his career on saving Muny Light, Kucinich had little choice. The result (rare in American politics) was that an elected chief executive of a major city not only resisted the demands of the banks but publicly attacked them.

Analysis of the four conditions necessary for the exercise of elite power in default (exclusion from the national bond market, a politically united local banking establishment, an uneven bargaining relationship, and a mayor willing to resist the demands of the banks) reveals that all, with the exception of the degree of collusion among local bankers, are closely related to the underlying economic and fiscal crisis besetting Cleveland.

Clearly, Cleveland's growth crisis is not primarily the result of directly political investment decisions, as in default. Cleveland's fiscal crisis is rooted in structural changes in advanced capitalism. The strength of the new political economy lies not in its ability to explain local government policy (economic structuralism) but in its ability to expose the contradictions of advanced capitalism that produce the problems and crises of urban politics. Whether it be showing that the benefits of growth are bottled up in the monopoly sector, generating a fiscal crisis in the state, or showing that market relations generate, by their own logic, uneven development, the new political economy demonstrates that investment decisions, notwithstanding that their intent is immediate economic gain, have profound political effects.[48] In this case, structurally induced investment decisions created the preconditions, both subjective and objective, for the instrumental manipulation of Cleveland politics by a financial elite.

The Cleveland example suggests that there is a dialectic of economic structure and political agency in local politics. Normally, the operations of the credit and investment markets are sufficient to keep local governments within safe bounds; disinvestment or withdrawal of credit will automatically occur if there is too radical an effort at redistribution. Contradictions within the "normal" operations of these investment markets, however, create urban problems and crises. Those who suffer these costs mobilize politically in an effort to shift the burden. Economic crisis creates political crisis.

The economic dominants, in turn, mobilize to deal with the threat to their political hegemony. In Cleveland, this happened twice in the postwar period: once in response to urban populism of the 1970s and once in response to the black nationalist threat of the 1960s, when business reluctantly bankrolled a black liberal for mayor, Carl B. Stokes. Business later withdrew its support when Stokes proved incapable of protecting property during the 1968 Glenville riots.[49]

The Business Climate Issue

The bankers had two political goals: eliminate Muny as a competitor to CEI and politically embarrass Kucinich, preventing his reelection. On the issue of Muny Light, the bankers lost. Voters overwhelmingly opposed the sale in the February election. Muny Light remains in the public sector today.

But the bankers achieved their second goal: Kucinich was defeated for reelection in November 1979 by Republican George Voinovich (56 to 44 percent). Although it is difficult to determine how many votes default cost Kucinich, there is no doubt that it hurt him politically. Kucinich was damaged both by the general onus of default and by the tax increase he was forced to support to cope with default.

For years, Kucinich had criticized the city's income tax as regressive and in the 1977 mayoral campaign had stated categorically, "Under no circumstances will I ever increase the income tax." In December 1978, however, Kucinich had little choice. Because Cleveland's property tax base was stagnating, raising the income tax was the only viable course of action. Kucinich used his popularity in the ethnic wards to help carry the income tax increase even though, ironically, under Ohio law, neither banks nor utilities pay any local income taxes.[50]

More than the tax increase, the general onus of default, related to the issue of the business climate, hurt Kucinich with the voters. Kucinich's electoral appeal, urban populism, was based on the claim that he could deliver economic benefits to the inner city that other mayors could not. If the argument here is correct (that Cleveland was discriminated against regarding credit because it elected a populist mayor and chose to retain the municipal light plant), then, at least in the short run, urban populism meant economic sacrifice, not economic gain.

The particular nature of the banks' power in the case of default should be made clear. The banks exerted power over the size and shape of the local public sector, not over particular allocations. Forced to seek an income tax increase, Kucinich nevertheless controlled the allocation of tax receipts and made the banks wait in line behind the city payroll. By withdrawing their credit, however, the banks convinced many voters that keeping Kucinich as mayor would hurt the city economically. The banks did not take over city government, they laid siege to it—a siege, it was implied, that would not be lifted as long as Kucinich was mayor. As one voter in a lower-income ethnic ward put it the weekend before the 1979 election: "There's the business people and the common people. The two got to work together. I'm a straight Democrat, but you can't tell people with money to go to hell."[51]

The business climate issue, then, proved very damaging to Kucinich. I would argue, however, that, with the important exception of default, Kucinich's short-lived administration had little impact on capital investment in Cleveland. To be sure, Kucinich took actions that were perceived as having a negative effect on the business climate, but this does not mean they actually had a negative impact. Kucinich, for example, killed a tax abatement program for downtown. Existing studies overwhelmingly support the conclusion that local tax abatements have little effect on investment.[52] Indeed, shortly after Kucinich killed tax abatement, downtown Cleveland experienced a building boom. In this case, just the opposite of default, there was no investment conspiracy to punish Kucinich for acting against business. Competition created economic space for a populist policy rejecting tax breaks for business.

The impact of the business climate issue, however, is not based solely on objective effects; because of the importance of perceptions, it is open to a great deal of political manipulation. Although Kucinich's stand against abatement was economically successful, it was a failure politically. Kucinich's opposition to abatement was used effectively, along with default, as evidence of his baneful effect on Cleveland's economy. Unlike the banks in their refusal to lend money to the city, most business people were not in a position to exercise political discretion in their investment decisions. What they could do, at no cost to themselves, was exercise political discretion over the reasons for their investment behavior, distributing praise or blame for ongoing investment trends. When Diamond Shamrock, the nation's 178th largest industrial corporation, announced that it was moving its headquarters from Cleveland to Dallas, papers gave front-page headlines to the charge of its president that the main reason was "the anti-business attitude on the part of the city administration." Overwhelming evidence shows that the move was dictated by economic considerations internal to the corporation, but this did not allay the impression created in the minds of the voters.[53]

In short, the economic pressures on the political system were mediated in crucial ways by politics. A hostile media fostered the impression that Kucinich was a disaster for the local business climate. For the most part, this was simply not true; local governments have little leverage over private investment. Default, however, was an exception, and investment really was pulled out; default helped to validate the impression that business was boycotting Cleveland because of Kucinich. To a certain extent, Kucinich was a victim of his own rhetoric. His headline-grabbing fights with business played into the theme of a deteriorating business climate, and his lack of a positive economic program meant that he had no way to reassure voters that something was being done about Cleveland's growth crisis.

Conclusion: The Space for Populist Reform

Economic structuralism, the argument that external economic factors tightly constrain local policy making, denies any significant role for political discretion, or agency, in the decisions of either investors or governments. In the case of Cleveland's default, an economic elite exercised political discretion in its decision to call in loans. Likewise, local governments can exercise political discretion within the interstices of structural economic determinations. Different public policies may have the same effect on mobile wealth—requiring political discretion to decide between them.[54] In addition, the mobility of capital varies across time and across industries. The economic pressures on cities, therefore, will also vary. In short, the degree of discretion that is available to local governments and to investors must be determined empirically; it cannot be postulated in the theory. Economic pressures are not unimportant for political decision making, but their effects are mediated in complex ways by political variables.

Moving from theory to practice, what does the Cleveland example suggest for the future of populist reform in American cities? The lesson seems to be that it is futile for economic reformers to participate in electoral politics at the local level. After all, Cleveland had a mayor whose main accomplishments were negative: ending tax abatements for downtown and preventing the sale of the municipal light plant. Nevertheless, he came under severe attack from business. Led by a financial elite, which precipitated the city's default for political reasons, business succeeded in convincing the electorate that urban populism had poisoned Cleveland's business climate. Little room for electoral reform exists if finance capital can withdraw badly needed credit for political reasons and then brand insurgent mayors as responsible for the city's growth crisis.

This extreme pessimism is unwarranted because there is economic space for reform. Even the most depressed industrial cities, for example, are enjoying substantial growth in downtown service employment, which offers opportunities for redistributive reforms. Cities do not have to offer tax abatements to attract this investment; they can do just the opposite: cities can tax this sector to provide funds to ameliorate the problems of uneven development such as neighborhood decay and a shortage of low-income housing.

The most recent policy innovation for spreading the benefits of the downtown service sector is called "linkage." Linkage requires downtown office developers to contribute to a fund for low-income housing. Between 1981 and 1983 San Francisco raised over $19 million for this purpose from office developments. The program has had no visible effect on investment. Boston enacted a linkage policy in 1983. Under the leadership of populist mayor Ray Flynn, the linkage program was expanded. By the end of 1992, linkage had contributed almost $70 million, helping to develop over 10,000 units of affordable housing.[55] Although such programs are clearly not commensurate with the scope of the problems, they do provide evidence that economic space exists for redistribution. It is a prime function of scholars, it seems to me, to determine exactly how great that space is.

Although the economic constraints leave room for discretion, the Cleveland case highlights the severe political constraints on policy making. Political constraints are different from economic constraints, however, for they can be altered by policy changes—short of radical restructuring of the economic system. At the most rudimentary level is the political organization of insurgent movements themselves. The nature of Kucinich's political organization, its reliance on confrontation politics, antipathy to political parties, and focus on personal appeal as opposed to grassroots organization made it vulnerable to destabilization. Strong political organization is necessary to counter the impression, fostered by the mass media, that all redistributive reforms are bad for the business climate.

It is much more difficult, however, to counter default, for investment really was withdrawn from city government because of its political coloration. Looking at the four conditions necessary for the exercise of such monopoly power, however, shows that only rarely in American politics does a city possess all four. Most cities, for example, retain access to the national bond market. Direct political allocation of municipal credit is rare. Yet if the fiscal pressures on central cities intensify in the years ahead, if the economy is hit with a deep recession, the number of governments vulnerable to financial blackmail will increase.

These tendencies to fiscal crisis are not rooted in the nature of modern capitalism but are the product of political practices chosen by each society. C. G. Pickvance argues convincingly that the link between economic crises and urban fiscal crises is weak and that "the occurrence of urban fiscal crises is primarily due to the character of political institutions in a society."[56] In Great Britain, for example, clearly a capitalist economy, there is no general tendency for urban fiscal crises.

Ironically, among Western liberal democracies, it is in the United States, where local governments have probably the greatest formal powers, that the political structures and practices most seriously undermine local political autonomy. Unlike most Western European countries, the United States also lacks any coherent policy to counteract uneven development.[57] Furthermore, local governments in the United States rely more on locally generated revenues than do local governments in Western Europe. "By not providing capital resources to subnational governments from the central government, the United States stands apart from almost every other advanced capitalist state, even other federal states."[58] Local governments in the United States, therefore, are almost totally dependent on wealthy private lenders. In Western Europe most central governments lend money directly to local governments and in many countries municipalities band together to establish lending cooperatives. Many major German cities control their own municipal savings bank from which they can borrow.[59] In short, many of the economic constraints on local governments in the United States are the result of political choices, especially the political structure of American federalism, not the inevitable result of a capitalist economic system.

Notes

1. David A. Gold, Clarence Y. H. Lo, and Erik Olin Wright, "Recent Developments in Marxist Theories of the Capitalist State," *Monthly Review* 27 (November 1975): 29–43.

2. See Harvey Molotch, "The City as a Growth Machine: Toward a Political Economy of Place," *American Journal of Sociology* 82 (1976): 309–32; Robert Goodman, *The Last Entrepreneurs* (New York: Simon and Schuster, 1979); Barry Bluestone and Bennett Harrison, *The Deindustrialization of America* (New York: Basic Books, 1982); Roger Friedland, *Power and Crisis in the City* (New York: Schocken, 1983); and Michael D. Kennedy, "One Fiscal Crisis of the City," in *Cities in Transformation*, ed. Michael P. Smith (Beverly Hills, Calif.: Sage, 1984), 92–110.

3. Fred Block, "The Ruling Class Does Not Rule," *Socialist Revolution* 33 (1977): 6–28.

4. Frances Fox Piven and Richard A. Cloward, *The New Class War* (New York: Pantheon, 1982), 90–91.

5. Charles M. Tiebout, "A Pure Theory of Local Expenditures," *Journal of Political Economy* 64 (1956): 416–24.

6. See Gurney Breckfeld, "Refilling the Metropolitan Doughnut," in *The Rise of the Sunbelt Cities*, ed. David C. Perry and Alfred J. Watkins (Beverly Hills, Calif.: Sage, 1977); William E. Simon, *A Time for Truth* (New York: Berkley, 1978), chap. 5; President's Commission for a National Agenda for the Eighties, *Urban America in the Eighties: Perspectives and Prospects* (Washington, D.C.: Government Printing Office, 1980); *President's National Urban Policy Report* (Washington, D.C.: GPO, 1982); Douglas A. Hicks, "Urban and Economic Adjustment to the Post-Industrial Era," in *Hearings Before the Joint Economic Committee, Congress of the United States, Ninety-Seventh Congress, Part 2* (Washington, D.C.: GPO, 1982).

7. Paul E. Peterson, *City Limits* (Chicago: University of Chicago Press, 1981).

8. Michael P. Smith, "Urban Structure, Social Theory, and Political Power," in *Cities in Transformation*, 14. Davida Glasberg criticizes my interpretation of Cleveland's default for ignoring economic structural factors. See Glasberg's critique, my rejoinder, and her response in *Journal of Urban Affairs* 10, no. 3 (1988): 219–52.

9. Eric H. Monkkonen, "The Politics of Municipal Indebtedness and Default, 1850–1936," in *The Politics of Urban Fiscal Policy*, ed. Terrence J. McDonald and Sally K. Ward (Beverly Hills, Calif.: Sage, 1984), 150.

10. Default literally means the failure of a borrower to make payments on time. Strictly speaking, New York was the first city to default. The New York State Legislature, however, declared the failure of the city to meet payments on $2.4 billion in outstanding notes on time in November 1965 a "moratorium" rather than a default.

11. U.S. Congress, *The Role of Commercial Banks in the Finances of the City of Cleveland*, Staff Study by the Subcommittee on Financial Institutions of the Committee on Banking, Finance and Urban Affairs (Washington, D.C.: GPO, 1979), 265, Kucinich Letter (hereafter cited as *Finances of Cleveland*).

12. Ibid., 240.

13. Tom Johnson, *My Story* (1911; reprint, Kent, Ohio: Kent State University Press, 1993), 192–94.

14. Nuclear Regulatory Commission, *Nuclear Regulatory Commission Issuances*, vol. 5 (Washington, D.C.: GPO, January 1–March 31, 1977).

15. U.S. Congress, House of Representatives, *Role of Commercial Banks in Financing the Debt of the City of Cleveland*. Hearing before the Subcommittee on Financial Institutions, Supervision, Regulation and Insurance of the Committee on Banking, Finance and Urban Affairs (Washington, D.C.: GPO, 1980), 317–20, Kucinich Press Release (hereafter cited as *Debt of Cleveland*).

16. Joseph D. Rice, "2 Issues Take Lead: Pollster Finds Sizable Margins on Tax Hike, Muny Light Sale," *Cleveland Plain Dealer,* January 23, 1979.

17. *Finances of Cleveland,* 317–20.

18. See Robert Cady as cited in Edward S. Herman, *Conflicts of Interest: Commercial Bank Trust Departments* (New York: The Twentieth Century Fund, 1975), 151. Given major structural and legal impediments to complete separation, as well as lack of any enforcement mechanism, Herman concludes that these "Chinese Walls" are rarely completely effective in practice.

19. Channel 8 WJW-TV read a retraction, exactly as dictated by lawyers for National City Bank, on the evening news for the following two nights. The reporter who originated the story, Bob Franken, resigned in protest.

20. Quoted in Julie Wiernik and Thomas Geidel, "Weir Warms to Rhodes' Plan for City," *Cleveland Plain Dealer,* January 12, 1979.

21. *Finances of Cleveland,* 231.

22. Quoted in Mark Hopwood, "Why Saltzman Gave Up," *Cleveland Press* (December 18, 1978).

23. On the day of default an officer of Cleveland Trust confirmed the newspaper reports linking Muny Light and default. See Peter Phipps, "Default Time Arrives as the Nation Watches," *Cleveland Press,* December 15, 1978.

24. The letter is reprinted in *Finances of Cleveland,* 304–7.

25. According to Ohio law, cities may borrow for capital projects using short-term notes renewable for up to eight successive one-year periods. Cities are required to pay only interest for the first five years, after which they must begin to amortize the principal. At any time in the eight years, the notes may be converted into long-term bonds, thus enabling a city to time its entry into the bond market. The Cleveland notes in question were still several years short of the five-year limit.

26. *Finances of Cleveland,* 235–36.

27. John H. Beck, "Is Cleveland Another New York?" *Urban Affairs Quarterly* 18 (1982): 214.

28. Mark Hopwood, "Assets of City Set at $1 Billion, Budget Balanced," *Cleveland Press,* May 12, 1981.

29. Ronald Berkman and Todd Swanstrom, "A Tale of Two Cities," *The Nation,* March 24, 1979.

30. Beck, "Is Cleveland Another New York?" 215.

31. In 1977, Price Waterhouse declared the city's books unauditable. Reportedly, Cleveland used a single-entry method of bookkeeping that predated Medici banking.

32. Quoted in *Debt of Cleveland,* 35–36.

33. Shortly after Kucinich's defeat, top bankers expressed a willingness to help the new mayor, including raising bond money. Less than a year later, the banks approved, without a major tax increase, a $36.2 million bond issue at a highly favorable 8 ⅞ percent interest rate, that got the city out of default. See Mark Hopwood, "Business is Ready to Aid Voinovich," *Cleveland Press,* November 8, 1979; Ronald Alsop, "Bankers in Cleveland Are Clearly Jubilant City Has New Mayor," *Wall Street Journal,* December 8, 1979.

34. In 1982, Voinovich charged that CEI was trying to cripple Muny by lobbying in council against needed legislation. "We still have a battle going on," said Voinovich. "They [CEI] are as dedicated as ever to laying away the Municipal Light system." Quoted in Gary R. Clark, "CEI Fighting Muny Legislation, Mayor Charges," *Cleveland Plain Dealer,* February 26, 1982.

35. John Lawless, "Voinovich Kills Deal with CEI," *Cleveland Plain Dealer,* January 6, 1984; Roldo Bartimole, "Tired City," *Point of View* 17 (1984): 2.

36. Block, "The Ruling Class," 19. Cleveland's default, of course, is not the first time elites have used their control over credit to exert political influence. As early as the fifth century B.C., there is recorded the example of a banker taking over the administration of a Persian city in Ionia, Atarneus, to collect on a loan. A. M. Hillhouse, *Municipal Bonds: A Century of Experience* (New York: Prentice Hall, 1936), 38. Much later, Karl Marx described how the "finance aristocracy" ruled in France during the regime of Louis Philippe (1830–48) by keeping the state "artificially on the verge of bankruptcy" and how later, in a similar fashion, financiers hamstrung the process of revolutionary change during the tumultuous years 1848–50. Karl Marx, *The Class Struggles in France 1848–1850* (1850; reprint, Moscow:

Progress Publishers, 1968). Otto Kirchheimer likewise analyzed the period of mass democracy following World War I as a period of conflict "between public control of government and private control of central banks," showing how the left reformist tendencies of the French electorate in the 1920s and 1930s were held in check by the machinations of the banks. Otto Kirchheimer, "Changes in the Structure of Political Compromise," in *The Essential Frankfurt School Reader,* ed. Andrew Arato and E. Gebhardt (New York: Urizen Books, 1978). Today, of course, many Third World countries have huge external debts and the International Monetary Fund (IMF) frequently conditions rollover of loans on specific policy changes such as cutting subsidies of essential foodstuffs.

In the advanced industrial countries today, however, central governments have simply become too big and powerful, exerting too much leverage over foreign commerce and exchange, to allow banks to attach specific political conditions to the extension of credit. In particular, the demise of the cherished doctrine of a balanced budget has left the United States government in a much more independent position vis-à-vis financial capital. At the local level, the situation is different. Local governments cannot run deficits year after year, print money, or engineer inflation to lighten their debt load; like underdeveloped countries, they are vulnerable.

37. The following analysis, which attempts to synthesize the valid insights of economic studies with the power elite perspective, has similarities to the approaches proposed by J. Allen Whitt, "Structural Fetishism in the New Urban Theory," in *Cities in Transformation;* Susan S. Fainstein, et al., *Restructuring the City* (New York: Longman, 1983); and Friedland, *Power and Crisis in the City.*

38. Richard E. Ratcliff, "Declining Cities and Capitalist Class Structure," in *Power Structure Research,* ed. G. William Domhoff (Beverly Hills, Calif.: Sage, 1980), 136.

39. John Gelbach, Cleveland Bank Clearing House president, in a draft of a letter rejecting the city's request to purchase $3.3 million in city notes, wrote: "This decision [to reject the notes] has been reached on an individual as well as on a collective basis." In the final letter to the city, the phrase "on a collective basis" was deleted. *Finances of Cleveland,* 232.

40. United States Congress, *Commercial Banks and Their Trust Activities: Emerging Influence on the American Economy,* Staff Report for Subcommittee on Domestic Finance of the Committee on Banking and Currency (1968; reprint, New York: Arno Press and the *New York Times,* 1969).

41. Ibid., 633.

42. *Finances of Cleveland,* 196.

43. No implication is made here that the rating agencies were politically motivated. Although the agencies refuse to divulge their exact formulas, it is clear that subjective factors are important. From an objective point of view, if Cleveland deserved a below-investment-grade rating in 1978, it also deserved the same rating in 1977 or 1976. For discussion of the subjective factors in bond rating, see Twentieth Century Fund Task Force on Municipal Bond Credit Ratings, *The Rating Game* (New York: Twentieth Century Fund, 1974) and Dennis R. Judd and Todd Swanstrom, *City Politics: Private Power and Public Policy* (New York: HarperCollins, 1994), 324–27.

44. *Finances of Cleveland,* 272.

45. Todd Swanstrom, *The Crisis of Growth Politics: Cleveland, Kucinich, and Challenge of Urban Populism* (Philadelphia: Temple University Press, 1985), 185; Robert B. Avery and Thomas M. Buynak, "Mortgage Redlining: Some New Evidence," *Federal Reserve Bank of Cleveland: Economic Review* (Summer 1981): 18–32; Roldo Bartimole, "Ameritrust," *Point of View* 13 (1981): 1–4.

46. *Finances of Cleveland,* 195.

47. Swanstrom, *Crisis of Growth Politics.*

48. James O'Connor, *The Fiscal Crisis of the State* (NewYork: St. Martin's, 1973); Stephen Hymer, "The Multinational Corporation and the Law of Uneven Development," in *Economics and World Order,* ed. Jagdish Bhagwati (New York: World Law Fund, 1971); Barry Bluestone, "Economic Crises and the Law of Uneven Development," *Politics and Society* 3 (1972): 65–82; Bluestone and Harrison, *Deindustrialization,* 203–4.

49. Carl B. Stokes, *Promises of Power* (New York: Simon and Schuster, 1973).

50. Quoted in Fred McGunagle, "Two Candidates Tax Each Other in Debate," *Cleveland Press,* October 26, 1977; Swanstrom, *Crisis of Growth Politics,* 172–73.

51. Quoted in John Judis, "Decline and Fall," *Progressive* 54, no. 1 (January 1980): 38.

52. John F. Due, "Studies of State-Local Tax Influences on the Location of Industry," *National Tax Journal* 14 (1961): 163–73; David Mulkey and B. L. Dillman, "Location Effects of State and Local Industrial Development Subsidies," *Growth and Change* 7, no. 2 (April 1976): 37–42; Bennett Harrison and

Sandra Kanter, "The Political Economy of State 'Job-Creation' Business Incentives," in *Revitalizing the Northeast*, ed. George Sternlieb and James W. Hughes (New Brunswick, N.J.: Center for Urban Policy Research, Rutgers University, 1978); Jerry Jacobs, *Bidding for Business* (Washington, D.C.: Public Interest Research Group, 1979); Michael J. Wasylenko, "The Location of Firms: The Role of Taxes and Fiscal Incentives," in *Urban Government Finance*, ed. Roy Bahl (Beverly Hills, Calif.: Sage, 1981); Michael Kieschnick, *Taxes and Growth: Business Incentives and Local Development* (Washington, D.C.: Council of State Planning Agencies, 1981); Advisory Commission on Intergovernmental Relations, *Regional Growth: Interstate Tax Competition* (Washington, D.C.: GPO, 1981); Roger W. Schmenner, *Making Business Location Decisions* (Englewood Cliffs, N.J.: Prentice Hall, 1982).

53. Quoted in Michael Kelly, "Diamond Shamrock to Leave Area," *Cleveland Plain Dealer*, May 30, 1979; Daniel J. Marschall, "Why Did Diamond Shamrock Go?" *Cleveland Plain Dealer*, June 25, 1979; "Media Distorts Reason, Purely Economic," *Northern Ohio Business Journal* 17 (June 11, 1979): 22.

54. "Investor discretion" is a key concept in Charles Lindblom's *Politics and Markets* (New York: Basic Books, 1977). In *City Limits*, Peterson acknowledges that governments may exercise political discretion over what he called "allocational policies," but, in my view, he underestimates their importance.

55. J. Werth, "Tapping Developers," *Planning*, January 1984. Advisory Group, *Report to the Mayor on the Linkage Between Downtown Development and Neighborhood Housing* (Boston: Boston Redevelopment Authority, 1983).

56. Chris G. Pickvance, "Theories of the State and Theories of Urban Crisis," *Current Perspectives in Social Theory* 1 (1980): 32.

57. James L. Sundquist, *Dispersing Population: What America Can Learn from Europe* (Washington, D.C.: Brookings Institution, 1975); Susan S. Fainstein and Norman I. Fainstein, "Federal Policy and Spatial Inequality," in *Revitalizing the Northeast*, ed. George Sternlieb and James W. Hughes (New Brunswick, N.J.: Center for Urban Policy Research, 1978).

58. Thomas H. Boast, "A Political Economy of Urban Capital Finance in the United States" (Ph.D. diss., Cornell University, 1977).

59. Arnold J. Heidenheimer, Hugh Heclo, and Carolyn Teich Adams, *Comparative Public Policy* (New York: St. Martin's, 1983), 290–92; Alberta Sbragia, "Cities, Capital, and Banks: The Politics of Debt in the United States, United Kingdom, and France," in *Urban Political Economy*, ed. Kenneth Newton (London: Frances Pinter, 1981), 200–202.

Black Civil Rights

Christopher Wye

THE HISTORY of the quest for black civil rights in Cleveland reflects many unique aspects of the city. Historically, black citizens of Cleveland were more likely to be treated as almost equals than in virtually any other city of the same size.[1] Partly, this liberalism was an outgrowth of historical geography and its implications. As a northern urban industrial city, Cleveland was far removed from the economic, political, social, ideological, and even psychological currents that underlay the southern plantation system with its dependence first on the enslavement of blacks and, following the Civil War, their subordination through custom and law. But Cleveland's liberal views on race were also a reflection of the city's early settlement pattern, for the Western Reserve attracted a large infusion of settlers from northern New England who brought with them a strong evangelical religious commitment and an inclination toward reformist movements.

In the early years of the nineteenth century Clevelanders were barely and perhaps even indifferently aware of their black neighbors. With only a handful—probably fewer than a hundred—black residents in a total population of several thousand, the city's black community was not sharply defined in the minds of local whites.[2] The views of the latter on race issues were indistinguishable from those of many others who lived in similarly situated midwestern urban centers. There was a pervasive sense of distance from the national debate, then just beginning, over the issues of slavery and race. Many had only a vague sense of the human rights side of the issue and felt that preservation of the Union was the only issue of real merit. Clevelanders roundly condemned the militant position being articulated by New England abolitionists as a dangerous threat to the peace, prosperity, and even survival of the Union.[3]

The views of Cleveland's black citizens in the early years of the nineteenth century, especially before 1830, are unknown because no written record has sur-

Abridged from "At the Leading Edge: The Movement for Black Civil Rights in Cleveland, 1830–1920," in *Cleveland: A Tradition of Reform*, ed. David D. Van Tassel and John J. Grabowski, © 1986 by The Kent State University Press. Reprinted with permission of The Kent State University Press.

vived to provide a direct account or reflection. We know that George Peake, his wife, and their two sons crossed the Ohio River into the Western Reserve on a journey from Pennsylvania, purchased one hundred acres of land, and became Cleveland's first permanent black settlers in 1806.[4] We also know that Peake and his family were followed by a very small number of other black families.

Beginning in the 1830s, the attitudes and activities of both whites and blacks toward race issues changed significantly, and Cleveland became more liberal on the question of civil rights. The immediate impetus for the change in white attitudes was the infusion of new settlers from northern New England. These new settlers, born and raised in a section of the country that spawned a rich variety of evangelical religions and reformist causes, brought with them a dynamic, activist, liberal inclination toward a broader and higher definition of the quality of life. Many of them supported the abolitionist movement and the underground railroad.[5]

If the 1830s marked the beginning of Cleveland's reformist tradition on the issue of race, it also marked the beginning of recorded black activity and expression on civil rights. As the country became increasingly divided over the issue of slavery in the years before the Civil War, leading black Clevelanders publicly supported the abolitionist movement, and some actively helped escaped slaves reach Canada and, ultimately, freedom. As the city became a major terminus on the road to freedom, local black citizens formed vigilance committees to coordinate activities in support of fugitive slaves, including the provision of food, clothing, shelter, and assistance in securing passage across the Great Lakes.[6]

By their active support of runaway slaves, Cleveland blacks showed the strength of their opposition to the institution of slavery. In terms equally clear, they demonstrated their rejection of any future that included a separate status for blacks. Local blacks wanted nothing to do with a movement whose goal was the removal of black citizens from the mainstream of American life.[7]

In every way, black Clevelanders of this period confirmed their commitment to the ultimate achievement of full citizenship rights. They labored to improve their skills, supported and contributed to community activities, participated eagerly where they could, and waited impatiently where they could not. They encouraged their children to hope for a better future than theirs and worked hard to help them achieve it. When the outbreak of the Civil War threatened the dissolution of the Union, they were among the first to volunteer for active combat. And when they were initially rejected on the grounds that the Ohio constitution forbade their enlistment, many served in an all-black regiment established in Massachusetts until in 1865 the state of Ohio authorized the recruitment of black troops.[8]

Beginning around the 1870s and gaining considerable momentum in the years just before and after the turn of the century, new strands of thought increasingly influenced the civil rights strategies of black leaders. The Civil War, which settled the issues of sectionalism and slavery, left the country weary of intense debate, especially regarding blacks. In a different but related development new schools of thought emerged, some in the highest academic circles, around the notion that blacks were biologically inferior to whites and hence lacked the natural aptitude required to exercise full citizenship rights.[9]

In roughly the same period but especially during World War I, a related demographic trend had an important impact on race relations. Seeking to escape the increasingly hostile environment of the South and, especially during the war years, hoping for better jobs in northern war industry, black migrants streamed into the Forest City. In the fifty years following the Civil War, the Cleveland black population grew from just under one thousand to about eighty-five hundred, reflecting a very modest annual increase of about one hundred persons a year. But between 1910 and 1920 it grew to almost thirty-five thousand—nearly a 400 percent increase in ten years. Virtually overnight these migrants transformed the black presence in Cleveland from a relatively unobtrusive racial cluster to a full-blown ghetto.[10]

This influx of southern blacks substantially increased the pressure on race relations at every point along the margins of interracial contact, generating friction and discrimination in contexts ranging from employment to education to recreation. Although still more liberal than many midwestern cities, Cleveland now joined other northern urban centers in redefining and circumscribing the status of black citizens.

Although the Ohio legislature had passed a civil rights law in 1883, by the beginning of World War I almost every public and semipublic facility it covered—including restaurants, theaters, amusement parks, and swimming pools—had manifested some form of antiblack prejudice. In this period, discrimination became more evident in hotels, playgrounds, drugstores, hospitals, public schools, and train cars.

At the same time that the growth in the black population led to increased friction in race relations, it gave rise to increased race consciousness and community development. Almost all of Cleveland's blacks lived on the city's East Side, in the Central Avenue section bordered on the north by Euclid Avenue, on the east by East 55th Street, on the south by the New York Central Railroad tracks, and on the west by the downtown business district. As the black community grew in size and complexity, it developed a distinct identity, including its own tradesmen and professionals, newspapers and journals, churches and lodges, banks and insurance companies, drugstores and groceries. By the early twentieth century black Clevelanders lived in an area that resembled a city within a city.[11]

Members of the new entrepreneurial group of black businessmen moved up the economic, political, and social ladder within the black community and came to occupy key leadership positions in civic and political organizations.[12]

Against this backdrop of changing circumstances and uncertain times, black leaders all over the country were divided in their thinking. In the mid-1890s Booker T. Washington, then headmaster of Tuskegee Institute, emerged as the spokesman for those who favored a strategy of accommodation. While affirming a commitment to the ultimate achievement of full citizenship rights, Washington advocated a public posture that deemphasized civil and political protest in favor of self-help, thrift, hard work, and racial solidarity. In the same period, W. E. B. Du Bois, a noted black sociologist and author, espoused a more integrationist position. Du Bois felt closer to the racial leadership of the early nineteenth century, to such men as Frederick Douglass who worked actively to overcome the limitations faced by blacks. Like them, he believed that blacks should exercise full civil and political rights and that they should reject the establishment or use of separate facilities or services.[13]

Cleveland's new black leaders naturally reflected the national pattern of black thought. Among those leaders committed to an integrationist approach, John P. Green exemplified the position often espoused by upper-status moderates. As an active Republican, Green had a long and distinguished career. In the 1870s he was repeatedly elected justice of the peace, in the 1880s he was twice elected to the lower house of the state legislature, and in 1891 he became the first northern black elected to a state senate. Throughout his career Green maintained extensive social and political contacts within the white community—including the influential politician Marcus A. Hanna. Most of Green's electoral victories were based predominantly on white votes.[14]

Because of his heavy dependence on the white electorate and easy access to white leadership circles, Green developed a very cautious approach to the public discussion of race issues. While recognizing the virtues of hard work, self-help, and discipline, Green rejected the implicit assumption underlying the Washington philosophy—that the only immediate opportunities available to blacks were in the black community itself. His whole life testified to a strong belief that a successful and aggressive career could be won in the white community.[15]

If John P. Green represented the moderate wing of the integrationist group, Harry C. Smith represented its more militant wing. Smith was born in West Virginia in 1863 and came to Cleveland as a young child. An active Republican like Green, Smith was appointed deputy inspector of oils in 1885, and he was elected three times to the Ohio General Assembly for terms in 1894–96, 1896–98, and 1900–1902.[16]

A biting critic of what he referred to as Washington's "fool" accommodationist racial philosophy, Smith stridently condemned the "Uncle Tom" tactics of "white folks Negroes" who favored the establishment of separate organizations and espoused a compromising approach to the white community. From the beginning of his career in the 1880s through to his death in 1941, the militant editor of the stridently integrationist newspaper *Gazette* argued for the right to complete and immediate participation in every aspect of American life.[17]

Green and Smith, as well as others who shared their integrationist outlook, tended to share organizational affiliations such as the Cleveland branch of the National Association for the Advancement of Colored People (NAACP). This branch, founded in 1914, evidenced a muted version of the legalistic protest strategy set forth by the national office. Reflecting its roots in the relatively more comfortable racial atmosphere of earlier years as well as a tendency to underestimate the increasing erosion of the city's liberal heritage, the Cleveland NAACP pursued a cautious and unobtrusive program of local community activity.[18]

But the integrationism that Smith so ardently supported increasingly lost ground to the new strain of accommodationism. This new emphasis was evident in the thinking of J. Walter Wills, a prominent businessman and civic leader of the period. Following college he came to Cleveland to learn the insurance business, holding a number of positions until 1904, when he became co-director of the Central Avenue Funeral Home. Several years later Wills established his own funeral home, and he soon dominated the business in Cleveland.[19]

Wills also participated in community affairs, developing a reputation as a leading advocate of the economic self-help theory. In 1905 he founded the Cleveland affiliate of Booker T. Washington's National Negro Business League. The primary function of the league was to mobilize community support for black business. Wills also actively supported the local NAACP and sometimes lent his support to lawsuits against discrimination in public and semipublic accommodations.[20]

As much a businessman as Wills and even more of an ideologue—in fact, *the* Cleveland ideologue—on the self-help issue was Nahum D. Brascher. Born in rural Indiana and educated in southern Ohio, Brascher came to Cleveland in the 1890s in search of a career. He worked at selling real estate and advertising before joining Thomas W. Fleming and Welcome T. Blue in establishing the *Cleveland Journal*, an all-black newspaper, in 1903. With Brascher as its managing editor, the paper was published on a weekly basis until 1912.[21] Brascher and the *Journal* were the accommodationist counterpart to Smith and the *Gazette*. Through the pages of the *Journal* Brascher became the most articulate spokesman for the conservative ethic.[22]

Brascher, Wills, and others who supported Washington's self-help philosophy gave their support to a variety of community organizations with a wide range of purposes. Prominent among these were the Phillis Wheatley Association, a social welfare institution similar in function to a Young Women's Christian Association, and the National Negro Business League. But most, if not all, felt especially close to the work of the Cleveland Urban League, the local affiliate of the National Urban League. Founded in 1917 under the leadership of William R. Connors, a bright young black social worker with a doctorate from the University of Pennsylvania, the league evidenced a strong commitment to Washington's emphasis on racial elevation by means of self-improvement and a tactful approach to the white community.[23]

By the early 1930s a rising tide of discrimination against blacks as well as the economic collapse engendered by the onset of the Depression contributed to a worsening of the racial climate. As Cleveland entered the first years of the Depression, its black labor force suffered severe dislocation. Within the black community, which by now included over seventy thousand persons, unemployment among wage earners averaged 50 percent and in some neighborhoods was as high as 90 percent.

This worsening racial climate combined with the severe economic collapse to place new pressure on Cleveland's black leadership. Although the basic ideological division among black leaders continued to be between those who emphasized accommodation, self-help, and gradualism on the one hand, and those who stressed protest, activism, and institutional change on the other, during these years new leadership groups and positions began to appear across the full spectrum of black thought, especially within its more activist segments. Both wings of the established leadership were challenged by the new clusters, one associated with the Communist party, another advocating an alliance with the labor movement, and another espousing the use of economic boycotts and pickets.[24]

The Communist party was especially active among blacks in this period, although its blatant effort to exploit the hopelessness and despair among unemployed workers for political reasons, as well as its ideological extremism and commitment to the ultimate destruction of American capitalism "root and branch," severely limited its appeal to blacks.[25]

Another of the new groups to emerge in this period called for greater attention to the economic problems of the black masses and advocated an alliance with the labor movement, especially the industrial union movement that was just beginning to gather steam under the leadership of the Congress of Industrial Organizations (CIO). They felt that the economic problems faced by black workers could be solved only if mass pressure was brought to bear on the white power structure and that the best avenue for the expression of that pressure was the labor movement.[26]

In 1935 those who held this view became active in establishing a Cleveland affiliate of the National Negro Congress (NNC), an organization then being established nationally to revitalize and redirect the overall thrust of the black community's advancement effort. Although the congress supported legal action and public demonstrations on many community issues, its primary mission was to mobilize support for the unionization of black workers. Charles W. White, Cleveland's most influential black exponent of this view, remarked that it would be "the tragedy of the twentieth century . . . for the American Negro to permit a proletarian movement to develop without his being an integral part of it."[27] The NNC never really got off the ground in Cleveland, however, largely because the Communist party tried to push it in a more radical direction, but also because the success of the CIO in organizing black workers in the middle and late 1930s seemed to obviate the need for its existence.[28]

The final new leadership cluster that arose in these years espoused the use of economic pressure tactics to obtain jobs for blacks. Apparently influenced by a similar movement launched in Chicago in 1929, a campaign involving boycotts and picket lines was started by several Cleveland organizations to force employment of blacks in white-owned stores located in the ghetto. The most prominent of these local groups was the Future Outlook League (FOL). In the mid-1930s the FOL employed pickets and boycotts against dozens of white-owned businesses, ranging from small groceries and pharmacies to large food and theater chains, eventually securing hundreds of clerical and sales positions for young blacks.[29]

As the league became more successful, it expanded its activities to include a wider range of targets and in the process substantially broadened its spectrum of mass pressure techniques. The organization ventured outside the ghetto for the first time in 1941, when it simultaneously conducted a picket line and a telephone campaign in an effort to get the Ohio Bell Telephone Company to hire blacks at its downtown office.[30]

By the late 1930s and early 1940s it was clear that the FOL, the NNC, and despite its almost total rejection by blacks, even the Communist party had achieved a considerable impact on Cleveland's established black leadership. Race leaders associated with both ends of the traditional ideological spectrum—from the gradualist Urban League to the activist NAACP—were beginning to take into account the newer strands of thought. Both showed greater concern for the economic problems of black workers and understood the increasing importance of the labor movement.[31]

These two emerging characteristics—greater assertiveness and sharper focus on economic matters—were a direct outgrowth of the black experience in the dark years of the Depression. The economic collapse created a sense of urgency, fear, and impatience. Among the burgeoning number of black citizens who were unemployed or otherwise adversely affected by the hard times, there was a rising feeling of desperation, a sense that something had to be done. These tensions were exacerbated by the failure of the existing leadership groups to adapt their strategies to the times.

Underlying the evolution of black thought in this period, and in part responsible for it, was a series of interwoven generational, career, and class imperatives. In general, at the outset of the Depression, the age, career status, and class position of black leaders followed an ascending path from the newer groups like the FOL and NNC through to the Urban League and NAACP. The key leaders of the NAACP were older individuals such as John P. Green and Harry C. Smith, who were at or beyond the middle of their careers and who had achieved recognition in the early years of the twentieth century.

The composition of the newer groups, like the FOL and the NNC, was quite different. Though both tended to attract younger people who were just beginning their careers, the similarity between the two groups ended there. The FOL was made up of lower-middle-class individuals, the sons and daughters of the working poor. Most had a high school education, some had attended college for a few years, and a small number had college degrees. They aspired to entrepreneurial or middle management positions, as well as to solid middle-class respectability. The NNC, by contrast, was composed of middle- and upper-middle-class people, the progeny of those who were aggressive aspirants to upper-class status.

As the NAACP and Urban League selectively took into account some of the emerging strands of thought, groups like the FOL and the NNC began to decline in importance. This is not to say that the established leaders officially endorsed the new thinking. The street tactics of the FOL and the ideological radicalism of the NNC were far beyond the social and intellectual limits of the upper-status individuals who constituted the inner leadership core of the NAACP and Urban League.

Ultimately, however, the extremism of newer groups like the FOL and the NNC was deflated by the return of economic prosperity. When the country entered World War II, American industry was strained to capacity to meet the needs of defense production. Although the first jobs in war industry went to whites, and though blacks had to wait on the sidelines until local labor shortages made their employment inevitable, by the early and mid-1940s black workers were streaming into Cleveland's steel and ironworks, many moving into skilled positions, most of which had never before been open to them. When the entire community—white and black—returned to full employment, many holding better positions at higher wages than ever before, the radical ideologies of the discouraging 1930s lost their relevance.[32]

Also, the war was fought on the basis of an antifascist, prodemocratic ideology. In Cleveland this was symbolized by a renewed commitment on the part of the municipal government to consider the needs of its black constituents. In 1943, the Cleveland Welfare Federation announced the beginning of a two-year study of the black community. The Central Area Social Study, as it came to be called, was designed to provide a full look at racial and economic conditions in the city's black community.[33] Although the study never fulfilled its action-oriented promise to identify the "real potentially organizable forces" that might be used as a "channel for implementing programs of community welfare," it did provide the informational base for a new concept of the predominantly black area.[34]

In the same year that the Central Area Social Study began, the city's mayor, Frank Lausche, established the Committee on Democratic Practice composed of the city's leading black and white civil activists. The committee was assigned the task of developing a broad educational program against racial intolerance and of working toward the eradication of specific problems such as discrimination in employment, housing, and public accommodations.

Many issues contributed to the broadening of a black protest movement during the Depression and World War II. The judicious receptiveness of the established black leaders to newly emerging protest groups with different ideas, the return of economic prosperity with the beginning of war production, the essential commitment to the American way of life which the wartime emergency elicited among blacks, the democratic and antiracist ideology of the war against fascism, the Central Area Social Study with its effort to view the black population as a distinct community, and the Committee on Democratic Practice with its attempt to focus public attention on race issues all contributed to a new atmosphere in which a debilitating sense of pessimism was replaced by optimism and despair gave way to hope.[35]

But in later years, especially in the 1950s and 1960s, and despite a continuing reputation as one of the country's most liberal urban environments for black Americans, the future of race relations in Cleveland became increasingly unclear. On the one hand, the city's black citizens made steady, though incremental, progress in municipal civil rights and local politics. On the other hand, they faced deteriorating conditions in housing and public schools. Both of these trends, though reflecting divergent outcomes, were closely related to a single impelling force—a large increase in the city's black population caused by the continued immigration of southern blacks.

Following the large increase in Cleveland's black population during World War I, the city's black community continued to grow in size each decade, although at a reduced rate. Whereas the black population increased 400 percent to 35,000 between 1910 and 1920, it increased by a much smaller 100 percent to 72,000 by 1930 and by only 18 percent to 85,000 by 1940. But again, as had been the case during World War I, during World War II the black migration to Cleveland accelerated dramatically as poor, rural southern blacks streamed into the Forest City hoping for jobs in the burgeoning war production effort. Between 1940 and 1950 Cleveland's black population almost doubled to 148,000; in the 1950s, as the city's industrial production continued at high levels and southern blacks continued to come north in search of jobs, the black population again almost doubled to 251,000. The white population shrank, leaving a black presence in the city that was becoming more and more sharply defined.[36]

One effect of this growth in the black community was an increased role for blacks in local politics, for as the black population increased so did black voting strength and political representation. Also related to the growth of the city's black population was the enactment of new municipal civil rights legislation. In these years the increasing importance of the black electorate, together with the continuing influence of the city's liberal heritage, gave rise to broadened legal recognition for black civil rights. In 1945 a new city ordinance transformed the city's Committee on Democratic Practice into the Cleveland Community Relations Board. In 1950 the council enacted the first Fair Employment Practices Law in the country. The law gave the Community Relations Board the responsibility to receive complaints, conduct investigations, and make recommendations relative to discrimination in employment.[37]

But if the World War II influx of blacks had the positive effect of increasing black political strength and broadening black civil rights, it also had the negative effect of heightening tension in many areas of race relations. This was especially the case in regard to the adequacy of housing. In the 1950s, slum conditions were intensified by the urban renewal program, which, though intended to rebuild some of the worst areas, actually accelerated the spread of urban blight as whole neighborhoods were demolished in preparation for the construction of new units and facilities, many of which were never completed.[38]

The most notorious of these areas was the Hough neighborhood in the northeastern section of the city's East Side black community. As recent migrants streamed into the neighborhood, housing conditions that were already strained to their limits went from bad to worse. Building code and sanitary violations became an accepted standard.

While the incoming migrant families put increased pressure on the ghetto housing market, their children strained the capacity of public schools. One problem was that many migrant children had begun their education in segregated, rural southern schools, which did not adequately prepare them for the Cleveland system, and were in need of special remedial education courses. Another problem was the sheer number of new students. The school program serving the black community was taxed far beyond its limit by the incoming migrant families.[39]

In 1964 the issue came to a head in an escalating spiral of protest by blacks and counterprotest by whites. Angered by continuing discrimination and segregation in the city schools, blacks picketed the Board of Education; in response, whites staged a countermarch into black neighborhoods, overturning cars, breaking store windows, and beating black citizens; blacks then staged spontaneous sit-ins in school headquarters and buildings.[40] As blacks became more and more frustrated with their inability to influence important areas of community life, such as housing and public education in spite of their growing political importance within the city, black protest thought again moved in a more aggressive direction.

The Congress of Racial Equality sought to unite all black action groups in support of community self-determination. The Southern Christian Leadership Conference, founded by Dr. Martin Luther King, Jr., worked with churches in support of black youth, as well as on consumer and family-related issues. At the extreme end of the ideological continuum and representing the most militant elements of the black community were organizations that shared an orientation toward black separatism or black nationalism such as the Black Panthers, United Black Alliance, United Black Student Alliance, Republic of New Africa, and Afro Set. By the early 1960s the divergent forces set in motion by the rapid increase in the size of the black community—one tending toward increasing black political power and the other toward growing black frustration over ghetto conditions—came to a head at virtually the same historical moment when the city almost simultaneously elected the first black mayor of a major urban center and experienced a major race riot.[41] In 1966, following a barroom argument between a white bartender and a black customer, the Hough section of Cleveland erupted in four days and nights of interracial violence. Two years later violence erupted in the Glenville area when a gun battle took place between black nationalists and local police in what became known as the Glenville shootout.[42]

In between those two events, in 1967, Carl B. Stokes was elected as the first black mayor in Cleveland. Two years later he was again successful, defeating Robert J. Kelly in the Democratic primary and Republican Ralph J. Perk in the general election.[43]

More than any other, these two events—the eruption of the Hough riot and the election of Carl B. Stokes—symbolized the emergence of a new element in Cleveland's race relations: uncertainty. True, the election of the first black mayor of a large city was an event of tremendous significance. But so, too, was the Hough riot, for it showed that, at least in some respects, race relations in Cleveland were not much different from race relations in other cities. By the middle 1960s it was apparent that Cleveland's liberalism, at least that part of it related to black issues, stood at a crossroad.

Postscript to Black Civil Rights by Wye

NORMAN KRUMHOLZ

Carl B. Stokes, who served as mayor of Cleveland for two terms (1967–71), declined to run for reelection in 1971. Instead, he attempted to orchestrate the election of a chief aide, Arnold Pinkney, to succeed him so that a black would remain in the mayor's office. This attempt failed, and Republican Ralph J. Perk won the mayor's office in 1971. White ethnic mayors then controlled Cleveland City Hall until the election of Michael R. White in 1989. During this period of white ethnic control of the mayor's office, however, the City Council, under the leadership of its president, George L. Forbes, continued to exert great political strength. Forbes used the growing clout of Cleveland's black voters and the issues of racial parity and fairness to win minority contracts and to deflect criticism.

Black employment rose sharply in public agencies, including the city, county, and federal governments and such quasi-governmental agencies as the Regional Transit Authority, Cuyahoga Metropolitan Housing Authority, and Cleveland Public Schools. Black leaders were using their political power to provide the rewards of government to their constituency, much as had other ethnic groups that had come before them. But with Cleveland in decline rather than growing, fiscal crises became the order of the day, and public patronage was more limited than previously.

White reactions to black claims were also a concern. The Cleveland Firefighters Union, for example, successfully sued against affirmative action provisions in 1990. The city of Parma was sued by the NAACP alleging a deliberate violation of affirmative action rules. A black vice-president for affirmative action, whose contract was withdrawn by Cleveland State University, alleged that the reason for the rupture was the university's insincerity in seeking more black personnel. The controversy resulted in a six-month strike by black students. Still, progress was being made.

While black Clevelanders struggled more or less successfully for their fair share of jobs in the public sector, positions of wealth and power continued to elude them in the private sector. There were few black faces among the chief executive officers of Cleveland's banks, large corporations, or major law firms, and black-owned businesses of significant size were also in short supply. The number of black members of the city's exclusive Union Club could still be counted on one hand.

A key event in 1976 was the finding by the U.S. District Court that the Cleveland Public Schools had deliberately violated the Fourteenth Amendment to the

Constitution and had maintained racial segregation in the schools. Citywide busing of school children was ordered as part of the remedy, setting off a bitter public debate that still raged in 1994. The case Reed v. Rhodes remains alive, and its influence on the schools and the city continues to be strong.

During the 1970s and 1980s, both black and white families economically able to make the move left Cleveland for the suburbs. In 1990, Cleveland's population stood at about five hundred thousand, split about equally among blacks and whites. Although many low-income blacks migrated into adjacent suburbs like East Cleveland, which had many of the same problems as Cleveland, fair housing laws now made it possible for middle- and upper-income blacks to enjoy a wider choice of residence in metropolitan Cleveland, particularly in some of the eastern suburbs. Shaker Heights, Cleveland Heights, Warrensville Heights, and a few other suburbs absorbed a large number of black residents and continued to maintain both a desirable environment and an integrated population.

While many black families were becoming solid members of the suburban middle class, fundamental problems remained. The loss of Cleveland's manufacturing base resulted in much structural unemployment as businesses moved to outlying suburbs or to the Sun Belt. The loss of manufacturing jobs hurt both races, but blacks were injured disproportionately. In 1990, Cleveland led all large American cities with a black unemployment rate of 20 percent. Bitter racial segregation in housing continued and 1994 poverty rates in the city reached 42.2 percent—the highest in the city's history. By virtually any measure, Cleveland's black neighborhoods were worse off than they were twenty years ago.

As Cleveland reached the millennium, the future was cloudy for its black citizens, and it was unclear whether local political power could be used to benefit the poor even they made up a majority.

Notes

1. Kenneth Kusmer's work develops this thesis for the years 1870–1930. Kenneth Kusmer, *A Ghetto Takes Shape: Black Cleveland, 1870–1930* (Urbana: University of Illinois Press, 1976). This essay supports Kusmer's argument and extends it through the Depression and war years.

2. Kusmer, *Ghetto,* 10. There are no statistics available to indicate the number of blacks in Cleveland through the first half of the nineteenth century. In 1850, the first year for which data are available, there were 200 blacks in a total city population of 17,034. By 1870 there were 1,293 blacks in a total city population of 92,829.

3. A. G. Riddle, "Rise of Anti-Slavery Sentiment on the Western Reserve," *Magazine of Western History* 6 (1887): 54; *Herald,* November 14, 1820.

4. Russell H. Davis, *Memorial Negroes in Cleveland's Past* (Cleveland: Western Reserve Historical Society, 1969), 6–8.

5. Riddle, "Anti-Slavery Sentiment," 145–46; Karl Geiser, "The Western Reserve in the Anti-Slavery Movement, 1840–1860," Mississippi Valley Historical Society, *Proceedings* 5 (1811–1912): 73–98; *Herald,* November 14, 1820, and October 5, 1839; and *HG,* September 23, 1838.

6. Davis, *Memorable Negroes,* 11; and Benjamin Quarles, *Black Abolitionists* (New York: Oxford University Press, 1969), 153.

7. *Herald,* April 9, 1846. The brief quotation is reported in Kusmer, *Ghetto,* 28.

8. Benjamin Quarles, *The Negro in the Civil War* (Boston: Little, Brown & Company, 1953).

9. John Hope Franklin, *From Slavery to Freedom* (New York: Knopf, 1967), 439–41.

10. *U.S. Census Reports, 1890–1930.* For a discussion of the factors related to the World War I migrations see Kusmer, *Ghetto,* 157–60.

11. Christopher G. Wye, "Midwest Ghetto: Patterns of Change and Continuity in the Black Social Structure, 1930–1945" (Ph.D. diss., Kent State University, 1974), 2; Kusmer, *Ghetto.*

12. Kusmer, *Ghetto,* 113–54.

13. Wye, "Midwest Ghetto," 9–14.

14. Kusmer, *Ghetto,* 114; John P. Green, *Fact Stranger than Fiction: Seventy-Five Years of a Busy Life with Reminiscences of Many Great and Good Men and Women* (Cleveland: Riehl Printing Company, 1920).

15. Green, *Fact Stranger than Fiction.* The quotation is from the *Leader,* October 30, 1902.

16. William J. Simmons, *Men of Mark: Eminent, Progressive, and Rising* (Cleveland, 1887), 194–97.

17. *Cleveland Gazette,* November 15, 22, March 7, 9, 1931; Davis, *Memorable Negroes,* 32–43.

18. Kusmer, *Ghetto,* 260; Charles W. White to Walter White, February 25, 1927, "Cleveland Branch NAACP, Annual Report," November 21, 1929, and David H. Pierce to Herbert T. Seligman, October 23, 1930, in NAACP Branch Files, Western Reserve Historical Society; Dudley S. Blossom to Charles W. White, October 24, 1928, in George A. Myers MSS, Ohio Historical Society; *Cleveland Gazette,* July 6, December 23, 1929, and May 10, 1930; and interview with author, August 4, 1972.

19. Davis, *Memorial Negroes,* 45.

20. *Cleveland Journal,* March 25, 1904; *Cleveland Gazette,* April 22, 1905, November 27, 1909.

21. *Cleveland Journal,* April 8, 1905; *Cleveland Gazette,* January 1, 1910.

22. *Cleveland Journal,* April 11, 1903, April 16, 23, 1910.

23. *Cleveland Gazette,* March 10 and November 17, 1917, May 25, 1918; interview, January 18, 1972; Board of Trustees Meeting minutes, March 8, 1928, and March 27, 1930, Cleveland Urban League MSS, Western Reserve Historical Society.

24. Wye, "Midwest Ghetto," chaps. 1, 9.

25. *Cleveland Gazette,* December 19, 1931, February 21, 1941; *Cleveland Eagle,* April 17, 1936.

26. Interviews, October 2, 1969, February 19, 1972.

27. *Cleveland Gazette,* January 24, 1931; David H. Pierce to Walter White, April 1, 1933, and David H. Pierce to Herbert T. Seligman, October 25, 1930, NAACP Branch Files, Library of Congress.

28. *Cleveland Call and Post,* May 15, 1935, February 27 and May 28, 1936; *Cleveland Gazette,* April 25, 1936; *Cleveland Eagle,* April 24, October 17, and November 6, 1936; *Cleveland Union Leader,* September 30, 1937.

29. Charles H. Loeb, *The Future is Yours: The History of the Future Outlook League, 1935–1946* (Cleveland: The Future Outlook League, Inc., 1947), 15–18, interviews, October 19, 1969, May 16, 26, 1972; *Cleveland Call and Post,* May 5, 1938; John O. Holly to William O. Walker, September 12, 1935, Future Outlook League MSS, Western Reserve Historical Society.

30. *Cleveland Gazette,* June 22, 1935; *Cleveland Call and Post,* May 11, August 8, September 19, 1935, June 4, August 15, 1936; John O. Holly to Joseph Solomon, September 19, 1935, Future Outlook League MSS.

31. For Urban League see Board of Trustees Meeting minutes, June 17, 1938, and April 16, 1941, Cleveland Urban League MSS. For the NAACP see *Cleveland Call and Post,* March 24, 1938, May 17, 24, June 14, 1941.

32. This interpretation of the generational, class, and career imperatives underlying black leadership patterns is developed in Wye, "Midwest Ghetto," chap. 9.

33. Cleveland Welfare Federation, *Central Area Study,* 1943, p. 125, on file at Cleveland Public Library.

34. Ibid.

35. *Cleveland Press,* September 23, 1943; *Cleveland Plain Dealer,* September 23, 1942.

36. Wye, "Midwest Ghetto," 81, 82, 91.

37. Russell H. Davis, *Black Americans in Cleveland, From George Peake to Carl B. Stokes, 1796–1969* (Cleveland: Associated Publishers, 1972), 271–304.

38. Wye, "Midwest Ghetto," 1–30, 66–110.

39. Interview, January 1972; Davis, *Black Americans*, 377–85.

40. Davis, *Black Americans*, 353, 376, 377–85.

41. Interview, February 19, 1972; Davis, *Black Americans*, 351.

42. "Escape Burning," *Saturday Evening Post*, July 29, 1967, 38–42; "You Can't Stop the Riot from Coming," *Look*, May 30, 1967, p. 96.

43. Davis, *Black Americans*, 407–13; "Stokes Elected," *Newsweek*, November 17, 1969, p. 36.

Part 5

GOVERNANCE

Public and Private

Introduction

THE INTIMATE relationship between public authority and the private sector is the theme of this section. Historically, city, state, and federal politics have involved an interplay between government and the institutions controlling private investment. National and local governments in the twentieth century have vastly increased their responsibilities. These responsibilities expanded during three periods of crisis which were perceived to be linked with the possibility of social disorder.

The first great expansion of government power took place during the Progressive Era from about 1900 to 1920. In Cleveland, this time was linked forever with Mayor Tom L. Johnson (1901–9). The second increase in power took place during the Great Depression of the 1930s, when President Franklin D. Roosevelt expanded government as a vehicle for hope. The most recent expansion was during the administrations of Presidents John F. Kennedy and Lyndon B. Johnson in the turbulent decade of the 1960s, which saw racial rioting in many of America's cities.

The substantial growth of the public sector during these times did not eclipse the power and authority of private institutions to make critical political decisions involving jobs, land use, and investment. The American private enterprise system exerts great influence over decisions affecting public policy. As a result, key decisions on what will be produced, where it will be produced, where corporate headquarters will be located, what production technologies will be used, how manpower will be allocated—all momentous decisions with great public impact—are decided by businessmen, not public officials. Although such decisions have enormous consequences for all American society, corporate executives make them using great personal discretion.

Despite the expansion of government responsibilities, then, the private sector retains control over critical resources and decisions. The frequent tension between public and private is outlined in the three essays that follow.

W. Dennis Keating, Norman Krumholz, and David C. Perry describe the almost century-long struggle between the city's Municipal Light plant, initiated in Tom Johnson's Progressive administration shortly after the turn of the century, and the investor-owned Cleveland Electric Illuminating Company. The battle over public versus private electric power illustrates the conflicting interests of the two sectors. Through the years, CEI has attempted in various ways to extinguish Muny's lights and restore its earlier monopoly. Most recently, Muny's survival depended on the refusal by Mayor Dennis Kucinich to sell the plant to CEI, an act that helped plunge Cleveland into fiscal default in 1978. This essay offers a rationale for the maintenance of public power plants as a means of improving citizen participation in setting rates as well as a means of lowering the cost of electricity.

Fortune magazine and its viewpoint contrasts with Keating et al. Its view is clear from the title: "How Business Bosses Saved a Sick City." Its author, Myron Magnet, argues that Cleveland was on the bottom, overwhelmed by all the recent ills of industrial America. Its river had burst into flames and its ghettos had erupted in violence in the 1960s, municipal services were "a shambles," and it had gone into default in 1978 under its populist "boy mayor," Dennis Kucinich. In Magnet's view, fifty of the city's leading and most senior businessmen responded to this crisis by taking charge of the "grittiest aspects of civic life." Together, they formed the Cleveland Tomorrow organization, financed a candidate for mayor who defeated Kucinich and cooperated with business, restructured the city's finances, and promoted heavily subsidized downtown development projects. This self-described "conspiracy" has succeeded in turning the city around, according to Magnet.

Roldo Bartimole, a Cleveland legend, presents an opposite view. For twenty-five years, Bartimole has been the editor and publisher of *Point of View*, an independent newsletter presenting a sharp and incisive critique of Cleveland politics. His essay is an analysis of who actually governs in Cleveland. Bartimole argues that from the administration of Ralph Locher in the 1960s through that of Michael R. White in 1991, the not-so-invisible hand of corporate Cleveland has been in control regardless of which mayor was in power. One question he raises is profoundly disturbing for our democracy: can lower-income and minority citizens make their local government do their bidding, even when they constitute well over half of the population? Or is local control by elites so well entrenched as to make citizens' wishes largely irrelevant and ineffective?

The Ninety-Year War Over Public Power in Cleveland

W. Dennis Keating, Norman Krumholz, & David C. Perry

Progressive Politics to Consumer Advocacy

PUBLIC CONTROL and ownership of utilities has been a recurring issue of urban politics. It is one of the tenets of Progressive reform and presently is manifested most clearly in the concerns of consumer and environmental advocates over such issues as rate increases and safety hazards resulting from the use of nuclear power.

At the turn of the twentieth century, a hallmark of Progressive political faith was the municipalization of utilities as a defense against the abuses of private trusts that had attempted to monopolize entire industries. It also reflected a belief that basic necessities should be subject to democratic control to ensure fair pricing and equitable distribution of services.

The debate over public versus private power today contains many of the past concerns over democratic control, pricing, and equity. In cities all over the country, rising prices have been a common concern among consumers.[1] Environmental activists have joined consumers, citing environmental hazards, as well as runaway costs associated with nuclear power. These issues are at the center of contemporary issues over the control and delivery of utility services in the post-Reagan era of privatization and deregulation.

For the entire twentieth century, a political struggle over the control of electric power has been waged in one form or another. Nowhere has the battle for public power been fought harder than in Cleveland, Ohio, where John D. Rockefeller organized the first and greatest private monopoly trust—Standard Oil. During four terms as mayor of Cleveland (1901–9), Progressive Tom L. Johnson championed the public ownership of utilities. He led the fight that eventually resulted in the formation of the city of Cleveland's Municipal Light Company (Muny Light). Muny Light was formed after Johnson's defeat and death, despite determined opposition from the Cleveland Electric Illuminating Company (CEI).

Originally published in the *Journal of Urban Affairs*, Vol. 13, no. 4, 1991. Reprinted with permission.

The formation of Muny Light began a protracted conflict over the next nine decades over public versus private electric power. This political conflict in Cleveland continues despite changes in the electrical energy industry and shifts in the region's economy and politics. This article reviews this ninety-year struggle in Cleveland.

The Contemporary Debate over Public versus Private Power

Today, environmental and consumer activists in cities as diverse as Kansas City and New Orleans have expressed concern over pricing, cost overruns, and environmental hazards associated with the investment of private, investor-owned utilities (IOUs) in nuclear power.[2] They have also fought for energy conservation to reduce consumption and costs to consumers. In response, the IOUs, which are subject to state regulation, have countered that public ownership would be too expensive a capital investment, would duplicate existing private facilities, and could not operate efficiently.

The debate of the 1980s and 1990s echoes the one that took place in the early twentieth century. The difference is that this debate is now occurring within the context of privatization of many municipal services and federal deregulation of private producers by the Reagan and Bush administrations. The extent to which electric utilities should be deregulated is a major issue.[3]

The Reagan administration's deemphasis on antitrust policy meant that IOUs had less to fear in competition with public power. For example, in March 1991, the U.S. Supreme Court refused to review a decision by the First U.S. Circuit Court of Appeals which reversed a trial court decision finding Boston Edison guilty of antitrust violations (*Concord* v. *Boston Edison*).

In the United States, 87 percent of electricity users obtain their power from IOUs. Only 13 percent obtain their electric power from public power systems, municipal, state, and federal.[4] Of approximately fifteen hundred cities and towns with municipal power systems, more than nine hundred buy all or part of their power from competing private companies.

In Los Angeles and Seattle, which have long had municipal power systems, there has been no sustained political conflict with private competitors. For example, in Seattle, voters approved creation of municipal power in 1902, and Seattle City Light began to operate a plant in 1905 (before Cleveland's Muny Light). Like Muny Light and CEI in Cleveland, there was initially fierce competition between Seattle City Light and the Puget Sound Power and Light Company, but eventually price competition ended and an accommodation was reached. Finally, in 1951, the city purchased its private competitor.[5]

The private power companies are subject to regulation by federal, state, and municipal utility commissions, primarily at the state level. Consumer groups have long criticized state public utility regulatory commissions as being too favorable to the interests of IOUs in regulating rates and guiding energy policies. They have fought for lower rates, especially for low-income electricity users.[6]

The electrical power industry is in a state of flux. Energy sources are changing. In the wake of opposition to nuclear power in the United States, "rate shock" caused by rate increases triggered by nuclear power construction costs and the bankruptcies of utilities in New Hampshire, New York, and Washington because of cost overruns in nuclear plant construction, electric utilities are rethinking their options. Cogeneration of electric power is becoming more important because it allows for the relatively inexpensive transmission of excess power from existing resources through regional energy grids.[7]

The debate over public versus private power has long focused on comparative prices. Public power advocates argue that public power is cheaper because of efficient management and its nonprofit status. The latest available data from the American Public Power Association (APPA), based on data compiled by the U.S. Department of Energy, show that the average residential electricity rates paid by the customers of public power in 1988 were 21 percent lower than those paid by IOU customers. The APPA data include comparative production, transmission, and distribution costs.[8]

The Edison Electric Institute, representing the IOUs, argues the opposite. It claims that private companies operate more efficiently and are at a price disadvantage compared to public power companies. They can charge artificially lower rates because they do not pay local property taxes or federal income taxes, they can raise capital through tax-exempt financing, and they may receive indirect public operating subsidies.

Comparative studies of public and private electric power have not proven to be conclusive. In reviewing such studies, E. S. Savas, a leading advocate of privatization, admits that they have not proven the superiority of private companies over municipal power agencies.[9]

It has been argued that utility consumers would benefit more from direct competition than from regulation of private producers. W. J. Primeaux argues that competition causes firms to operate at lower costs, sell electricity at lower prices, operate without engaging in price wars, and avoid excess capacity.[10]

Although we do not resolve these issues, our study of Cleveland is an instructive example of the politics involved in them. Cleveland is unique (even when compared to Seattle and Los Angeles) in its long-standing competitive conflict between public and private power. Cleveland is the only city in which the full history and contemporary experience of the public power debate may be studied.

Tom Johnson, the Progressive Era, and Cleveland's Municipal Light System

Cleveland experienced tremendous growth as a burgeoning industrial city in the late nineteenth century, reaching a population of 382,000 in 1900. The city was a vibrant center of industrial activity attracting a massive influx of European immigrant labor. Active annexation of adjoining communities contributed to the city's territorial expansion.

The introduction of electrical energy enhanced Cleveland's transformation. In 1890, Populist Louis Tuckerman proposed that the city build and operate its own light company. This proposal met with substantial opposition. In 1892, Charles Brush, noted inventor and pioneer in the use of electricity, and a group of investors formed the Cleveland Electric Lighting Company, a private utility renamed Cleveland Electric Illuminating two years later. CEI constructed a generating plant and, by 1900, was supplying most of the electrical needs of the city of Cleveland and its adjoining suburbs.

The idea of public power did not die. Instead, it gained a powerful champion in Tom Johnson, the streetcar magnate who, influenced by the socialist economist Henry George, mounted a Progressive reform campaign for mayor of Cleveland in 1900. One of Johnson's campaign proposals called for the municipalization of CEI and the Cleveland Vapor and Light Company. Johnson believed in the municipal ownership of all public service monopolies because "[it] will work betterment in service, reduce its cost to the people and purify politics by extinguishing a powerful interest hostile to good government."[11]

In 1901, Johnson was elected to the first of four terms as mayor, and he immediately tried to municipalize private utilities. He and his supporters argued that this would reduce inefficiency and corruption, while providing essential services to working-class residents at more affordable rates. Rather than take over CEI, as he had proposed in his first mayoral campaign, Johnson instead introduced an ordinance in May 1903 authorizing the approval of a $200,000 bond issue to finance the construction of a municipal power plant. The Cleveland Chamber of Commerce argued strongly against the bond issue, and CEI, according to Johnson, effectively lobbied the City Council so that only twenty of thirty-two members voted for the proposal, two short of the number needed to authorize issuance of the bonds.[12] The historic war over public power in Cleveland was joined.

Undeterred by the City Council vote, Johnson called for a special election in September 1903 on the bond issue. The Ohio attorney general, acting on behalf of CEI according to Johnson, successfully argued against holding such an election on the ground that the enabling legislation was unconstitutional. A determined Johnson persisted, and in 1904 Cleveland voters approved the creation of Muny Light. Johnson proceeded to annex the town of South Brooklyn in 1905, thereby acquiring its small electric light plant. Johnson had a source of municipal power, but the City Council continued to oppose its operation. Johnson countered by charging that his political opponents had accepted campaign contributions and bribes from CEI.

It was not until 1911, two years after Johnson's defeat for reelection, that Cleveland voters approved a $2 million bond issue to build a power plant. After another delay because of a legal challenge, construction began, and in 1914 the plant and several substations were opened. The new Muny Light system served only Cleveland's West Side neighborhoods.

The Expansion of Muny Light and Competition with CEI

In keeping with Johnson's pledge of cheap public utility rates, Muny Light charged three cents per kilowatt hour, in contrast to CEI's rate of ten cents. Johnson's successor and former city law director Newton D. Baker was dubbed "the three cent mayor" for having defeated a CEI proponent in 1911. Baker wanted Muny to serve as a "yardstick" against which consumers could measure the reasonableness of CEI's charges.[13] Under Baker and his successors, Muny Light's customer base grew rapidly, totaling 24,304 in 1919. In 1917, after passage of a bond issue, Muny Light expanded its generating plant.

CEI considered Muny Light's expansion an invasion of its territory. CEI appealed the validity of Muny Light's three-cent rate to Ohio's Public Utility Commission (PUCO), claiming that its rate of ten cents per kilowatt hour was the only reasonable rate. Progressive advocates of public power have always criticized appointed state public utility commissions for being dominated by commissioners overly sympathetic to the positions taken by the IOUs.[14] In 1919, PUCO found in favor of CEI and required Muny Light to increase its rate to five cents per kilowatt hour for five years, starting in 1920.

As a result of this compromise, Muny Light, while continuing to expand, was relegated to a yardstick role and lost much of its dynamic and progressive character. In 1920, the city commissioner of light and heat instructed the Muny Light plant superintendent to cease any further expansion of lines into CEI territory: "From this point on, when the private utility accepted the five cent rate, and the City Plant refused to build duplicate lines in order to serve customers of the Illuminating Company, there resulted an ever-decreasing interest by the public to the affairs of the plant. This fact was more the result of the refusal by the Plant to replace the services of the private utility than due to the decrease in rate differential. The public gradually assumed an attitude of indifference."[15] The Progressive Era had ended. Although in 1921 Cleveland adopted the city manager form of government favored by Progressives, the city managers during its brief period of operation (1924–31) were not supportive of Muny Light. Two former plant managers appointed by Cleveland's city managers were prominent supporters of CEI's successful campaign to defeat a bond issue to expand Muny Light in 1931.[16]

Following continued growth in the 1920s, Muny Light's customer base stabilized in the 1930s, influenced in part by the Great Depression's devastating impact on economic activity. By 1938, Muny Light had fifty-three thousand residential customers. This number would grow only slightly during the next two decades.

The Depression threatened Muny Light's very existence because the financially strapped city of Cleveland had used the utility's reserves for welfare relief and had not repaid this debt from its general fund. In 1936, alarmed by Muny Light's fiscal problems and its possible demise, a group of supporters, led by conservative lawyer Paul Walter, organized the Cleveland Municipal Light and Power Association (CMLPA) and set out to separate Muny Light from the direct control of the City Council. Their aim was to protect Muny Light's fiscal independence while expanding its generating and distribution capacity and reducing rates.

CMLPA was successful. The city began to repay its debt and, at CMLPA's urging, applied for a federal grant from the Works Progress Administration. This grant together with the issuance of mortgage revenue bonds was intended to improve Muny Light's operation. CEI strongly opposed both funding efforts, forcing a referendum on the bond issue. CEI waged what was termed the best organized, best financed campaign of opposition ever seen in Cleveland. It was aided by the *Call and Post,* the city's black newspaper, which criticized Muny Light for discriminatory hiring practices and praised CEI. Nevertheless, Muny Light won a resounding victory by a vote of eighty-nine thousand to thirty-five thousand.[17]

In the early 1940s, CMLPA, along with some sympathetic City Council members, attempted to carry out Tom Johnson's original strategy of buying out CEI. The conditions seemed right. In 1942, the city had finally realized Johnson's dream of public transit with the municipalization of the Cleveland Railway Company. The North American Holding Company, parent company of CEI, was under a Securities and Exchange Commission order to sell the utility. In March 1942, the prominent industrialist Cyrus Eaton assured the City Council that he could arrange financing for the purchase. CEI and influential business interests strongly opposed the buyout, and in June 1943 the City Council voted against it, nineteen to thirteen.[18] After World War II, Muny Light remained in a steady state with a stable customer base.

Resumption of Competition

In the late 1950s and early 1960s, Muny Light again began to compete with CEI for customers within Muny Light's territory. Prospective customers were offered inducements, and the city proposed to expand Muny Light's generating capacity. Based on a 1966 consultant's report, Muny Light was considering a direct connection with the Power Authority of the State of New York (PASNY) and its Niagara Falls source of power through the Ohio-Pennsylvania Association of Co-ops and Municipal Utilities. CEI countered by offering such a transmission interconnection only if Muny Light would agree to increase its rates to conform to CEI's rates. This set the stage for another dramatic chapter in the saga of conflict over public power in Cleveland.

By the mid-1960s, Muny Light's role as a competitive yardstick was jeopardized. Countless power interruptions and overloaded infrastructure had caused customer dissatisfaction, resulting in desertions to CEI, which offered free rewiring to former Muny Light customers. Muny Light urgently needed an expanded source of power.

Mayor Carl B. Stokes, a liberal Democrat elected in 1967 as the first black mayor of a major American city, had pledged to sell the increasingly troubled and deficit-ridden Muny Light.[19] The East Side black wards, which were critical to his narrow victory, were not served by Muny Light so Stokes could take this position with little political risk. But he failed to win the support of the City Council for the sale of Muny Light to CEI.

Stokes's desire to sell the utility reflected the city's escalating fiscal woes. Confronted with rapidly rising costs and declining revenues, Stokes twice unsuccessfully proposed tax increases. Muny Light was running deficits, adding to the city's financial problems. CEI argued that Muny Light was a "financial albatross" costing the city revenue in the form of taxes (paid by CEI but not by Muny Light) and that its services demanded an unfair subsidy from the majority of taxpayers, who were not served by Muny Light, to the minority, who were Muny Light customers.

In 1971, Ralph J. Perk, a Republican, was elected as a populist mayor on a platform of economy in government and no tax increases. Determined to maintain city ownership of Muny Light and to increase its service, Perk introduced and the City Council passed a $13 million bond issue for long overdue improvements. The bonds, however, did not sell and Perk accused CEI of sabotaging their sale. The Perk administration filed a $330 million antitrust suit against CEI in 1975 based on this and related charges that CEI was trying to undermine Muny Light as a competitor.[20]

Perk was aided in his conflict with CEI by the Cleveland Planning Commission, then under the direction of Norman Krumholz.[21] The city planners were drawn into the controversy because they were responsible for preparing Cleveland's annual capital improvements program. Initially, the planners tried to identify the capital improvements required to correct the frequent power outages then plaguing Muny Light, but it became apparent that the issue was more complex.

The planners concluded that CEI's refusal to provide Muny Light with a permanent interconnection with other power sources was the major cause of Muny Light's problems. Nearly all electric power companies have such tie-ins to other power systems as a backup so that they can continue uninterrupted service should their own facilities fail or need repair. In the past, CEI had refused any tie-in at all (absent an equalization of rates to eliminate Muny Light's price advantage) and was forced to provide a temporary interconnection under court order.

The planners proposed to the mayor that the city condemn and purchase CEI's transmission and generating capacity in the city of Cleveland. This would expand Muny Light into a citywide network, eliminate blackouts, and provide electricity at much lower cost to city residents and businesses. Mayor Perk rejected the planners' proposal, deciding instead to pursue the antitrust lawsuit.

The city's chance for success seemed strong. The U.S. Justice Department filed a brief in support of the city, based on a finding of the Atomic Safety and Licensing Board of the U.S. Nuclear Regulatory Commission (NRC) that confirmed that CEI "had deliberately rigged its interconnecting policies to cause Muny's power failures" and alleged that CEI and its allied private power companies had acted "individually and collectively to eliminate one or more electric entities and to preclude competition."[22]

But Mayor Perk reversed his long-standing support for Muny Light and in 1976, as part of a complex, short-term response to the city's financial troubles, proposed to sell Muny Light to CEI. Under the proposal, CEI would pay $150 million and forgive the city its $16 million debt in return for the city dropping its antitrust suit. The proposed sale of Muny Light was part of a retrenchment program that included the sale of other city assets.

Mayor Perk finessed the city's fiscal problems until he left office in 1977 after being defeated in his reelection bid, but they were ticking like a bomb for the new mayor, Dennis J. Kucinich. Kucinich had pledged to block the sale of Muny Light to CEI if he was elected, and that was one of the first acts of his administration.[23] His action infuriated the City Council, which had voted over a year before to sell Muny Light. This action also frustrated CEI, whose long war against Muny Light had appeared so close to being finally won.

Kucinich viewed his actions as an extension of the Progressive politics of Tom Johnson. But his defense of Muny Light exacerbated the city's fiscal problems. Muny Light was in severe financial trouble, having accumulated millions of dollars of debt for power purchased from CEI. Kucinich's repayment plan was invalidated by the Ohio Supreme Court in June 1978 (*State* v. *Tegreene*), forcing the new mayor to choose between taking the money out of operating funds or failing to pay the debt by the end of the year, which would have required that the city abandon its antitrust suit. Kucinich chose the former course of action. The City Council responded by prohibiting Kucinich from using bond money for operating expenses. Kucinich's veto was overridden by the City Council.

Cleveland's political turmoil, much of which pivoted on the Muny Light–CEI issue, led directly to a weakening of the city's credit rating. By the fall of 1978, following a bitter recall election that Kucinich narrowly won by 236 votes, it was clear that the city would have to pay the CEI debt out of the general fund. Apart from the debt problems directly associated with CEI, Kucinich also faced the prospect of default on $14 million in short-term notes issued by the city and held by six local banks. Four of the six banks holding the notes in question had interlocking directorships with CEI.

Kucinich tried to persuade the banks that the city would fulfill its obligations if the banks would roll over (refinance) the notes. These banks had been purchasing and routinely rolling over city notes during the Perk administration, and the request seemed reasonable. Kucinich, swallowing a lifetime of antitax rhetoric, proposed a tax hike and a bond sale in 1979 to redeem the notes and consolidate other debts. But the City Council and the Cleveland Trust Company, Ohio's largest bank, balked. They would roll over the notes only if Kucinich agreed to the sale of Muny Light to CEI.

The City Council steadfastly refused to put Kucinich's tax increase on the ballot unless he agreed to sell Muny Light. But Kucinich was not about to sell Muny Light, the keystone of his mayoral campaign and the cornerstone of his populist economic philosophy. Nor was he about to drop the antitrust suit against CEI. He decried what he saw as collusion and conspiracy among Cleveland Trust, CEI, and the City Council. On December 15, 1978, the city of Cleveland became the first major American city to default on its fiscal obligations since the Depression. A few days later, the City Council agreed to put the tax increase on the ballot, but only after Kucinich also agreed to put Muny Light's fate to the ballot test as well.

The 1979 Referendum of the Sale of Muny Light to CEI

The Cleveland newspapers gave comprehensive coverage to the Muny Light issue in the 1979 special election. The *Cleveland Press* gave a balanced summary of the arguments for and against the sale of the electric utility, as well as in-depth historical background and a political roll call of supporters and detractors of Muny Light. In contrast, the *Cleveland Plain Dealer* sought to discredit Muny Light and Mayor Kucinich, whose recall it had supported in August 1978. Nevertheless, when CEI criticized its coverage of the Muny Light–CEI conflict, the paper removed the reporter, leading to a protest by its Newspaper Guild unit. The result was uncensored coverage, which is credited with affecting the outcome of the election.[24]

Both papers ultimately endorsed the sale of Muny Light for the same reasons, that Muny Light had become a "millstone" around the neck of the city. Both acknowledged, however, that a combination of politics, mismanagement, and the not-so-hidden hand of CEI had contributed to Muny Light's precipitous decline. The papers concluded that the city's plant had outlived its usefulness; it was badly in debt and in need of major investment that could be better used for other civic purposes.

At times the debate in the press took on a carnival atmosphere because of the flamboyant campaigning of the mayor. Kucinich cast the issue as the Municipal David versus the CEI (and associated banking interests) Goliath. Kucinich's denunciation of CEI's role in the Muny Light crisis frequently took on the tone of a holy crusade. Kucinich said that CEI had "plotted for years to ruin Muny Light" and that it had "used its influence to destabilize the municipal government in a manner reminiscent of greedy, ruthless, immoral corporate oligarchies in Latin America." The sale of Muny would let CEI off the hook for its "crime against our community."[25]

The mayor's populist rhetoric also contained less dramatic but compelling arguments. There was an authentic argument over the selling price. The arguments against the sale did not stop with its finances. A case against CEI as an active obstacle to the efficient administration of Muny Light was made repeatedly during the campaign. For example, the newspapers reported documented instances when CEI refused to sell power to Muny Light, causing failures of service, followed immediately by customer solicitations by CEI.

Proponents of the sale were well represented and just as active in presenting their case. The sale was endorsed by both major newspapers, the Citizens League, the Growth Association (Cleveland's Chamber of Commerce), and the major banks and corporations.

The election was held on February 27, 1979, and the outcome was clear and unambiguous. By a vote of 69,957 to 38,817, twenty-five of the city's thirty-three wards opposed the sale.[26] Although Kucinich immediately took credit for the victory, Muny Light was supported by a far greater margin than had voted for him in the recent recall election.

Ironically, the most decisive influence on the outcome of the election was CEI. During the campaign period, CEI submitted a request to the PUCO asking for a 12 percent rate hike for residential customers and an even greater increase for commercial customers. Analysts of the election later concluded that this, more than any other factor, accounted for the defeat of the sale proposal.[27] CEI defended its decision knowing that the rate hike was coming and concluding that announcing it before the election would sacrifice some support but was preferable to losing the election and then announcing the hike, which could be interpreted as vindictive behavior.

The Outcome of the Antitrust Case (1980–1981)

Following Kucinich's term as mayor, the antitrust suit went to trial in September 1980. CEI's defenses were that as a regulated private utility, it was not subject to the antitrust laws; it had not illegally achieved a monopoly position; and as a "natural" monopoly, its refusal to deal with Muny Light was legitimate competitive conduct. A mistrial was declared after a hung jury (five to one in favor of Muny Light) deliberated for thirteen days. The retrial began in July 1981, and on October 8, 1981, the second jury found in favor of defendant CEI after deliberating only six hours.[28]

Despite CEI's efforts over several decades to prevent the creation of Muny Light, to limit its operations and block its expansion, to deny it a permanent interconnection, and to block the one attempt to municipalize CEI, CEI prevailed in the city's legal attempt to prove that its conduct was anticompetitive. The reasons for the city's legal defeat included the holdout juror in the first trial, the second jury's negative reaction to the presentation of the city's case by its legal team, and CEI's lawyers' successful defense arguing that Muny Light's problems were the result of its own incompetence rather than anticompetitive actions by CEI.[29]

Continuing Political and Legal Conflicts

The brief but highly volatile Kucinich era ended in 1979 with the election of business-backed conservative Republican George Voinovich as Cleveland's mayor. Although he was supported by the corporate community that had fought Kucinich so hard, Voinovich was publicly committed to upholding the results of the 1979 referendum.

In 1984, Muny Light, renamed Cleveland Public Power (CPP), again was under attack. A City Council member proposed that the city either sell CPP to CEI (for the incredibly deflated price of $40 million) or lease the utility to CEI for twenty-five years. If the lease agreement was approved, all CEI customers would be given a 10 percent decrease in rates, matching those already enjoyed by CPP customers. CEI also agreed to become an anchor tenant in a new downtown revitalization project known as Tower City. In return, if after twenty-five years the city decided to retain ownership of CPP, CEI would be reimbursed for any investment it had made in the CPP facilities.[30]

Because there was no public sentiment to sell CPP, this new proposal was intended to circumvent the 1979 referendum. CEI was threatened on two fronts: first, CPP was readying an expansion effort and second, CEI's customers were about to experience a rate shock because of CEI's costly investment in nuclear power plants at Perry and Beaver Valley. A further influence was the potential ability of CPP to purchase increased amounts of cheap power from PASNY. To win public support for the lease effort, CEI mounted an extensive lobbying campaign.

In August 1984, Mayor Voinovich publicly rejected the CEI proposal, citing the city's business interests as the owner of a utility and his disgust with the pressure he was under as a result of the issue: "I have never experienced any more pressure than this since I have been mayor." Voinovich admitted that he had ended secret negotiations with CEI in part for political reasons.[31] His arch-foe, Dennis Kucinich, was back on the City Council, as was Kucinich's brother, who became Voinovich's unsuccessful opponent in the 1985 mayoral election. Both Kuciniches were outspoken opponents of the proposed lease. Voinovich, whose major claim as mayor was the restoration of peace in city politics, wanted to avoid another divisive confrontation over public power.

The pressure from Voinovich's key ally, the powerful black City Council president George Forbes, who supported CEI, was intense. Forbes attacked the mayor's decision, arguing that rejection of CEI would result in CEI's nonparticipation in the downtown redevelopment effort that was anchored by the Tower City project. Predictably, Forbes was joined in his argument by the Cleveland Growth Association. The Tower City project proceeded and opened in March 1990 without CEI's participation.

Forbes continued his attack, attempting unsuccessfully to put the CEI proposal before the voters in yet another referendum in 1984. Forbes's other efforts to block CPP's expansion were successful. When Voinovich sought City Council approval in early 1985 for a $35 million bond issue as part of a ten-year $100 million expansion program designed to increase CPP's customer base from forty-eight thousand to one hundred thousand, Forbes was able to delay approval until 1987.

Finally, the City Council did unanimously approve the bond issue.[32] The black members, whose wards would be served by CPP expansion, all supported the bond issue. The sale of $50 million in bonds to finance expansion affirmed CPP's solvency and improved operation.

The Territorial War

The private utilities, including CEI, have regularly turned to the Ohio legislature in their attempts to limit the authority of public power companies. This was especially true during the Tom Johnson era, when he constantly fought corporate attempts through the legislature to limit or eliminate the power of charter cities to operate public enterprises and regulate competing private enterprises.

In 1989, the battle was once again joined in Columbus. At issue was legislation introduced at the behest of Ohio Edison, intended to restrict the right of municipal utilities to sell power outside their own boundaries. The private utilities claimed that this would eliminate unnecessary duplication of services and prevent "unfair" competition from public utilities.

This bill was defeated by the public utilities, including CPP; the Ohio Public Interest Campaign (OPIC), representing consumers; environmental groups; and the Republican mayors of Cleveland and Columbus (which also has public power), who claimed that the legislation was simply intended to prevent price competition. CPP believed that the bill was intended to prevent its expansion inside the city of Cleveland.

As CPP prepared for expansion, it had increased its customer base to 52,000 (88 percent residential) by 1989, compared to CEI's regional customer base of 735,000. Between 1982 and 1989, CPP gained a net increase of 6,689 meter accounts that switched from CEI. CPP enjoyed a rate differential of 30 percent in early 1990, which was projected to grow to as much as 33 percent by 1996, taking into account CEI's proposed rate increases based on its increased costs (largely because of inclusion of its nuclear power costs in its rate base). CPP's justification of its expansion was based on survey research indicating that it could compete for new residential customers in Cleveland as long as it enjoyed a 25 percent rate advantage. Once CPP's expansion is completed, it could win over a much larger share of the city's residential customers.[33]

CEI launched a legal attack against CPP through a 1984 taxpayer's suit to force it to reimburse the city's general fund for $29 million advanced between 1971 and 1982, which allegedly violated Cleveland's City Charter requiring utilities to be "non-tax supported." By a four-to-three vote (with former Cleveland mayor Ralph Locher dissenting), the Ohio Supreme Court ruled in CEI's favor in 1988 and remanded the case for a payment plan to be worked out.[34] With interest, the repayments could force CPP to raise its rates by approximately 25 percent, just below CEI's rates, which was undoubtedly the object of CEI's lawsuit. The city appealed this decision.

Meanwhile, the city placed a charter amendment on the November 6, 1990, ballot, authorizing the city to provide financial aid to its public utilities, if necessary. CPP had the support of Michael White, Cleveland's second black mayor, who was elected in 1989 largely because voters from Cleveland's West Side (which is served by CPP) overwhelmingly rejected City Council president Forbes, a CPP foe.

Centerior, CEI's parent holding company, through a committee to "protect city services," opposed the charter amendment. Mayor White charged that this CEI-supported group engaged in false and misleading advertising, claiming that the charter amendment would result in reduction of the city's police and fire protection services. Nevertheless, the voters overwhelmingly approved the measure by a two-thirds majority. Once again, Cleveland voters supported municipal power.[35]

Brook Park

In 1991, CEI faced yet another competitive threat. The city of Brook Park, adjacent to Cleveland, announced its interest in the creation of a municipal power system and hired CEI's old nemesis Dennis Kucinich as a consultant. Faced with the potential loss of one of its five largest commercial customers—Ford Motor—CEI strongly opposed the city's action. It surveyed city residents by telephone on the issue and announced that it would seek $75 million in compensation if the city built its own power system. A study commissioned by the city estimated that Brook Park residents and businesses would save about 30 percent through conversion to public power. In November 1991, a voter-approved referendum authorized Brook Park as the eighty-fifth Ohio municipality to establish a municipal power system.[36] However, in 1993, after lengthy negotiations, Brook Park agreed not to proceed with municipal public power. In return, CEI agreed to reduce its residential and commercial rates 20 percent for five years to its Brook Park customers.[37]

Nuclear Power, Rate Shock, and the Economics of the Contemporary Electric Power Debate in Cleveland

Rate shock in the early 1990s attributable to nuclear power construction costs became an important factor in the rate rivalry between CPP and CEI. In the early 1970s, CEI announced its participation in the construction of a complex of nuclear facilities. CEI, Toledo Edison, Ohio Edison, Pennsylvania Power, and Duquesne Light agreed to share the cost and output of a series of nuclear plants.

The first plant, Perry One, was to be completed by 1978 at a cost of $600 million, followed by the Beaver Valley plant in Pennsylvania. Investment in such plants, argued CEI, would keep the region economically competitive and environmentally safe. The construction plans for Perry, however, were subject to extraordinary delays and operational problems, which significantly increased the unit's cost, while the economic and demographic decline of the region during the period of the Perry plant construction called into question the need for the additional capacity provided by the plant.

In 1985, when the nuclear project remained uncompleted, CEI proposed a reorganization of the ownership, creating a holding company with Toledo Edison to reduce costs for completion of both Perry One and Beaver Valley. This proposal generated opposition from consumer advocates: "The new generating subsidiary to run the nuclear plants would be under federal rather than state regulatory control, guaranteeing weaker regulation and higher rates. Further, public power systems such as the Cleveland municipal would be at a disadvantage in purchasing power from the private companies at competitive rates now that they operated under a single roof."[38]

Perry One was finally completed in 1987, sixteen years after construction had begun. It is jointly owned by the Centerior group (CEI, Toledo Edison, and Ohio Edison), Pennsylvania Power, and Duquesne Light. Thirteen percent of all of CEI's electrical output now comes from Perry One.

The rate shock occurred the next year. In fall 1988, Centerior applied to the PUCO for a 23.4 percent rate increase over three years to cover cost overruns for the Beaver Valley and Perry nuclear power plants. The overruns reduced CEI's net income by 69 percent in 1988 and its regulated return on investment to only 2.9 percent, compared to an average of 12.7 percent during 1984–87.[39]

Centerior's request became the subject of lengthy negotiations with the state Office of Consumer Counsel and the Industrial Energy Consumers. In January 1989, a settlement was reached. Although $495 million in costs associated with Perry and Beaver Valley were disallowed and Centerior promised to comply with nuclear power plant operating standards to increase efficiency, PUCO approved a total increase of 24.2 percent (9 percent, 7.2 percent, and 6.3 percent annually) over three years, which was slightly more than Centerior had originally requested. CEI agreed, for the first time, to create a Consumer Advisory Board. In November 1989, a stockholder's suit resulted in a settlement under which Centerior agreed to greater oversight of its nuclear operations.[40]

OPIC refused to join in this agreement. To ease the rate shock for large businesses with heavy consumption, the PUCO approved rate abatements for industrial users, shifting the difference to residential customers. To reduce rate shock, low-income residential users were to be charged 2 percent less than other residential users. But rate shock and the impact of CEI's rate increases on its residential customers remain critical factors in the competition between CEI and CPP. In 1991, CEI's electrical rates were the highest in Ohio.[41]

In 1990, about 40 percent of Cleveland's population of 505,000 was below the poverty line. These residents could ill afford to pay the large utility rate increases engendered by the costs of nuclear power facilities, especially since CEI's rates were already higher than CPP's. In contrast, CPP's purchased energy is almost entirely non-nuclear. The current rate gap may widen because CEI was projecting the need to construct the second phase of the Perry project.[42]

Conclusion

What lessons are to be learned from this case study of the creation and survival of an embattled public power enterprise in Cleveland? The first and most obvious conclusion is that public power does serve a very useful public purpose that justifies its creation and continued existence, namely, providing electric power at the lowest possible rate to consumers. The rate gap between CPP and CEI constitutes a real benefit to consumers (both residential and business) and the city. The offsetting taxes that CEI and its employees pay must be measured against the economic benefits of competitive, lower rates. The precise costs and benefits of this economic trade-off are difficult to identify, and we do not attempt to do so here.

Nevertheless, lower utility rates are especially important in cities like Cleveland, where the climate requires higher than average usage of utilities and a very high percentage of the population of the old central city lives below the poverty line. Without either direct public competition or public power simply serving as a yardstick, a private monopoly could charge much higher rates. It is impossible, however, to calculate what CEI's rates to Cleveland residents would have been without Muny Light. Public utility regulators generally favor the interests of IOUs over those of utility consumers so consumers cannot necessarily rely on state and federal regulatory agencies to keep utility rates as low as possible.

Second, public power is more accountable to the public than are IOUs. The positions taken by local officials such as Cleveland's mayors about public power can affect their political future. Appointed state regulators are not directly accountable to consumers. In addition to electing the mayor and City Council, voting consumers may express their views about utility rates and policies through the referendum. Despite heavy expenditures by CEI, Cleveland voters have often shown their support for public power, from the initial 1904 referendum authorizing its creation, to the 1938 referendum supporting its modernization, to the decisive 1979 defeat of the proposal to sell it to CEI, and finally to the 1990 approval of the change in the city charter authorizing city financial support of public power. If those administering public power are not acting in the public interest, then there is a possibility that this can be corrected by local politicians susceptible to voter oversight.

It must be conceded that Muny Light has not always been a model public enterprise, despite its public accountability. It has been accused of racial discrimination and political cronyism in its employment practices. Accusations of racial discrimination against Muny Light, including employment practices and the location of its service areas, are hardly surprising in Cleveland, one of the most racially segregated American cities.[43] Muny Light has behaved no differently from other municipal agencies. It has not been known as a notable leader in encouraging consumer participation. Nevertheless, as a public enterprise, it can be influenced to adopt "progressive" policies. In the 1980s, CPP showed marked improvement in its operations.

In contrast, CEI is susceptible only to such influence through the PUCO. The PUCO was somewhat more protective of consumer interests in the 1980s in the administration of liberal Democratic governor Richard Celeste. Nevertheless, consumer groups such as OPIC still consider PUCO much too favorable to producers in its role as regulator and ratesetter.

Third, the Cleveland case reinforces the credo that the price of enjoying the benefits of public power is eternal vigilance. Although other major municipal utilities have not had to withstand the protracted opposition of an IOU as had Muny Light/CPP in its ninety-year battle with CEI, this saga illustrates the implacable opposition of profit-driven IOUs to public competition. Progressive mayor Tom Johnson's warning of the corruption of civic politics proved true many times when CEI attempted to influence Cleveland mayors and City Council members. CEI's opposition has heightened the pressure on IOU profits from the cost overruns from their investment in nuclear power, making lower public power rates even more threatening to them.

It cannot be said that Muny Light has always enjoyed widespread grass-roots support. Part of the reason is the compromise of 1920 that limited its service areas and reduced it to serving the role of a passive yardstick. Its own past deficiencies, publicized by the media and exacerbated by CEI, have contributed to this limited role. Nevertheless, when put to an electoral test, Muny Light/CPP has almost always triumphed. A political "savior" has appeared in Muny Light's times of trial, beginning with mayors Tom L. Johnson and Newton D. Baker in the Progressive era, Paul Walter's CMLPA in the Depression era, and Mayor Dennis Kucinich in 1978–79. Even conservative mayor George Voinovich publicly sang the praises of public power in 1984. As CPP expands in the 1990s, it may once again need political support in the face of CEI opposition.

Finally, Cleveland's long struggle between public and private power suggests that, although public power may survive intensive attack by an IOU competitor, it is most unlikely to completely supplant IOUs. The only serious attempt to buy out CEI failed in 1942–43, although because of the wartime emergency, this was more a trial balloon than a serious attempt at exclusive public ownership. Competition in local markets, however, has been shown to be important in keeping rates lower.[44]

Ultimately, the most compelling reason for municipal ownership is democratic control. Although there are marginal benefits—lower rates being the most obvious—keeping the complicated and changing issues of electric power prominent in the public discourse of local governance, where the people can debate and vote their will, is most important. Democratic control makes for a better and more responsive public service because in the end, power, a by-product of natural resources, is a public service.

Notes

1. Richard Rudolph and Scott Ridley, *Power Struggle: The Hundred Year War Over Electricity* (New York: Harper & Row, 1986).

2. Ibid., 251–53, 256.

3. Paul L. Joskow and Richard Schmalansee, *Markets for Power: An Analysis of Electric Utility Deregulation* (Cambridge, Mass.: MIT Press, 1983), 179–98.

4. Edward S. Savas, *Privatization: The Key to Better Government* (Chatham, N.J.: Chatham House, 1987), 150.

5. Richard Hellman, *Government Competition in the Electric Utility Industry: A Theoretical and Empirical Study* (New York: Praeger, 1972), 343–51.

6. David Sweet and Kathy W. Hexter, *Public Utilities: Rights and Responsibilities* (New York: Praeger, 1987). Also see W. Gormley, *The Politics of Public Utility Regulation* (Pittsburgh: University of Pittsburgh Press, 1983).

7. Office of Technology Assessment, *Electric Power Wheeling and Dealing: Technological Considerations for Increasing Competition* (Washington, D.C.: Government Printing Office, 1989).

8. "Public Power Costs Less," *Public Power* 26 (January–February 1991): 16.

9. Savas, *Privatization,* 150.

10. Walter J. Primeaux, Jr., "Competition Between Electric Utilities," in *Electric Power Deregulation and the Public Interest,* ed. J. C. Moorhouse (San Francisco: Pacific Research Institute for Public Policy, 1986).

11. Tom L. Johnson, *My Story* (1911; reprint, Kent, Ohio: Kent State University Press, 1993), 27.

12. Ibid., 192.

13. Clarence H. Cramer, *Newton Baker: A Biography* (New York: World, 1961), 51.

14. Rudolph and Ridley, *Power Struggle,* 180–209.

15. Edward J. Kenealy, *The Cleveland Light Plant* (Cleveland: Privately printed, 1935), 8.

16. R. Husselman, *Cleveland's Municipal Light Plant Still Pesters Power Trust* (Chicago: Public Ownership League of America, 1931); Howell Wright, *Cleveland's Municipal Light Plant or Municipal Government in the Electric Light and Power Business* (Chicago: Utilities Publication Company, 1930).

17. Hellman, *Government Competition,* 306.

18. Thomas Campbell, "Municipal Ownership," in *The Encyclopedia of Cleveland History,* ed. David D. Van Tassel and John J. Grabowski (Bloomington, Ind.: Indiana University Press, 1987), 701.

19. Hellman, *Government Competition,* 307.

20. Campbell, "Municipal Ownership," 702.

21. Norman Krumholz, "A Retrospective View of Equity Planning," *Journal of the American Planning Association* 48 (1982): 163–74. See also N. Krumholz, Janice Cogger, and John Linner, "The Cleveland Policy Planning Report," *Journal of the American Institute of Planners* 41 (1975): 298–304.

22. Todd Swanstrom, *The Crisis of Growth Politics: Cleveland, Kucinich, and the Challenge of Urban Populism* (Philadelphia: Temple University Press, 1985), 159.

23. Ibid., 157.

24. Ellen S. Freilich, "Cleveland 'Plain Dealer,' Pressured by Reporters, Prints a Story it Stifled," *Columbia Journalism Review* 18 (May–June 1979): 49–57.

25. David T. Abbott, "CEI Plotted for Years to Ruin Muny Light, Mayor Tells City Club," *Cleveland Plain Dealer,* February 17, 1979; Peter Phipps, "Kucinich Goes to Big Screen at City Club to Sell His Stand," *Cleveland Press,* February 28, 1979.

26. Fred McGunagle, "Tax Bite Starts Tomorrow; Muny to Woo CEI Customers," *Cleveland Press,* February 28, 1979.

27. Al Thompson, "Muny Vote Called a Rebuke to CEI," *Cleveland Press,* February 28, 1979.

28. Arthur D. Austin, *Complex Litigation Confronts the Jury System: A Case Study* (Frederick, Md.: University Publications of America, 1984), 21.

29. Ibid.

30. Steven Luttner, "Council to Get Plan for Muny Lease Monday," *Cleveland Plain Dealer,* December 14, 1984.

31. Gary R. Clark, "Good Deal, Bad Deal? How CEI–City Pact Failed at the Last Minute," *Cleveland Plain Dealer,* August 12, 1984.

32. Campbell, "Municipal Ownership," 703.

33. V. Reiner, "Cleveland Public Power Expanding," *Public Power* 22 (May–June 1987): 10–16.

34. *City of Cleveland* v. *CEI,* 37 Ohio St. 3d 50, 524 N.E. 2d 441 (1988).

35. Bob Becker, "Voters Give Support to City Light System," *Cleveland Plain Dealer,* November 7, 1990.

36. The entire three-year scenario in Brook Park, from threat to action to compromise, may be seen in the following articles by Michael O'Malley in the *Cleveland Plain Dealer:* "Brook Park's Moth Drawn to Municipal Power Light," June 13, 1991; "Power Plan Generates Legal Threat: CEI Would Seek $75 Million if City Sets up Own System," August 29, 1991; "Study Says Residents Can Save 30% if City Builds Power System," August 21, 1991; "Brook Park O.K.'s a City Power System," November 6, 1991; "Brook Park O.K.'s Deal for Cut in CEI Rates," April 30, 1993.

37. Michael O'Malley, "Brook Park O.K.'s Deal for Cut in CEI Rates," *Cleveland Plain Dealer,* April 30, 1993.

38. Rudolph and Ridley, *Power Struggle,* 232.

39. Harry Stainer, "Consumers' Counsel Assails Utility Profits," *Cleveland Plain Dealer,* August 10, 1989.

40. Tom Breckenridge, "Centerior, Sued by Shareholders, to Enact Reforms," *Cleveland Plain Dealer,* January 13, 1990.

41. Mark Holley, "Cleveland Zapped by Top Power Bill," *Cleveland Plain Dealer,* July 27, 1990.

42. James T. Lawless, "Completion of Perry Unit 2 Studied," *Cleveland Plain Dealer,* September 10, 1989.

43. Norman Krumholz, "Twenty Years After Kerner: The Cleveland Case," *Journal of Urban Affairs* 12 (1990): 285–97.

44. Walter J. Primeaux, Jr., *Direct Electric Utility Competition: The Natural Monopoly Myth* (New York: Praeger, 1986).

How Business Bosses Saved a Sick City

Myron Magnet

ONE LESSON Americans learned in the 1980s was that they had to take responsibility for their own fates. For companies, in the age of raiders and Darwinian global competition, this was luminously so—and hence the restructuring wave that defines this business era. Individuals, their jobs and expectations rattled by the corporate convulsions, discovered that they and not some institution must shape their careers, a perception that bred legions of new small businesses. Cities, especially old industrial centers, made the same discovery. With their economy, politics, and social fabric frayed by vast forces seeming to make them as obsolete as Pompeii or Atlantis, they were said to be turning ungovernable, unlivable, and bankrupt. But instead of subsiding gracefully into the dustbin of history, some cities stood and fought. And some—Baltimore, Pittsburgh, and Lowell, Massachusetts, for instance—are winning.

No city has battled more cannily than Cleveland. A microcosm—almost a caricature—of all the recent ills of urban industrial America, the nation's twelfth largest metropolitan area had much to overcome. Two decades ago it seemed a place decomposing into spontaneous combustion. In 1969, for instance, its oil-smeared Cuyahoga River—the *river*—burst into sooty flames, a presage of the inner decay of Cleveland's crucial heavy industries. In 1966 the Hough ghetto, and two years later the Glenville neighborhood, flared into wild rioting that left scores of stores scarred and gutted. Today weed-grown lots mark where burned buildings were bulldozed.

The town's political framework threatened to go up in smoke too, an immolation that had more the air of farce than tragedy. When Cleveland needed strong leaders to navigate these urban ills, its mayors seemed to have stepped out of a Three Stooges movie. In 1972, Mayor Ralph Perk—whose wife had just declined a chance to meet with President Nixon because it interfered with her bowling night—

made Cleveland a national laughingstock: while wielding an acetylene torch to cut the metal ribbon at a bridge opening, he set his hair alight.

His successor, the boy mayor Dennis Kucinich, wrote the City Hall farce's last act with a wild-eyed, publicity-hungry, populist style of government that ended by bringing Cleveland into default, the only major U.S. city to have suffered that fate since the Depression. Elected as a thirty-one-year-old to a single two-year term in 1977 and nearly recalled nine months later, he treated business as the archenemy of "the people." His business-bashing helped drive Diamond Shamrock out of town in horrified disgust.

With the city till empty and municipal services a shambles, Clevelanders decided to take their civic fate in hand. Says Richard Pogue, managing partner of Cleveland-based Jones Day Reavis & Pogue, the nation's second-largest law firm: "In a sense, Kucinich was the best thing that ever happened because he became a unifying element. People looked at him and said, 'Enough is enough here. Let's get together and change things.'" In response, Clevelanders achieved a unity almost startling in this every-man-for-himself epoch.

E. Mandell de Windt, the now retired CEO of Eaton Corporation and unofficial dean of Cleveland businessmen, organized the troops and devised a strategy, setting in motion a benign conspiracy of executives and entrepreneurs that still operates. The impressive feat of organizing that cabal and persuading Cleveland's most senior businessmen to take charge of the grittiest aspects of civic life was the real key to the town's turnaround. Cleveland bosses are arguably more public-spirited than most, but they had hitherto focused that spirit on their especially successful United Way or their superb art museum or the world-famous Cleveland Orchestra, not on bread-and-butter civic matters. By the start of the 1980s, though, top executives realized they had to get their hands dirty if they wanted to keep viable the Cleveland life they liked so much—the Cleveland of excellent cultural institutions and big-league athletic teams, the Cleveland ringed by enviably comfortable, old-fashioned, family-oriented suburbs, where $300,000 buys you $1 million worth of house by New York City or Boston suburban standards.

The civic rescue operation was more than a personal extracurricular activity for these executives. Says Del de Windt: "It was an extension of my role as a CEO of a major corporation to recognize that we had to do something about the environment in which we lived." Tackling civic problems in concert rather than singly gave top bosses the necessary confidence to invest their time and their corporations' money in Cleveland—when they could have followed Diamond Shamrock out of town. They knew they wouldn't be left alone holding the bag, like the last person in a chain letter.

The business cabal's first campaign was political. Shortly after Cleveland defaulted in 1978, de Windt sent an emissary to implore Republican lieutenant governor George Voinovich, a former Cuyahoga County commissioner, to come back and run for mayor. Financed largely by the corporate leaders, he beat Kucinich handily.

"All they wanted was somebody to bring some saneness and just establish a city administration, so the city would function," says Voinovich. But they got much more. They got a mayor with a gift for nurturing all the incipient impulses toward unity and cooperation that the town's revulsion for Kucinich had engendered. According to lawyer Pogue, "Voinovich always says, 'I don't like to make war. I like to make love.'"

In agreeing to run, Voinovich had extracted from the executive cabal a promise that cemented its cooperation with the city. Executives agreed to scrutinize the operations of city government with the hard-nosed skepticism of a bank workout squad, looking for ways to impose corporate efficiency on City Hall. Almost ninety executives took up the task. From over 650 of their proposals—ranging from a new financial management system to contracting out car and truck maintenance—Voinovich adopted about 500, saving Cleveland $200 million in his nine-and-a-half year tenure. Besides modernizing the city administration, this exercise gave business leaders a personal stake in municipal government's success. They have kept volunteering.

Voinovich also established harmony between the mayor's office and the entirely Democratic City Council, in place of the Beirut-like dissension of the Kucinich era, when in two years the mayor vetoed more council measures than in all the rest of Cleveland's modern history. Council president George Forbes met the Republican mayor halfway—a potentially problematic move for a big-city black Democrat to make. But Forbes and the council were sick of all the fighting and failure. Voinovich, Forbes recognized, had a mandate to revitalize the city, doable only in concert with the business community. "I recognized that we politicians don't provide the jobs," Forbes says. "Those are the guys that provide jobs, and if we don't make them viable, we don't have jobs for our people."

Clevelanders have their differences, often sharp ones, but today's prevailing tone of cooperation gives local politics an oddly unideological character. The city's cold season of adversity has persuaded Clevelanders of the importance of economic development. Most of them agree that you have to create wealth before you can think of redistributing it. Most believe that the long-term way to help the poor is to make the local economy flourish.

For beyond its race riots or Keystone Kops former politicians, Cleveland's fundamental problem was, and is, economic. Like other Rust Belt capitals, it saw its heavy industries—steel, auto parts, iron ore—dwindle in the face of global competition. Compounding its problem, Cleveland had execrable labor relations; remote, dictatorial bosses were in constant confrontation with unionized workers, whose work rules were rigid and wages uncompetitively high. In the early 1980s recession and the strong dollar hit Cleveland companies with bewildering suddenness. They cut back and restructured with a vengeance.

As a result, unemployment in greater Cleveland 4.7 percent when Kucinich took office in 1978, peaked at a vertiginous 11.3 percent in 1983. Manufacturing employment, from its 1979 high of 276,300, slid to a 1987 low of 200,600. But in 1988 unemployment was only estimated at 5.5 percent, and even manufacturing employment had risen to an estimated 201,700. In 1988 employment finally recovered to its 1979 level.

Cleveland's CEO conspiracy led the economic as well as the political turnaround. Just after Voinovich took over City Hall, Del de Windt, along with now retired TRW chief Ruben Mettler, recently deceased Harris Corporation chief executive George Dively, and other local powers, hired the McKinsey & Company consulting firm to figure out how to brighten Cleveland's economy. The first prescription: Set up a *formal* conspiracy of CEOs to provide leadership.

The beauty of that organization—called Cleveland Tomorrow and founded in 1982—is that it unified the formerly cliquish, factionalized chief executives of Cleveland's top fifty companies into an almost irresistible force. Says former Ohio governor Richard Celeste: "Cleveland Tomorrow derives its strength from the fact that the CEO is the only participant. There's no delegating it to someone else. He can commit real resources in a way that only a CEO can."

The CEOs didn't have the option of turning Cleveland into a heartland Silicon Valley or Route 128, as they saw it, but they certainly could help put the shine back on the heavy Rust Belt industries that, if somewhat diminished, would remain Cleveland's economic anchor for a long time. That meant improving the sorry labor relations that made Cleveland workers, despite their well-developed skills and work ethic, so uncompetitive. Like most Cleveland Tomorrow efforts, this one produced a new institution, the Work in Northeast Ohio Council.

Under the aegis of a board of union and management representatives and now heavily financed by the state of Ohio, the council's staff spreads the gospel of productivity, product quality, and quality of work life on the factory floor and in union halls. Staff members do extensive consulting, promoting the whole array of modern management techniques that get workers and managers to see themselves as partners rather than adversaries. Meanwhile, the Greater Cleveland Roundtable, a separate group of CEOs, union chieftains, and political leaders formed just before Cleveland Tomorrow, fostered labor-management cooperation among the panjandrums. The result is an utterly transformed labor climate in Cleveland, where today you can find hot-metal shops managed like Silicon Valley start-ups.

Not just labor relations but also manufacturing technology needed modernization. Cleveland Tomorrow mobilized the resources of local colleges and universities, helping Cleveland State University, for example, set up a research center that solves quality improvement and industrial engineering problems for area companies. A program at Cuyahoga Community College provides customized training for companies. For example, it taught a small, growing defense subcontractor how to choose a CAD/CAM system and then taught the company's employees how to use it.

To foster new businesses, Cleveland Tomorrow in 1984 established a venture capital fund of $30 million raised from Cleveland Tomorrow companies and the Ohio state pension system. Investing mainly in Cleveland-area start-ups, most based on innovations in old industries, the fund has done well enough so that it recently had no trouble raising an additional $75 million.

With Cleveland's spirit of cooperation, which makes the whole greater than the sum of the parts, small businesses have flourished by pooling know-how in the nation's largest self-help organization for small enterprises. Thousands of these firms trade expertise in how to market or computerize or do cost accounting, and their bosses regularly exchange advice on specific problems.

Without exotic cultivation, Cleveland's big law and accounting firms have prospered, with demand for their services largely unruffled by the vicissitudes of their big-corporation clients. The health services industry has expanded to become, unexpectedly, Rust Belt Cleveland's No. 1 employer. The Cleveland Clinic, which brings $300 million from out of town into the city each year, has become a center for civic improvement, joining with other institutions to restore economic vitality to their sadly decayed neighborhood.

All these happenings add up to a sea change, but it is subtle and hard to discern if you don't look attentively. Says developer Albert Ratner, president of Forest City Enterprises, "The real thing that's changed is open heads." But Ratner and another Cleveland-based developer—Cleveland Indians co-owner Richard Jacobs, Chief of Jacobs Visconsi & Jacobs—are close enough to see how profoundly the city's civic culture and economic climate have improved. These developers are just starting to give outward form to that change with big projects that in three or four years will transform downtown.

Like crocuses forlornly peeping through the snow, a few brave projects, starting with the new BP America headquarters, finished in 1984, have shown that Cleveland isn't frozen lifeless. In 1986, Dick Jacobs's son Jeffrey built a bar, restaurant, and boardwalk on the Flats by the newly cleaned-up Cuyahoga River, setting off a wave of recreational development that in summer produces traffic jams and boats rafted up three deep by waterfront restaurants. Neil and Myron Viny have refurbished parts of the handsome but derelict warehouse district nearby for now bustling offices and apartments. The last drop of paint dried in April 1988 on the spectacular restoration of three adjacent splendid 1920s theaters, and now concerts, plays, and ballet draw big crowds downtown.

The new downtown is springing up as rapidly, extensively, and glitteringly as if by Prospero's magical conjuration. In October 1987, Dick Jacobs and his brother opened a suave, glass-vaulted galleria, where two levels of such tony shops as Ann Taylor and Williams-Sonoma have lured suburban matrons back into the city. The Jacobs brothers broke ground recently in the center of downtown on the first of two striking towers, designed by world-class architects, to house Cleveland's two biggest banks and two new hotels, a Hyatt Regency and a Marriott. Representing a total investment of some $750 million, they were to be built in 1992 and 1993, and at sixty stories, the taller will be Ohio's tallest building. (Society Tower was completed in 1992, but the Ameritrust building was delayed due to market conditions.)

Nearby, Albert Ratner is completing a $15 million renovation of Cleveland's landmark 1920s Terminal Tower office building. He is putting up two smaller office complexes, one containing a Ritz-Carlton hotel, and constructing another office building in the shell of the old post office. These will all be joined to the Terminal Tower by Tower City, a vast, three-level, vaulted mall containing restaurants, movie theaters, a new commuter rail station, and 120 shops. A walk through the site suggests that the $400 million project—to be finished in the spring of next year and partly built on the foundations of a similarly ambitious project aborted by the Depression—has the makings of a truly sophisticated urban forum. [Tower City opened in 1990.]

All this building will take Cleveland's comeback a step further. Says managing director James Bennett of McKinsey's Cleveland office: "You need big symbols of physical progress. They are momentum-building and pride-building. You can't move the city without physical splashes."

The city is providing plenty of encouragement. It has helped builders get hefty federal grants and produced a master plan to guide development. It has also enlarged the Cleveland convention hall and offered a twenty-year full tax abatement to encourage new hotel construction, hoping to turn Cleveland into a regional convention center. Attracting more revivifying downtown activity is only part of the benefit a convention industry would provide. Says council president Forbes: "It means young people can be hotel managers and desk clerks and cooks and waiters. They won't be making $20 an hour, but they damn sure can make $10." A city law sponsored by Forbes ensures that one-third of all jobs created with the help of a tax abatement or an urban development grant must go to minorities.

For Clevelanders aren't kidding about wanting to spread the benefits of recovery through the whole community. The Cleveland Tomorrow companies have provided $2.5 million, for example, to help an innovative organization buy and refurbish houses to sell to poor people on a lease-purchase plan. The corporate community and local charitable foundations are putting up $16 million to motivate disaffected public school students by offering scholarship money for good grades. To keep kids in school, companies offer hiring preference to graduates of Cleveland high schools. Says former BP America chief James Ross: "You've got to get to the social fabric of the city, or you have the politics of envy ruling. I don't believe that a BP can exist as a wealthy company in a society where you have such a substantial underclass that it will pull the whole structure down with it."

Listening to Clevelanders' earnest talk about how they are turning their town around, and looking at what they've accomplished, is an impressive, oddly moving experience—and not just because it's exhilarating to see people take their fate in their hands instead of complaining about irresistible, impersonal forces. Beyond that, you can't help thinking that *this* is what community is all about. Doubtless it sounds comic to speak of Clevelanders in the same breath as Athenians, but isn't this at least a little like what the Greeks meant by the civic ideal—the public life in which people achieve their fullest humanity?

Who Governs: The Corporate Hand

Roldo Bartimole

THE EYES of America were upon Cleveland in 1967 as this old, troubled, northern industrial city faced a historic mayoral election that would pit the great-grandson of a slave against the grandson of a president.

Elections can be looked upon from many perspectives, and certainly this election, during the stormy days of the civil rights movement, of Carl B. Stokes as the first black mayor of a major American city, was historic and the focus of national attention. Stokes's mayoralty represented only a brief interlude of black control of Cleveland City Hall, however, and control reverted to mayors of eastern European ancestry until the election of Michael R. White in 1989. Yet, despite the racial or ethnic background of individual mayors and the often brutal clashes of ethnic groups for control of political power, Cleveland over the last twenty-five years represents a classic study of the historic question in American city politics—who governs?

This essay provides a subjective view of big city politics in Cleveland viewed through twenty-five years of the mayoral terms of Ralph Locher, Carl Stokes, Ralph Perk, Dennis Kucinich, and Michael White. It argues that, despite who sat or sits in the mayor's chair—ethnic or black—from 1965 to 1993, the corporate community and institutions dominated by business interests decisively controlled the issues and dominated the public agenda, often to the detriment of ordinary Cleveland residents. Indeed, the managing partners of Cleveland's great law firms often seem to have more clout than the mayor.

Cleveland of the late nineteenth and early twentieth centuries produced an enormous concentration of wealth and power, exemplified by John D. Rockefeller, the Mathers, Hannas, Severances, and Boltons. It also produced a civic legacy of noblesse oblige—a strong social welfare system, cooperating foundations, and corporate-dominated charity committees—that has extended its hand into the present. Long before the 1960s, the wealthy had abandoned Cleveland as a place to live, but they left behind a sophisticated network of foundations and social institutions to do their bidding and protect their places of business and their rich cultural infrastructure. They also left behind a city whose production of wealth was declining sharply, bringing widespread poverty, crisis, and political upheaval.

The beginning of this era can be placed in the fall of 1964, when a school boycott successfully shut down the public school system and marked the growing political power of blacks. It also belatedly awakened the business community. John "Jack" Reavis, the managing partner of Jones, Day, Reavis and Pogue, Cleveland's largest (and now the nation's second largest) law firm, formed the Businessmen's Interracial Committee on Community Affairs (BICCA), the first of many mechanisms used by Cleveland's corporate community to quiet social unrest.

The election in 1965 was a three-way race among then incumbent Democratic mayor Ralph Locher, Republican Ralph J. Perk, and Carl B. Stokes running as an independent. Locher barely held City Hall as Stokes came within twenty-one hundred votes of staging an amazing upset. The 1965 race set the stage for Stokes's victory over Locher in the 1967 Democratic primary (Stokes ran as a Democrat because of promises of support from the national Democratic party). In the 1967 general election, Stokes defeated a member of the establishment and Jack Reavis's partner, Seth Taft, the grandson of President William H. Taft.

The Undermining of Mayor Ralph Locher

Crisis was commonplace during the two years between the 1965 and 1967 elections, and Mayor Locher was buffeted by the upheaval of civil rights aspirations and long-standing economic problems. The 1966 U.S. Civil Rights Commission hearings in Cleveland uncovered problems of poverty, poor housing, education, employment, and police misbehavior. Later that summer, five days of rioting exploded in Hough. Locher became the riots' victim.

The Hough riots had their roots in decisions made by corporate interests in the late 1950s and early 1960s, which sought to revive the economic boom days of Cleveland's past. The major focus of corporate interests—as it so often is in American cities—was the revitalization of the city's downtown under the federal urban renewal program. Cleveland was led by corporate interests into placing 6,060 acres of land into renewal projects, more than any other city in the nation. The renewal projects, which covered most of Cleveland's East Side, where blacks lived, were promoted by the Cleveland Development Foundation (CDF) created for that purpose by members of the corporate elite.

Money to pay for CDF's plans was readily available from various foundations, particularly the Leonard C. Hanna fund, administered by the Cleveland Foundation. CDF became in essence the city planning and urban renewal department for the city, subject to no public scrutiny. Though people believed the CDF was to help with serious urban problems, Edward "Pike" Sloan, a former chairman of Oglebay Norton Corporation and president of CDF, said, "It would be a mistake to think that the foundation ever had as its main concern housing. The main thing was to make land available for industrial and commercial use."[1]

Cleveland's city government did not have the resources to execute or manage the vast urban renewal projects pushed on it by CDF. The plans, particularly the St. Vincent and University-Euclid projects, displaced thousands of primarily black and poor residents. Many migrated to overcrowded Hough, fueling the 1966 riots. Said Tom Westropp, a banker, who also sat on the city's planning commission, "For some, the urban renewal program has worked very well, indeed. Hospitals and education institutions have been constructed and enlarged. So have commercial and industrial interests and many service organizations, all with the help of urban renewal dollars. With respect to housing, however, the urban renewal program has been a disaster. I wish I could believe that all of this was accidental and brought about by the inefficiency of well-meaning people—but I just can't. The truth, it seems to me, is that it was planned that way."[2] A federal urban renewal official in 1967 took an even dimmer view, comparing it to the Vietnam quagmire: "We'd like to get out but we don't know how."[3]

By early 1967, while President Lyndon B. Johnson promised to support Stokes, Housing and Urban Development secretary Robert Weaver took unprecedented action in denying any new renewal funds to Cleveland as the city's vast program ground to a halt. Stokes wrote later that "Locher's loss of federal funds gave us a chance to attack him at a most vulnerable point. When those attacks were coupled with my frequent and visible trips to Washington, it began to seem to people that President Johnson wanted Carl Stokes to be mayor of Cleveland."[4]

With business interests threatened by the funding shut-down, Ralph Besse, chairman of the local electric utility, the Cleveland Electric Illuminating Company, and a former partner of the city's second largest law firm, Squire, Sanders and Dempsey, offered to assist the city's urban renewal program. A series of meetings with Mayor Locher in early 1967 were not encouraging. Locher believed Besse was willing to offer help only on his own terms. Again in March, Besse offered the assistance of the business community, demanding a quid pro quo, the replacement of Locher's urban renewal director with Major General Stanley Connelly, director of Besse's Inner City Action Committee. Locher rejected the offer, and Besse severed relations with the administration to blazing headlines. The *Cleveland Plain Dealer* used its largest headline type on the top of page 1: "Besse's Inner-City Group Quits Locher."[5] It was a powerful blow.

In a bitter letter released publicly, Besse accused Locher of spurning help because of the administration's inadequate personnel and ineffective coordination. Locher hit back that the business community was not really interested in helping but wanted to take control over City Hall. The break with Besse added to the collapsing public confidence in the Locher administration.

Local and national foundations also played a role in undercutting Locher's administration. The Ford and Cleveland foundations funded the Greater Cleveland Associated Foundation (GCAF), a mechanism to deal with urban issues, because trustees of the Cleveland Foundation found involvement with such issues distasteful. The two foundations also provided support for various voter registration activities before the 1967 primary election.

Ford gave $127,000 to Reavis's BICCA committee; another $175,000 to the local Congress of Racial Equality for a voter registration drive; and $200,000 to GCAF for a program to work on problems of racism among ethnics. At about the same time, the Reverend Martin Luther King, Jr., announced that the Southern Christian Leadership Conference (SCLC) would begin a program in Cleveland to register voters, a program that had been planned for a year later. King said he would help register forty thousand blacks. SCLC spent $500,000 but never publicized the source of its funding.[6] Ford had granted SCLC $230,000 for staff training in 1967. Reavis's BICCA also presented SCLC with a $5,000 check.

Added to these well-publicized efforts were less publicized programs by corporate elites. Ralph Besse and other business leaders put together a private fund of some $40,000 for an under-the-table program, directed out of the Cleveland Foundation offices. Black militants were paid each week at the *Call and Post*, a weekly newspaper serving the black community, for patrolling the ghetto and preventing black violence. "Keep the peace for Carl" was the cry. The payments stopped the weekend after the Democratic primary, leading some to believe that the elites intended that Stokes defeat Locher and clear the way for Seth Taft, the Republican candidate and Jack Reavis's law partner, to win the general election. They apparently assumed that if Stokes won the primary, Taft would win the general election because race would determine the victor, and whites, at the time, far outnumbered black voters.

Indeed, as insurance, a second white Democrat, Frank Celeste, was entered into the race by business leaders, presumably to take white votes from Locher and aid Stokes's challenge. Celeste got only 8,500 votes: Stokes won by 18,700 votes, making Celeste's spoiler role inconsequential. Celeste was bankrolled by a $100,000 campaign fund which was led by Jack Reavis.

Republican lawyer Ralph Besse may have had another, more self-serving, reason for wanting Locher eliminated. Locher and his major white ethnic supporters were strong supporters of the city's municipal electric system (Muny Light), a competitor of Besse's Cleveland Electric Illuminating Company (CEI) and long a major bone of contention between city politicians and corporate leaders. CEI wanted to absorb the city's system and restore its monopoly. Stokes, indeed, made one of his campaign pledges to sell the city system, which at that time served few black citizens because of its geographical distribution. As mayor, Stokes did not deliver on his pledge.

Muny Light was to become a major campaign issue years later and a central factor in Cleveland's default in 1978, when Mayor Dennis J. Kucinich claimed bankers promised to renew a $14 million city bond issue only if Kucinich would sell Muny Light to CEI. Kucinich refused, and Cleveland Trust (later AmeriTrust) forced the city into default by calling the bonds for payment.

Another lawyer, James C. Davis, of Squire, Sanders and Dempsey, also helped discredit Locher with a widely covered speech to the Cleveland Bar Association in May 1967. Thousands of copies of his speech, entitled "Cleveland's White Problem—A Challenge to the Bar," were printed and distributed. Davis declared that he was "disturbed about the future climate of Cleveland as a place in which to practice law." He went on to blame the problems of Cleveland on white ethnic or "nationality groups."[7] This was another slap at Locher and his white ethnic supporters, as well as a bow toward rising black power.

Carl B. Stokes as Mayor

Stokes won the 1967 primary with 52 percent of the vote, winning by 18,000 votes over Locher. The general election was closer, Stokes upsetting the "smart money" and being declared the winner over Taft with a margin of less than 2,000 votes. Stokes received 129,396 and Taft 127,717, with 79 percent of the voters participating.

Cleveland's corporate community quickly took advantage of the positives of the Stokes victory. Here was a mayor who might avert another Hough riot (and maybe sell Muny Light to CEI). The Greater Cleveland Growth Association took full-page ads in the *Wall Street Journal* advertising Cleveland as an old blue-chip city with bright new leadership. The local Democratic party, still antagonistic to blacks, never took to Stokes, but the historic victory put Cleveland in the national spotlight, and the glare of attention demanded good behavior.

When Stokes personally walked the streets in early April 1968 and kept peace after the assassination of Martin Luther King, the business leadership could not have been more indebted. The result was a major program by Stokes called Cleveland Now. The newspapers treated it as if it were the solution to the problems of poverty and gave it positive headlines. It was planned as a $177 million program that was to work on all facets of city problems, particularly housing. Stokes saw the program as a way to draw Cleveland corporations into dealing with the social problems of the city. But it also contained the seeds of disaster when some of the same black militants who had been paid by the businessmen the summer before to "keep the peace for Carl" got money from Cleveland Now. In July 1969 a gun battle between the militants and police ended with three policemen and six civilians killed, rioting, and an order by Stokes to keep white police out of the Glenville area, scene of the gun battle. Funds used by the militants to buy weapons were traced to Cleveland Now. Business leaders who had embraced Stokes now shrank from controversy.

The funding of Cleveland Now, never really more than a cosmetic approach to solving the severe problems of the city, evaporated. In releasing the final report less than two years after it announced ten-year goals, Stokes called it only a "first step" and said that it "did not correct the deplorable housing situation . . . alter the city's unemployment problem . . . nor solve the crisis of the growing number of old, young, and handicapped people who find today's society continually harder for them."[8]

Privately, Stokes was more bitter. He felt the corporate leaders had deserted him and Cleveland and that they simply did not want conflict. With few exceptions, Stokes felt that they were more concerned about not rocking the boat than with seeking solutions. "He became more and more conscious of his blackness and this disturbed the business establishment," said his press secretary, who quotes Stokes retorting to the retrenchment of the business community, "I'm not going to be their house nigger."[9]

Stokes won another term in 1969, easily defeating a Democratic opponent in the primary, and then, in a close contest, overcoming county auditor Ralph J. Perk in the general election. Stokes got 120,464 votes to Perk's 117,013, with again a high turnout of 75 percent of the voters. But the hope that the first black mayor would make significant change dissipated in the gunfire in Glenville and the return to conventional politics.

In 1971, Stokes decided he would not run for a third term. Instead, he wanted a chief aide, Arnold Pinkney, to succeed him so a black would continue in the mayor's chair. Stokes's complicated strategy, however, proved ineffective, and Pinkney came in second to Ralph Perk. Perk was the beneficiary of the support of a popular Democratic councilman—Dennis Kucinich—who gave crucial support to Republican Perk in a predominantly Democratic city. Perk got 88,664 votes and Pinkney 74,085 with a 72 percent turnout.

Six Years of Mayor Ralph J. Perk

Perk, a Czech whose wife is Italian, marked a return of city hall to white, though Republican, ethnic hands. Cleveland's corporate leaders felt at home because they had long backed ethnic politicians with conservative views. As county auditor, Perk had long had a reputation of opposition to most any taxes, and his image of frugality fit the mood of Cleveland's strong white ethnic community, which had grated under the leadership of the flamboyant Stokes and a civil rights era that had begun to wane.

Ethnic control of City Hall, however, would not erase the political gains made by blacks. Indeed, both black political power and corporate entrée into public decision making grew strongly during the eight years of the Perk administration, as Perk maintained his position by sharing power with George L. Forbes, a former Stokes lieutenant who had become City Council president. Forbes was to become the longest serving council president in the city's history (1973–89) and possibly the most powerful and feared ever.

Through Perk's six-year term (1971–77), Perk and Forbes maintained power by cooperating in conventional city politics and sharing the political spoils. The problems of the city continued to cut away at its economic well-being as population and industrial jobs continued to decline and poverty continued to increase. The Perk administration—marked by a great diversity of interests from left reformers to some appointees allegedly affiliated with local organized crime elements—was a mishmash of performance.

Perk, whose image was carefully nurtured as a man of the people, simple and close to the grass roots, began to get fanciful ideas for his future. A disastrous run for the U.S. Senate in 1974 revealed an egotistical image and a movement away from his closeness to the "little people" who had elected him.

Perk's strong reliance on never asking for a tax increase forced him to seek financial resources elsewhere. He presided over the sale and transfer of many city assets. Lakefront parks went to the state of Ohio; for $32 million, quickly spent by Perk, the sewer system went to a regional authority; and the city's $70 million transit system also went regional. Debt began to be increased, leading to the misspending of capital bond funds for current general fund expenses, which eventually led to the city's default after Perk left office. Perk's reputation as a patsy of the business community grew. He began to see cracks in his own political base.

Perk tried to ingratiate himself with corporate interests and their continuing desire to revitalize downtown. Two issues hurt Perk badly and led to criticism by his old supporter, Kucinich. First, under pressure from business, Perk backed a policy of tax abatements for new downtown buildings, and second, in 1976 he reversed his long support for Muny Light and proposed to sell the system to its archfoe, CEI. In 1977, Perk pushed through two tax abatements, one to National City Bank and another for a new headquarters building for Standard Oil of Ohio (now BP America). The attempt to sell Muny was thwarted by Kucinich. Kucinich had his eager and always potent campaign staff hit the streets. He soon had collected thirty thousand signatures to put the issue on the ballot. Perk retreated, and the sale move was ended.

By 1977 Perk's image had been thoroughly tarnished. Popular and populist Dennis Kucinich, the youthful councilman, who had, as a Democrat, helped Perk get elected in 1971, was complaining about Perk's policies and had broken with the mayor. A renegade who often used the successful Cleveland political stratagem of being the political outside crusader for the "little people," Kucinich began to make plans to run for mayor himself. His issues were opposition to tax abatement and support for Muny Light.

Most observers thought that the nonpartisan primary election would be between Edward Feighan, a member of the Ohio House of Representatives, and Kucinich for the second spot and a run-off against Mayor Perk. But surprisingly, in a heated primary, Perk failed to make the cutoff, finishing behind Feighan and Kucinich, both of whom had attacked Perk and his willingness to sell Muny Light.

With Feighan, also a strong supporter of Muny Light, in the race, Kucinich needed another issue. Tax abatement became that issue. Feighan, as a state representative, had chaired the committee that passed the tax abatement enabling legislation in the Ohio House and could not erase his support for abatements.

Urban Populism and "Destabilization" under Dennis J. Kucinich

In a close race, Kucinich won by 3,000 votes (Kucinich 93,047, Feighan 90,074 with a 64 percent turnout) to become the fifty-second and youngest mayor of Cleveland. His brief tenure (1977–79) became the most explosive two-year term for any mayor in Cleveland history. It was marked by an attempted recall election, a vote on an income tax increase, and a referendum on the sale of Muny Light. Kucinich won them all in the face of enormous opposition.

No local politician so touched the nerve of leadership-starved Clevelanders as did Dennis Kucinich when he became mayor. A willing symbol of anticorporate resistance, Kucinich unabashedly pushed his way onto the front pages of the nation's major newspapers and nudged his image onto national television, even luring late night talk show host Tom Snyder's TV show to Kucinich's then favorite working-class diner, Tony's. His flamboyant popularity caused dismay among Cleveland's stodgy corporate leadership.

Kucinich attracted attention by doing the unexpected, poking his finger into the belly and face of corporate Cleveland over important decisions. He had successfully thwarted the sale of Muny Light and actively continued an antitrust suit in federal court against CEI, claiming damages of a third of a billion dollars. He ended tax abatements by refusing to sign legislation for new projects. He fought public subsidies for an iron-ore dock, dearly desired by Republic Steel. Business interests found themselves frustrated at every turn by Kucinich, who proudly proclaimed a "new urban Populism."

Kucinich was invited to the National Press Club in 1978 to expound on his Cleveland experience. He stated his philosophy in pre-Reagan Washington: "You may have noticed that I didn't touch on any of the great debates over social issues. The basis of genuine reform is economic reform. We can solve economic problems if we refuse to be distracted. The failure of courage among reformers to attempt to mobilize popular support for basic economic issues which challenge the economic interests of big business dooms their efforts to failure. The substitution of social issues in place of economic issues trifles with people's problems. Trifling with social issues evades our responsibilities to face economic issues. It diminishes the potential of economic issues to rally popular support."[10]

Business leaders did not like the populist rhetoric of Kucinich's philosophy. They were determined to fight it to the end. With political allies, led by council president Forbes, and with a well-disposed news media, particularly the *Cleveland*

Plain Dealer, Kucinich became Public Enemy No. 1. For his part, Kucinich seemed to cooperate in creating a siege mentality in Cleveland during this period.

Business leaders formed a united front against Kucinich, revealing how private interests can call upon informal networks of power to exercise extreme political clout. Playing a game of political checkmate, with Forbes's help, the business leaders conducted a political civil war with the Kucinich administration. The climax was a battle over a $14 million bank loan made during the Perk administration. Cleveland Trust had rolled over (renewed) the loan automatically during the Perk administration. Now, Cleveland Trust said it wanted payment in full.

At the same time, a well-connected, highly political Republican federal judge ordered the administration to pay contested debts of some $15 million owed by Muny Light to CEI. The debts were part of long-contested bills charged by CEI for electric power bought by Muny Light. Although cheaper power was available, CEI surrounded Muny's territory and refused to "wheel" (essentially the transfer of electric power over lines to another utility) power through its lines from other electric companies willing and able to provide the city's system with much cheaper power. Eventually, the U.S. Nuclear Regulatory Agency found CEI guilty for refusal to "wheel" and ordered it to do so.

CEI began to tag city property, claimed to meet the debt. Kucinich chose to begin paying the debt, making it increasingly clear that he could not possibly repay the bank loans by the December 15, 1978, deadline. In a dramatic final day, the closed-door negotiations among council, administration officials, and business leaders all failed, and as the clock ticked away past midnight, Cleveland slid into default.

Kucinich claimed that in a closed-door meeting, on the morning of December 15, the chief executive officer of Cleveland Trust and his political allies offered him a deal: sell Muny Light to CEI and the loans would be rolled over. Further, Cleveland banks would then provide the city with $50 million in new financing. Kucinich refused. Observers said Kucinich had been "destabilized," much as the Central Intelligence Agency had "destabilized" the Allende regime in Chile in the 1970s.

The default case dramatically raised the question of who governs? Right or wrong, Kucinich had challenged the invisible government, that finely textured network of institutions which establishes the community agenda to fit the desires of those who hold economic power. Kucinich had gone beyond conventional political rhetoric, actually challenging the informal decision making of the business oligarchy. To survive, he had been forced to win three elections within his two-year term, just to assert the legitimacy that he was supposed to have won by his original election.

Ten years later, Cleveland's business establishment took credit for usurping the political will of the people of Cleveland in a fanciful paean to itself in the March 27, 1989, *Fortune* magazine. The piece, entitled "How Business Bosses Saved a Sick City," more clearly than any textbook told a story of who really governs.

Cleveland's business leaders boasted that they had led a renaissance of the city by ridding it of Kucinich and urban populism and returning the city to an agenda espoused by business leaders. *Fortune* quotes Richard Pogue, a successor to Jack Reavis as managing partner of Jones, Day, Reavis and Pogue: "In a sense, Kucinich was the best thing that ever happened because he became a unifying element. People looked at him and said, 'Enough is enough here. Let's get together and change things.'"

The next paragraph makes clear the warlike mind-set of the Cleveland establishment when challenged by the "rabble" of Cleveland: "E. Mandell de Windt, the now retired CEO of Eaton Corporation and unofficial dean of Cleveland businessmen, organized the troops and devised a strategy, setting in motion a benign conspiracy of executives and entrepreneurs that still operates. The impressive feat of organizing that cabal and persuading Cleveland's most senior businessmen to take charge of the grittiest aspects of civic life was the real key to the town's turnabout." The author had undoubtedly been touched by the flavor of a coup, as related by the businessmen who had participated in essentially the overthrow of a duly elected government.

To replace Kucinich, the businessmen chose Republican George V. Voinovich, in 1990 elected governor of Ohio but then another of the ethnic politicians with conservative backgrounds cultivated by corporate Cleveland.Voinovich was then Ohio lieutenant governor and had a reputation for running for higher office as soon as he won an election. He had been a state representative, county auditor, and county commissioner and had run unsuccessfully in the past for mayor in Republican primaries. Despite his political leanings, in 1977 he had endorsed Kucinich for mayor.

Now he had plenty of financial aid and business support to end the Kucinich administration. In the primary, Voinovich outpolled Kucinich, 47,000 to 36,000, with three other candidates splitting another 40,000 votes. Everyone expected a bruising battle in which Kucinich would slam Voinovich as the candidate of big business. "I like Fat Cats" was Voinovich's reply. But a few days after the primary, Voinovich's nine-year-old daughter was struck by a van and killed, essentially bringing the campaign to a halt. Kucinich never had the time or the opportunity to continue the slashing attack upon the bereaved Voinovich. Voinovich, in a turnout of only 56 percent, won with 94,541 votes to Kucinich's 73,755.

"Normalcy" Returns under Mayor George V. Voinovich

Voinovich welcomed special task forces of corporate volunteers to help straighten out the city's various functions, including a state controlling board that could oversee the city's finances as a result of the default. But Voinovich moved cautiously on some of the issues that had propelled Kucinich to office and still retained strong support in the community. Voinovich continued to support the legal case brought against CEI until it was lost by the city. The trials had gained support for Muny Light, and Voinovich moved to improve its service. Voinovich avoided tax abatements, including an abatement for the new Sohio (now BP America) headquarters on Public Square. Sohio had been given a tax abatement for its headquarters during the Perk administration but had not built on its designated site. Now it moved to a new site and never sought an abatement.

Voinovich, who served from 1979 to 1989, was a low-key politician who avoided confrontation. Instead of fighting with the all-Democratic City Council, he shared power with council president George Forbes to maintain peace. He had little trouble winning reelection in 1981 and 1985.

Indeed, as the years passed, many believed Forbes was the real mayor while Voinovich played a mainly ceremonial role. Forbes maintained power from 1973 through 1989, when, after Voinovich decided to run for governor, Forbes sought the mayor's seat himself. Voinovich was elected; Forbes was defeated.

Forbes had built his power during a period when federal funds, particularly through community development block grants (CDBG), flowed to the city. Voinovich, during much of this period, allowed Forbes the major voice in distribution of those funds. Forbes, as wily a politician as ever held office, carefully distributed funds to maintain power among his council members. During the ten-year Voinovich-Forbes era, for example, more than $34 million was spent on sidewalks and curbings. Other CDBG funds went to various social service agencies, often controlled by Forbes's loyal council members.

Meanwhile, the city's housing and neighborhoods declined dramatically. Poverty, according to the Council for Economic Opportunities in Greater Cleveland, increased 49 percent during the Voinovich reign to give the city a 40.6 percent poverty rate in 1991. In one neighborhood, the Kinsman area, 83 percent of the population lived in poverty. No Cleveland East Side neighborhood had a 1991 poverty rate lower than 23 percent. Since 1979, said the report, more than sixty-two thousand factory worker jobs had disappeared from Cleveland, taking with them an annual $2.8 billion reduction in local manufacturing production earnings. The report also noted that "the real estate sales value of the average Cuyahoga County home declined by 30 percent between 1979 and 1987" at a time of rapid housing inflation in the rest of the United States. Cleveland's population dropped another 12 percent during the 1980s and in 1990 barely exceeded five hundred thousand, a 45 percent drop since 1950.[11]

Though business leaders had bought political peace with Voinovich and Forbes, despair in the city over the operation of its major institutions, from the school system to the public housing authority, to the regional transit system, had only increased and solidified. The result was an increased exodus from the city.

Despite the increasing poverty and the spreading deterioration, business leaders continued their campaign to force a renaissance centered in downtown. Business leaders wanted to take advantage of a mayor they could trust. As the *Fortune* magazine article put it, "Cleveland's CEO conspiracy led the economic as well as the political turnaround," resulting in a new mechanism, Cleveland Tomorrow, that brought together the top fifty corporate leaders to push economic development in Cleveland.

The result was the fiction of "Comeback City," heralded nationwide by another corporate-created institution, the New Cleveland Campaign, with ads in national publications and a public relations campaign that led to such articles as the one in *Fortune*.

The "comeback" rested heavily on massive tax abatements, as Voinovich in the late 1980s changed policy toward downtown abatement about the same time he began seeking heavy contributions to run for the U.S. Senate against Senator Howard Metzenbaum.

With Forbes in firm control of the City Council, Voinovich gave some $250 million in tax abatements to two major complexes, both on Public Square, where Sohio had built several years before without abatement. The new developments—both offices for banks, one AmeriTrust Center, the other Society Center—were projects of Jacobs, Visconsi and Jacobs, and each included a hotel, a longtime dream of business leaders thirsting to make Cleveland a tourist mecca.

Other tax gimmicks followed, including a new form, tax increment financing (TIF), that would divert 75 percent of property taxes to help finance other private and nonprofit ventures. The most significant TIF took tax revenue from another Public Square project, Tower City, diverting all new tax revenue to a proposed Rock 'n Roll Hall of Fame. Tower City, a combined renewal and new construction project, has become the center of downtown shopping, attracting luxury retail outlets. It included a full-tax-abated Ritz-Carlton Hotel. The Tower City TIF transferred about $42 million in property taxes away from the public schools toward the construction of the Rock Hall, another heavily publicly subsidized entity highly desired by corporate leaders.

Having spent sixteen years as the powerful president of the City Council, Forbes decided to cap his career by formally assuming the office and power most people believed he had actually held under Mayors Voinovich and Perk. Forbes had spent those sixteen years representing a ward of some twenty-two thousand, almost all black, constituents. He had fashioned his political career as a black politician. Now he wanted to be the mayor of all Cleveland's people, many of whom he had insulted by some action or word during the years. He carried additional baggage as someone who delivered for downtown interests, to the detriment of neighborhoods and their residents.

Forbes got solid support from the elites who had backed Voinovich. He found himself in a race with several potentially potent white candidates and one black candidate, Michael White, a former business partner and political ally when he served in the City Council. White had moved to the Ohio Senate, an appointment originally engineered by Forbes for his political friend. White, who had been promised Forbes's support before Forbes decided to run himself, refused to move over for his mentor.

White proved to be a more formidable competitor than anyone thought. As in the 1977 race, the primary election provided a surprise. Forbes and White finished first and second, and for the first time in the city's history, two black politicians faced off in a general election. Whites voted more than 80 percent for White, who gathered enough black votes to win the mayor's office. White got 86,112 votes to Forbes's 68,429, with a 53 percent turnout.

Mayor Michael White: Changing the Guard?

White campaigned strongly as a progressive who saw the need to turn public attention back to the neighborhoods. Though he did not spurn future downtown development, he did give people the hope that long-neglected problems of the city's neighborhoods would be addressed. In practice, however, the new mayor set a course not much different from the Voinovich-Forbes record. He quickly showed the establishment that he saw progress in much the same way it did by providing vigorous support for many subsidized downtown developments. Some of this support came from CDBG money that could have been used for neighborhood housing. That action did not match White's inaugural rhetoric that called for the city to show the nation how to deal with the problem of homelessness. "We must treat it as a disaster," he had said.[12]

Even those moves paled against what White did next. Having promised no new taxes and to pay attention to the problems of low-income housing and declining neighborhoods, White led a campaign to pass a $275 million regressive "sin" tax on liquor, beer, wine, and cigarettes to build a new baseball stadium and basketball arena for the Cleveland Indians and the Cleveland Cavaliers. White campaigned for the tax as vigorously as he had campaigned to become mayor. It passed countywide, though the vote in the city was strongly negative. Nearly two to one, Clevelanders voted against the tax, with only one ward—an affluent far West Side ward—approving the measure.

In his campaign to sell the sin tax, White promised sixteen thousand permanent jobs and tax revenues for the neighborhoods. He promised to forbid any tax abatement to the stadium and arena and to benefit the Cleveland schools with $15.6 million in "additional" taxes. A year after the vote, White went to Columbus to plead with state representatives to award a tax abatement in perpetuity to the stadium and arena, again breaking his pledge and aligning himself with the agenda of those old corporate business interests that have long set the public agenda of this major American city.

Who governs? When Mayor White celebrated his fortieth birthday with a fundraiser in his second year of office, the co-sponsors of the event were heavy with the names of Cleveland's major business leaders. Leading them was the strong supporter of George Forbes, White's opponent in the 1989 election, Dick Pogue, managing partner of Jones, Day, Reavis and Pogue, who had followed, obviously, in the footsteps of his predecessor at Jones, Day, Jack Reavis.

Notes

1. *Cleveland Development Foundation: A Review* (New York: The Ford Foundation, 1964).

2. *The Cleveland Papers* (Cleveland: The Illuminating Company, a Cleveland Radical Research Group, 1972), 42.

3. "Cleveland: Recipe for Violence," *The Nation,* June 26, 1967, 814–17.

4. Carl B. Stokes, *Promises of Power: A Political Autobiography* (New York: Simon and Schuster, 1973), 97.

5. *Cleveland Plain Dealer,* February 1, 1967.

6. *Cleveland Papers,* 18.

7. James C. Davis, "Cleveland's White Problem—A Challenge to the Bar," *Cleveland Bar Journal,* April 1967.

8. *Cleveland Press,* March 23, 1970.

9. Roldo Bartimole, "Keeping the Lid On: Corporate Responsibility in Cleveland," *Business and Society Review* 5 (Spring 1973): 103.

10. *Cleveland Plain Dealer,* September 29, 1978.

11. Council for Economic Opportunities in Greater Cleveland, *Poverty Indicators, Vol. 9, 1991,* 20; U.S. Bureau of the Census, Department of Commerce, *Census of Population and Housing, 1990.*

12. Mayor Michael White, Inaugural address, "A Vision For A New Decade," January 1, 1990.

Part 6

NEIGHBORHOODS
City and Suburbs

Introduction

Like comparable American cities, Cleveland became a city of neighborhoods. Urban historian Edward Miggins presents a graphic account of the development of ethnic villages in Cleveland as it was transformed from a commercial to an industrial city. The first two immigrant groups to follow the New England settlers of the Western Reserve were the Germans and the Irish. They were followed after the American Civil War by waves of immigrants from eastern and southern Europe. World War I and postwar legislation ended mass migration from Europe. Then came the Great Migration of African Americans from the black belt north to cities like Cleveland, seen by the rural black poor as the promised land. Miggins explains the ethnic and racial rivalries among these groups, vying for jobs and a better life in Cleveland. Describing the central city's decline with the resulting deterioration of the city's neighborhoods as post–World War II suburbanization almost halved the city's population, Miggins concludes with reference to the rise of a neighborhood movement in the 1970s which has attempted to arrest this decline.

Claudia Coulton and Julian Chow address the modern form of poverty that afflicts contemporary Cleveland, different from the poverty that faced the immigrants, which Miggins describes, and the temporary poverty of the Great Depression of the 1930s. They identify the spread of poverty into more neighborhoods (including some older suburban communities) and the persistence of high rates of poverty in many Cleveland neighborhoods. They analyze the many negative impacts of poverty on inner-city neighborhoods and their residents.

Mittie O. Chandler addresses public housing in Cleveland, which was originally transitional housing meant to replace cleared slum areas and to shelter the deserving poor only temporarily displaced, and has become housing of the last resort for the nonmobile poor. In Cleveland, this group has increasingly become African Americans, especially female-headed households and the elderly. The projects, several dating to the 1930s, are located in some of the city's poorest neighborhoods, badly need repairs and improved maintenance, and have very high vacancy rates. Chandler details the origins and gradual decline of public housing in

Cleveland, especially since the 1960s, as neighborhoods and their political representatives opposed the development of new public housing, fearing an influx of the poor, particularly when the neighborhoods were white and feared an infusion of poor, black residents.

Chandler explains how, despite a 1972 federal court order mandating racial integration in newly built public housing, political opposition and the drastic cutbacks in funding in federal support for new public housing since 1980 have combined to prevent effective implementation of the decision. Likewise, she recounts how Cleveland's public housing authority failed in its effort in the 1970s to force suburbs to cooperate and provide at least some low-income housing throughout the metropolitan area. She analyzes the politics of exclusion which have mostly denied Cleveland's poor decent housing in most of the city's neighborhoods and confined them to an isolated existence with little prospect of future improvement.

Thomas E. Bier describes the decline of the city's housing and residential neighborhoods since 1950. He analyzes how federally subsidized housing, insurance "redlining," and highways helped to fuel the tremendous exodus from the city to the suburbs through the 1970s. This trend continued in the 1980s, abetted by the relocation of employment to suburban office corridors and industrial parks and the flight of whites opposed to racial transition in their neighborhoods and court-ordered desegregation of Cleveland's public schools in 1977.

Bier explains how housing filtering, combined with economic transformation and suburbanization, has emptied out many inner-city neighborhoods, leaving a surplus housing stock, much of which is vacant and deteriorating. At the same time, overbuilding of new housing in the outer ring of newer suburbs, aided by federal and state subsidies for housing ownership, infrastructure, and roads, has acted as a magnet for even greater suburban dispersal of the population in metropolitan Cleveland. The result is an eroding tax base, declining population, and deteriorating neighborhoods in the city of Cleveland, despite several decades of attempts at redevelopment. Bier argues that only regional planning can prevent the further weakening not only of the city of Cleveland but also of adjacent older suburbs, which are beginning to lose population and are declining in comparison to newer suburbs located on the fringes of the metropolitan area.

Between Spires and Stacks: The People & Neighborhoods of Cleveland

Edward M. Miggins

Growth of Cleveland

BETWEEN THE Civil War and the Great Depression America's commercial cities located in the North and dependent on retail trade, agriculture, and commerce, were transformed into industrial metropolises. This transition was achieved by rapid spatial, socioeconomic, and demographic expansion. In 1886, an observer was amazed at the growth of Cleveland, Ohio, into a "great manufacturing city": "The old Pasture grounds of the cows of 1850 are now completely occupied by oil refineries and manufacturing establishments, and the river, which but a generation ago flowed peaceful and placid through green fields, is now almost choked with barges, tugs and immense rafts. The whole valley shows a black background, lit up with a thousand points of light from factories, foundries, and steam boats, which are multiplied into two thousand as they are reflected in the waters of the Cuyahoga, which looks like a silver ribbon flowing from the darkness."[1]

The account left out the smoking chimneys of the factories and commercial businesses in the Flats area along the river and the spires of nearby churches serving the spiritual needs of immigrant workers. Between the "spires and stacks" were the neighborhoods that segmented the city's people into areas defined by social class and nationality background—the social mosaic of modern cities like Cleveland. The social and economic forces that created this urban landscape had transformed the city from its first stage as a rural outpost of transplanted New Englanders into a commercial-industrial city with a large foreign-born population.[2]

The commercial city—the second stage of Cleveland's economic development—depended on its location on the Great Lakes and the Cuyahoga River, agriculture, and trade. Its success as a mercantile community in the antebellum era was also based on a transportation revolution that linked the area to the surrounding region and nation and the arrival of immigrant workers. The city's third phase as an industrial center consisted of enormous growth of its manufacturing establishments, foreign-born population, and physical size. Today, Cleveland is witnessing another stage with the decline of its industrial base, blue-collar jobs, and central city population as service industries and suburbs dominate the region. All phases of its development overlapped and connected to one another.[3] Changes in the size and composition of the city's population played a key role during its different phases of social and economic evolution from a rural village to an industrial metropolis.

The Ohio Canal, opened to Portsmouth in 1832, accelerated the growth of lake traffic, wholesale and retail trade, and population. The village grew from five hundred to five thousand people between 1825 and 1837. The temporary influx of approximately five hundred Irish immigrants as canal workers was the harbinger of demographic changes that would lead a writer to suggest later that Cleveland should change its title from the "Forest City" to the "Foreign City."[4]

Between 1830 and 1840, Cleveland's population increased from 1,365 to 6,071 inhabitants, or over 400 percent—the greatest decennial increase in the city's history.[5] It is estimated that the village's population was overwhelmingly native-born (96 percent) in 1830. In 1836, Ohio incorporated it as a city. The growth of commercial activity attracted foreign immigrants and changed its household population to 25 percent foreign-born by the end of the decade. As the population expanded, social and economic differences gradually segmented the neighborhoods as people either were forced or chose to associate with others of their own background.

Elegant homes of merchant capitalists appeared along ridges overlooking the lake and river. Charitable workers from churches and philanthropic organizations, supported by the city's elite, began to visit the homes of impoverished families in immigrant neighborhoods in the Flats area along the river.

Germans and Irish

New Englanders and other native stock from surrounding areas and the Northeast constituted the majority of Cleveland's population of forty-three thousand in 1860. Twenty-two percent were foreign-born. Approximately eight hundred African Americans also lived in the city. Germans made up 33 and Irish 22 percent of the immigrant population as Cleveland attracted both skilled and unskilled workers for its burgeoning job market. They built a network of churches, schools, and fraternal organizations to help them survive in the New World.

German and Irish groups demanded neighborhood or territorial churches which celebrated their ethnic life or customs and clashed with Bishop Amadeus Rappe, who favored Americanization. He resigned over the issue in 1870. Each nationality group resisted the forces of assimilation into the mainstream of Anglo-Saxon America. The Irish were famous for their impoverished ghettos in Whiskey Island, Irishtown Bend on the Cuyahoga River, and the Angle located from West 25th and Washington streets down to the river. But escapees from the Irish potato famine, who worked as unskilled day laborers on the ore docks, could proudly point to the construction of St. Malachi's Church (1870) in the Angle and St. Patrick's Church (1853) on Bridge Avenue in Ohio City.[6]

The Irish feared the domination of the Protestant religion in the Cleveland public education system, which took over the Ragged School after its incorporation in 1836. Established by the Bethel (House of God) Union Church in the Flats, this Sunday school found it necessary to teach impoverished immigrant children (dressed in ragged clothes) how to read the Bible. The tradition of reading the Protestant Bible continued in the public schools and influenced Irish Catholics and other nationality groups to establish a parochial school system.[7] Edwin Cowles, the editor of the *Leader,* attacked the "popery" and the political loyalties of the Irish.[8]

Equally suspicious in the eyes of many native-born Clevelanders was the growth of another large foreign-born group, which also maintained their own nationality culture against the attacks of Anglophile reformers or critics and nativist hatred. Between 1840 and 1846, German immigrants constituted one-third of the city's demographic growth. Taking advantage of the new railway system, German refugees escaping the political and economic turmoil of their homeland increased the community's size to 2,590 people by the end of the decade—almost equal to that of all other foreign groups combined. Their previous background as skilled workers allowed them to find similar occupations in Cleveland. Lacking the religious homogeneity of the Irish Catholic population, Germans supported a variety of Catholic or Protestant churches, fraternal organizations, and nationality schools.

The Germans supported the construction of St. Peter's Church (1854) on East 17th Street and Superior Avenue and St. Joseph's Church (1857) on Woodland Avenue. After worshiping at St. Mary's in the Flats, which first served the Irish working on the canal, the city's West Side Germans built St. Mary of the Assumption in 1865. The Turnverein Society, a fraternal organization, held its first meetings at Huron Road and Ontario Street on Cleveland's East Side in 1849. A wide variety of nationality newspapers and gymnastic and musical societies also maintained the German community's heritage during the antebellum era of social and economic expansion.[9]

Cleveland grew for several reasons in the 1850s. Its next-door rival, Ohio City—the home of most of the city's Germans and Irish—was annexed in 1854. Commercial activity dramatically increased with another addition to the transportation revolution—the steam locomotive. By the outbreak of the Civil War, several railroads served the city and changed the focus of long-distance trade from a north-south to an east-west direction.[10]

Cleveland was now able to take advantage of its strategic position midway between the rich iron-ore deposits discovered in Minnesota and Michigan and the coal deposits in southern Ohio, western Pennsylvania, and West Virginia. Lake traffic between the Great Lakes was facilitated by the construction of the Sault Sainte Marie Canal to link Lake Michigan and Lake Erie in 1856.

The coal and ore from these regions became the catalyst for growth in another major industry. William Otis, a former resident of Massachusetts and descendant of James Otis of revolutionary war fame, found that the demand for new metals exceeded the supply of iron ore from Ohio's Trumbull and Mahoning counties. But Cleveland's steamboats shipped more than enough iron ore from the upper Great Lakes to solve his problem. He expanded his ironworks and established a rolling mill on Whiskey Island, located to the west of the mouth of the Cuyahoga River. In 1857, David and John Jones started the Cleveland Rolling Mill in Newburgh, next to the Cleveland-Pittsburgh Railway, to produce iron rails. Sam Mather, a son of the prominent Mather family of Massachusetts, founded Cleveland Iron Company, later named Cleveland Cliffs, and personally arrived with the first boat of iron ore in 1854.[11]

The Civil War

The Civil War accelerated Cleveland's population and economic growth as the city became a major supplier for the Union army. From 1860 to 1865, Cleveland's population increased 50 percent—a proportional increase greater than that of any other northern city. At the war's end, it had fifteen foundries and fourteen steel rolling mills to satisfy the local and national demand for rails, structural beams, bridges, and pipes. Led by John D. Rockefeller, a graduate of Cleveland's Central High School, the city became the oil refining capital of America. He first built a refinery at Kingsbury Run above the Cuyahoga next to the Atlantic and Great Western Railroad, which ran directly to the oil fields of western Pennsylvania. Capitalizing on the demand for kerosene, he pioneered the purchase of all industries involved in the production of oil and merged his competitors into Standard Oil Company, founded in 1870. The city's skyline could count the smokestacks of eighty-six refineries in 1884, representing an investment of over $27 million. The development of the internal combustion engine eventually made gasoline the most important product of the oil industry.[12]

By 1870, Germans (15,855), Irish (11,964), English (4,522), and Czechs (3,252) were the largest foreign-born groups. By 1880, the immigrant population totaled 59,409 out of a population of 160,146 residents. Cleveland's economic growth in the post–Civil War era required a greater number of workers than was available from either the native-born people or immigrants from northern and western Europe. A Cleveland newspaper strongly advocated the recruitment of immigrants as the answer to the city's labor shortage.[13] Private corporations organized large-scale recruitment of laborers at the end of the Civil War through hired labor agents and organizations such as the Emigrant Company.

The New Immigrants from Europe

Throughout the nineteenth century, the federal government practiced an open-door policy, except for the Chinese Exclusion Act of 1882, to encourage foreign newcomers. Like other industrial cities, Cleveland became the home for the "new immigrants" from eastern, southern, and central Europe. As Oscar Handlin, the historian, stated: "The European movement started in the peasant heart of Europe."[14] Substantial numbers preferred the risk of leaving to the uncertainties and pain of remaining behind in their homelands. Faced with rising population, poverty, oppressive taxes, and political or religious tyranny, millions of European people began to see America as the solution to their problems. Steamship lines also made safe and inexpensive passage increasingly available after 1870.

The immigrant ordeal started as soon as the decision was made to move. In addition to the strain of uprooting themselves from their homeland, they faced weeks of travel, hardship, and expense along with the distant possibility that many might fail to reach their destinations. After their perilous voyage and grueling experience at Ellis Island, the depot established in New York Harbor in 1892 to control the flood of immigration to America, foreign-born people often found themselves wondering how much exaggeration was contained in those glowing letters and reports about their new homeland.[15]

Described as the "new immigrants" because they arrived later and came from areas outside northern and western Europe, twenty-three million foreign newcomers arrived in America between 1880 and 1919. As they moved westward, they joined their predecessors from northern and western Europe to swell the population of cities like Cleveland, Detroit, Chicago, Milwaukee, and other regional centers in the Midwest. By the 1920s, 75 percent of the population in these urban areas was either foreign-born or the children of immigrants.[16] America increasingly became, as Walt Whitman had described it before the Civil War, a "nation of nations."

Cleveland's population of foreign-born residents increased from 54,409 in 1880 to 97,095 in 1890. Between 1870 and 1890, the German population almost doubled to reach 39,893. The number of Irish increased from 11,958 in 1880 to 13,512 people in 1890. The English grew from 7,565 to 10,621 residents but declined from third to fourth place during that decade because the Czechs barely outnumbered them. Canadians reached a population of 8,611 by 1900, but older groups of northern Europeans were soon overshadowed by newcomers from eastern and southern Europe.

The new immigrants increased in number from 21,073 in 1890 to 43,281 in 1900 and from 115,870 in 1910 to 170,198 in 1920. The older groups declined by 2,436 in the first decade after the turn of the century. Newer groups accounted for three-fourths of the foreign-born. The Slavic nationalities of the Austro-Hungarian Empire, Hungarians, Russian Jews, and Italians were the leaders of this influx.[17]

The increase of the foreign-born kept pace with the growth of Cleveland between 1870 and 1910. They accounted for one out of three persons at each decennial enumeration. While Cleveland's population increased sixfold in this period, the foreign-born group quadrupled to a total population of 196,170 in a city with 560,663 people by 1910.

Clevelanders took pride in its demographic growth for, like smoking chimneys, it symbolized progress. New factories and businesses arrived as a result of the abundance of low-cost fuel, power, and water, a supply of trained workers, a burgeoning population of inexpensive immigrant laborers, and proximity to materials and markets. The automobile was another link in its transportation network and added to its local industrial base. Although Detroit eventually became the leading manufacturer of automobiles, Cleveland was a major producer of cars, trucks, and auto parts. The city also thrived with foundry and machine shops, clothing establishments, brick and textile businesses, and chemical, steel, and lithographing plants.

By 1900, Cleveland was the largest city and the industrial heart of Ohio. Twenty years later, its population totaled 796,841, making it the fifth largest city in America. Rapid growth of Cleveland's population had accompanied and made possible its economic development into an industrial metropolis. By 1930, manufacturing employed 33 percent of the city's work force, or approximately 181,000 people, a fourfold increase since the turn of the century.[18]

After the Civil War, Euclid Avenue became known as Millionaires' Row because wealthy industrialists and commercial entrepreneurs built elegant mansions overlooking Lake Erie. Many of the new foreign groups, like their Irish predecessors, lived in the poorest sections of the city, closest to their places of work. Cleveland's more affluent and older groups, assisted by the interurban trolley line, gradually moved to streetcar suburbs such as Glenville or Hough on the city's East Side. By 1910, all but one of the city's five leading nationality groups were from the new immigrants. Many were recruited by labor agents, newspaper advertisements, or affected by the "American fever" in their homelands.

Like previous groups from Europe, Cleveland's new immigrants were attracted by economic opportunities, social or political freedom, and the presence of early settlers from their homeland.

Ethnic Villages

The ethnic neighborhoods of immigrant newcomers cushioned the difficulties of living in a foreign, often hostile, country. They eased the painful process of adjustment and assimilation, for many of the new immigrants were poor, illiterate, rural peasants, unable to speak English. They would become, like their Irish predecessors, a ghettoized people, but their neighborhoods provided the social and cultural resources to withstand the harsh realities of a highly competitive, individualistic, and industrialized society.

As a Slovenian writer who grew up on Cleveland's southeast side later remarked, "The neighborhoods provided the early immigrants with a buffer zone, a place of shelter among their own kind to insulate them from the cultural shocks of the larger society."[19] Foreign newcomers could find familiar churches, cultural traditions, stores, and people who shared the same language, customs, and values—an island in a foreign ocean threatening to drown them.

By the turn of the century, their ethnic enclaves or "villages" added to the rich cultural variety of Cleveland's social mosaic: Warszawa or Little Poland, Big and Little Italy, Goose Town, the Cabbage Patch, Chicken Village, Cuba, and the Ghetto. Often immigrants from southern and eastern Europe took over areas vacated by older groups as their neighborhoods grew between the spires and stacks of industrial Cleveland.[20]

Perhaps the most infamous neighborhood at the turn of the century in Cleveland was the Haymarket, an area southwest of Public Square on lower Central and Ontario avenues. Named after the site where farmers sold their hay before the Civil War, it also became known as the Baghdad on the Cuyahoga because of the multiplicity of foreign tongues spoken by its inhabitants. The presence of over thirty nationalities in the neighborhood's public schools indicated its rich diversity. Filled with boardinghouses and tar-papered shacks, without water or sanitation facilities, on streets running down to the Cuyahoga River, it became the first home for many impoverished immigrants and migrants, "birds of passage," who wanted to live cheaply and return home with their earnings, and injured or elderly workers.

A report on Cleveland's "alien" colonies remarked how "pitiful" was the sight of half-naked children lying in the alleys or seeking shelter under a wagon or car, as well as people sleeping on roofs to escape the summer heat in the Haymarket. He contended: "Any Clevelander can appreciate his home twenty fold if he will but spend a few hours in going through this congested district. . . . We see here, the ideal sweat shop, the father and mother 'sewing on' cheap garments at poor pay with possibly one or more children ill and in bed in the same room and the whole surrounded by dirt and filth."[21]

Immigrant Pioneers and Brokers

Many of Cleveland's foreign colonies or ethnic neighborhoods began when immigrant pioneers first settled in an area. Like early settlers from New England, they developed economic and social networks to attract and maintain newcomers from their homeland. Pioneers played the role of entrepreneurs and brokers or intermediaries between immigrant communities and the host society.

Joseph Carabelli, an Italian stonemason, immigrated to America in 1870 and arrived in Cleveland a decade later. He established a large group of stonecutters from the Campobasso Province in Italy.[22] They settled next to the cemetery in the Mayfield–Murray Hill Road area that became known as Little Italy. Carabelli helped organize the first Italian mutual benefit society, the Italian Fraternal Society, in 1888. He assisted both Protestant and Catholic churches in the neighborhood and helped establish, with the financial support of John D. Rockefeller, the Alta House social settlement in 1900. Named after Rockefeller's daughter, it provided a kindergarten, gymnasium, playground, English classes, and other social welfare programs. By the 1920s, almost a dozen social settlements were serving to the city's poor, immigrant neighborhoods.

Joseph Turk, one of the first Slovenes to live in Cleveland, settled next to a steel mill in Newburgh in 1881. Four years later, a dozen of his compatriots joined him in what was called Chicken Village and built homes around East 80th Street in the Broadway neighborhood.[23] Turk acquired a grocery and three boardinghouses, then moved close to the Otis Steel Company along Lake Erie and opened a saloon, restaurant, general store, and boardinghouse to serve the needs of a growing Slovenian community along St. Clair Avenue from East 30th to 79th streets. White Motor Company became its major employer. Turk often met new immigrants on their arrival and lent money and clothes or posted bond for them during times of trouble. Concerned about the religious needs of his compatriots, he invited to Cleveland the first Slovenian priest, Reverend Vitus Hribar, who helped establish St. Vitus Church on East 61st Street in 1894.

David and Morris Black, Jewish immigrants and political refugees after the failure of the Revolution of 1848, were the first Hungarians to come to Cleveland. They achieved great success as entrepreneurs, especially in the clothing industry. Hungarian immigrants coming to Cleveland often had the Black family name pinned to their clothing in expectation of assistance upon their arrival. By 1872, fifty Hungarian families lived in Cleveland. Most were Jewish and resided on Oregon Street, near St. Clair Avenue.[24]

In 1880, a Hungarian immigrant, Joseph Schwab, settled with his family on Holton Avenue on the East Side. His son and grandson opened a restaurant on Superior Avenue. John Weizer, a boarder, lived with the Schwab family until he found a job at the Eberhardt Manufacturing Company near what became the city's largest settlement of Hungarians, the Buckeye-Woodland neighborhood. Weizer owned a small grocery store and organized a political club to encourage the naturalization of immigrants from his homeland. He sold two thousand building lots to his countrymen in the area in which resided a variety of manufacturing and commercial businesses.[25] St. Elizabeth's Church on Buckeye Road was the first church (1893) established for Hungarian Roman Catholics in America.

By 1900, there were more than nine thousand Hungarians living in Cleveland. Seventy-six percent of the male heads of their households in Cleveland were laborers. Approximately 70 percent of Hungarian married women earned wages or kept boarders. More than half of the Hungarian immigrants who came to America between 1908 and 1914 were "birds of passage," who returned home with their earnings. Others were part of a chain migration, as whole districts moved to different areas of America.

Theodore Kundtz, who came from Hungary to Cleveland at the age of twenty-one, was responsible for establishing a colony of his compatriots on the city's West Side. He organized a shop to supply cabinets to the White Sewing Machine Company and by 1900 employed twenty-five hundred skilled craftsmen, mainly from his former village of Metzenseten and the upper Hungarian counties of Zzepes and Abavj. They settled around Lorain and Abbey avenues near the West Side market and within walking distance of factories in the Flats.[26]

Polish immigrants also lived in inexpensive housing close to their jobs. By 1919, they made up 50 percent of the labor force at American Wire and Steel near the Fleet-Broadway neighborhood or Warszawa (Little Poland).[27] Michael Kniola, who arrived in the neighborhood in 1880, became its broker. He first served as a foreman in the steel mill because he was fluent in English. He then opened a grocery store and a travel brokerage company for incoming Polish immigrants and became an unofficial banker for his community. He also led a Republican club which he founded.

By 1890, Cleveland's Polish-American people formed two additional communities: Krakowa, around Marcelline Avenue (East 71st Street) and Grant Avenue, and Jackowa, near Tod and Francis avenues. They also settled west of the Cuyahoga River, working in the docks and steel mills on the West Side. Jobs at National Carbide also attracted Poles and other Slavic workers to an area around Madison and West 117th Street, known as Birdtown, after the names of local streets.[28]

The Nationality Churches and Synagogues

The majority of Slavs who arrived in Cleveland between 1880 and 1920 were initially hired as manual laborers in local industries and commercial businesses for long hours and little pay. But they could point not only to their burgeoning ethnic neighborhoods and voluntary associations but also to the spires of the growing number of nationality churches as a proud symbol of the strength of their cultural and religious life in a new homeland. These spiritual homes for foreign newcomers maintained the language, customs, and liturgy of the Old World.

The religious institutions of both old and new immigrant groups struggled with the growing diversity of the city's immigrant population—the threat of a modern "Babel" in an industrial city. Proselytizing work among the city's Congregationalist churches led to the organization of the Schauffler Missionary Training School, which prepared foreign-speaking young women to work among their countrymen. It was named after Henry Albert Schauffler, who spoke ten foreign languages and was invited by Pilgrim Congregational Church to missionize among Cleveland's Czech community.

The church was located in the Tremont neighborhood, originally settled by New Englanders, Irish, and Germans. They were replaced in the 1880s and 1890s by Poles, Ukrainians, Slavs, and Russians. Pilgrim Church and its older congregants, mainly from families that originated in New England, decided "to remain and serve, rather than run from the changes that confronted it."[29] It provided a gymnasium, reading room, library, recreation room, social parlor, and classrooms—the core of nonreligious services of what was described as an "institutional church" for the Protestant community.

Cleveland's Jewish community also witnessed the efforts of older groups to assimilate later arrivals of their religious faith from different countries. Before the Civil War, the city's German Jewish settlement was mainly located southeast of Huron Road and East Sixth Street along Scovill, Woodland, and Central avenues. Jewish people prospered in the commercial business and retail trade in downtown Cleveland. As they moved eastward, a new group of Jews from eastern and central Europe succeeded them in the 1880s. They would find that German Jews had already built a network of social, educational, and religious organizations that helped them adjust to their new environment. The religious and social traditions of recently arrived Russian Jews derived from religious orthodoxy, and life in "the Pale" competed with and even threatened the more Americanized customs of German Jews. Cleveland's Jewish population grew from twenty-five thousand in 1905 to seventy-five thousand in 1917.[30]

The older segment of the community established such organizations as the Jewish Orphan Asylum (1868), the Council Educational Alliance, which acted as a social settlement, and a variety of other philanthropic and social welfare programs.

The newly arrived European Orthodox Jews established traditions and a way of life in the ghetto which sustained the ways of their homelands. They built numerous schools and synagogues in their overcrowded, impoverished Central-Woodland neighborhood. Some supported Zionism and socialism to the great alarm of older groups. Jewish synagogues resembled nationality churches of the new immigrants because each was maintained by a specific nationality group. Anshe Emeth was established for Polish Jews, Anshe Chesed for German members, B'nai Jeshurun (1886) for Hungarian Jews, and Beth Israel Chevra Kadisha (1860) for Russian Jews.[31]

German Jews led the reform movement to modernize or Americanize religious services. By 1900, Anshe Chesed's congregation conducted all services in English. Jews from such eastern European countries as Romania, Lithuania, Hungary, Poland, and Russia preferred a more orthodox religion to preserve the customs and languages of their homelands. The religious traditions of other groups of new immigrants also faced a similar debate and conflict.

When a Protestant church (Plymouth Congregational) established a mission to work with Cleveland's Slovak community, Bishop Richard Gilmour of the Catholic Diocese, who had mixed feelings about supporting separatist nationality churches not based on the territorial model, invited Stephen Furdek in 1882 to work with

Czech and Slovak immigrants. He first served as a priest at St. Wenceslas Church (1867) at East 37th—the city's first Bohemian parish—and helped organize Our Lady of Lourdes (1883) at East 55th in the Broadway area. Both congregations were the result of a chain migration from villages in their homeland. Father Furdek also founded St. Ladislas Church (1889) on East 92d Street to serve, temporarily, the needs of both the Slovaks and Hungarians in the Buckeye-Woodland neighborhood.

Fraternal or Self-Help Organizations

Furdek helped develop the St. Stephan Society, a fraternal organization that collected mutual aid dues to pay social insurance. In an era without federal or state entitlement programs, ethnic fraternal organizations became the linchpin of community life, for they provided sickness, old age, and death benefits to their members. Furdek also founded the First Catholic Slovak Union, a national fraternal insurance program, whose membership grew to forty-five thousand by 1915, and *Jednota* (Union), a local journal, which enabled Slovaks to learn about significant events in their own language. Foreign-born readers could also read nationality newspapers, which flourished in Cleveland by serving their needs. Twenty-five existed by 1929.

Czech immigrants arrived earlier than their counterparts. Escaping the Revolution of 1848, the earliest Czechs, or Bohemians, were political refugees. By 1869 they numbered over three thousand and worked more than thirty occupations. Many were farmers or skilled tradesmen with a high rate of literacy. They first settled in the rural area of Brooklyn on Cleveland's West Side and were quick to assimilate.[32]

From 1880 to the turn of the century, Cleveland gained over eight thousand Czechs. A second settlement was established on Croton Street, near East 40th Street and Woodland Avenue. Martin Krejci, who owned a general merchandise store, steamship agency, and public utility office, acted as the community's broker.

Others resided near the Standard Oil Company along the south side of Kingsbury Run, Trumbull Avenue, and East 37th Street. Rockefeller hired Czechs as barrel makers, and as the population grew, Broadway and East 55th Street became the center of the community. They built St. Adelbert's Catholic Church (1883) on East 83d Street. During this period, Czechs from Brooklyn moved to a new settlement (Kuba or Cuba) at West 41st Street, between Clark and Denison avenues. Goosetown and the Cabbage Patch—other urban villages belonging to this nationality—were also located near this settlement on the city's West Side.

In 1863, Cleveland's Czechs established Slovenska Liba, the first fraternal lodge in their community. At least five Czech Sokols or gymnastic societies were built between 1869 and 1906. In 1889, the Bohemian National Hall was constructed at

4939 Broadway to provide a social center to preserve their language, music, drama, and gymnastic traditions in a community split into Catholic or Protestant denominations and freethinkers. Despite religious differences, the Czechs were fiercely nationalistic and participated in the Bohemian National Alliance, which joined the Slovak League in 1915 to promote the independence of Czechoslovakia.[33]

Often the scope of activities within a church and affiliated fraternal associations reflected the background of an ethnic group. The "hometown" societies of Big Italy stood in contrast to the regional or national organizations of Cleveland's Slovak and Czech communities. Located next to the produce and retail businesses on lower Woodland, Broadway, and Central avenues, Cleveland's Big Italy was characterized by a chain migration.[34] Over half of the Italians in Cleveland came from ten villages in southern Italy.

By 1890, approximately nine hundred Italians in Big Italy lived in the vicinity of Orange and Ontario streets. Ninety percent were from Sicily. At the heart of the neighborhood was St. Anthony of Padua's Church, established, on Prospect Avenue, as the first Italian nationality church in 1887. The church honored the religious customs of its congregants' hometown societies, which celebrated annually the patron saint of their former villages. More than half had their own bands. The Feast of Saint Anthony was the largest as twelve bands led the congregation around the neighborhood.

Cleveland's Italians were more isolated than any other ethnic group by the turn of the century. Concentrating on hometown and family life and finding the resources either to survive impoverished circumstances or to return to their homeland with their earnings, many retreated from the concerns of the larger society. Unable to speak English and often belittled by the lack of sympathy or understanding among outsiders, one of Cleveland's Italian-Americans remarked that their ethnic neighborhood helped them escape "the well of misunderstanding."[35]

The city's Polish community also shared in this sense of isolation and anxiety about the host society. Equally important as proximity to steel mills for their settlement in the Fleet-Broadway neighborhood was the establishment of St. Stanislaus Church in 1881. Like other nationality churches, it provided a wide variety of social services and programs, fraternal insurance clubs, a school that taught in the Polish language, a place for business and neighborhood meetings, and a welfare agency in times of need. Under the leadership of Father Frances Kolaszewski, the parish undertook an ambitious building program, costing approximately $150,000, to meet the needs of the burgeoning Slavic neighborhood.[35]

Often portrayed as strikebreakers, radicals, or illiterate peasants, Warszawa's residents could point with pride to the tall spires of St. Stanislaus Church on Forman and East 65th streets, one of the largest Gothic churches in America. Reacting to the large debt of $90,000 to build the sacred landmark, the Catholic Diocese and a group of the church's parishioners asked for the removal of Father Kolaszewski. Returning to Cleveland against the wishes of Bishop Gilmour, he established Immaculate Heart Parish in 1894 and championed community control over the church.

Part of the source of his defiance against the hierarchy of the Catholic church which excommunicated him can be detected in his earlier letter to the bishop explaining why he was too busy to prepare for junior clergy exams:

> They do not speak or write the English language. So with everything, the first thing they do is come to me to seek my advice. . . . I am their advisor, their contractor, their friend, their brother and very often their judge. With everything, they come to me. So you see how my time is occupied. I rise at five o'clock in the morning and go to bed at eleven at night and many times at twelve. I work eighteen hours a day, day after day; I never take a vacation, I am never at rest. I also take many sick calls when I should have five or six hours of sleep. What else do you want from me? Do I not work enough; should I go to my room and study a few definitions by heart?[37]

World War I and the End of Mass Foreign Migration

Although ethnic neighborhoods and groups often served as a path for immigrants to Americanize or assimilate into the larger society, the advent of World War I created a deep sense of anxiety in Cleveland concerning the loyalty of its German-American population as well as that of other "hyphenated" ethnic groups. During the wartime campaign for "100 percent Americanism," they were told to separate totally from their homelands and nationality cultures. The Cleveland School Board dropped the teaching of German and required a loyalty oath from teachers. Events surrounding the May Day riot and Red Scare of 1919 aroused more paranoia about immigrants during a time of great stress from postwar unemployment, labor strikes, race riots, and inflation.[38]

On May 1, 1919, the Socialist party's march to Cleveland's Public Square in support of its imprisoned leader, Eugene Debs, and the Russian Revolution incited a riot and arrest of 116 demonstrators. Only 8 were American citizens, offering support to nativist fears. An eyewitness later recalled: "The sight of these men and women and children marching peacefully drove the business leaders absolutely berserk. . . . All they could see was another Russian Revolution."[39] The *Cleveland Plain Dealer* reported with alarm that Cleveland's "foreign colonies" contained over 85,000 unnaturalized males and estimated that the number of unnaturalized foreigners was approximately 212,000 out of a total population of 796,841 people. The melting pot had not worked.[40]

Poland had the largest nationality group (35,024) in Cleveland by 1920. The Hungarians (29,724), Czechs (23,907), Russians (21,502), Italians (18,288), Yugoslavs (15,898), which included Serbs, Croats, Slovenians, and Montenegrans, and Austrians (15,228) were other major groups among the new immigrants. Though declining in numbers, Germans (26,476) still led the older immigrants numerically. In 1920, Cleveland's foreign-born population reached its peak of 240,173 people.[41]

The postwar arrival of millions of southern and eastern Europeans created a sense of panic throughout America. The nation was judged incapable of assimilating such huge numbers on several grounds.

Critics of public education pointed to the high failure rate of immigrant students and predicted an even greater disaster if their size increased. The Dillingham Commission, a federal investigation (1911) of America's immigrants, had found that less than 1 percent of Cleveland's Slovak children attended high school. A Cleveland Foundation survey of the city's youth in the early 1920s revealed that 33 percent of the student population had not gone beyond grammar school and 80 percent had not graduated from high school. Most left school early to supplement their families' income.[42]

A settlement worker from Hiram House, a social settlement in the Central-Woodland neighborhood, despaired about the arrival of what she described as "fiery Italians and the Slavish and Polish with their duller minds, their drunkenness and immorality."[43] Increasingly, the American public endorsed the arguments of social scientists and politicians who favored restricting immigration of what were believed to be inferior races from southern and eastern Europe. Quotas drastically reduced the number of people coming from these countries and totally excluded Asians in the National Origins Act of 1924.

The Great Migration

With the decline in European immigration, Cleveland employers turned to the American South as a source of cheap labor. The city's African American population grew from approximately 10,000 before World War I to 34,451 people by 1920. African Americans attempted to escape the bitter legacy of slavery and the economic injustices of the South by migrating to northern cities like Cleveland, especially during the economic expansion of war industries during World Wars I and II. Life in the North did not completely solve their problems. The Urban League helped this growing minority group to find jobs and housing and, assisted by the NAACP, to fight racial discrimination, but Cleveland still became the second most racially segregated city in America.

Cleveland's African American community supported the Phillis Wheatley Association, established in 1911 by Jane Edna Hunter, a graduate of Hampton Institute and a nurse. She saw the need for housing and vocational training of young black women who had migrated from the South. Equally important were the recreational and cultural activities of Karamu House, a social settlement that opened its doors in 1915 to both blacks and whites in Cleveland. Older blacks, as well as recent migrants, often centered their lives around their churches.[44]

The number of Cleveland's African American churches expanded from 17 in 1915 to 150 by 1930. Two-thirds of black church members were Baptists. Several congregations, such as Zion Hill Baptist Church, were literally transplanted from the South. Many recent migrants attended newly organized Baptist congregations or storefront churches of the Holiness and Spiritualist sects.

By 1930, Cleveland's African American churches had approximately forty thousand members, almost 60 percent of the community's population. Older black churches, such as Mount Zion Congregational Church or St. Andrews Episcopal Church, attracted an elite group but expanded their social welfare activities to help recent migrants. Many African American newcomers from the rural South sought help from storefront churches. Impoverished migrants felt left out or looked down on in the more established black congregations. In 1929, approximately 10 percent (four thousand congregants) of all black church members belonged to these groups. Their religious services were informal but charged with emotional singing and reading of Scripture. In 1928, a study indicated that 109 storefront churches were located mainly in the Central area—the heart of the city's black ghetto.

The Great Migration of the World War I era accelerated the residential segregation that had begun earlier for Cleveland's African American community in the lower Central-Woodland neighborhood. By 1930, twelve census tracts on the city's East Side were between 60 and 90 percent black. African Americans constituted 8 percent of the city's population, or 71,899 residents.

Competition from returning soldiers and cutbacks in wartime industries decreased the community's employment in manufacturing from 63 to 48 percent between 1920 and 1930. The proportion of black males working as domestic servants increased from 15.1 to 18.9 percent during that decade. The proportion of black women employed as domestics rose to 86.7 percent.[45] Faced with hostility from local craft unions and without the appropriate training as a result of their previous background as agricultural laborers in the South and exclusion from training programs, the majority of the city's African American migrants were confined to low-paying domestic or unskilled and semiskilled jobs.

Unlike older groups of white residents, who were pushed upward by the arrival of new immigrants who took over menial jobs, Cleveland's black community suffered a decline in occupational status after the pre–Civil War era, when one-third of its population was employed in skilled trades. Nor did blacks disperse when large numbers of new migrants arrived from the South. By 1960, they reached a total of 251,000 people as a result of the Great Migration. Unlike ethnic communities, which developed new settlements or dispersed their upwardly mobile or second-generation members among the host society, the city's African American population expanded in size while simultaneously becoming more segregated or restricted to impoverished and physically deteriorating neighborhoods.

Because of racial bigotry in both the housing and employment markets, the black experience was different from that of white ethnic groups. By 1910, only a few of the city's Irish and German neighborhoods still existed, even though both groups expanded in size during the latter half of the nineteenth century. Blacks who ventured beyond the "enduring ghetto" of their community were met with a wall of racial hostility.[46]

Suburbanization

In the 1920s Cleveland's African Americans expanded beyond East 55th Street, along Central, Woodland, and Scovill avenues. Often they followed in the footsteps of the city's Jewish community, who, like other immigrant groups, used the street arteries of their original settlements as "ethnic corridors" or "conveyor belts" to move to other areas within Cleveland as well as to outlying suburbs.[47] With the advent of the automobile, transportation was available to the new housing developments in areas adjacent to the central city. The suburban population jumped from 76,762 to 146,654, or 91.1 percent, between 1900 and 1910 and increased to 301,026, or 105.3 percent, by the end of the next decade.

Established first as enclaves of native white Protestants, suburban communities increasingly attracted foreign-stock Catholic and Jewish families and their descendants after the turn of the century. Nationality groups moved along the city's arterial routes from their original settlements to outlying regions. The following communities have been major "conveyor belts" for ethnic groups: Detroit for Irish; Lorain for Germans; St. Clair for Slovenians and Croatians; Mayfield and Euclid for Italians; Kinsman and Woodland for Jews, Italians, and Hungarians; Broadway for Poles and Czechs; and West 25th for Ukrainians and Poles who migrated from Tremont to Parma, Ohio.[48]

Suburban areas, like the immigrant settlements in the central city, were not an amorphous or random collection of individuals. Jewish residents migrated, for example, along Superior, Woodland, and Kinsman avenues to the eastern suburbs. By 1961, 35 percent lived in Cleveland Heights, 18 percent in Shaker Heights, 15 percent in University Heights, 10 percent in South Euclid, and 6 percent in Beachwood. Only 5 percent were left in Cleveland.

Moving from Collinwood, many Italians settled in East Cleveland and Euclid. Residents of Little Italy followed the direction of Mayfield Road to Cleveland Heights, South Euclid, and Mayfield Heights. Polish residents from Warszawa were found in Garfield and Maple Heights. Significant numbers of Slovenians moved to Euclid. They opened a Slovene Home for the Aged on Neff Road in 1962.

The Ethnic Mosaic: Conflicts and Differences

For the second and third generations, the arteries that brought them to the suburbs also returned or connected them to churches and organizations of their parents and grandparents which remained in the central city. Many no longer felt the emotional ties to European cultures or folk traditions that molded the experience of their immigrant ancestors and the ethnic mosaic of Cleveland. Very few nationality churches were established in suburban areas. Membership dropped from a peak of

202,237 parishioners in thirty-two nationality churches to 75,166 parishioners by 1972.[49] Suburbanization, economic mobility, and attrition of cultural tradition from the Old World with modernization and assimilation into the values of the majority society played a major role in their decline. This was especially true for urban-born descendants of rural European peasants.

That immigrants were often in conflict with their Americanized children is not surprising for they could not instill in them the vivid impressions of the homeland or the reasons for leaving their family and village behind. Their children often grew up with conflicting values, those learned at home, in city schools, and at play in the streets. Shin Miller, a son of a Jewish family from Russia, expressed the conflict between generations in "House Divided," an autobiographical novel of life in a Central-Woodland neighborhood in the 1920s. After his brother informed his family that he had adopted a more Americanized name (Leroy Chase), his father commented: "Children I brought up and raised and they defied me. One works, one slaves for them, sends them to schools, and they don't even like their name, disdain to be called by that name."[50] After finding out the meaning of his son's new name, the father threatened to "chase" him out of both the family and the neighborhood.

There were many differences between and among immigrant groups depending on their time of arrival, occupational skills, and the cultural backgrounds they brought with them from Europe. Some were able to progress at a quicker pace economically than those who followed later or arrived with no urban experience. Historian Josef Barton has studied the comparative mobility of Cleveland's Italians, Romanians, and Slovaks between 1890 and 1950. Their secular, middle-class, and urban background and retention of children in school helped Romanians achieve more rapid mobility and economic success than the other two groups. One-third of the sons born in the first decade of the twentieth century improved their social class standing during their careers. No Romanian son who had begun his occupational career as an unskilled laborer in the 1930s and 1940s remained so at the age of thirty.[51] By contrast, children from families with an agricultural or lower social class background often left school early to supplement their family's income. Such was the case of second-generation Italians, who fared poorly in skilled and nonmanual occupations in comparison with children whose parents were artisans and petty merchants. Even the Italian fathers who learned a skilled trade had only a 50 percent chance of passing on a similar status to their sons.

Often the differences among immigrants were directly related to their reasons for coming. Those who planned to return to their homes were often resigned to the backbreaking manual labor of the industrial city; for them, it was only a temporary means toward a greater goal that did not include permanent residence in the United States. For the many who did not return, both to accept their fate and to resign themselves to their low status in American society was an admission of defeat they found difficult to accept.

The American Dream

For many immigrants, the experience of living in America was neither the melting pot nor the road to instant affluence but constant practice in the art of living under difficult circumstances. The reality of the struggle behind the American Dream was poignantly expressed by one of Cleveland's Italian immigrants: "If one does not work hard and without stopping for even one day, one cannot, will not live. The dollar is made of sweat and endless sacrifices. But for those who came as we did, not knowing the language, and in the era in which we came, life was cruel. Other immigrants who had been fortunate to live in countries where English was spoken treated the tongue-tied newcomers like beasts. . . . Poor immigrants, how many dreams that vanished all too quickly when they came into contact with reality."[52]

America also fulfilled the hopes of immigrants who were aware of the opportunity that America had provided for a people who were economically and socially oppressed in the Old World. John Kovacs, who emigrated from Hungary in 1881, wanted to stay only long enough to be able to purchase a farm in his homeland but changed his mind: "I had made nine dollars the first week, more—much more—than the amount I received for one year's service as a farmer's hand in the old country. This was indeed the country of golden opportunity for me."[53] For many immigrants, the freedom to organize a church, an ethnic newspaper, a fraternal organization, or a nationality holiday or to obtain a better job was a real improvement over life in the Old World. A Hungarian worker wrote to the *Szabadsag* in 1892: "I feel as though I know ten times as much as I did in Europe, where there is the idea that newspapers are only for the gentry. Had I known the joy of newspaper reading then I would gladly have parted with my cow in order to afford it!"[54] The celebration of nationality cultures and contributions to America and the city of Cleveland was partially an expression of this new freedom.

Far less dramatic, but equally important, was the day-to-day encounter between immigrants and older groups. A son of a Serbian Orthodox priest and student in Waring Elementary School was unable to explain to his Scotch-Irish teacher that he celebrated Christian holidays at a later date according to the Julian Calendar. Because he was "Orthodox," she had incorrectly assumed that he was Jewish and told him that this group did not observe Good Friday.[55] In contrast, the Mayfield Merchants Association sponsored a banquet in 1948 to honor Florence Graham. Of Irish descent, she had faithfully served and fought discrimination against the city's Italian-American community during her tenure as a teacher and principal of Murray Hill School since 1908.[56]

Similarities existed between the new immigrants' and black migrants' neighborhood life in the industrial city. Pioneers, the first to settle an area, usually served as community leaders. Often they became involved not only with the social, cultural, and economic life of the city but later became politically active as ward leaders, often delivering the votes of their people in return for commitments and favors to their communities.

The church was often the center of both black and white settlements in Cleveland. Religion had played a large part in the newcomers' former lives. In their new environment, they attempted to retain that same spiritual dynamism, but it was often frustrated by conflicts between the congregation and clergy or among different religious factions. The greater freedom of the industrial city allowed individuals and groups to pursue their own course and is illustrated by the number of groups that broke away from the main body of their church to form new congregations or schismatic factions. Religious leaders were almost always revered. Many became important community leaders in their own right.

The majority of the newcomers, especially those of Slavic background and the black migrants, were hired as unskilled manual laborers and worked long hours for little money. Immigrant and migrant neighborhoods served as "decompression chambers" for they cushioned people from the often dehumanizing physical and psychological brutality of noisy, dangerous factories. Within the familiar surroundings of their own cultural and social life, they were able to adjust to an environment that differed greatly from rural or small town life.

The new immigrants and the black migrants were an important part of Cleveland's economic, social, and cultural development. As the unsung heroes of industrial America, they retained their pride and human determination in the face of alien, often dehumanizing circumstances. Their settlements enriched Cleveland's urban mosaic despite constantly changing conditions as a result of internal and external pressures. A study of the Civil War neighborhood around Hiram House has demonstrated that, in the first decade of this century, over 90 percent of the residents moved.[57]

The Decline in the City's People and Neighborhoods

The decline in nationality churches as well as ethnic neighborhoods in Cleveland's central city was directly related to changes within its foreign-born population. Movement to the suburbs and demographic changes after the passage of restrictive immigration laws impeded their growth. During the 1920s, Cleveland showed a net loss of its foreign-born residents. The Great Depression also had a negative impact. The foreign-born population decreased from 230,946 in 1930 to 179,183 in 1940, a loss of 22 percent. By 1950, only 132,799 persons of foreign birth, or 14.5 percent of the total population, were enumerated in Cleveland and 50,868 in the suburbs.[58]

Both the people and the neighborhoods of Cleveland declined after World War II, as the city's population plunged from 914,808 in 1950 to 505,000 in 1990. In the 1980s, the city lost sixteen white and four black people each day. The number of new migrants and immigrants, such as the Hispanic and Asian groups, could not replace those leaving the city. A historic cycle had ended.[59] Highway systems facilitated the movement of jobs and people, fearing urban blight and the growing minority population, to the suburbs. Their formidable inner belt systems also destroyed older areas. Businesses, churches, and residences in the city's near East and West Side neighborhoods that stood in the automobile's way were soon destroyed. Urban renewal projects as well as demolition and abandonment of older housing also wreaked havoc on inner-city neighborhoods.

The influx of poor people—Appalachian and black migrants from the South, Asians, Puerto Ricans, Arabs, and other groups from foreign countries—and the flight of more affluent residents and businesses to the suburbs deeply affected the city's neighborhoods. The removal of quota restrictions with the passage of the National Origins Act of 1965 shaped the growth and location of Cleveland's immigrant population. The new law gave preference to newcomers with technical or professional skills, who often settled in suburban areas that restricted the entry of minority and poor people.

Cleveland was left with a "predominance of households with low educational attainments, and low incomes" and a disproportionate amount of poverty, crime, and delinquency.[60] By 1988, approximately 40 percent of its households were at or below the poverty line. Almost 50 percent of its public school children failed to graduate from high school. To escape these and other problems, such as a busing program to integrate the educational system, parents with school-age children who could afford to move elsewhere or have their children attend parochial schools increasingly left Cleveland's public schools. As industries shut down and moved to the South or overseas, the city's unemployment rate was much higher than that of the rest of the nation. It has the second worst record for the employment of adult workers and the worst for minorities in the nation.[61]

The Modern Neighborhood Movement

The neighborhood movement that emerged in the 1970s fought against the deterioration of living conditions in Cleveland's central city. A variety of programs and strategies—housing rehabilitation, free enterprise zones, low interest loans for home improvements, mandatory reinvestment for local banks, citizen political groups, federal community block grants, and shelters or services for the homeless and hungry—attempted to reverse the decline.[62]

The neighborhood movement, like local social settlements and fraternal organizations of ethnic and minority groups, hoped to restore what Alexis de Tocqueville, the French author who visited the United States in the 1830s, saw as the genius of this new nation's democracy—the voluntary group or association. Based on self-reliance, cooperation, and mutual aid, voluntary groups maintained democratic life in America by taking responsibility for problems. Through involvement with other citizens in common concerns or issues, Americans learned "the habits of the heart" or local autonomy, community initiative, civic intelligence, and participation in public life.[63]

An Alternative Vision

Certainly the concern for one's neighbor was the highest achievement in Cleveland's ethnic and minority communities that stood between the spires and stacks. America's individualism and materialism were restrained or tempered by the values of nationality or family life and religious traditions celebrating peace, justice, and loving fellowship. Jobs below the "stacks" made people leave their social enclaves, but they realized the importance of the connection of economic activity or steady work to their familial and neighborhood life. Our age celebrates the divorce of the two in the worship of acquisitive individualism or materialism, mobility, and destruction or replacement of the old with the new. America can find an alternative moral and social vision by understanding and recapturing the creativity and courage of its immigrant and migrant people who built churches, fraternal organizations, and schools in their urban neighborhoods as a communal strength against the economic and social turmoil of their day.

Notes

1. William Glazer, *Peculiarities of American Cities* (Philadelphia: Hubbard Bros., 1886), 148–49.

2. See David Van Tassel and John J. Grabowski, eds., *The Encyclopedia of Cleveland History* (Bloomington: Indiana University Press, 1987), xvii–xlii.

3. Carol Beal and Ronald R. Weiner, "The Sixth City: Cleveland in the Three States of Urbanization," in *The Birth of Modern Cleveland 1865–1930*, eds. Thomas Campbell and Edward M. Miggins (Cleveland: Western Reserve Historical Society and Associated University Presses, 1988), 24–53.

4. Wellington Fordyce, "Immigrant Colonies in Cleveland," *Ohio State Archaeological and Historical Quarterly* 45 (1936): 87.

5. Justin Galford, "The Foreign Born and Urban Growth in Cleveland, 1850–1950," 2–3, manuscript at Western Reserve Historical Society, Cleveland, Ohio. The manuscript was derived from the author's "The Foreign Born and Urban Growth in the Great Lakes, 1850–1950: A Study of Chicago, Cleveland, Detroit and Milwaukee" (Ph.D. diss., New York University, 1958).

6. See Nelson Callahan and William Hickey, *Irish Americans and Their Communities in Cleveland* (Cleveland: Cleveland State University's Ethnic Heritage Studies, 1976), and Nelson J. Callahan with Anthony J. Schuerger, *History of St. Malachi Parish* (Cleveland: St. Malachi, 1990).

7. See Edward M. Miggins, "Cleveland Public Schools" and "Americanization," in *Encyclopedia*, 28 and 263.

8. Edward M. Miggins, "Becoming American: Americanization and the Reform of the Cleveland Public Schools," in *Birth of Modern Cleveland*, 350.

9. Michael S. Pap, ed., *Ethnic Communities in Cleveland* (Cleveland: John Carroll University, 1973), 110; John R. Sinnema, "Germans," in *Encyclopedia*, 447; and Charles J. Wolfram, "The Germans in the Making of Cleveland," manuscript at Cleveland Public Library, derived from the author's speech before the Temple Woman's Association on February 15, 1928.

10. Robert Wheeler, "A Commercial Hamlet is Founded, 1796–1824," in *Encyclopedia*, xxv; and Ronald Weiner, "The History of Land Use Decision Making in Cleveland, 1880–1930" (Ph.D. diss., Case Western Reserve University, 1974), 15.

11. Harlan Hatcher, *Giant from the Wilderness: The Story of a City and Its Industries* (Cleveland: World, 1955), 98.

12. Ronald Weiner, "The New Industrial Metropolis: 1860–1929," in *Encyclopedia*, xxix–xliii; and Harold C. Livesay, "From Steeples to Smokestacks: The Birth of the Modern Corporation," in *Birth of Modern Cleveland*, 54–70.

13. Edward M. Miggins and Mary Morgenthaler, "The Ethnic Mosaic: The Settlement of Cleveland by the New Immigrants and Migrants," in *Birth of Modern Cleveland*, 105.

14. Oscar Handlin, *The Uprooted: The Epic Story of the Great Migrations That Made the American People* (Boston: Little, Brown, 1973), 7.

15. Maxine Seller, *To Seek America: A History of Ethnic Life in the United States* (Englewood, N.J.: Jerome S. Ozer, 1988), 104.

16. Edward M. Miggins, "Labor Reform and the Social Base," in *Birth of Modern Cleveland*, 101.

17. Galford, "The Foreign Born," 12–14.

18. See Naphtali Hoffman, "The Economic Development of Cleveland: 1825–1910" (Ph.D. diss., Case Western Reserve University, 1980); and Beal and Weiner, "Sixth City," 41–43.

19. Frank Kuznic, "The Ethnic Myth," *Cleveland Magazine*, February 1960, p. 56.

20. See Charles E. Hendry and Margaret Swendsen, *Between Spires and Stacks* (Cleveland: Welfare Federation of Cleveland, 1936). The author used the title of this pioneering study of juvenile delinquency in Cleveland's Tremont neighborhood as the metaphor for all immigrant groups.

21. "The Foreign Population in the City of Cleveland and Where They Live," manuscript at the Cleveland Public Library. This study was probably done by a local church group in Cleveland around the turn of the century.

22. Eugene Veronesi, *Italian Americans and Their Communities of Cleveland* (Cleveland: Cleveland State University's Ethnic Heritage Series, 1977), 198. See also Charles Ferroni, "The Italians in Cleveland: A Study in Assimilation" (Ph.D. diss., Kent State University, 1969).

23. Miggins and Morgenthaler, "Ethnic Mosaic," 111. See also Frank Turk, "History of the First Slovene Settler in Cleveland" (1955), manuscript at the Western Reserve Historical Society.

24. Karl Bonutti et al., *Selected Ethnic Communities in Cleveland* (Cleveland: Cleveland State University's Ethnic Heritage Series, 1974), 36; and *Peoples of Cleveland* (Cleveland: Writers' Program of the Works Progress Administration, 1942), 108.

25. *Peoples of Cleveland*, 61.

26. Susan Papp, *Hungarian Americans and Their Communities in Cleveland* (Cleveland: Cleveland State University's Ethnic Heritage Series, 1981), 105.

27. John J. Grabowski et al., *Polish Americans and Their Communities in Cleveland* (Cleveland: Cleveland State University's Ethnic Heritage Series, 1976), 159–61.

28. James Borchert and Susan Danziger-Borchert, "Migrant Responses to the City: The Neighborhood, Case Studies in Black and White, 1870–1940," *Slovakia* 31 (1984): 9–43.

29. Michael J. McTighe, "Babel and Babylon on the Cuyahoga: Religious Diversity in Cleveland," in *Birth of Modern Cleveland*, 237.

30. Miggins and Morgenthaler, "Ethnic Mosaic," 117. See also Lloyd P. Gartner, *History of the Jews in Cleveland* (Cleveland: Western Reserve Historical Society, 1978).

31. McTighe, "Babel and Babylon," 251.

32. Celia Frances Beck, "From Grist Mill to Steel Mill" (M.A. thesis, Western Reserve University, 1929), 32–33.

33. Marian Mark Stolarik, "Immigration and Urbanization: The Slovak Experience, 1870–1918" (Ph.D. diss., University of Michigan, 1974), 213–21.

34. Josef Barton, *Peasants and Strangers: Italians, Rumanians and Slovaks in an American City* (Cambridge, Mass.: Harvard University Press, 1975), 53.

35. *Peoples of Cleveland*, 129.

36. Grabowski, *Polish Americans*, 177–81.

37. Ibid., 232.

38. Edward M. Miggins, "Becoming American: Americanization and the Reform of the Cleveland Public Schools," in *Birth of Modern Cleveland*, 364.

39. Emil Bolek, "The Ethnic People's Contribution to the Life of Cleveland" (1976), 14, manuscript at Western Reserve Historical Society.

40. *Cleveland Plain Dealer,* May 3, 1917.

41. Galford, "The Foreign Born," 42.

42. Ernest G. Brooks, *The History of Fenn College* (Cleveland: Fenn Educational Fund, 1974), 39.

43. John J. Grabowski, "A Social Settlement in a Neighborhood in Transition: Hiram House, Cleveland, Ohio" (Ph.D. diss., Case Western University, 1977), 161–62.

44. Miggins and Morgenthaler, "Ethnic Mosaic," 132; see also Kenneth Kusmer, *A Ghetto Takes Shape: Black Cleveland, 1870–1930* (Urbana: University of Illinois Press, 1976).

45. Ibid., 133.

46. Ibid., 136–37.

47. Daniel A. Stillman, "The Excluding Metropolis" (M.A. thesis, Harvard University, 1963), 60.

48. Ibid., 60–69.

49. See Barbara Gartland, "The Decline in Cleveland's Roman Catholic Nationality Parishes" (M.A. thesis, Cleveland State University, 1973).

50. Shin Miller, "House Divided" (ca. 1920–22), 37, manuscript at the Western Reserve Historical Society.

51. Barton, *Peasants and Strangers,* 99–104.

52. Frank Aleschi, *It Is Never Too Late: A True Life Story of an Immigrant* (Cleveland: St. Francis Publishing House, 1963), 9–10.

53. *Peoples of Cleveland,* 111.

54. Ibid., 115–16.

55. Michael B. Petrovick, "Thoughts on the Eastern Orthodox Experience in America," in *Studies in Ethnicity: The East European Experience in America,* ed. Charles A. Ward et al. (Boulder, Colo.: East European Monographs, 1980), 171.

56. Veronesi, *Italian Americans,* 233.

57. See John J. Grabowski, "Immigration and Migration," in *Encyclopedia,* 544.

58. Galford, "The Foreign Born," 27–28.

59. *Cleveland Plain Dealer,* March 31, 1991.

60. Edric A. Weld, "The Demographic Setting for the Eighties for the Cleveland Region" (Cleveland: Cleveland State University, 1980), 23.

61. *Cleveland Plain Dealer,* May 16, 1991.

62. Edward M. Miggins, ed., *A Guide to Studying Neighborhoods and Resources on Cleveland* (Cleveland: Cleveland Public Library, 1984), 23–25.

63. Robert Bellah et al., eds., *Habits of the Heart: Individualism and Commitment in American Life* (New York: Harper & Row, 1985), 167–69.

The Impact of Poverty on Cleveland Neighborhoods

Claudia J. Coulton & Julian Chow

Modern urban poverty is embedded in a set of mutually reinforcing economic and social forces at the regional, neighborhood, and individual levels. How these forces interact to produce distinct patterns of poverty and social conditions in specific neighborhoods is the focus of this essay. We demonstrate how regional forces have affected the growth and distribution of poverty in the Cleveland area. We identify the differential operation of particular factors in areas of high poverty.

The essay examines two aspects of poverty today that make it more intractable and amplify its effects on people and places—its concentration in particular geographic areas and its persistence for some individuals and families; clarifies aspects of regional and neighborhood economic and social structures that shape the particular patterns of poverty that we see today; traces the impact of poverty on social conditions and the quality of life in Cleveland area neighborhoods; and draws distinctions among high poverty areas that suggest alternative interventions.

The analysis is based on an extensive data base compiled by the Center for Urban Poverty and Social Change at Case Western Reserve University, measuring poverty and related social and physical conditions in Cleveland neighborhoods. We used the census tract as the unit of analysis because it is the smallest geographical unit for which data are available. The measures of physical and social conditions were calculated from official records produced by administrative agencies. Indicators of demographic and economic characteristics came from the censuses of 1940 through 1990 and from estimates provided by several individuals and organizations covering the period 1979–90. Trends in Cleveland are compared with those in other cities in the United States.

This analysis was supported in part by grants from the Rockefeller and Cleveland foundations. The opinions expressed are those of the authors.

Poverty in Cleveland: The Numbers and Distribution

Poverty in the Cleveland area in 1991 had several important features. The absolute size of the poor population had expanded despite the economic recovery of the late 1980s. The number of neighborhoods with a sizable group of poor persons was growing and, at the same time, there were more areas with high concentrations of poverty. Finally, a sizable portion of the poor population was suffering from long-term poverty. Although most persons in the nation who are ever poor will be poor only temporarily, the majority of poor persons in Cleveland at a given point in time are persistently poor.

The Cleveland metropolitan area, like other northern industrial cities, saw a rise in the poverty rate after 1970. Table 1 demonstrates that the increased poverty rate for the city of Cleveland from 1970 to 1980 was due primarily to population loss. The number of poor persons actually declined during this period.[1] After 1980, population continued to fall, but the actual number of poor grew considerably, leaving approximately 30 percent of Cleveland's residents below the poverty line. The increase in the number of poor persons was somewhat higher in the suburbs than in the city. Suburbs, however, lost less population and their poverty rates remained relatively low.[2]

One of the most troubling aspects of poverty is its concentration in particular geographic areas. It has been suggested that geographic concentration of the poor may lead to social isolation, further limiting the ability of residents to improve their economic situations. A potential contagion effect for social problems in these areas has also been identified.[3] The consequences of extended poverty may be particularly devastating for families and children.

Concentration of poverty is typically measured as the percentage of a geographic area's residents who are poor according to the official threshold used by the Census Bureau. The boundaries used to define an area are often dictated by the availability of data. We use the census tract as the unit of analysis.[4] We sometimes use census tracts as proxies for neighborhoods, even though we recognize that neighborhood boundaries are defined subjectively by residents. Census tracts with 40 percent or more of the population classified as poor are considered high poverty areas.[5]

One way of determining whether poverty is becoming more geographically concentrated is to look at changes over time in where the poor live. Table 2 presents information for 1970 through 1990 on the total population of poor areas and the numbers and percentages of poor who live in each of three groupings of tracts: areas of low poverty (<20 percent poor), areas of moderate poverty (20 to 39 percent poor), and areas of high poverty (40 percent or more poor).

The portion of the poor population living in areas of high poverty changed slightly from 1970 to 1980, but it nearly doubled by 1990. This suggests that geographically concentrated poverty is a phenomenon of the 1980s. In the city of Cleveland in 1991, 46 percent of the poor population resided in high poverty neighborhoods.

Table 1
Trends in Poverty, Cleveland and Cuyahoga County, 1970–1990

Area	*1970*[a] *census*	*1980*[b] *census*	*Percent change 1970–80*	*1990*[c] *estimate*	*Percent change 1980–90*
Cuyahoga County					
Population	1,720,835	1,498,400	-12.93	1,412,140	-5.76
Number poor	168,132	169,226	+00.65	213,430	+26.12
Percent poor	9.77	11.29		15.11	
City of Cleveland					
Population	750,879	573,822	-23.58	505,616	-11.89
Number poor	128,389	124,846	-2.76	151,211	+21.12
Percent poor	17.10	21.76		29.90	

[a] U.S. Bureau of the Census, 1972, Census of Population and Housing, 1970, Fourth Count Population Summary Tape, Cleveland, Ohio. Number of poor is based on 1969 income.
[b] U.S. Bureau of the Census, 1982, Census of Population and Housing, 1980, Summary Tape File 3, Cleveland, Ohio. Number of poor is based on 1979 income.
[c] U.S. Bureau of the Census, 1991, Census of Population and Housing, 1990, Summary Tape File 1, Cleveland, Ohio. In the city of Cleveland, the census tract data in the 1990 STF-1A tape has 255 more persons than the actual reported 505,616 because of the misclassified boundaries. 1990 poverty estimates were prepared by Morton Paglin, Center for Regional Economic Issues, Case Western Reserve University, based on 1989 public assistance levels.

The effects of concentrated poverty are even more evident for the nonwhite population of Cleveland than for the white population. The percentage of the nonwhite population living in high poverty areas is about ten points higher than that of whites, although there has been a recent shift toward more predominantly white high poverty neighborhoods. The proportion of high poverty area residents who are white was 12 percent in 1970, 10 percent in 1980, and 22 percent in 1990.[6]

Most of Cleveland's areas with highly concentrated poverty were more prosperous in 1970 and 1980 than in 1990. A minority of these areas, however, have housed large numbers of poor families for decades. We have classified census tracts into four groupings of high poverty areas based on when the tract passed the 40 percent threshold for concentrated poverty: original high poverty areas with a poverty rate of 40 percent or more continuously since 1970; early high poverty areas that reached a 40 percent poverty rate after 1970 but before 1980; emerging high poverty areas that reached high poverty between 1980 and 1990; and former high poverty areas, no longer home for large numbers of poor.

Original poverty areas declined in total population and in the number of poor persons between 1970 and 1980. The estimates show a decline in the number of

Table 2
Geographic Concentration of Poverty, Cleveland & Cuyahoga County, 1970–1990[a]

Poverty levels	*1970*[b]		*1980*[c]		*1990*[d]	
	Cleveland	*County*	*Cleveland*	*County*	*Cleveland*	*County*
Low poverty (< 20% poor)						
Population	516,298	1,486,254	298,040	1,187,081	158,014	1,017,315
Percent of Population	68.76	86.37	51.94	79.22	31.24	72.04
Number poor	52,173	91 ,916	31,562	67,736	17,658	64,851
Percent poor	40.64	54.64	25.28	40.03	11.68	30.39
Number census tract	128	331	90	283	46	203
Moderate poverty (20% to 39% poor)						
Population	172,233	172,233	206,189	241,726	217,741	258,742
Percent of population	22.94	10.01	35.93	16.13	43.04	18.32
Number poor	45,802	45,802	57,191	65,397	64,251	76,523
Percent poor	35.67	27.24	45.81	38.64	42.49	35.85
Number census tract	55	55	75	85	78	92
High poverty (40% or more poor)						
Population	62,348	62,348	69,593	69,593	130,086	136,053
Percent of population	8.30	3.62	12.13	4.64	25.72	9.63
Number poor	30,414	30,414	36,093	36,093	69,127	71,871
Percent poor	23.69	18.09	28.91	21.33	45.72	33.67
Number census tract	21	21	39	39	73	77

[a] Nonresidential census tracts were excluded in the analysis.
[b] U.S. Bureau of the Census, 1972. Census of Population and Housing, 1970: Fourth Count Population Summary Tape, Cleveland, Ohio. Number of poor is based on 1969 income.
[c] U.S. Bureau of the Census, 1982. Census of Population and Housing, 1980: Summary Tape File 3, Cleveland, Ohio. Number of poor is based on 1979 income.
[d] U.S. Bureau of the Census, 1991. Census of Population and Housing, 1990: Summary Tape File 1, Cleveland, Ohio. 1990 poverty estimates were prepared by Morton Paglin, Center for Regional Economic Issues, Case Western Reserve University, based on 1989 public assistance levels.

poor in these areas from 1980 to 1990 and clearly indicate that original poverty areas contain a much smaller portion of the total poor population than they did in 1970. Original poverty areas that still exist today housed almost one-fifth of the poor in 1970 but now account for less than 10 percent of the poor in Cuyahoga County.

Early poverty areas lost significant population between 1970 and 1990 as the number of poor persons grew. These areas have represented a consistent percentage of the county's poor, however, housing about eight percent of the poor in 1970 and about seven percent in 1990. Rapid population loss throughout the 1970s elevated the poverty rate in these areas.

Emerging poverty areas show the greatest absolute increase in the number of poor persons along with continued population decline. Emerging areas account for a larger portion of the poor than either original or early poverty areas and, unlike these areas, have shown notable increases in the number of poor residents. In fact, this is the type of poverty area in which the largest proportion of poor individuals live.

Only two tracts are former poverty areas, and they account for a very small proportion of the population. These tracts in the center of the city gained population between 1970 and 1980 and remained stable through 1990. Located in the downtown area, they increased their poor population between 1970 and 1980; by 1990, their poor population had declined significantly.

Map 1 displays the locations of these high poverty areas along with lower poverty tracts in the remainder of the county. Original poverty areas are confined to the center of the city and include most of the statistical planning areas[7] known as Hough, the western portion of Central, small parts of Kinsman, and Ohio City. Early poverty areas are in the eastern portion of Central, part of Kinsman, and much of Fairfax, and some scattered tracts in St. Clair–Superior, Woodland Hills, and University. Emerging poverty areas are on the outskirts of the city and in a few eastern suburban areas. They represent much of Detroit-Shoreway, Tremont, Glenville and parts of Goodrich–Kirtland Park, University, St. Clair–Superior, and Ohio City. A few emerging poverty tracts are scattered in the Clark-Fulton and Archwood-Denison areas to the west and in Union-Miles, Buckeye-Shaker, Woodland Hills, and Mt. Pleasant to the east. Former poverty areas are confined to downtown.

Although it seems contradictory to use both spread and concentration to describe the geographical distribution of poverty, that is what we see in the Cleveland area. There is a growing concentration of poverty; more of the poor live in high poverty areas. There is also a spread of these concentrated poverty areas outward, toward the edges and suburbs of the city. Moreover, the number of high poverty areas has grown geometrically since 1970. If this trend were to continue, nearly three-quarters of city of Cleveland tracts would reach high poverty levels before the year 2000.

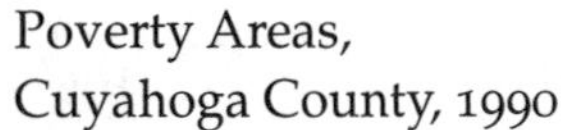

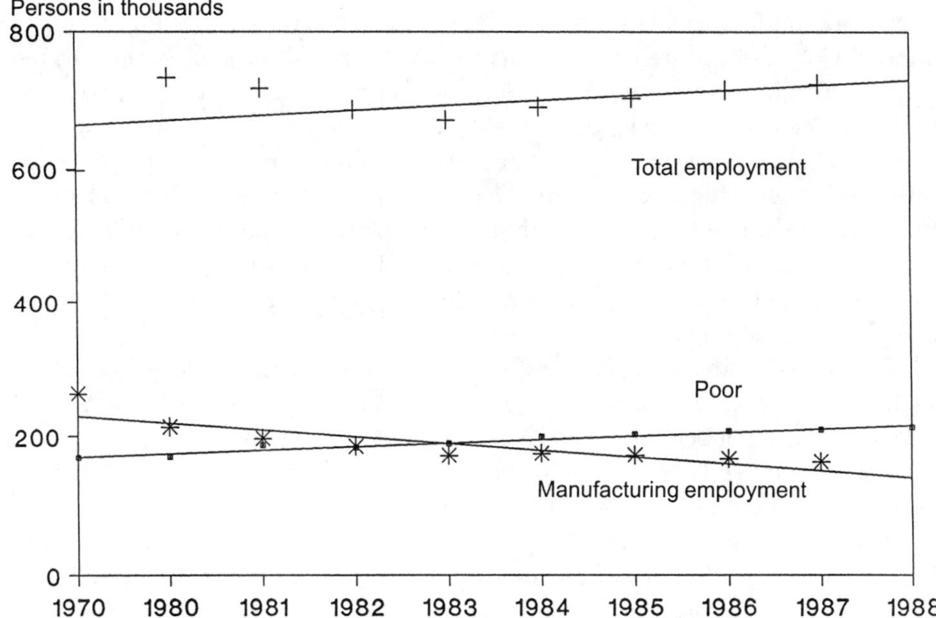

Source: U.S. Bureau of the Census. Analysis by Center for Urban Poverty and Social Change, Mandel School of Applied Social Sciences, Case Western Reserve University.

Growth of Poverty: Explanatory Factors for Cleveland

The persistent and geographically concentrated poverty in the Cleveland area arose within a context that is economic and demographic, local and regional. The decade of the 1980s brought a steady loss of manufacturing jobs in the city of Cleveland and Cuyahoga County as a whole. Many of the remaining manufacturing jobs moved to the suburbs. The geographic shift of manufacturing jobs to outlying areas was accompanied by population losses as employed persons moved their residences further out from the central city.

Nonpoor employed persons exited the city at a much faster rate than the unemployed poor. Particular neighborhoods, once traditional entry points for new immigrants, suffered significant net population losses as the rate of in-migration slowed drastically. Residents left in these areas are the ones most affected by the loss of jobs for low-skill workers. In their neighborhoods, poverty rises and steadily increases in concentration.

Economic Change and Poverty

The Cleveland area economy grew steadily throughout the 1950s, 1960s, and much of the 1970s with major emphasis on a wide base of manufacturing enterprises. From peak employment of 918,000 in 1979, jobs declined rapidly until 1983. Ninety thousand jobs disappeared in this short period. Most of these jobs were recovered in the economic upturn of the mid-1980s, and employment for the region returned to approximately the 1979 level.[8]

The regional recovery in the total number of jobs obscures some fundamental shifts in the Cleveland area economy. One important change is in the mix of industries and occupations. Specifically, employment in manufacturing has decreased as employment in service industries has increased. In 1970, nearly 40 percent of area jobs were in goods-producing industries. By 1985, this sector represented only 28 percent of jobs, or one-third fewer jobs than in 1969.[9]

Fast growth in executive and professional jobs along with rapid decline in low-skill, blue-collar employment characterizes the situation. Low-skill jobs in the service sector have not begun to replace the numbers of lost blue-collar jobs. Existing low-skill, service sector jobs offer lower wages and fewer benefits than jobs previously occupied by the least skilled individuals in Cleveland's work force.[10]

The geographic location of employment is another important change. Most growth has occurred in the far distant suburbs, leaving the city of Cleveland with only about one-third of all jobs in the Standard Metropolitan Statistical Area (SMSA). During the early 1980s, the central city lost 27 percent of its manufacturing jobs, while surrounding suburbs lost only 4 percent. Current growth in city of Cleveland jobs is largely confined to the downtown area's professional and business services sector, which requires highly skilled employees.[11]

Evidence that the loss and relocation of manufacturing jobs played a key role in the formation of central city poverty areas comes from a comparative analysis of urban areas by Mark A. Hughes.[12] He demonstrates that both the absolute loss of central city manufacturing jobs and the shift of these jobs to outlying areas are responsible for a growing concentration of poverty in northern industrial cities such as Cleveland. By contrast, suburban relocation of manufacturing jobs has not led to similar concentrations of poverty in the South and West. Hughes speculates that the extreme concentrations of poverty seen in older northern cities are the result of racial segregation and transportation systems that make it difficult to reach outlying suburbs from the central city. Blacks have been most adversely affected by the loss of manufacturing jobs and, in the North, these residents are clustered in particular parts of the city. The public rail and bus systems of older cities were designed for jobs in central locations, not for the widely dispersed employment destinations brought about by suburban job expansion.

Change in the regional economy can affect some neighborhoods more adversely than others. Vulnerable neighborhoods may be those that contain disproportionate numbers of workers who were particularly dependent on the types of industries that declined or who were in close proximity to the locations where crucial employers were lost. Neighborhoods with large numbers of low-income workers (i.e., working poor) will feel economic shifts more strongly than poor areas with low labor force participation.

To explore the effects of a shrinking manufacturing job base on specific city of Cleveland neighborhoods, we used census data to examine employment levels and compare the proportions of blue-collar and professional workers in original, early, emerging, and low poverty areas. We hypothesized that emerging poverty areas had a large contingent of blue-collar workers in manufacturing industries in 1980. Labor market shifts beginning in 1979, therefore, would have had strong effects in these tracts that fell into high poverty during the 1980s. We also anticipated that the working population had been proportionately larger in the emerging poverty areas than in the early and original areas so that these areas would be more responsive to economic changes.

Table 3 demonstrates that the emerging high poverty census tracts of 1990 were indeed those with fairly high overall employment levels in 1980 but with high proportions of blue-collar workers.[13] The early poverty areas had a similar proportion of blue-collar workers among the employed population, but a much smaller proportion of the adult population was actually employed in 1980. Regional economic changes affecting job opportunities would, therefore, have fewer effects in these neighborhoods. Census tracts maintaining low poverty levels had a more diversified base of occupations, including professionals, in 1980. This pattern is consistent with a regression analysis demonstrating that neighborhoods with high proportions of blue-collar workers experienced the largest increases in poverty rate while those with high proportions of professionals experienced the lowest increases.[14]

As can also be seen in Table 3, employment levels in the city of Cleveland generally declined after 1970. By 1980, however, they had reached very low levels in original poverty areas (only 32 percent of individuals ages sixteen to fifty-nine worked), while remaining fairly high in emerging poverty areas (more than half the residents worked).

It is the overall type and level, rather than the specific location, of employment in the metropolitan area that affects poverty. The relationship is clarified in Figure 1, which plots over time the number of total jobs and manufacturing jobs along with the number of poor persons in Cuyahoga County. Poverty rates have gone up as manufacturing jobs have declined in spite of the increase in the total number of jobs.

MIGRATION AND POVERTY

Differential migration appears to be an important factor in the rise of concentrated poverty in some areas of Cleveland. Cleveland and the entire region have experienced major population losses since the 1970s. The population in the SMSA declined from approximately 2,064,000 in 1970 to 1,831,000 in 1990. This population

Table 3
Employment Levels and Occupation by Type of Poverty Area, Cuyahoga County, 1980

Poverty areas	*Percent adults employed*[a]		*Percent blue collar*[b]		*Percent professional*[c]	
	1970[d]	*1980*[e]	*1970*	*1980*	*1970*	*1980*
Original poverty areas	47	32	48	29	6	9
Early poverty areas	64	44	46	32	11	10
Emerging poverty areas	63	53	49	32	11	11
Low (city) poverty areas	71	68	46	29	14	13
Low (suburb) poverty areas	71	76	28	14	31	28

[a] This is the ratio of adults aged sixteen and over who worked twenty-six weeks or more in 1979 to the total population aged sixteen to fifty-nine.
[b] This is the percent of the employed population classified as operators, fabricators, and laborers.
[c] This is the percent of the employed population classified as professional, managerial, and specialty.
[d] U.S. Bureau of the Census, 1972, Census of Population and Housing, 1970: Fourth Count Population Summary Tape, Cleveland, Ohio.
[e] U.S. Bureau of the Census, 1982, Census of Population and Housing, 1980: Summary Tape File 3, Cleveland, Ohio.

loss of 11 percent will affect poverty rates in specific locations if the nonpoor move out at a higher rate than the poor.

Table 4 shows the change in poor and nonpoor populations for areas that became impoverished in the 1970s.[15] From 1970 to 1980, a combination of poor in-migration and nonpoor out-migration formed the early poverty areas. We estimate that approximately 4.47 percent of the increased concentration of poverty between 1970 and 1980 was the result of poor persons moving in and approximately 51.54 percent was the result of the higher rate of out-migration of the nonpoor. In-migration of the poor from surrounding areas is important, but out-migration of the nonpoor appears to be the stronger factor in the creation of Cleveland's early high poverty areas during the 1970s.

The role of differential migration in the emerging poverty areas of the 1980s is summarized in Table 5. Growth of poverty in the county in the 1980s was more pronounced than in the previous decade, moving from 169,226 to 213,430 (an in-

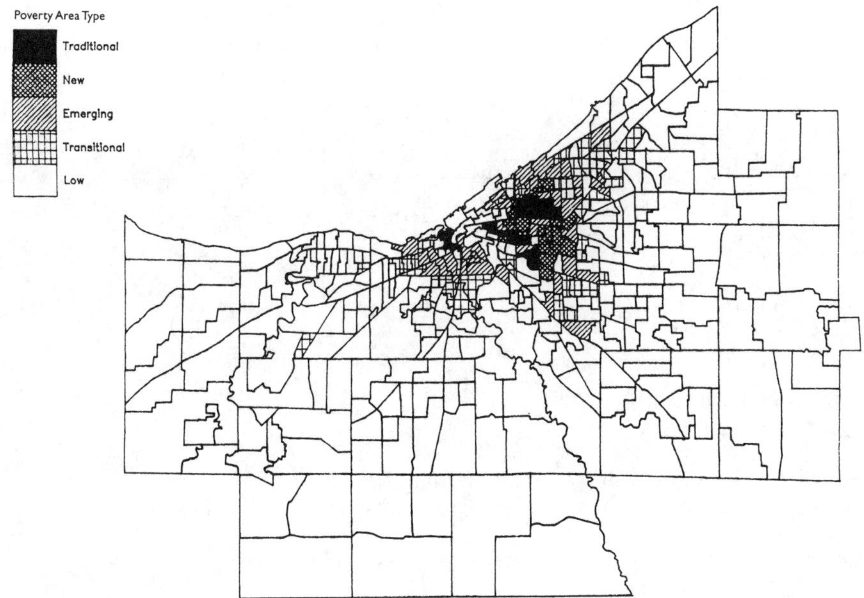

Source: Ohio Bureau of Employment Services, Prepared by Center for Regional Economical Issues, Case Western Reserve University. Analysis by Center for Urban Poverty and Social Change, Mandel School of Applied Social Sciences, Case Western Reserve University.

Figure 1
Trends in Poverty and Employment, Cuyahoga County, 1980–1988

crease of 26 percent). We find that both the in-migration of the poor and the out-migration of the nonpoor from emerging poverty areas proceeded at a lower rate than it did in the early poverty areas of the 1970s. Nevertheless, differential migration remains a crucial factor in the creation of emerging poverty areas.

This analysis of migration rests on relatively conservative assumptions about the growth of poverty. With higher estimates of the expected increase in the poverty rate, the effect of nonpoor migration is less dramatic, but it still accounts for a substantial portion of the growth in concentrated poverty. Although there is evidence that poor households move more frequently than nonpoor households, most of these moves are within the city of Cleveland itself.[16] The net effect on the Cleveland poverty rate is marginal.

SEGREGATION

Douglas S. Massey offers an additional explanation for the geographic concentration of poverty in northern cities experiencing declines in manufacturing employment. Northern cities are more geographically segregated by race than cities in the South and West. Blacks are disproportionately affected by regional losses in lower-

Table 4
Estimation of the Role of Migration in Creation of New Poverty Areas, 1970–1980

	1970[a]	*1980*[b]	*Change*	*Percent change*
Total	48,636	31,216	-17,420	-35.82
Number poor	13,564	14,262	+698	+5.15
Number nonpoor	35,072	16,954	-18,118	-51.66
Percent poor	27.89	45.69	+17.80	
Number of poor increased in county, 1970–80 (169,226 - 168,132 = 1,094)			+.65%	
Estimated number of poor in 1980 without migration (i.e., 0.65% of 13,564)			13,652	
Estimated number of persons who became poor, 1970–80 (13,652 - 13,564)			88	
Estimated number of poor who moved in, 1970–80 (698 - 88)			+610	
Estimated number of nonpoor who moved out, 1970–80 (17,420 + 610)			-18,030	
Percent poor who moved in			+4.47%	
Percent nonpoor who moved out			-51.54%	

[a] U.S. Bureau of the Census, 1972, Census of Population and Housing, 1970: Fourth Count Population Summary Tape, Cleveland, Ohio. Number of poor is based on 1969 income.
[b] U.S. Bureau of the Census, 1982, Census of Population and Housing, 1980: Summary Tape File 3, Cleveland, Ohio. Number of poor is based on 1979 income.

skill jobs. When blacks are clustered in segregated neighborhoods, the regional economic shift has a neighborhood effect. Cleveland and Cuyahoga County are highly segregated by race. On most segregation indices, Cleveland is second only to Chicago in the degree to which blacks are segregated residentially.[17]

TRANSPORTATION

The concentrated effects of suburban job relocation on segregated city of Cleveland neighborhoods are likely to affect low-skill, employed residents of these neighborhoods in two ways. Those who can, move their homes nearer to their jobs; those who cannot move must change jobs or commute.

Table 5
Estimation of the Role of Migration in Creation of Emerging Poverty Areas, 1980–1990

	1980[a]	*1990*[b]	*Change*	*Percent change*
Total	101,042	87,091	-13,951	-13.81
Number poor	31,276	39,992	+8,716	+27.87
Number nonpoor	69,766	47,099	-22,667	-32.49
Percent poor	30.95	45.92	+14.97	
Number of poor increased in county, 1980–90 (213,430 - 169,226)			+26.12%	
Estimated number of poor in 1988 without migration (i.e., 26.12% of 101,042)			39,446	
Estimated number of persons who became poor, 1980–90 (39,446 - 31,276)			8,170	
Estimated number of poor who moved in, 1980–90 (8,716 - 8,170)			+546	
Estimated number of nonpoor who moved out, 1980–90 (13,951 + 546)			-14,497	
Percent poor who moved in			+1.38%	
Percent nonpoor who moved out			-23.54%	

[a] U.S. Bureau of the Census, 1982, Census of Population and Housing, 1980: Summary Tape File 3, Cleveland, Ohio. Number of poor is based on 1979 income.
[b] U.S. Bureau of the Census, 1991, Census of Population and Housing, 1990: Summary Tape File 1, Cleveland, Ohio. 1990 poverty estimates were prepared by Morton Paglin, Center for Regional Economic Issues, Case Western Reserve University.

There is considerable debate about how the poor are affected by the geographic proximity of employment and place of residence.[18] There is no question that traveling farther to work adds expense and burden, particularly in this area where many companies outside the city of Cleveland are difficult or impossible to reach via public transportation from high poverty areas. In 1980, a majority of workers in Cleveland traveled to work by private vehicle, but those in high poverty areas were more reliant on public transportation. Nearly 35 percent of workers in original and early poverty areas relied on public transportation, while only a little more than 20 percent of those in emerging poverty areas used public transportation.

Using individual data from a 5 percent sample of the 1980 census, John D. Kasarda estimates that the burden of traveling to work is considerable for black males in Cleveland with low educational levels. He reports that 83.6 percent of black males without high school degrees who held full-time jobs in 1980 commuted to work by private vehicle. Their mean travel time was fully ten minutes longer than that of whites with similar credentials. This suggests a greater disadvantage in reaching the workplace for those whose wages make them least able to afford it.[19]

HOUSING

Availability of livable housing is another factor of importance in these areas. Between 1977 and 1987, the number of residential structures (one to four units) increased in Cuyahoga County by 5.3 percent but declined by 1.1 percent in the city of Cleveland. Housing stock dropped more precipitously in some areas of the city: 11.7 percent in original poverty areas, 6.8 percent in early poverty areas, 2.5 percent in emerging poverty areas, and less than 0.1 percent in low poverty areas.[20] Reduction of suitable housing stock through demolitions and abandonments may add impetus to large population losses in high poverty areas.

The decline and abandonment of housing in Cleveland's central city has been attributed to several factors, including the predominance of single-family, wooden structures and a surplus of affordable suburban housing drawing potential buyers and renters away from the central city.[21] This suggests a push-pull process in Cleveland's emerging poverty areas; the nonpoor are pulled away by affordable housing in outlying areas and pushed away by deteriorating neighborhood conditions.

The reciprocal relations between poverty and housing conditions in the city of Cleveland clearly contribute to the maintenance of geographically concentrated poverty. As the nonpoor moved out through the 1980s, housing values declined steadily. Original high poverty neighborhoods had the lowest values, followed closely by early and emerging poverty areas, and finally affecting areas approaching the high poverty threshold. The housing stock declined in a similar progression. The diminished supply, quality, and value of housing in the city of Cleveland reflects regional economic change and the resulting conditions that begin to institutionalize concentrated poverty over time.

FAMILY STRUCTURE

The female-headed household is a growing American phenomenon among families at all economic levels.[22] Today, more than 80 percent of black and 40 percent of white families will spend a period of time headed by a woman. Although many female-headed households are not poor, the poverty rate is much higher in this type of family; more than 50 percent are poor at some time. Female-headed families also make up a substantial proportion of poor families.

Poor, female-headed households are also more likely to be persistently poor. In the city of Cleveland, an estimated 26.1 percent of households headed by black women are poor for ten years or more, as compared to 6.2 percent of households headed by black men. Among white household heads, the persistent poverty rate for females is 12.5 percent and for males 2.0 percent.[23]

Male-headed families are much more likely to earn their way out of poverty than are female-headed families both because of increased male earnings and increased earnings of adult females likely to be present in male-headed families. For individuals who earn minimum wages, both parents must typically work to bring family income above the poverty level. Single-parent families generally have only one wage earner. A single parent in a family of four must earn at least six dollars per hour to escape poverty; the ability to work, as well as the expense of doing so, is often complicated by child care responsibilities. The majority of poor, female-headed households receive welfare benefits. For female-headed families, marriage and transfer payments are more important in ending spells of poverty than are increased earnings.[24]

Between 1970 and 1980, there was an increase nationally in the proportion of female-headed households from 9.1 percent to 11.6 percent for whites and from 28.3 percent to 40.3 percent for blacks. Table 6 shows that the rates of female-headed households have also grown in Cleveland and have reached extremely high proportions in original and early poverty areas. This growth has been attributed to many factors, including the changing roles of women, increased acceptance of divorce and children born to unmarried mothers, availability of Aid to Families with Dependent Children (AFDC), and declining labor force participation among black men.[25]

Known as the "marriageable male pool" hypothesis, this last factor is particularly visible in Cleveland's areas of highly concentrated poverty. Table 6 shows the ratio of males over sixteen years of age, who are employed or in school, to females aged fifteen through fifty-nine. The assumption is that males who are unemployed and high school dropouts are seldom desirable partners for marriage. In the original poverty areas in 1980, females outnumbered "marriageable" males by more than two to one. Ratios were more favorable in the emerging poverty areas in 1980, but this was before the impact of regional economic changes on employment levels was felt in these areas.

In their search for suitable marriage partners, females are not, of course, confined to their neighborhoods. The neighborhood effects are likely to occur through a combination of proximity factors as well as their influence on residents' expectations for marriage over time. Nevertheless, rising male unemployment in these neighborhoods, especially among young adults, is likely to erode further the formation of two-parent families in these neighborhoods. At wages close to the minimum, two earners in a family are necessary to escape poverty.

Table 6

Percent Female-Headed Households and Ratio of Females (aged 15–59) to Males (aged 16+) Employed or in School (aged 16–19), Cuyahoga County, 1970–1980

	Percent female-headed households[a]		*Ratio of females to males*[b]	
Poverty areas	*1970*[c]	*1980*[d]	*1970*	*1980*
Original poverty areas	54	77	1.49: 1	2.19: 1
Early poverty areas	39	65	1.24: 1	1.61: 1
Emerging poverty areas	30	46	1.13: 1	1.31: 1
Low (city) poverty areas	17	30	1.05: 1	1.14: 1
Low (suburb) poverty areas	8	14	0.98: 1	0.96: 1

[a] This is the percent of households with children that were headed by females.

[b] Figure for males included all males aged sixteen and over who were employed twenty-six weeks or more and males aged sixteen to nineteen who were in school. The figure for females included all females aged fifteen to fifty-nine.

[c] U.S. Bureau of the Census, 1972, Census of Population and Housing 1970: Fourth Count Population Summary Tape, Cleveland, Ohio.

[d] U.S. Bureau of the Census, 1982, Census of Population and Housing 1980: Summary Tape File 3, Cleveland, Ohio.

Poverty and Neighborhood Conditions

Concentrated, persistent poverty brings with it an array of phenomena with important consequences for neighborhoods and cities. As the poor are increasingly confined to particular neighborhoods, their isolation from the mainstream may act to limit avenues of escape from poverty. Areas of intense poverty are commonly associated with a convergence of undesirable conditions, from deteriorated housing and physical environments to family disintegration, school failure, delinquency, crime, and substance abuse. When these conditions become acute and widespread in particular geographic locations, they may have powerful effects on individuals who live in their midst. The conditions themselves may become forces that tend to keep residents in poverty. As more neighborhoods of a city become troubled in these ways, the overall quality of life in a metropolitan area declines.

ISOLATION OF THE POOR

In his ground-breaking work, *The Truly Disadvantaged,* William J. Wilson argues forcefully that the growing isolation of the inner-city poor is a phenomenon that makes poverty more alarming and increasingly resistant to traditional economic solutions. As geographic concentration separates the poor from other segments of society, their experience changes. The isolated poor are unable to receive information and assistance from nonpoor friends and neighbors who might help them gain access to resources, services, and opportunities that could reduce their poverty (e.g., jobs, training programs, transportation, health care, education). Children growing up isolated from the nonpoor have few role models for working, achievement, and other behaviors that can help them advance in society. As a result, the beliefs and attitudes of isolated people may diverge from those of the larger society. They may become alienated from mainstream ways of life.[26]

Researchers have only recently begun to study how and to what degree geographic concentration of poverty results in long-term social isolation. Further, there have been few attempts to measure or quantify isolation of the poor. L. J. D. Wacquant and Wilson, reporting on one of the largest studies of families in Chicago's high poverty areas, offer evidence of a relationship between concentrated poverty and social isolation.[27]

Although no survey research comparable to that for Chicago has been done in Cleveland, we can examine the degree of isolation of Cleveland's poor by calculating an index (*P*) developed by Stanley Lieberson.[28] This index reveals how likely it is that the poor will come into contact with the nonpoor in their places of residence. Table 7 shows that the degree of residential isolation of the poor in the county has increased since 1970, a finding consistent with Wilson's thesis. The chance that poor persons living in the city of Cleveland will encounter nonpoor persons has declined considerably (see column 2) as their chance of interacting with other poor persons has increased (see column 1). Although the isolation of the suburban poor has risen slightly, it is clear that poor residents of the suburbs are much less isolated geographically than those living in the city of Cleveland.

One of the most devastating aspects of isolation is that it limits exposure of the poor to role models who might help economic advancement. To see whether this is true in Cleveland, we use data from the 1970 and 1980 censuses to identify adult residents of high poverty tracts who were working full- or part-time.[29] If, over the decade, we see a growing proportion of the poor living in areas in which few of the adults are employed, we can infer that role models are becoming increasingly scarce in poor neighborhoods.

In 1970, about 16 percent of Cleveland's poor lived in tracts where labor force participation was low—less than 50 percent. By 1980, almost 40 percent of the poor lived in tracts where fewer than half of all adults were working. This trend is a result of the overall decline in labor force participation in poor areas and the concentration of the poor in high poverty areas.

Households without regularly employed individuals require alternative sources of income. Some critics suggest that some income sources further isolate groups of the poor, specifically those who receive Aid for Dependent Children and General Assistance for nonelderly and nondisabled households without children. Studies

Table 7
Mean Isolation Index of the Poor, City of Cleveland and Suburbs of Cuyahoga County, 1970–1990

Year	*Poor with poor*[a]	*Poor with nonpoor*[b]	*Nonpoor with poor*[c]	*Nonpoor with nonpoor*[d]
		City of Cleveland		
1970[e]	.27	.73	.15	.85
1980[f]	.32	.68	.19	.81
1990[g]	.40	.60	.25	.75
		Western Suburbs		
1970	.04	.96	.03	.97
1980	.05	.95	.03	.97
1990	.07	.93	.05	.95
		Eastern Suburbs		
1970	.07	.93	.05	.95
1980	.12	.88	.06	.94
1990	.18	.82	.08	.92

[a] Probability of poor interacting with poor.
[b] Probability of poor interacting with nonpoor.
[c] Probability of nonpoor interacting with poor.
[d] Probability of nonpoor interacting with nonpoor.
[e] U.S. Bureau of the Census, 1972, Census of Population and Housing, 1970: Fourth Count Population Summary Tape, Cleveland, Ohio. Number of poor is based on income reported in 1969.
[f] U.S. Bureau of the Census, 1982, Census of Population and Housing, 1980: Summary Tape File 3, Cleveland, Ohio. Number of poor is based on 1979 income.
[g] U.S. Bureau of the Census, 1991, Census of Population and Housing, 1990: Summary Tape File 1, Cleveland, Ohio. In the city of Cleveland, the census tract data in the 1990 STF-1A tape has 255 more persons than the actual report 505,616 because of misclassified boundaries. 1990 poverty estimates were prepared by Morton Paglin, Center for Regional Economic Issues, Case Western Reserve University, based on 1989 public assistance levels.

have repeatedly shown that availability of welfare benefits has minimal effect on family structure and adult decisions to work.[30] We know much less, however, about how welfare dependency affects neighborhoods. The effects are difficult to isolate; in most states, the majority of welfare recipients fall well below the poverty level so that the effects of welfare per se cannot be separated from the effects of poverty itself.

Nevertheless, we examine welfare dependency levels over the 1980s for two reasons. First, we suspect that the stigma associated with welfare programs may further isolate recipients. Second, decisions of service providers, businesses, and property owners in high poverty areas may be colored by their perceptions of welfare programs and beneficiaries.

The ratio of AFDC cases to total households in Cleveland rose throughout the decade. In original poverty areas, it was 338 per 1,000 households in 1980 and 467 by 1990. In early poverty areas, the change in AFDC cases was from 250 per 1,000 households to 490. In emerging poverty areas, the increase was from 200 cases per 1,000 households to 318.

Since 1970, Cleveland's poor have become more isolated, both physically and socially. Their neighborhoods are increasingly characterized by low labor force participation, widespread reliance on public assistance, and diminishing opportunities for contact with employed role models. These neighborhoods, isolated from the mainstream, provide a context for our examination of social problems and quality of life in poverty areas.

SOCIAL PROBLEMS AND QUALITY OF LIFE IN POVERTY AREAS

It is commonly observed that neighborhoods with high concentrations of poverty are also scenes of intense social problems such as crime, delinquency, family disruption, school failure, and substance abuse. The mechanisms responsible for this pattern are often unclear, however. Does the experience of poverty itself lead individuals to behave in these ways regardless of where they live? Or does living in an area of highly concentrated poverty have a detrimental effect on the individuals who live there? Is it poverty per se or the multitude of deficiencies found in poor environments that leads to problematic social responses? Do some of these social behaviors actually work to trap individuals in poverty?

To date, there are no answers to this complex set of questions. In this analysis, we are interested in how concentrated poverty may affect neighborhoods rather than individuals. Some of our questions have to do with changes in poverty and related problems over time. Specifically, is a rise in a neighborhood's poverty rate accompanied by a rise in the rate of selected social problems? Are there particular levels of poverty concentration at which the rate of these problems rises steeply?

Another objective is determining whether some high poverty areas reach extremely high levels of social problems while others maintain more stable patterns. It may be that some of the detrimental effects of concentrated poverty on individual behaviors are more directly related to high rates of associated social problems than they are to the fact of poverty itself. We also suspect that problems associated with poverty are equally, and perhaps more, responsible than economic deprivation for the population, residential, and commercial declines of some areas. Thus high poverty areas with relatively low rates of social problems would have more benign influences on their residents and greater viability as places to live and do business than poverty-intense areas with high levels of social problems.

We identify several available indicators of neighborhood conditions that we hypothesized would be affected by a growing concentration of poverty. As is often the case with administrative agency data, these indicators serve as proxies for complex, unobserved processes. Nevertheless, they are practical tools for monitoring the changing well-being of neighborhoods and their residents and can point the direction for more in-depth studies of processes. Because the incidents of several indicators may fluctuate, a three-year average of data is used for the analysis.

The following are indicators of social conditions: the low birth weight (LBW) is the number of infants born weighing less than 2,500 grams per thousand live births. The infant death rate (INFD) is the number of infants who died before their first birthday per thousand live births. The teen birth rate (TNBR) is the number of infants born to teenage mothers, aged eleven to nineteen, per thousand females aged eleven to nineteen. The rate of births to unmarried mothers (ILBR) is the number of births to mothers classified as unmarried at the time of the birth per thousand live births. The crime rate (CRIM) is the total number of FBI index crimes reported to the Cleveland Police Department and confirmed as valid reports per thousand population. Eight types of crimes are included: homicide, rape, robbery, assault, aggregated assault, burglary, larceny, and auto theft. The juvenile delinquency rate (JUVD) is the number of children in the census tract who were charged with delinquency in the County Juvenile Court per thousand population aged ten to eighteen. The drug violation arrest rate (DRUG) is the number of arrests by the Cleveland Police Department for drug-related offenses per thousand population. Median housing values (MEDV) for one-to-four-unit structures are calculated for each census tract using evaluations provided by the county auditor and compiled by the Housing Policy Research Program of Cleveland State University. All values are reported in 1987 dollars.

The rates of occurrence for these social conditions in each type of poverty area are presented in Table 8. An examination of the patterns suggests that there are differences among original, early, emerging, and low poverty areas on all indicators with the exception of infant death rate. There was no significant growth over the decade, however, in low birth weight or infant death rates even though poverty rates grew by more than 30 percent. The most visible differences among types of areas in rates of change can be seen in housing values, birth rates to unmarried mothers, and drug arrests. An examination of means reveals that the most notable changes in social indicators during the 1980s were in the emerging poverty areas, as anticipated. Whereas all other areas either declined or remained the same in crime rates, the rate in emerging poverty areas increased. Emerging poverty areas also experienced the greatest proportionate decline in median housing values and a large increase in the rate of births to unmarried mothers.

Thus the areas in which poverty became concentrated during the 1980s began to decline rapidly on various indicators of social conditions. They have yet, however, to reach the extreme negative levels of areas that have experienced concentrated poverty for one or more decades. On most indicators, the original poverty

Table 8
Three-Year Average for Selected Social Conditions by Type of Poverty Areas, City of Cleveland, 1980–1989

Variable names	*Traditional poverty areas (n = 17)*	*New poverty areas (n = 18)*	*Emerging poverty areas (n = 38)*	*Low poverty areas (n = 115)*	*Overall city (n = 187)*
LBW rate					
1980–82	155.96	157.74	117.69	90.98	105.29
1987–89	158.32	136.83	126.32	95.74	108.82
INFD rate					
1980–82	26.68	37.70	23.82	17.71	20.79
1987–89	22.39	19.90	15.90	14.97	16.03
TNBR rate					
1980–82	72.69	62.62	50.15	28.39	38.15
1987–89	101.50	90.88	72.65	49.33	59.53
ILBR rate					
1980–82	842.17	769.84	577.42	336.93	448.53
1987–89	886.04	812.22	700.36	477.43	571.42
CRIM rate					
1980–82	176.07	175.49	115.61	82.06	99.03
1987–89	164.35	167.71	122.53	81.92	97.68
JUVD rate					
1980–82	76.90	57.41	53.03	40.49	46.72
1987–89	136.90	118.24	92.30	69.42	81.08
DRUG rate					
1980–82	2.91	6.10	2.40	1.22	1.79
1987–89	33.33	18.86	12.22	4.07	7.86
MEDV rate					
1982	6,201.13	7,732.83	13,396.30	29,237.96	22,101.11
1987	5,060.63	6,481.47	11,330.81	25,339.83	19,051.22

Key: LBW=low birth weight; INFD=infant death rate; TNBR=teen birth rate; ILBR=rate of births to unmarried mothers; CRIM=crime rate; JUVD=juvenile delinquency rate; DRUG=drug violation arrest rate; MEDV=median housing values.

areas still appear to have the most adverse conditions.

Neighborhood social conditions seem to decline following passage into high poverty status, but the longer an area has experienced high poverty seems to lead to an even greater deterioration. It is unclear whether this is merely an effect of the length of deprivation, the historical conditions present at the time the area declined economically, or the fact that areas that have been poor longer are also more isolated in the central portions of the city.

This analysis supports the growing concern that the poor are more geographically and socially isolated and suggests that the forces impinging upon them from their neighborhood environments are worsening. Coupling this with the finding that a growing portion of one city's poor persons are living in these environments suggests that the circumstances of the poor are indeed becoming more intractable and limiting of their opportunities.

Geographically defined neighborhoods may have more profound influences on the poor and their life chances than they do for the more affluent. Poor people are more likely than nonpoor to have social networks that are restricted geographically to their neighborhoods, and the poor are less likely to participate in organizations outside the immediate geographic area.[31] Furthermore, poor children and adolescents whose future life chances are being formed may be most affected by their location of residence.

Summary and Implications

The 1980s brought a dramatic increase in poverty in the Cleveland area, whether it is measured by the absolute number of poor or by poverty rates. The growth of poverty, however, is not a phenomenon of pure numbers. Where and how the poor live and the duration of their economic adversity tell us much about the development, nature, and dimensions of the problem. In the Cleveland area, poverty has become geographically concentrated and increasingly long term.

The result is a growing physical and social isolation of people and neighborhoods circumscribed by poverty. As Cleveland's poor have grown in number, they have also grown into a social and environmental milieu separate from other segments of society. The growth in the number of poor living in areas of concentration and the persistence of poverty have taken place in a context of forces at the regional, metropolitan, and neighborhood levels.

STRUCTURAL FACTORS

Directly related to the growth of poverty in specific areas and to its becoming more persistent is the growing disjuncture between employment opportunities and employment skills. As manufacturing jobs in the region have declined, so have the demands for unskilled labor, especially in the city of Cleveland. Today's thriving industries require a work force with high levels of basic and employment-related skills inconsistent with the dropout rates and school performance of youth in high poverty areas.

Inner-city workers' employment prospects have been further constrained by the relocation of low-skill jobs to outlying areas. The regional public transportation system was designed to serve the city and later to bring people into town on selected suburban routes. Private vehicles, however, have become increasingly important for city residents whose workplaces are located throughout the suburbs and even in areas outside the county. As low-skill, low-wage jobs have moved to the outskirts, travel time and costs have become significant for city residents.

Out-migration has played a large part in the formation of high poverty areas. Particularly the nonpoor have left the early and emerging poverty areas at a much faster rate than the poor. This process seems to have been fueled by a push-pull process, with housing in outlying areas becoming more affordable and declining quality of life in some poor neighborhoods influencing people who can afford to do so to move. If current trends continue, the emerging poverty areas are expected to experience further out-migration of the nonpoor.

Residential segregation has contributed to the geographic concentration of poverty among the black poor. Economic changes that disproportionately affect black families also affect their neighborhoods, which are already isolated along racial lines. But racial segregation does not fully explain today's economic segregation or concentration of poverty. Even though the black population is more likely to live in high poverty areas than the white population, a rapidly growing percentage of residents of high poverty areas are white. Clearly, the manufacturing downturn of the early 1980s adversely affected blue-collar neighborhoods in general, both black and white.

Family structure is an important mediating factor through which regional economic forces and societal trends affect neighborhood economic conditions. Labor force participation among men has reached an all-time low, especially in original and early poverty areas. Families officially headed by females now predominate in these poverty areas. A female-headed family typically has just one wage earner, and her earning potential is tied to the generally lower wages of females. Family structure interacts with poverty to produce difficulties in child rearing and supervision of adolescents that are associated with higher rates of school failure, crime and delinquency, and teenage pregnancy.

Housing affects who can and wants to live in an area. Patterns of investment in housing construction and housing rehabilitation and decisions about public housing affect the location of the poor and their quality of life. The striking differences across types of poverty areas in housing values, conditions, and amount of public housing suggest that housing affects whether a neighborhood becomes high in poverty and the quality of life for both poor and nonpoor residents. The tremendous loss of housing structures in original and early poverty areas compared with the retention of housing in emerging areas implies that they are in different stages with respect to housing supply. Although quality of housing does not create poverty, there seems to be a point at which deterioration in housing supply and quality encourages heavy out-migration and serves to maintain geographically concentrated poverty.

SOCIAL CONDITIONS AND QUALITY OF LIFE

Some Cleveland high poverty areas are distinguished by very high incidences of social problems such as crime, delinquency, teenage pregnancy, school dropouts and failure, and substandard housing. These phenomena can be seen both as effects of concentrated poverty and as factors leading to the further concentration and persistence of poverty. The devastating effects of poverty on individuals and families are partly attributable to these accompanying conditions. And these conditions are of vital concern to surrounding neighborhoods because of perceived and real spillover effects.

The confluence of these social problems in many high poverty areas is not an unexpected finding. More telling, however, is the fact that high poverty areas are neither universally troubled nor troubled in the same ways. Areas that have experienced high poverty for longer periods, that have a lower ratio of adults to children and women to men, that have a higher ratio of general assistance cases to AFDC cases, and where the poor themselves are poorer seem to be more likely to reach an intensity of problems. These economics and demographics, however, do not explain even most of the differences. Individuals, institutions, leaders, and policy decisions not studied in this essay have undoubtedly played a part in alleviating or exacerbating social problems at the neighborhood level.

The concentrated and persistent poverty that we see today presents a complex set of interconnected problems that seem qualitatively different from those of the past. For families and able-bodied adults, poverty is all too rarely a temporary state resulting from unemployment or marital disruption. It is often a chronic condition. In the current economy, many heads of families can earn only a poverty-level wage; others are now out of the work force entirely.

The concentrated poverty now covering vast portions of the city of Cleveland is especially alarming in view of the social conditions that tend to follow. These negative social circumstances have the potential to limit avenues of escape from economic deprivation. As they proliferate and persist, they bring devastating consequences for residents of these areas, the city, and the region as a whole.

Strategies for addressing the new problems of persistent and concentrated poverty will need to embrace both the causes of these conditions and their consequences, both the elements of the social and economic structures and the resulting quality of life in the neighborhoods. The strategies must be tailored to particular neighborhoods because poor neighborhoods differ significantly and the long-term poverty areas are the most troubled.

An understandable reaction to this description of original and early poverty areas might be to conclude that we should focus our strategies where success seems most achievable, the emerging poverty areas. Such a focus has merit, especially for the purpose of preventing further decline, out-migration, and social disruption. Neglecting the higher-risk original and early poverty areas, however, may carry an enormous economic and human cost. These neighborhoods are geographically contiguous to many of the city's key institutions and to areas designated for industrial and commercial redevelopment. This proximity of high risk and high potential suggests a cornerstone for investment to rebuild and restore the human, economic, and physical assets of the areas.

Notes

1. We distinguish here between the poverty rate and the number of poor persons. The rate is an indication of the concentration of poverty while the number of poor persons is an indication of the amount of poverty. The poverty rate rises because the number of poor increases, the total population decreases, or both.

2. The low poverty rates in the suburbs suggest that poverty is not concentrated in these areas. Nevertheless, there are more poor people there today than in 1980.

3. W. J. Wilson, *The Truly Disadvantaged: The Inner City, The Underclass, and Public Policy* (Chicago: University of Chicago Press, 1987), and J. Crane, *An Epidemic Model of Social Problems in Ghettos* (Cambridge, Mass.: Harvard University Press, 1988).

4. There are 204 census tracts in the city of Cleveland and 175 in the remainder of Cuyahoga County. The tracts in Cleveland can be aggregated upward to statistical planning areas (SPAs) which have names that correspond to identifiable areas of the city. The suburban tracts can be aggregated into the incorporated area. For analyses at the census tract level, we have eliminated seventeen nonresidential tracts because these tracts are particularly prone to errors of estimate. All of the eliminated tracts are in the city of Cleveland. Some tract designations changed between 1970 and 1980, and other changes occurred after 1980. Most of these changes occurred in the suburbs because of population growth. Typically, an existing census tract was divided into two and designated with .01 or .02 suffix. Some of our data sources combine the .01 and .02 tracts while others do not. Therefore, in some analyses the total number of census tracts will be less than 379 (or less than 341 tracts with .01 and .02 tracts added). When low population tracts are deleted, there will be 370 (or 332 wherever .01 and .02 tracts are added).

5. The cutoff of 40 percent is arbitrary but is the figure that has been used nationally. Because poverty rates are based on a 15 percent sample of the census population, there is a margin of error in their estimation even in 1970 and 1980. The 1990 rates are estimates based on a regression model so they have additional errors in estimation. Tracts that are slightly above or below the 40 percent threshold may be misclassified because of estimation error. If we assume the errors are unbiased, this will not affect the number of tracts that are high in poverty but will affect the particular tracts that are so designated. Therefore, the reader should not focus on the identity of specific tracts.

6. Persons of Hispanic origin are classified as white or black by the census. The vast majority of Hispanics are classified as white. Although we have intercensus estimates of race, we have no estimates for Hispanic ethnicity.

7. The statistical planning areas are aggregations of census tracts. They were designed to take into account natural boundaries and local perceptions but are often too large to be considered a neighborhood by residents. When we use the word *neighborhood* we are generally referring to the general concept rather than a specific area. The reader will already have noted that there is considerable diversity within many of the SPAs in economic status and other conditions.

8. Edward W. Hill and Heidi M. Rock, *Education as an Economic Development Resource* (Cleveland: Cleveland State University, College of Urban Affairs, 1989); *Cleveland Economic Analysis and Publications* (Cleveland: Center for Regional Economic Issues [REI], Weatherhead School of Management, Case Western Reserve University, 1987); Michael S. Fogarty, "Civic Vision Employment Projections Revisited," *REI Review* (Spring 1989): 29–31.

9. *Cleveland Economic Analysis Publications.*

10. Ibid.

11. Gasper A. Garofalo and Chul S. Park, "The Location of Manufacturing in CALE," *REI Review* (Fall 1987): 14-23; *Cleveland Economic Analysis Publications.*

12. Mark A. Hughes, "Misspeaking Truth to Power: A Geographical Perspective on the 'Underclass' Fallacy," *Economic Geography* 65 (1989): 187–207.

13. Blue-collar workers include individuals whose occupations are classified as operatives, fabricators, and laborers. Professionals include those whose occupations are managerial, professional, and specialty. Blue-collar jobs have traditionally been the jobs for low-skill workers that paid wages well above the minimum.

14. Edward W. Hill and Thomas E. Bier, "Economic Restructuring: Earnings, Occupations, and Housing Values in Cleveland," *Economic Development Quarterly* 3 (1989): 123–43.

15. The tracts we classify as former poverty areas are included here. They became poor between 1970 and 1980 but dropped below the 40 percent poverty threshold by 1990. Between 1970 and1980, the number of poor in the county rose from 168,132 to 169,226, an increase of 0.65 percent. Assuming no out-migration, an increase in poor persons proportionate to the county would result in a poor population of 13,652 in *early* poverty areas in 1980. If the 1970 population of 48,636 were the same in 1980, we would expect that 88 more people (i.e., 13,652 minus 13,564) would become poor in 1980. In *early* poverty areas, the poor population actually grew by 698 to 14,262. The difference between expected and actual growth in the number of poor is an estimate of the in-migration of the poor. In other words, 610 poor persons moved into these areas between 1970 and 1980. We know that the total population decline in *early* poverty areas was 17,420. If 610 poor residents moved in, then the remaining 18,030 people who left were not poor.

16. Mark Salling and Robert Van Der Velde, "Demographic and Housing Characteristics of Migrants and Non-Migrants in the Cleveland SMSA" (Cleveland: NODIS, The Urban Center, Maxine Goodman Levin College of Urban Affairs, Cleveland State University, 1985).

17. Douglas S. Massey and Nancy Denton, "Suburbanization and Segregation in U.S. Metropolitan Areas," *American Journal of Sociology* 94 (1988): 592–626.

18. David Ellwood, "The Spatial Mismatch Hypothesis: Are Teenage Jobs Missing the Ghetto?" In *The Black Youth Unemployment Crisis,* ed. R. Freeman and H. Holzer (Chicago: University of Chicago Press, 1989), 147–85; John D. Kasarda, "Urban Industrial Transition and the Underclass," *Annals of the American Academy of Political and Social Science* 501 (1989): 26–47.

19. Kasarda, "Urban Industrial Transition."

20. The number of structures comes from the county auditor's office and was compiled by Thomas Bier of Cleveland State University, Maxine Goodman Levin College of Urban Affairs. The structures counted in this analysis are those that have between one and four units and are residential. The findings do not include the effects of construction and demolition of apartment buildings.

21. Thomas Bier, Edric Weld, Mark Hoffman, and Ivan Maric, *Housing Supply and Demand: Cleveland Metropolitan Area, 1950–2005* (Cleveland: Cleveland State University, College of Urban Affairs).

22. I. Garfinkel and S. McLanahan, *Single Mothers and Their Children: A New American Dilemma* (Washington, D.C.: The Urban Institute, 1986).

23. T. K. Adams and G. J. Duncan, *The Persistence of Urban Poverty and its Demographic and Behavioral Correlates* (Technical Report). Ann Arbor: University of Michigan, 1988.

24. M. J. Bane and D. T. Ellwood, "Slipping Into and Out of Poverty: The Dynamics of Spells," *The Journal of Human Resources* 21 (1986): 1–23.

25. Garfinkel and McLanahan, *Single Mothers.*

26. W. J. Wilson, *The Truly Disadvantaged: The Inner City, The Underclass, and Public Policy* (Chicago: The University of Chicago Press, 1987).

27. L. J. D. Wacquant and W. J. Wilson, "The Cost of Racial and Class Exclusion in the Inner City," *Annals of the American Academy of Political and Social Science* 501 (1989): 8–26.

28. Stanley Lieberson, *A Piece of the Pie: Black and White Immigrants since 1980* (Los Angeles: University of California Press,1980). There are several *P* indices, each reflecting a somewhat different aspect of isolation. The first *(pPp)* refers to the probability that a poor person in a defined area will encounter a poor person. It is calculated as follows:

$pPp=\Sigma (p_i/P) * (p_i/T)$ where:

p_i = the total number of poor in each tract,

P = the total number of poor in the larger region, and

T = the total population of the tract.

Another indicator is the probability that a poor person will encounter a nonpoor person *(pPnp)*. This is equal to 1-*pPp*. The probability that a nonpoor person will encounter a poor person *(npPp)* reflects the degree to which the poor in their places of residence have firsthand experience with the nonpoor. All these indices are based on where poor and nonpoor live. They do not take into account the degree to which people interact outside their places of residence. Poor inner-city residents are thought to be more constrained in their movement throughout the region than are the nonpoor. Thus, *P* indices are probably a more accurate reflection of poor persons' encounters with the nonpoor than vice versa.

29. We attempt to represent the availability of working adults in each tract by counting those over age sixteen who are employed full- or part-time for twenty-six weeks or more. We compare this count with the number of persons of working age (sixteen to fifty-nine) in the area. This gives us a rough idea of the degree to which an observer would see work as a prevalent adult role in a neighborhood. This is not the equivalent of labor force participation or employment rates as defined by the census. People not in the labor force include those who have stopped looking for work as well as retired and disabled persons and those who have elected not to work so as to take care of home and children. Employment rates are typically calculated by dividing the number employed by the number in the labor force.

30. D. Ellwood, "The Spatial Mismatch Hypothesis: Are Teenage Jobs Missing in the Ghetto?"

31. R. S. Ahlbrandt, *Neighborhoods, People and Community* (New York: Plenum Press, 1984).

Politics and the Development of Public Housing

Mittie Olion Chandler

THIS ESSAY considers some key political dimensions related to the evolution of public housing in Cleveland under the auspices of the Cuyahoga Metropolitan Housing Authority (CMHA), formerly the Cleveland Metropolitan Housing Authority, established in 1933. The provision of publicly subsidized housing for low-income people has historically been engulfed in political controversy emanating from the national level and permeating local settings as well. Cleveland offers a unique opportunity to explore the public housing issue in Ohio where public housing legislation originated.

In 1933, Ohio was the first state to pass enabling legislation for the creation of local housing authorities. The legislation allowed housing authorities to accept federal aid and to take over some existing operations from the federal government. The 1937 Housing Act subsequently provided a formula for federal funding to underwrite local public housing programs. Passage of the federal law was delayed because of debate over various aspects of the law, including potential competition with the private housing market, reducing the construction and purchase of housing among those who could afford to buy, and charges of socialism.

The challenges facing public housing in Cleveland have been a product of the changing environment in which CMHA has existed. Cleveland got an early start in public housing because of Ernest Bohn. Ernest Bohn, known as the father of public housing, was the first and longest-serving executive director of the Cleveland-based public housing authority. He held the position of director for thirty-five years, from 1933 to 1968. Bohn, a conservative Republican, was a resolute advocate (maybe a zealot) who took charge of the housing authority.[1] He was a co-founder and the first president of the National Association of Housing and Redevelopment Officials. Bohn was a one-term member of the Ohio General Assembly and later chaired the Committee on Housing of the Cleveland City Council. He was able to take advantage of early programs that were precursors of the 1937 Housing Act to develop some of the nation's first public housing.

For its first thirty-five years, CMHA operated in relative obscurity when compared to the high visibility it experienced later. The external environment of any agency depends greatly on the particular society and era in which it exists; hence, any analysis of agency behavior must take into account prevailing social conditions, including the level of relevant technologies.[2] A number of factors contributed to the tranquil environment in which CMHA initially functioned: the influential role of Ernest Bohn; the compliant support for the public housing program; and a lack of controversy at the local level. Consideration of these issues must be placed within the context of the national framework for the establishment of public housing. The national perspective undergirds all public housing policies and, early on, deflected local controversy over the program.

National Debate over Public Housing

The debate at the national level over the 1937 Housing Act considered problems and unclear objectives associated with earlier programs under the Resettlement Administration and Public Works Administration (PWA). The discussion was marked by uncertainty surrounding the objectives of early programs under the Resettlement Administration and the PWA. Supporters alternatively cited putting people to work, providing a cultural bridge between urban and rural life, or adapting the earlier British greentowns experiments as the main purpose of public housing.[3]

Clearing slum dwellings and replacing them with new, low-cost housing was first initiated under the PWA. This program, born of the New Deal emergency, was criticized for its centralized administration, site controversies, high development costs, long delays in completion, and high rent levels. The rents were considerably above what many had hoped for and expected, although below those in comparable private market housing.[4] Congress responded to the crisis in housing and construction employment that plagued the country by passing the legislation—despite opposition from the real estate industry.

Federal support under the 1937 act only covered payment of the principal and interest on bonds issued by local housing authorities to finance construction. Operations and maintenance were to be covered by the rents charged. During the 1950s and 1960s, inflation increased the operating and maintenance costs, the aging buildings needed more repair, and residents' incomes were declining relative to the rest of the population. When rents were raised to cover the costs, Congress acted to restrict the increases and to quell tenant unrest and rent strikes in cities such as Newark and St. Louis.[5]

The Brooke Amendment, passed in 1969, limited rents to twenty-five percent of residents' adjusted gross income. The unintentional effect of the Brooke Amendment was to reduce the dollars available to housing authorities for maintenance and other operations. Although the legislation called for operating subsidies to cover the gap between residents' rental payments and the actual operating costs, the funding was never adequate. The resultant structural deterioration of some public housing contributed to its negative image, particularly when linked with racial attitudes directed toward the largely African American clientele in Cleveland.

Transfiguration: National Goals to Local Implementation

If a new bureau is designed to inhibit the activities of powerful social agents, it will be severely opposed from the start.[6] The first public housing in Cleveland did not challenge social norms. It encountered little resistance because it was located in slum neighborhoods; it was expected to serve an acceptable purpose for an acceptable clientele, the deserving poor; the ambiguity of the concept caught policy makers and others off guard; and political acumen enabled Ernest Bohn to head off controversy.

The survival of the agency and conventional public housing became imperiled over time as proposals surfaced to locate public housing in other than "undesirable" areas; as it became long-term housing for the "undeserving, long-term poor"; as forces beyond the control of the CMHA influenced its evolution in unanticipated ways; and as questions regarding changes in organizational leadership developed. Figure 1 portrays the major components of the functional environment of CMHA. These elements form the context of the changes in public housing policy and their implementation in the city.[7]

The persons and entities associated with CMHA interact to form its political environment or its power setting. The environment of CMHA has varied depending on the social conditions and regulations in effect during different periods. Its power setting has influenced operations of the agency in ways that have encumbered its functions more than they have enhanced them.

As shown on the figure, the elements that are most relevant to CMHA's operation are a sovereign, the organization or person with legal authority over the bureau; beneficiaries, persons who benefit from the social functions of a bureau; adversaries, who oppose the functions of the bureau for a variety of reasons; suppliers, who provide goods and services used by the bureau and whose survival may be dependent upon them; and allies, actual or potential supporters, or those who service the same clientele.

The disposition of Cleveland's public housing has been deeply affected by the juxtaposition of the internal and external environments in which the agency operated. When the internal goals and objectives of the agency were consistent with those of the community, the agency prospered. The most salient goals and objectives involve the location of public housing, who its clientele should be, tenant selection and placement procedures, and the benefits or outcomes of public housing

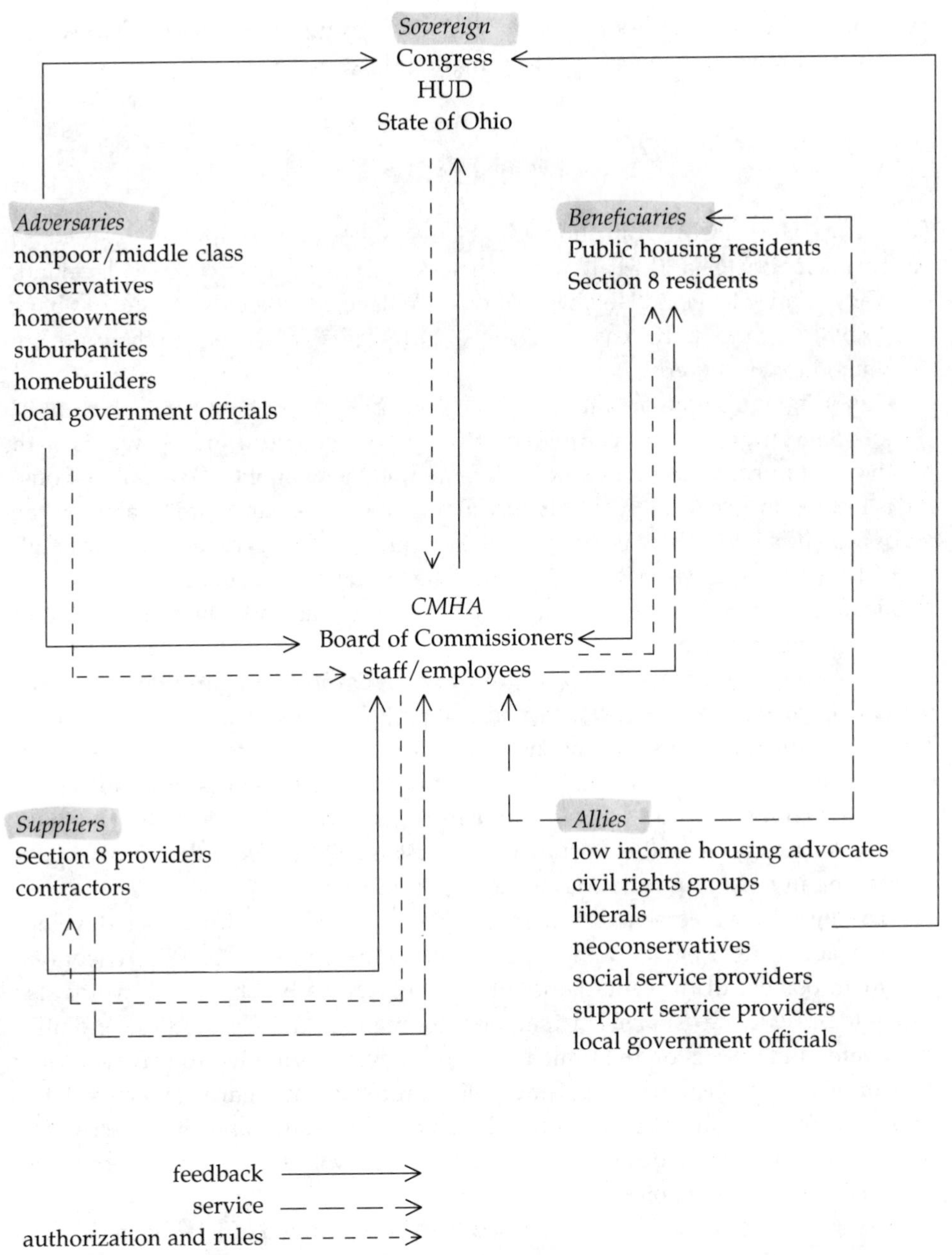

Figure 1
Power Setting of the Cuyahoga Metropolitan Housing Authority

residency. When agency goals clashed with community preferences, CMHA was heavily scrutinized and restrained in pursuing those goals.

Locational Issues

The service area of CMHA includes all of Cuyahoga County with the exception of one municipality, Chagrin Falls. Nonetheless, only five jurisdictions (Cleveland, East Cleveland, Cleveland Heights, Oakwood Village, and Berea) of fifty-eight have any public housing. In the cases of Cleveland Heights and Berea, all the units are designated for the elderly.

Public housing units operated by CMHA are highly concentrated in the central city of Cleveland. The city is divided into twenty-one councilmanic wards with relatively uniform areas of jurisdiction. Fifty-three percent of CMHA public housing is located in two of these wards. Seventy percent of all units are located on the predominantly black East Side. In part, the placement of units reflects the availability of land in areas deemed as blighted. The actual or anticipated resistance to public housing in other areas of the city and county was an additional factor that affected siting decisions.

The siting of public housing requires a cooperation agreement between the public housing authority and the local municipality where the housing is proposed. The cooperation agreement is the instrumentality for the protection of federalism in the public housing program.[8] The intent of the agreement is to establish the financial commitments of the public housing authority and the locality. The mandate for the execution of this document has obstructed the wider dispersal of public housing in most municipalities in Cuyahoga County.

Through the agreement, the municipality indirectly subsidizes the development by accepting a payment in lieu of property taxes (known as PILOT) equivalent to 10 percent of the rental amount received annually. The municipality also agrees to provide the usual municipal services (police and fire protection) and utilities (water and sewer) on the same basis that they are provided to private users.[9] This provision, particularly regarding police protection and garbage removal, has been a subject of contention between the city of Cleveland and the CMHA. The housing authority provides for these services directly by hiring a police force and contracting for garbage pickup.

In 1973, U.S. District Judge Thomas D. Lambros ordered officials from six suburbs to sign cooperation agreements with CMHA on the grounds that their refusal "had the effect of preventing the construction of badly needed housing for the predominantly black applicants who seek residence from the squalor of the central city."[10] This order has not resulted in any significant change in the location of public housing. The Nixon administration's moratorium on subsidized housing (imposed in January 1973 for twenty-eight months) was in force when the ruling was handed down, so it had no immediate impact. Suburban communities were required to show cause for rejecting public housing. Some officials responded by citing the high cost of land acquisition and the lack of undeveloped land.

A thrust begun during the 1970s to locate public housing in suburban communities met with a great deal of resistance. Objections included such comments as "I think in its attempt to force this [public housing] upon political subdivisions we are trying to destroy the basic philosophies on which this country was founded" from one suburban mayor.[11] Another mayor objected to the tax-free status of public housing. Conformance to local building codes was raised by other municipal officials. Zoning, building, and housing codes have typically been among the devices used to halt construction of housing for lower-income people.

Resistance to public housing has both racial and economic dimensions. Residents' trepidation regarding a racially changing neighborhood is compounded by fears of diminished property values. Although research has failed to prove that the location of subsidized housing has a negative impact on housing property values, it remains a prevalent notion. During the first year of his mayoralty, Carl Stokes promoted a subsidized housing program in the Lee-Seville area on the city's southeast side. No homes were constructed after black middle-income residents opposed placing units on the available vacant land.

In 1971, the Cleveland City Council authorized the construction of 2,500 units throughout the city on scattered sites. In the waning days of his administration, Mayor Stokes decried the number of units as inadequate. Stokes was quoted as saying, "Political expediency, not community need, was allowed to dictate the figure."[12] CMHA had proposed to build 6,750 units.

During 1971, controversy erupted around plans to construct 132 units of public housing on Cleveland's southwest side. The issue served as a rallying point for anti-Stokes council members and citizens. The ward councilman, Richard Harmody, spoke fervently against the proposal. Plans for public housing for the elderly in the city's fourth ward, represented by then City Council president James V. Stanton, met similar opposition. After a construction permit was issued for the building, Stanton charged that the plans did not meet the city's building code. Additional plans for seven two-family detached homes proposed on the site were ultimately dropped.

Between 1969 and 1976, 1,050 scattered-site homes were approved for Cleveland by the Department of Housing and Urban Development (HUD). Negative reactions from some neighborhoods meant that fewer than 40 percent were built during that time. The more affluent neighborhoods have been largely successful in excluding public housing, and the suburbs remain practically off-limits.

Other efforts since 1972 have done little to deconcentrate public housing. Two types of scattered-site housing are managed by CMHA. One provides multifamily housing in groups of twelve to twenty-five units constructed as duplexes or town houses. The architecture of these buildings tends to differ noticeably from surrounding homes. The second version, known as the Acquisition Housing Program, consists of one- and two-family houses purchased and renovated by CMHA. The buildings are part of the existing stock in the neighborhoods and are virtually indistinguishable from adjacent properties. A study of the latter program found that it had no negative impact on property values.[13]

The vast majority of public housing in the United States and Cleveland was built before 1973. After that time, influenced by the 1973 Nixon administration moratorium on federal housing programs, less than a thousand of the approximately twelve thousand units in Cleveland were built. Well over three-fourths of these newer units are designated for the elderly and not for families. There has been little opportunity to reverse the segregative effects of decisions regarding the location of public housing since the early 1970s because the construction of new units has been drastically curtailed.

The compounding effects of the concentration of public housing and related ills is very apparent in the Central Statistical Planning Area (SPA) of Cleveland. Of approximately 12,000 units that CMHA owns and operates, 4,366 are located in the Central neighborhood. In addition, 1,460 units of privately owned subsidized housing are in the area, resulting in nearly 6,000 units of subsidized housing in less than a one-mile radius.[14] On nearly every measure of decline, Central, along with the adjacent Kinsman neighborhood, is high in poverty, physical deterioration, crime, and other social dislocations. The unemployment rate is consistently among the highest in the city, median incomes among the lowest, homeownership minimal, and the out-migration of businesses and jobs astounding. The stability of public housing communities has been severely affected by the exodus of income-generating activities and individuals. The HUD area office determined that conditions in Central rendered the area nonviable and suggested that rehabilitation resources should be targeted to more vital areas. Congressman Louis Stokes (D-Ohio) and others have accused CMHA of making expenditure decisions on the basis that discriminated against East Side residents.

Public housing, once the habitat of the upwardly mobile working class, is now labelled as "the housing of last resort" by its detractors. This perception relegates the program and its residents to a secondary status in the eyes of some policy makers, government officials, and the general public. Often surrounded by signs of decline such as abandoned properties, vacant lots, deserted commercial strips, and empty factories, public housing developments appear isolated from the rest of the city. The emergence and acceptance of the notion of an urban underclass has condemned many residents of public housing to a fate of hopelessness and futility. This condition contrasts sharply with the push for self-sufficiency and empowerment among the poor, particularly in public housing developments.

The Case of Banks *v.* Perk: *The Response to Segregation*

Within the first six months of his administration, newly elected mayor Ralph Perk acted on his campaign pledge to follow area residents' wishes against scattered-site public housing. His stance set the stage for a major lawsuit, *Banks* v. *Perk,* when he revoked building permits for the 132 units. He further announced that all future public housing siting proposals would require prior approval by the city administration and the ward councilperson. After canceling the permits, he sought the resignations of two CMHA board members appointed by Mayor Stokes because they did not share his public housing philosophy. He subsequently sought to nullify the agreement between the city and CMHA. The City Council ordinance canceling the agreement was declared unlawful by Chief Federal Judge Frank J. Battisti, who ordered Perk to reissue all rescinded building permits.

Banks v. *Perk* might have had monumental impact on public housing in Cleveland if funds for development had been available from the federal government or other sources, but because it affects only public housing acquired after the case was settled, its impact has been minimal. The original lawsuit was filed by three parties: the American Civil Liberties Union, the National Association for the Advancement of Colored People, and the Legal Aid Society. The suit was brought on behalf of "Negroes and nonwhite tenants and applicants for public housing" who were forced to live in segregated housing and those on the waiting list who were denied an opportunity for integrated housing because of the site selection and tenant selection processes. The city of Cleveland and CMHA were named as defendants.

The original ruling by Judge Battisti prohibited the placement of units in areas already impacted by concentrated public housing on the East Side until such time as it was dispersed on the city's West Side. By mutual agreement, the parties to the suit did not pursue a final decision and order by the judge then.

Changes at the local and federal levels moderated the zeal of the plaintiffs over time. Mayor Perk became less vocal on this issue, as were his successors. On the federal level, conservative policy changes reduced public housing production and fewer funds were available for construction. A minimal amount of building did occur. For about ten years after the ruling, no progress was made toward integration.

In 1982, CMHA and the plaintiffs in the *Banks* v. *Perk* suit reached a final settlement. CMHA and the plaintiffs agreed that public housing could be acquired or built in areas where it did not exist, including areas on the East Side that had large black populations. The city was divided into three areas: prohibited areas where CMHA could acquire no additional housing; restricted areas where CMHA could acquire not more than one-third of any additional housing; and targeted areas where CMHA must acquire at least two-thirds of any additional housing. This order still dictates the location of public housing acquisitions in the city. CMHA was also required to prepare and implement a written affirmative marketing plan to encourage and promote the integration of new and old housing units. CMHA submitted a plan that was approved by the court in 1984.

The *Banks* v. *Perk* plaintiffs did not seek a remedy covering the entire metropolitan and suburban area. A subsequent lawsuit in 1973 (*Mahaley* v. *CMHA*) unsuccessfully attempted to require the inclusion of suburban communities to promote housing integration. The plaintiffs had sought a declaration that the federal regulation requiring cooperation agreements between the localities and the public housing authority be declared unconstitutional. The current trend seems to be going the other way, as evidenced by the city of Parma, which was permitted to establish an autonomous housing authority to construct subsidized housing under a 1980 housing desegregation order.

Clientele Issues

Public housing was initially conceived of as the home for the submerged middle class. Intermittently, questions of eligibility for public housing have surfaced at the national level as well as at the local level. In consideration of the 1937 Housing Act it was said that "the ideal housing act, then, would be one which would accept the new and reject the old poor; it would shut the doors on those with the ability to get housing privately, but would not open the doors to people on the dole and likely to stay there . . . [and] provide employment for workers."[15] A 1936 brochure for Cedar-Central homes in Cleveland stated that tenants for the apartments would be selected from "self-sustaining families of limited income."

Efforts to make public housing affordable for the lowest-income households combined with larger-scale demographic change to transform public housing in significant ways after the 1960s. Public housing was no longer perceived as designed for the working-class upwardly mobile family. Households were promptly required to vacate when their incomes exceeded established levels. On the other hand, rather than providing housing for one generation on the way up, public housing became the residence for generations of the same families. For some families, public housing became permanent housing. The majority of family households in CMHA receive public assistance as their major source of income. Further, the majority of CMHA residents and applicants are black.

Tenant Selection and Placement

At its inception, the population served by CMHA was segregated by race. During a transition period, the clientele was somewhat integrated but it is now predominantly African American. Of the first three public housing sites in Cleveland, Cedar-Central and Lakeview were designated for white families, while Outhwaite was designed specifically for blacks and southern European ethnic types. The color barrier at Cedar was not effectively broken until the late 1940s. As late as 1965, 75 percent of Cedar's units were occupied by whites, while close by, Outhwaite and Carver were 100 percent black, as they had been since opening.[16] All of the Central area estates are between 90 and 100 percent black with little prospect of being racially integrated, even after substantial rehabilitation. Only 10 percent of the applicants on CMHA's waiting list are white, and most of them are elderly. The cost of rehabilitating some of the most devastated units ($42,260 and $40,370 in Outhwaite and Carver Park, respectively) and the likely effects of the expenditure have led to discussion about the thinning out option, that is, dispersing residents to more affluent areas. Advocates for dispersal cite the advantage of a more stable environment as well as access to jobs and improved services as benefits. This option is obviously controversial, particularly because it would erode the electoral bases that the segregation (involuntary or not) of black people has created.

CMHA selection and placement procedures came under scrutiny in 1972 with the filing of *Banks* v. *Perk*. This lawsuit resulted in a ruling which dictates where public housing can be located in the future and seeks to prevent further segregation of public housing residents.

Program Benefits

During its birth and infancy, public housing was considered by reformers as necessary to improve the lot of poor people. A decent home and suitable living environment were considered as basic for entering the economic mainstream. With rare exceptions, public housing authorities did little to directly advance the notion of economic upward mobility. This task was left to other agencies or the free market. Typically, housing authorities have not provided social services for their residents. Residents have been employed by housing authorities and, at times, some employees have been required to live on-site at public housing developments.

Under the recently embraced rubric of empowerment, the functions of public housing have been enlarged. Not only should housing authorities be more concerned with self-help and the economic advancement of their residents, but the housing units may form the basis of upward mobility. The 1987 Housing Act codified the concept of resident management of public housing. Although residents have managed their own developments as far back as 1973 (Bromley Heath in Boston, Massachusetts), federal support was not forthcoming until the 1987 act and the backing of Republican Congressman Jack Kemp, who later became secretary of the Department of Housing and Urban Development. Amendments to the legislation in 1988 include provisions for resident management groups to assume ownership of their developments. Since its beginnings, therefore, public housing has changed from the provision of housing for the temporarily poor to a means of empowering the long-term poor. Skepticism accompanied the optimism associated with resident empowerment. Some advocates of affordable housing expressed concern that resident ownership disguised the desire of the federal government to relinquish its role in low-income housing.

Four groups in Cleveland received technical assistance grants from HUD to pursue resident management initiatives. The Lakeview Terrace Resident Management Firm (LTRMF) entered into a contract with CMHA in 1985 to run the Lakeview Terrace Estate and Tower. LTRMF experienced many difficulties and was required to participate in a dual management arrangement by HUD and CMHA in 1992. Under dual management, a private firm was hired to work side by side with the regular employees to upgrade their skills and improve the overall operation. In 1994, CMHA terminated the dual management arrangement and resumed responsibility for all management functions. LTRMF continued to exist and operate as a resident council. The other Cleveland resident management groups are in various stages of training and development. None of the groups has assumed major management responsibilities, such as leasing and maintenance, which LTRMF had at one time.

The administration of HUD under Secretary Henry Cisneros has changed the goal of resident empowerment. Under the Tenant Opportunity Program (TOP), the focus of resident empowerment has shifted from homeownership. The 1994 application kit for TOP funds states that resident management groups are allowed to establish their own priorities for achieving self-sufficiency goals. Alternatives to homeownership include business development, education, job training and development, and social services. Many more groups in Cleveland and other cities may seek HUD funding now that the emphasis on homeownership has been eliminated.

Governance and Conflict

Until 1983, the five-member boards of all public housing authorities in Ohio were appointed through the same process. One member was appointed by the probate court, one by the court of common pleas, one by the board of county commissioners, and two by the chief executive officer of the most populous city included in the territorial limits of the authority. Since a 1983 change in state law, two members of the CMHA board have been appointed by the mayor of Cleveland, two by the Cleveland City Council, and one by the city in the district with the second highest number of housing units owned or managed by the authority. At least one member must be a resident of public housing. In 1994, two residents were CMHA commissioners.

The city of Parma, Cleveland's largest suburb, built sixty subsidized family housing units as the result of a 1980 court order to remedy housing discrimination in the city. Parma officials successfully petitioned that the units not come under the administration of CMHA in light of its reputation for poor management and maintenance of its properties. CMHA was consequently deprived of an opportunity to expand within its jurisdictional boundaries.

CMHA Directors: The Fight over Leadership

Controversy has plagued every director of CMHA since the departure of Ernest Bohn. There have been four permanent executive directors of CMHA in the twenty-four years following his tenure. Bohn was succeeded by Irving Kriegsfeld in 1968. Controversy over expanding the location of public housing led to his firing after serving only two and a half years. Kriegsfeld was committed to dispersing public housing in Cleveland and other parts of Cuyahoga County and announced his intention to use every tool available to do so.

Within two years of assuming the directorship, he had used the turnkey approach provided in the 1968 Housing Act to place 2,290 units under construction, which represented about 67 percent of all new housing construction in Cleveland.[17] During Kriegsfeld's tenure, more than five thousand units were built, in contrast to the seven thousand built during the previous thirty-five years under the directorship of Ernest Bohn. Council members Stanton and Harmody led opposition to CMHA and Kriegsfeld for plans to build public housing in their wards, contending that it would reduce city tax revenue, that schools, sewers, and recreational facilities in project areas were inadequate, and that CMHA had a preference for certain developers and architects.[18] Kriegsfeld's swift action earned him the ire of former council president James V. Stanton, who called him a "superplanner trying to impose his plans on my constituents."[19]

When Kriegsfeld presented a plan to place 1,046 units of public housing in twelve different city wards to the City Council in 1970, it again attacked him. Apparently the City Council was not alone in its dissatisfaction with Kriegsfeld. In 1971, the CMHA board fired Kriegsfeld and replaced him with his deputy Robert Fitzgerald.

The firing of Irving Kriegsfeld triggered a variety of reactions from different quarters in CMHA including a "sick call" strike among maintenance workers, threats of rent strikes and the resignation in protest of William B. Hammer, one of three assistant directors. Kriegsfeld was considered responsive to the residents and was supported by Mayor Carl Stokes.

After the CMHA board appointed Fitzgerald, Congressman Louis Stokes pressed for his resignation. Fitzgerald expressed his belief that Stokes's motive was to pressure CMHA officials into appointing a black person to the director's post. Fitzgerald did not enjoy the unanimity of support among public housing residents that Kriegsfeld had. Nonetheless, Fitzgerald remained director of CMHA until 1981, then a bitter battle surfaced among board members seeking his replacement.

The search for a new director uncovered racial discord among CMHA board members and the general community. Although the first choice of the board was Elaine Ostrowski, a white woman, George James, the second choice of the group, was advanced based on community sentiment that the next executive director of CMHA should be a black person. With the support of black politicians in the city,

George James took over CMHA amid much adulation and optimism. During the last five years of his administration, however, charges of patronage and mismanagement constantly plagued CMHA. He was forced to resign under pressure in 1989 in the heat of a mayoral campaign during which CMHA's problems were a major issue. James lost the support of many of his original backers. His ultimate departure was forced by officials at the Chicago regional office of HUD, who threatened to withhold subsidy funds unless the board fired him immediately.

After a brief interim period during which three persons served as acting executive director, Claire Freeman, a top-ranking HUD appointee, was hired in 1991. Her salary and management style—publicly denouncing local political interference—drew attention during the first year. Under Freeman's direction, CMHA has shown visible signs of a transformation. The agency reports that its financial statements are auditable for the first time in nearly a decade. New social service programs, including Boys and Girls clubs and a residential chemical dependency treatment program, are offered on CMHA sites.

In 1994, CMHA operated outside the fray of local politics. Early negative reactions to projects undertaken by the current administration have seemingly been quelled by visible improvements and accomplishments. Changes in the mayor's office and city council have diminished political intrusion as well. Mayor Michael White has focused much personal attention on the Cleveland City School District and is apparently less directly involved with public housing. The previous city administration was frequently charged with seeking favors and benefits from public housing personnel.

CMHA in the 1990s

CMHA owned thirty-eight developments containing about 11,500 units which housed just over 18,000 residents in 1994. The units are in conventional apartments, townhouses, and scattered site homes. Although 29 percent of the units were vacant, 2,939 were under modernization and unavailable for leasing. The occupancy rate was 96 percent when adjusted for units that cannot be utilized and 71 percent when not adjusted. The waiting list for conventional public housing, composed of 5,492 applicants, was closed to new applicants in 1994.[20]

Under the Section 8 program, CMHA supervises the management of eight thousand units owned by private landlords. CMHA had a waiting list of another three thousand for its Section 8 housing program in 1987. By the middle of 1993, however, the number of applicants on the list was just 247. The list was reduced when CMHA updated it and expanded the inventory of available units and certificates.

In 1993, 90 percent of CMHA's residents were black and 10 percent were white. Black households constituted 82 percent and the white population was 16 percent just five years earlier. The average gross household income of all families was $5,234 in 1993. The major source of income for 79 percent of the residents was public assistance; about 5 percent derived their major income from employment.

CMHA's problems have resulted, in part, from the combination of very old and undermaintained structures, a very poor tenant population, and inadequate federal subsidies. Between 1983 and 1987, CMHA received approximately $40 million in modernization subsidies from HUD. Extensive renovation work began in 1992 on some of the most deteriorated Central area public housing estates. However, the remodeling cost of between $20,000 and $65,000 per unit was criticized by the manager of the Cleveland HUD office. HUD officials had previously proposed razing some of these units. Ohio Congressman Louis Stokes led a successful effort in 1989 to persuade HUD and CMHA to reverse their positions on the affected complexes. In 1993, CMHA received $26 million in operating subsidies from HUD, which constituted 70 percent of its overall budget of $36 million.

The roots of CMHA's problems go beyond its physical difficulties. It was the target of General Accounting Office and congressional investigations and the subject of eight critical reports between 1982 and 1990. It has been accused of mismanagement, financial irregularities, and political patronage. During the 1980s, HUD declared CMHA a "troubled" agency as a result of overspending its budget, inadequate operating reserves, and a very high vacancy rate. HUD's regional director called it the second worst public housing authority in the United States behind Chicago. At one time, HUD conditioned aid to CMHA and threatened withdrawal of support for the authority's failure to comply with HUD's conditions.

A confluence of recent events has occurred to alter the fate of public housing in Cleveland: the overt support of former public housing resident and Congressman Louis Stokes; the election of Councilman Frank Jackson, a strong supporter of public housing; the change in CMHA leadership; and a change in HUD modernization policies and viability determinations. Congressman Stokes is in a position to significantly influence the flow of federal dollars to Cleveland. He is a senior member of the House Appropriations Committee and chairman of the VA-HUD-Independent Agencies Subcommittee. Councilman Jackson is an outspoken advocate for the retention of low-income housing who questions any threat to maintaining and rebuilding the Central community that he represents. Director Claire Freeman held several sub-cabinet level posts with the federal government prior to becoming assistant secretary at HUD and moving on to CMHA. Her contacts and experience are undoubtedly assets in pursuing federal support.

After local HUD officials questioned the feasibility of rehabilitating units in the Central area, federal HUD policy changed to allow housing authorities to make viability decisions. HUD would not take a position to force the demolition of any public housing units. This cleared the way for CMHA to target resources to housing developments in Cleveland's most troubled East Side areas.

In 1992, HUD moved from the Comprehensive Improvement Assistance Program (CIAP) to the Comprehensive Grant Program to fund modernization in medium and large public housing authorities. Under the CIAP program, housing authorities competed annually for funding that was inconsistent and unreliable. Money in the Comprehensive Grant Program is awarded based upon a formula allocation established by Congress. Receipt of these dollars is more reliable and recipients have more flexibility in spending them. The average annual allocation of modernization funds to CMHA increased from $8 million per year prior to 1990 to $63 million per year from 1990 to 1994.

After Freeman's arrival at CMHA, the funds available to CMHA under the new funding formula almost doubled. Renovation support from Major Reconstruction of Obsolete Properties (MROP) funds was also received. MROP is a development appropriation for public housing buildings that are badly deteriorated, have high vacancy rates, and with high renovation costs. Further, CMHA received a $50 million Urban Revitalization Demonstration (URD) Program grant from HUD in 1993. The purpose of the URD grant is to renovate 500 units at the King-Kennedy and Outhwaite Homes in the Central area and to provide social and support services through the creation of urban villages. Residents will also have business development and job training opportunities. CMHA received the largest grant possible under this HUD initiative. The majority of these renovation funds have been spent on East Side housing developments.

Other changes within CMHA may account for a decline in negative media coverage and, hence, less local political intervention. The housing authority has expanded the scope of its concerns beyond bricks and mortar to include social and related services. An approach, described as holistic by an administrator, addresses concerns about police protection, tenant screening and selection, timely and quality maintenance, social service intervention, and resident employment through job opportunities. CMHA has stepped up its police department, increasing the number of officers from 21 to 272 in four years. Service was also expanded to station officers on duty at every high-rise development where elderly and disabled persons reside.

Miracle Village is a unique chemical dependency treatment program for women and their children. During the treatment and relapse prevention phases of the program, clients reside in renovated apartments in Outhwaite Homes. Several agencies work in collaboration with CMHA to run this program. A health care and wellness program offering services to adults and children is also operated from two developments, Outhwaite Homes and Riverview Tower.

Resident management in Cleveland has faltered. The Lakeview Terrace Resident Management Firm (LTRMF) received a HOPE I Homeownership Planning grant from HUD in 1992 amid opposition from CMHA. When the LTRMF sought a subsequent implementation grant from HUD, CMHA did not support the application. Since housing authority support was required, the movement toward homeownership at Lakeview was effectively terminated. Despite the frustrated outcomes of resident management efforts, CMHA Director Freeman is quoted as favoring maximum citizen involvement.[21] The new initiatives at CMHA include provisions for a high level of resident participation.

Among housing advocates, CMHA was viewed more positively in 1994. The success of grantsmanship efforts and the visible physical improvements at some developments have impressed some detractors. Public ratings of local government performance doubled for CMHA from 1989 to 1994.[22] HUD Secretary Henry Cisneros applauded CMHA reform efforts that encouraged resident self-sufficiency. HUD announced CMHA's removal from HUD's list of troubled housing authorities, after thirteen years, in July 1994.

The long-term impact of recent CMHA initiatives will be determined over the future. In 1994, it was clear that the agency had made significant progress toward improving its housing inventory, serving its residents, and changing its public perception. The agency, however, remains vulnerable to the vicissitudes of federal policies, financial support, and public perception.

Notes

1. The concept of zealot is described in Anthony Downs, *Inside Bureaucracy* (Boston: Little, Brown, 1967), 5–7.

2. Downs, *Inside Bureaucracy,* 44.

3. Semer et al., "Housing Programs," 88.

4. Ibid.

5. Allen R. Hays, *The Federal Government and Urban Housing* (Albany: State University of New York, 1985), 95.

6. Downs, *Inside Bureaucracy,* 10.

7. Adapted from Downs, *Inside Bureaucracy,* 44.

8. Charles E. Daye et al., *Housing and Community Development* (Durham, N.C.: Carolina Academic Press, 1989), 134.

9. Ibid.

10. Maxine Lynch, "Public Housing Finds Support in Suburbs," *Cleveland Plain Dealer,* December 23, 1985, p. 16-A.

11. John Sabol, "Suburban Mayors Cool to Public Housing," *Cleveland Press,* June 17, 1980, p. F-12.

12. Bob Kitchel, "New Public Housing Will Be Scattered in the City," *Cleveland Press,* May 11, 1971, p. A-3.

13. Mittie Olion Chandler, Virginia O. Benson, and Richard Klein, "The Impact of Public Housing Location on Urban Residential Property Values," *Real Estate Issues* 18, no. 1 (Spring/Summer 1993): 31.

14. Michael LaRiccia, "The Viability of Public Housing in Cleveland's Central Area" (unpublished), 1988, p. 2.

15. Lawrence M. Friedman, *Government and Slum Housing* (Albany: Rand McNally, 1968), 106.

16. LaRiccia, "Viability of Public Housing," 11.

17. The turnkey concept allows a private developer or building consortium to build units on sites they own and then sell them to a housing authority.

18. Bob Kitchel, "Cleveland's Future Public Housing Projects Struggle to a Standstill in Council," *Cleveland Press,* August 18, 1970, p. A-3.

19. Donald Sabath, "Stokes Led Public Housing Spree," *Cleveland Plain Dealer,* February 29, 1972, p. 5-A.

20. CMHA, data effective June 1, 1994.

21. *Cleveland Plain Dealer,* "HUD Chief Lauds CMHA For Innovative Reforms," May 13, 1994.

22. *Public Ratings of Local Government Performance, 1989–1994,* Citizens League Research Institute, March 3, 1994.

Housing Dynamics of the Cleveland Area, 1950–2000

Thomas E. Bier

THE TERM housing dynamics indicates that housing—what there is of it, how it is occupied, and by whom—is a constantly changing phenomenon. Typically, the change is so slow that, in any given year, it is hardly noticeable, but change occurs constantly. Every day, some people move; new homes and apartments are built; some are torn down; some communities grow, others decline. To understand this change and its implications, we need to take a metropolitanwide perspective, and we need to look over the long term—decades.

This essay examines basic factors that have affected the movement of people in the Cleveland metropolitan area and how that movement shaped, and continues to shape, the well-being of neighborhoods and communities. This overview analyzes the metropolitan area and how housing supply and demand affect subareas. The Cleveland metropolitan area covers Cuyahoga County and at least parts of the surrounding six counties.[1]

Housing and Automobiles

Housing and automobiles are interrelated. Housing is a consumer commodity just like automobiles.

Automobiles are manufactured; housing is constructed. New automobiles are sold to those who can afford to buy them; new housing is sold, or rented, to those who can afford it. As automobiles are used, they lose value, decline in price, and then typically are sold to people with less income. As housing is used and ages, it also typically loses value and often is sold or rented to people with less income. Eventually, possibly after several owners, when automobiles become fully worn out or in need of repair that is too costly compared to the vehicle's value, they are junked. Some are abandoned on city streets and in vacant lots. Homes and apartments in time become so worn out or in need of repair that would cost more than the property is worth that they are abandoned.

The average car goes through the process of usage, or consumption, in about ten years. For a house or apartment, the period of use is more like one hundred years, but the process is essentially the same. There are exceptions. Given proper maintenance, an automobile and a house could last many years. The Ohio City and Tremont neighborhoods on the near West Side of Cleveland have many homes that are more than one hundred years old. The suburbs of Lakewood and Shaker Heights have many homes that are seventy or more years old but they are so well maintained that they are likely to last for a very long time. But overall, automobiles and housing are products that are used, consumed, eventually worn out, or become obsolete.

The wearing-out process creates demand for a new product. If cars did not wear out, there would not be much of an automobile industry. The industry needs to have cars wear out. The same is true for the housing industry. The demand for new housing is partly created by population growth; more people require more housing. If there were no population growth (which is the case in the Cleveland area in the early 1990s),[2] production in both the housing and auto industries would depend on the existing product being used and worn out.

Automobiles are built at a pace set by the number sold. The more sold, the more are built. When sales drop, production drops. Automakers do not count the number of drivers in the United States and then say that the same number of cars are needed. They make and sell as many as they can. Indeed, there are more vehicles than licensed drivers.[3] But the more cars there are compared with the number of drivers, the more junked and abandoned cars there are likely to be.

If there were fewer cars than drivers, those who owned a car would be doing everything they could to keep it running as long as possible.

Housing Supply Exceeds the Number of Households

Like cars, there are more units of housing in the Cleveland area than there are households to occupy them, a situation typical of most metropolitan areas. Just as car makers do not build new cars based on the number of drivers, builders do not build houses and apartments based on the number of households living in the area. They build as many as they can sell or rent. The number of units builders usually are able to sell is such that, when added to the supply of existing housing, the total number of units in the area is greater than the number of households living in the area. That is why some units are vacant. In a normal housing market, a small percentage of units will be temporarily vacant after one occupant moves out and before the next moves in. But when housing stands permanently vacant, or abandoned, that is evidence of more housing in the area than households.

On January 1, 1990, there were 770,000 units of housing in the Cleveland metropolitan area and 720,000 households to occupy that supply. Because there were 50,000 more units of housing than households, 50,000 units had to be vacant. Of the

50,000 vacant, 25,000 were normal vacancies as occupancy changed, leaving 25,000 as abnormally vacant or abandoned. The abnormally vacant can be considered surplus; they really are not needed because there is no one to occupy them. On January 1, 1990, those units were the ones that no one wanted to buy or rent because other units were preferred. Where were the preferred units located?

Movement Keeps Suburbs Filled

The most preferred housing was in the suburbs. The suburbs extending out from the city of Cleveland were, and are, constantly being filled (except for normal, brief vacancy when units change owners).

Why does that happen? People want what a suburb offers. Surveys of movers tell us what attracts them.[4] People look at a house or apartment: its size, condition, age, yard, appearance, and so on. Schools are a very important factor for some. Parents want to live where they feel the schools will be good for their children. Security is an important factor. People do not want to live where they feel unsafe, particularly if they have children. Other factors include the quality of city services, the availability of parks, open space, clean air, and proximity to work, transportation, shopping, friends, and relatives.

Generally people buy (or rent) housing in the most attractive situation they can afford. After they have been in that location for a while, many move again; many move up to a better location. In a typical year, about 5 percent of all homeowners move (except in low-income neighborhoods, where owners move less frequently). Renters move four times more frequently than owners.[5]

There are factors that push some people to move when otherwise they would not. Crime is such a factor. Some people do not like busing of students to achieve racial balance in schools, so they move. Some whites move when blacks begin to move into their neighborhood.

Many people choose to live in a suburb rather than the city. Not everyone, however, wants to live in a suburb; many prefer the city. But the city is where there is more crime, poorer services (such as police response), and schools (and busing) that many parents reject. In 1991, about 25 percent of the metropolitan Cleveland area population lived in the city of Cleveland and 75 percent lived in suburbs.

Thus the overall pattern of movement in the metropolitan area is outward, even though movement occurs in all directions. Some people move inward toward the center of the city, but more move outward. In the 1980s, twice as many people moved out of the city of Cleveland into a suburb as moved into the city.

In the city of Cleveland, the outward movement is evidence that the outer neighborhoods are the most preferred and the most occupied. Generally, the close-in neighborhoods are the least preferred because of more crime, poorer condition of housing, and abandoned structures. As Cleveland residents move outward and away from negative conditions, they abandon the least preferred housing and locations. Thus it is mostly in the city of Cleveland that the twenty-five thousand surplus housing units exist. Some of these units are quickly demolished; others will stand vacant for a long time before they are torn down. Some probably will be burned purposely or by arson.

The process of suburbanization and outward movement does not mean that every city neighborhood inescapably must decline as incomes fall. It is possible that some neighborhoods, or parts of some neighborhoods, will be attractive enough to prevent income decline or to enable people to move in whose incomes are greater than those moving out (which is known as gentrification). Parts of the Ohio City and Tremont neighborhoods are examples. Downtown Cleveland is another example, as people who are far from low income have been moving into condominiums and apartments in the Flats and Warehouse District. But such examples are islands surrounded by the process of outward movement.

New Housing Spurs Movement

Just as the building of new automobiles enables and promotes the sale of used cars, the building of new housing enables and promotes the movement of people. One difference is that, in the case of cars, the car moves to the new owner, whereas in housing, the home or apartment is fixed in place and the buyer or renter moves to it.

Across the spectrum of movers is a spectrum of incomes. People typically move up in housing to something more expensive than that which they have been occupying. Buyers and renters of new housing typically have middle and upper incomes. Buyers and renters of moderately used existing housing typically have lesser incomes—and so on down the income ladder to the poor, who rent the cheapest housing available. Thus, over decades, most housing gradually is occupied by people with less and less income. Even the worst housing today was, at some time, brand new and expensive for its time. The process of change in the income level of occupants is known as "housing filtering" and has been the subject of much housing research.[6]

In 1990, the supply of housing in the Cleveland metropolitan area (770,000 units) was expanded by the construction of 6,000 new units, giving a total of 776,000 at the end of December.[7] Most new units were single-family homes (about 20 percent were apartments or condominiums) built at the outer edges of the area in suburbs such as Westlake, North Ridgeville, Strongsville, Brunswick, Solon, Twinsburg, Chardon, and Mentor. That was the largest number of new units that could be sold or rented in 1990, but it enabled some people to move up. As they sold or vacated their previous homes, they enabled others to move up. The end result of the filtering process occurred in the city of Cleveland, where more housing became surplus.

The extent of this surplus is known because, in addition to knowing the new construction in 1990, we also know the change in the number of households living in the Cleveland area. On January 1, 1990, there were 720,000 households. By the end of the year there were 723,000. In effect, the suburbs grew by 6,000 units of housing while household growth in the area was 3,000, resulting in a surplus increase of 3,000. Some new housing was built in the city of Cleveland, but because of the small number—about 300 units—it had little impact on the overall process.

In 1990, the city of Cleveland lost about 3,000 households (net, after all moves in and out) to the suburbs and had as a result about 3,000 more surplus and abandoned units, in addition to the 25,000 it had at the start of the year. The 3,000 households amounted to about 7,500 people (at an average of 2.5 per household). Most of those leaving the city were from among its better-income residents because they could best afford to move to a suburb. Thus in 1990 the city's population got a bit smaller and a bit poorer.

That change in one year was not noticeable because it was too small. A loss of 3,000 households out of 200,000, or 7,500 people out of 500,000, is virtually invisible. But the process of construction at the edges of the area and movement outward happens year after year. If we look at it over decades, the scale of the change becomes clear.

Suburbanization, 1950–1990

This process of change has been called "suburbanization" because it involves the residential development and expansion of suburbs, the movement outward of population, and the contraction of the central city. Suburbanization also typically involves retail and, in some cases, office and industrial development. The process began in the early 1900s with the invention and mass production of the automobile, which enabled people to live further from their place of work in the city and conveniently commute. Bratenahl, East Cleveland, and Lakewood were the earliest suburbs in the Cleveland area.

World War I interrupted the new phenomenon of suburbanization, but in the 1920s, development got under way in earnest in Cleveland Heights and Shaker Heights. A fifteen-year interruption occurred during the Depression of the 1930s and World War II. After the war, when many service men and women returned home, Cleveland was a very crowded place, with virtually no vacancies. In the census of 1950, Cleveland's population reached its all-time high figure of 915,000.

1950s

The federal government came to the rescue with programs to help people, particularly veterans, to buy homes. The Veteran's Administration enabled veterans to buy a home with no down payment (normally a down payment of at least 10 per-

Table 1
Cleveland Metropolitan Area

Decade	*Metro household increase*	*Metro new units*	*Suburban new units*	*Ratio units to households*
1950s	121,500	150,000	127,000 (85%)	1.2
1960s	82,000	130,000	118,000 (91%)	1.6
1970s	44,300	90,000	84,000 (93%)	2.0
1980s	25,300	46,700	44,700 (96%)	1.8
TOTAL	273,100	416,700	373,700 (90%)	1.5
1990s	10,600	55,000		5.2

Source: U.S. Census; various local construction reports.

cent of the purchase price would be required) and the Federal Housing Administration (FHA) enabled nonveterans to buy with down payments of about 3 percent. That government assistance assured home builders of buyers, and suburbs such as Parma, Maple Heights, and Euclid underwent massive development. For example, Parma's population in 1950 was 28,000; ten years later it was 82,000.

In the 1950s, 150,000 new units of housing were built in the Cleveland area (Table 1), the largest amount of residential construction in a single decade in the history of the area. Eighty-five percent of those new units were built in suburbs. But because the number of households living in the area increased by 121,500 and the city of Cleveland had been so overcrowded, the surplus that resulted in the city (from more units being built than the growth in households) simply returned vacancy to a normal level. Thus in the decade of the 1950s, there was no obvious indication that suburbanization was having a detrimental effect on the city.

1960s

The decade of the 1960s was different. Growth in the number of households living in the metropolitan Cleveland area was falling. Growth in the 1950s had been 121,500; in the 1960s it dropped to 82,000, and it would continue to fall each decade. In the 1990s, only about 11,000 new households are projected. In the 1960s, the push to move from the city to suburbs intensified as a result of rapid racial change in East Side neighborhoods and the Hough riot in 1966 and the Glenville shootout in 1968.

In the 1960s, 130,000 new units of housing were built in the Cleveland area. That number was 48,000 greater than the area's household growth. Since 91 percent of the new housing was located in suburbs, the movement outward resulted

Table 2
City and Suburban Population

Year	*Metro area*	*Cleveland*	*(change)*	*Suburbs (change)*
1950	1,533,000	915,000		618,000
1960	1,909,000	876,000	(-4%)	1,033,000 (67%)
1970	2,064,000	751,000	(-14%)	1,313,000 (27%)
1980	1,899,000	574,000	(-24%)	1,325,000 (1%)
1990	1,831,000	505,000	(-12%)	1,326,000 (1%)

Source: U.S. Census.

in major loss of population to the suburbs and major abandonment in Cleveland for the first time (Table 2). In the 1960s, Cleveland's population dropped 14 percent while the suburbs grew 27 percent overall. For the first time, surplus housing (mostly abandonments) was a serious problem—at the level of about 35,000 units.

1970s

The push to suburbs continued in the 1970s. Household growth continued to decline in the area, falling to 44,300 (about half the number of the 1960s), but suburban housing construction was double that number at 84,000 units. Housing was being built in the suburbs at twice the number of the area's household growth, and because the push from the city continued to be strong, all suburban housing was filled. The city of Cleveland lost 24 percent of its population, 177,000 people. About 40,000 units became surplus; abandonment was rampant. Suburban population grew by only 1 percent because declining birth rates meant fewer children, on average, in each household.

In 1977, the push to the suburbs was given added strength when a federal court ordered that public school students in Cleveland would be bused to achieve racial balance. Many city parents would not accept that imposition and left the city. Each year thereafter, a steady stream of families moved out of the city for that reason. An estimated twenty-five thousand families left Cleveland because of busing between 1977 and 1990.[8]

1980s

The decade of the 1980s in the Cleveland area was marked first by a serious economic recession and job loss, which began in 1979 and lasted until 1983. Suburban housing construction and movement decreased dramatically (about 50 percent). For the decade, construction totaled only 46,700 units. Household growth continued to drop as well, to 25,300. As in the 1970s, approximately twice as many units were built as the increase in households living in the area. Because almost all construction was suburban (96 percent) and the amount of construction was about half that of the 1970s, the movement to the suburbs (and the consequent housing surplus) was about half that of the 1970s. Cleveland's population loss was 69,000 (12 percent), putting it at 505,616 when the census was taken in 1990. Its housing surplus grew by about 20,000 units.

Because the city's population decline in the 1980s was roughly half that of the 1970s, and because so much office and entertainment development took place downtown in the 1980s, many people believed that Cleveland had recovered. Actually, the city's population decline was reduced by the fall in housing construction in the suburbs brought on by the recession early in the decade. The latter part of the 1980s reflected more normal economic times. If the amount of construction that took place between 1984 and 1989 had been constant across the decade, the city's population loss (and increased housing surplus) during the 1980s would have been just as great as in the 1970s.

During the four decades 1950-90, 373,700 units of new housing were built in the suburbs of the Cleveland metropolitan area, while only 43,000 were built in the city of Cleveland. The number of households living in the metropolitan area increased by 273,100. As a result, the population of the suburbs grew from 618,000 to 1,326,000, an increase of 115 percent; the city of Cleveland's population declined from 915,000 to 505,000, a drop of 45 percent. Many of the city's residents who were not poor moved out during that period, leaving the city proportionately more populated by people with lower incomes. In addition, approximately 100,000 units of housing in the city were made surplus, most of them abandoned or demolished. The changes are dramatic when viewed over the span of forty years. Over a single year, or even two or three, change was hardly noticeable.

Cleveland's 45 percent decline in population between 1950 and 1990 was not dissimilar to that in comparable cities. St. Louis lost 54 percent, Pittsburgh 45 percent, Detroit 44 percent, and Buffalo 43 percent. In each case, a thorough accounting of suburban housing construction in comparison with areawide household growth would in all likelihood show the same disparity as in Cleveland. For example, in the Detroit metropolitan area during the 1980s, 3.9 units of new housing were built for each additional household. The city of Detroit led the nation's major cities in population loss during the 1980s.

Public Policies Favor Suburbs

Government has been far from neutral about where people live. Federal, state, and local governments have strongly favored the development of suburbs and, concomitantly, movement out of the central city. This has not been conscious, explicit policy. Instead, it can be thought of as the unintended result of policies, programs, and actions. For example, when the interstate highway system was proposed, few, if any, foresaw that it would enable movement out of cities to suburbs.

The federal government led the way in suburban-oriented policies by providing funds to build superhighways (90 percent of the cost) which encourage people to live further out. Cleveland's first such roads were built around 1940 and included the Shoreway from downtown to Bratenahl and a piece of what would become I-77. In 1960, the Shoreway was extended through Euclid linking Route 2 (for all practical purposes an interstate road) with Mentor and beyond. The Euclid spur connected the Shoreway with I-271 and I-90 to the east, enabling people living in the northeast communities of Cuyahoga and Lake counties to commute conveniently to downtown Cleveland.

In 1968, I-71 opened Strongsville and Medina County for development. Also in that year, I-271 and I-480 to the southeast were completed. In 1970, I-77 was opened through Independence, Broadview Heights, and Brecksville. In 1978, I-90 to the west opened Westlake and northern Lorain County. In 1980, I-480 to the southwest did the same for North Olmsted and central Lorain County. In 1987, the I-480 crosstown route was completed, enabling people to live on one side of the county and work on the other. And in 1989, the last major road to affect the area's pattern of residential development, relocated 422, was opened from Solon into Geauga County.

That system of freeways, one of the best in the nation, encouraged people to move from Cleveland and even from older inner suburbs. Formerly rural communities that became popular new suburban communities were Brunswick in Medina County, North Ridgeville in Lorain County, Twinsburg in Summit County, Chardon in Geauga County, and Mentor in Lake County. The system of freeways also encouraged employers to locate in the outer suburbs. Employment centers emerged in Westlake, North Olmsted, Strongsville, Independence, Solon, Twinsburg, and Mentor.

The federal government also encouraged movement by offering to secure the mortgages of some home buyers through FHA mortgage insurance, thus enabling them to buy when they might not otherwise be able to, or to buy more quickly than they otherwise would have.

State and county governments helped promote movement out of the city (and even out of Cuyahoga County to an adjacent one) by improving roads and bridges. As people move to outlying communities, their cars cause road congestion. When a two-lane road is widened to four lanes by means of funding from the state and county, congestion is relieved, which in turn invites more people to move outward.

Expansion and improvement of sewer, water, and utility systems promotes movement as well. Even the city of Cleveland administration has been encouraging movement from the city by providing water to some of the growing suburbs—nearly all of the suburbs in Cuyahoga County and some outside of the county, Brunswick being an example.[9]

Most important, the costs of those systems and roads have been spread across all taxpayers and system users. The full range of infrastructure that has been pro-

Cleveland, Akron, Lorain/Elyria
Consolidated Metropolitan Area
with Interstate Highway System

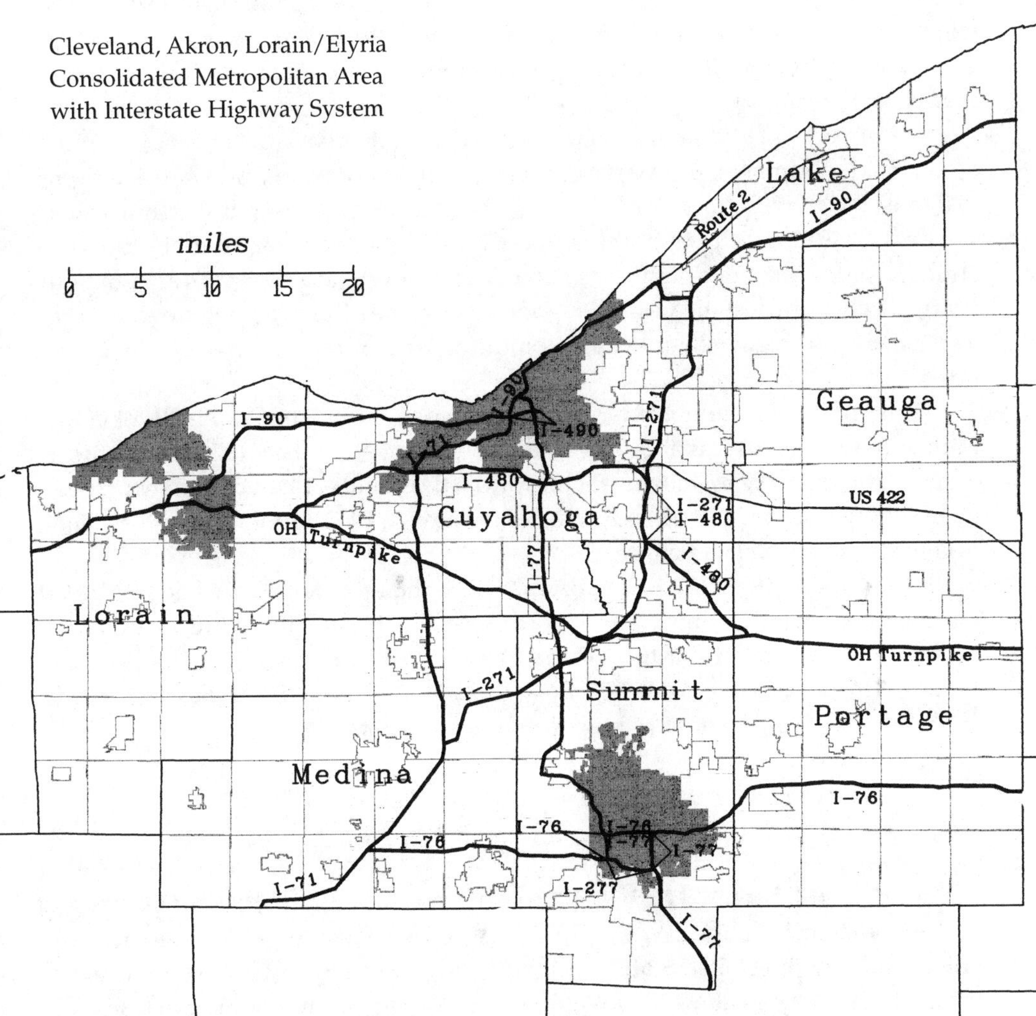

Prepared by: Northern Ohio Data & Information Service Cleveland State University

vided to people locating in developing communities has been highly subsidized.

Federal income tax law also has promoted suburbanization by encouraging homeowners to carry as large a mortgage as their income permits and to buy a more expensive house each time they move. Tax law permits homeowners to deduct the interest they pay on their mortgage and the amount they pay for local property taxes. Tax law also enables them to avoid paying any capital gains tax on their house when they move if they purchase a home that is more expensive than their previous one. Those provisions firmly push owners toward higher-priced suburban homes. For example, home prices in the city of Cleveland are on average half those of the suburbs.[10] Suburban owners would pay a tax penalty if they sold their suburban home to buy a lesser-priced Cleveland home. That discourages people from moving into the city or into any house in any community that is priced lower than the one being sold.

The impact of government policies and actions that have the effect of encouraging the development of suburbs and the movement of people outward has been extremely powerful—much more powerful than the policies and programs that were established to help central cities like Cleveland recover. For example, the construction of the interstate highway system in the Cleveland area cost over $1 billion (in 1991 value). In a single year, Cleveland-area home sellers moving up to a more expensive home legally avoid paying on the order of $300 million in capital gains taxes.

In the 1980s, the annual federal commitment to the city of Cleveland for community development was about $25 million. This money was to help the city deal with the consequences of movement outward—thousands of abandoned structures, increasingly poor neighborhoods, tens of thousands of deteriorating homes, and declining retail establishments.

If the superhighways had not been built, if the income tax law had not been written to favor owners moving to more expensive homes, if the full costs of the provision of suburban infrastructure had been borne by those moving to those locations, suburbanization would not have taken the course it did, and central cities like Cleveland would not have been undermined as they have been.

Cheap Land Made It Possible

Government policy would have had little effect if vacant land had not existed to accommodate new suburban development. The Cleveland area, like many metropolitan areas in the United States, has had a plentiful supply of land. The cheaper the land, the more feasible is development.[11] Before 1980, land for the expansion of outer suburbs around Cleveland was inexpensive. In the 1980s, land prices increased substantially but not enough to cause major reductions in housing construction. Developers and builders shifted their projects further out into the counties around Cuyahoga where land is cheaper.

Land availability on the east and west coasts of the United States is much more limited. So much development has occurred in recent decades that vacant land has become limited, very expensive, and, in many cases, far distant from city centers. As a result, the cost of new housing has increased greatly and dampened the pace of development.[12] The cost of all housing has risen, creating more demand for city living and resulting, in some cities, in gentrification.[13] There has been little gentrification in Cleveland because of the affordability of suburban housing, the proximity of suburbs to downtown Cleveland, and the absence of the type of housing (mainly brick) in the inner city which typically is attractive to gentrifiers.

The supply of vacant land within Cuyahoga County, however, is shrinking. By the year 2010, little developable vacant land is likely to be left. The implications of that change may well be serious enough to cause fundamental alteration in the dynamics of suburbanization in the Cleveland area.

The 1990s and Beyond

Several powerful factors may work in the 1990s to bring about change in the pattern of development in the Cleveland area. First is the amount of housing that could be built in the suburbs in comparison with the change in the number of households living in the area.

Growth in the number of households living in the Cleveland area has been slowing since 1950. Because of very low birth rates between approximately 1960 and 1980, there will be fewer young adults to form new households during the period approximately twenty-five years after those births—1985 to 2005. A projection of households for the Cleveland area shows an increase of 10,600 for the decade of the 1990s but a decrease between 1995 and 2005.[14] The figure of 10,600 is less than half the growth of the 1980s, which was only about half that of the 1970s.

Actual growth will depend on economic conditions in the 1990s. If the Cleveland area were to have a very strong economy in the 1990s compared with other parts of the country, people would move there for employment. That would boost the number of households. But it will take a dramatic increase in the number of jobs during the 1990s to attract enough people to increase significantly the extent of household growth.

As household growth has been slowing, so, too, has been the rate of new housing development in the suburbs. Nevertheless, in the 1970s and 1980s, twice as much housing was built as the increase in the number of households living in the area (see Table 1). In the 1990s, if household growth is 10,600, would housing construction therefore be twice that at 21,200 units? Probably not—21,200 units of new housing over a decade in a metropolitan area the size of Cleveland is a very small amount. It would be an average of 2,120 per year. In 1990, 6,000 units of housing were built (while households increased by only 3,000).

Housing construction is unlikely to fall much lower than 6,000 or 5,000 units a year, on average. Even if household growth were to be zero, there is likely, under normal economic conditions, to be a demand for new housing that would support 5,000 or 6,000 units per year. Assuming that future, 55,000 units for the decade of the 1990s are projected, an average of 5,500 per year.[15]

But if 55,000 units were to be built, and if household growth were to be 10,600, the implication for housing surplus would be very serious. Approximately 40,000 units would be surplus, double that in the 1980s and comparable to the level of the 1970s. Assuming the surplus would be concentrated in the city of Cleveland, the

40,000 would mean that about 20 percent of the housing units occupied in Cleveland in 1990 would be empty in the year 2000.

If household growth and suburban housing construction in the 1990s occur as projected, the pace of movement outward would accelerate over that of the 1980s. More people would have the opportunity to move to a suburb than was the case in the 1980s. The city's population could fall from 505,000 in 1990 to about 420,000 in the year 2000.

Even people with low incomes would have more opportunity to move to suburbs, those with the lowest-priced housing. These are the inner, older suburbs that share a boundary with Cleveland, such as Euclid, Cleveland Heights, East Cleveland, Maple Heights, Garfield Heights, Parma, Berea, and Lakewood. If income levels of residents in these suburbs fall, the suburbs will have difficulties in maintaining tax revenues for city services and schools, which would mean that those suburbs would be in decline. Conditions and problems that suburbanites had always associated with the city of Cleveland, and not suburbs, would indeed exist in some of its suburbs.

If the process of suburbanization and movement outward continued, in time the entire population of Cleveland could move into the suburbs. By continuously expanding the supply of suburban housing (at a rate greater than household growth), the day would come when enough suburban housing existed to accommodate *all* the households living in the Cleveland area. In 1990, there were about 200,000 households living in the city of Cleveland. If the amount of suburban construction were to continue at an average of 5,500 units a year, and if household growth in the Cleveland area were to continue to be slight, if any at all, at about the year 2030, there would be enough suburban housing to accommodate all households living in the metropolitan area; none would need to live in Cleveland. In 1990, compared with forty years earlier, Cleveland was almost half emptied. By the year 2030, under current policies which heavily support movement outward, the city of Cleveland could be virtually emptied into its suburbs.

That would indeed mean that some suburbs would become poverty or very low-income communities (assuming there will continue to be poor and near-poor people, an assumption which hopefully will turn out not to be the case). Poverty growth in some suburbs was evident in the 1980s. By 1990, the rate of poverty in the suburb of East Cleveland (42.8 percent) was higher than in the city of Cleveland (41.4 percent); in the city of Lakewood it was 10 percent and in Cleveland Heights it was 12 percent.[16]

That is a consequence of people with higher incomes moving farther out. Increasingly, farther out means out of Cuyahoga County and into adjacent counties. The implications for the suburbs of Cuyahoga County, for county government, and for the surrounding counties are serious.

The process of suburbanization could eventually result in serious economic decline within Cuyahoga County. Adjacent counties are outside of the tax jurisdiction of Cuyahoga County. By 1990, the spread outward of housing development had reached the point where 55 percent of all the single-family homes built in the Cleveland area were located in counties adjacent to Cuyahoga. Thirty-seven percent of all buyers of homes in adjacent counties were moving from Cuyahoga County. Cuyahoga County is losing property and income taxes to neighboring counties.

The situation can only worsen as the supply of vacant, developable land in Cuyahoga County suburbs diminishes. As that happens, development pressures in adjacent counties will grow and, for the most part, dramatically. For example, the number of homes that can be expected to be built in Medina and Lorain counties in the year 2010 (when the western suburbs of Cuyahoga County are likely to have little vacant land left) is three times the level of 1990.

Each of the surrounding six counties in the Cleveland area is looking at a future of increasing development and all that comes with it: traffic congestion, transformation from rural or semirural life to busy suburbs, demands on community services, environmental pollution. That represents progress for some people living in those counties, but for others it is a nightmare.

Thus suburbanization of the Cleveland metropolitan area has reached the point where serious negative consequences are increasingly metropolitanwide. It is no longer just the central city of Cleveland that is affected by the powerful complex of federal, state, and local policies that encourage building at the suburban fringe and the outward movement. Older inner suburbs are being affected—as is Cuyahoga County's tax base. Adjacent counties are facing increasing change.

Conclusion

The policies and subsidies that have supported movement outward in the Cleveland metropolitan area have been so powerful that no initiative aimed at contending with decline in Cleveland neighborhoods has had anything but marginal effect. The city, outside of downtown, has been in a continuing process of decline in which the only change has been the rate of decline caused by ebbs and flows of the regional economy. In light of the past forty years, and the national, state, and local commitment to policies and subsidies as they are, it is difficult to imagine the next ten or twenty years being anything but a continuation of the previous forty.

Yet the combined impact of the decline of older inner suburbs, the erosion of Cuyahoga County's tax base, and the accelerating development of rural areas in adjacent counties (in addition to further decline of Cleveland neighborhoods) could cause officials representing each of those interests to come together for the purpose of changing the course of events.[17]

To begin, each of the seven counties in the Cleveland region needs to assess its situation and trends. Cuyahoga County needs to determine where new housing development will be located, and how much, in the longer term as its suburbs run out of vacant land. To maintain the county's residential tax base, about three thousand new units of housing must be built each year for the indefinite future. And all must pay full property taxes. No tax abatement should be granted. Most of those units, at least two thousand, will have to be located in the city of Cleveland because that is where a growing amount of vacant land exists. What are the obstacles to building and selling or renting two thousand new housing units in the city during the year 2010 and each year thereafter? (The number built in 1990 was about three hundred, most of which were heavily subsidized.) What will be required to remove those obstacles?

Each of the six adjacent counties needs to determine the amount of development it is prepared to absorb over the next several decades. If two thousand units per year are not built in Cleveland, they will be built somewhere in the region because of normal market demand for new housing. If they cannot be built in the suburbs of Cuyahoga County, market pressures would have them built in adjacent counties, which would double or triple construction activity in each. How much development does each of the six counties want to have? What are the costs and benefits of various amounts? Would it be in the self-interest of adjacent counties to support the city of Cleveland in achieving the construction goal of two thousand units per year?

After each of the seven counties determines the number of new housing units it would prefer to have built over several decades, the seven could meet as a group to produce a regional plan. The regional total should average about six thousand units per year.

The seven counties then would need to determine the mechanisms through which their planned geographic distribution of new housing construction could be achieved. Possibly they would want to change the way infrastructure for new housing is paid for; possibly they would want the state to initiate subsidies or incentives for building new housing in the city of Cleveland; possibly they would lobby for change in the federal income tax code, which governs home capital gains.

The state of Ohio should review its role in affecting the dynamics of Ohio's metropolitan areas and central cities. Currently, its role is to support outer-edge development and movement away from the city. Its role could be to provide incentives or subsidies to balance outer development with development in the city and promote movement inward. The state also could take the lead in attempting to change federal policy and law that creates the large imbalance of subsidies that favors outer suburbs.

If state and local officials work cooperatively, the pattern of development and population movement in the Cleveland region can be altered, and the trends that have been extending for forty years, and are leading to increasingly costly consequences, can be broken.

Notes

1. Data are based on the Census Bureau definition of metropolitan area, which includes Cuyahoga, Lake, Geauga, and Medina counties. The data for those four counties approximate those for all of Cuyahoga and parts of each of the adjacent six which form the actual Cleveland area.

2. "Population and Household Projections: Cleveland Metropolitan Area, 1985–2020," Cleveland State University, Housing Policy Research Program, December 1988.

3. In 1989, Ohio had 7,393,000 registered drivers, 7,129,000 registered passenger cars, and 1,090,000 noncommercial trucks. Thus there were about 800,000 more vehicles than drivers.

4. "Sellers of Cleveland Homes, 1989," Cleveland State University, Housing Policy Research Program, November 1990.

5. Xu Du, "Residential Mobility in the United States," *Housing Economics* 38, no. 9 (September 1990): 12–14.

6. For a comprehensive review of housing filtering and the literature, see William C. Baer and Christopher B. Williamson, "The Filtering of Households and Housing Units," *Journal of Planning Literature* 3 (Spring 1988): 127–52.

7. "Suburbanization of Ohio Metropolitan Areas, 1980–2000," Cleveland State University, Housing Policy Research Program, June 1990.

8. The survey "Sellers of Cleveland Homes, 1989," shows that in 1988 and 1989, 1,400 sellers said that they "wanted children to attend suburban schools" and moved for that reason. An estimated 600 renters moved for the same reason, for a total of 2,000 households annually. The same survey recorded many parents as saying that they would not allow their children to be bused. On that basis, it is assumed that during the fourteen years 1977–90 of court-ordered busing, at least 25,000 households left the city to avoid busing.

9. Columbus became Ohio's largest city by refusing to provide water to a suburb unless the suburb merged with the city. If Cleveland had done the same, Strongsville, for example, would be part of the city and not an independent suburb.

10. In 1990, the median price of a single-family home in the suburbs of Cuyahoga County was $83,500; in the city of Cleveland it was $42,000.

11. William Alonso, *Location and Land Use: Toward a General Theory of Land Rent* (Cambridge, Mass.: Harvard University Press, 1964).

12. James W. Hughes and George Sternlieb, *The Dynamics of America's Housing* (New Brunswick, N.J.: Rutgers University, Center for Urban Policy Research, 1987).

13. Brian J. L. Berry, "Islands of Renewal in Seas of Decay," in *The New Urban Reality*, ed. Paul E. Peterson (Washington, D.C.: Brookings Institution, 1985).

14. "Population and Household Projections."

15. "Suburbanization of Ohio Metropolitan Areas."

16. "Poverty Indicators, Trends: 1970–1990, Cuyahoga County, Ohio, Council for Economic Opportunities in Greater Cleveland, v. 8-1990.

17. In 1989, an advisory committee was formed to work with housing researchers at Cleveland State University's College of Urban Affairs to formulate policy and programmatic responses to housing problems in the city of Cleveland, Cuyahoga County, and the rest of the Cleveland metropolitan area. The committee represented a range of perspectives from across the area. See the report "Toward the Year 2000: Housing Policy Recommendations for the Cleveland Metropolitan Area," Cleveland State University, Levin College of Urban Affairs, October 1990.

Part 7

RACE & DISCRIMINATION

Introduction

RACE AND racial conflict have played an important role in Cleveland's history. Kenneth L. Kusmer traces the origins and evolution of the African American community in Cleveland. He explains the early settlement patterns of black Clevelanders, when the black minority was not singled out from other ethnic groups for discriminatory treatment. He then examines the beginnings of the black ghetto in the late nineteenth and early twentieth centuries, when mass European immigration fueled a tremendous population growth and intense competition among the ethnic poor for employment. Kusmer explains how the end of this influx and the Great Migration from the South led to the formation of Cleveland's black ghetto. Kusmer reviews the emergence of black churches, social agencies, self-help organizations, newspapers, and prominent politicians, placing them within the context of the city's growth and change between World War I and the Depression.

William E. Nelson reviews the new black politics that emerged in the 1960s. A new breed of black liberal Democratic politicians which vied for power in the turbulent era of the civil rights movement and urban unrest was represented by Carl Stokes, whose 1967 victorious mayoral campaign marked the first election of a black mayor in a major American city. He then explains the downfall of Stokes and his allies and the eventual emergence of City Council president George Forbes as a political power broker. Finally, he discusses the victory of another reform candidate, Michael White, who was elected in 1989 as Cleveland's second black mayor, defeating his onetime mentor George Forbes.

W. Dennis Keating explains the prevailing pattern of residential racial segregation that characterizes the housing market and neighborhoods, both in the city of Cleveland and in its surrounding suburbs. He reviews the attempts to promote racial integration, which have been most enduring in some of Cleveland's suburbs.They have enjoyed mixed success, and some suburbs have seen resegregation in the face of black suburbanization. Keating argues that only metropolitan-wide policies can effectively address pervasive racial segregation in housing.

Black Cleveland and the Central-Woodland Community, 1865–1930

Kenneth L. Kusmer

THE HISTORY of black Clevelanders is, in many ways, not dissimilar to that of the myriad immigrant groups who by 1930 had transformed the Forest City into a multiethnic metropolis. Both African American and white immigrants underwent the experience of migration and the subsequent need to adjust peasant values to an urban world; both located in the poorer sections of the city; both encountered hostility from the established host society. The same elemental human problems face the white immigrant and the black newcomer: finding work, raising a family in a strange environment, building supportive institutions, securing effective group leadership.

Indeed, an observer set down on a busy corner on lower Central Avenue in 1920, witnessing the common poverty of the blacks, Italians, and Russian Jews who lived on or near that crowded thoroughfare, might readily conclude that, for good or ill, the fate of these minority groups would be similar. Social scientists of the time had come to exactly that conclusion. The prominent sociologist Eugene W. Burgess stated in his famous theory of ethnic succession in urban areas that concentrations of blacks in cities were little different from clusters of white immigrants near the industrial district, and he implied that the former, like the latter, would eventually move to outlying areas. The implication was that African Americans were the "last of the immigrants" and that they would gradually rise economically, gain acceptance, and be assimilated into the urban system in much the same manner as other groups.[1]

These conclusions—widely accepted at the time and still believed by many—were based on a faulty historical analogy. First, although black Clevelanders were clearly better off during the 1920s than they had been before World War I, the long-term history of the black economic structure between the Civil War and the Great Depression was hardly one of gradual upward mobility. Second, the black ghetto of the 1920s, though superficially having much in common with immigrant neighborhoods, was developing in an entirely different manner from that of the white ethnic concentrations. The model of ethnic succession postulated by Burgess would not be followed by blacks in Cleveland—or in most major cities. The long shadow of racial discrimination created fundamentally different conditions for the development of Cleveland's black community, conditions which ultimately made the historical experience of African Americans unique among the multitude of groups that made up the city's population.

The basic error of the optimistic "last of the immigrants" theory is that blacks in most northern cities did not arrive last at all. The movement of black peasants northward during World War I, however important, was preceded by a century of slow but steady migration to the cities.[2]

Cleveland's first black settler arrived in 1809, and by the eve of the Civil War the black community consisted of almost eight hundred souls out of a population of about forty-three thousand. By 1870, the black population had increased to almost thirteen hundred; by 1880, to over two thousand. Thus the arrival of the early black settlers (most of whom were free Negroes from the upper South) largely coincided with that of the Irish and German immigrants, but it preceded all but a handful of Italians, Russian Jews, or Poles. There was a black community in the city long before there was a Polish or Italian community; by 1915 some blacks were third-generation Clevelanders.

The mid–nineteenth century was an era of endemic and often virulent racism. In the North, however, there was considerable variation in the level of racial antagonism among whites, and Cleveland was certainly among the most "liberal" cities on the race issue. Although the Forest City had never dealt with blacks on a basis of complete equality, by the 1870s it had progressed further toward that goal than most other cities.

The average income and occupational level of black Clevelanders was considerably higher than that of most urban blacks in the North. In 1870 almost a third of all black men in Cleveland were skilled craftsmen, a substantially higher proportion than among the Irish immigrants residing in the city.[3]

Nor was the residential segregation a significant factor in black life at this time. By 1865, most of Cleveland's African Americans lived on the East Side, and the old Haymarket district on Central Avenue had become the center of the black community. Before about 1890, however, there was little noticeable tendency toward ghettoization. Although blacks were concentrated mostly within three wards, they were thoroughly integrated in each, and many black families lived side-by-side with whites. Blacks sometimes clustered together along portions of some streets, but no segregated neighborhoods as such existed.[4]

By the end of the Civil War, a sizable fraction of Cleveland's black community had been able to attain a middle-class standard of living. Family life was stable; two parents were present in over 85 percent of black households. Most blacks lived in single-family dwellings, and homeownership was increasing. About three of every ten black families owned their own home in 1870.[5]

The liberal racial atmosphere of nineteenth-century Cleveland did not make the city's blacks complacent. Instead, it engendered a spirit of pride and a belief in the need for militancy to surmount the racial oppression and inequality that existed throughout the United States. Before the Civil War, black Clevelanders were active in the abolitionist movement and often assisted escaped slaves.

Equal access to most public accommodations and the modest size of the city's black population in the nineteenth century retarded the development of separate black institutions in Cleveland.

The half-century between 1865 and 1915 was a significant time for black Clevelanders. In many ways the quality of life for blacks deteriorated, especially after 1890. In the new industrial city of the turn of the century, with its fully developed transportation system, segregation among many groups (ethnic, class, occupational) became more common.[6] But the growth of racial discrimination during the post-Reconstruction period intensified this trend for blacks, laying the groundwork for the ghettoization of the black population that would follow World War I.

Between 1880 and 1910, the growth rate of Cleveland's black population matched that of the city itself; the increase was more than fourfold, and by the eve of World War I there were close to ten thousand black Clevelanders. Migration from the upper South and border states accounted for most of this population growth.

Most of these newcomers moved into the Central Avenue district, and the area of black settlement gradually expanded northward between Central and Euclid avenues and to the south and east along Scovill and Woodland avenues. In 1910, almost 80 percent of the black community was housed within an area circumscribed by Euclid to the north, the Cuyahoga River industrial district to the west and south, and East 40th Street to the east. Blacks had begun to move into the area between East 40th and East 55th streets, but they were still restricted almost entirely to the streets between Central and Woodland. Only a small fraction of the black community, mostly middle-class families, lived in sections of the city well removed from the main area of black settlement.[7]

Before 1917, no genuine black ghetto existed in Cleveland. Even along lower Central and Scovill, blacks were still a minority of the population and lived in close proximity to impoverished Italians and Russian Jews. "We have no 'Little Africa' in Cleveland," a black clerk boasted in 1915. "There is not a single street inhabited by nothing but Negroes." Nevertheless, the increasing concentration of the black population was laying the groundwork for the future ghetto.The Central district was one of the oldest in the city, its dilapidated structures housing a population far larger than originally intended. When Jane Edna Hunter, a nurse who was later prominent in social welfare activities, arrived in the city in 1905, she had an experience undoubtedly shared by most black newcomers: "the despairing search for decent lodgings—up one dingy street and down another, ending with the acceptance of the least disreputable room we encountered." Many blacks, of course, settled in this area because they were too poor to live elsewhere, but there was also growing white opposition to the settlement of black families who could afford to reside in better areas.

At the same time that residential segregation was becoming more evident, black Clevelanders were suffering increasing discrimination in public accommodations. At this time black students were not segregated in separate schools or classrooms, as they often were in other cities. But black residents watched with dismay as institutional racism reared its ugly head. Of course, the growth of segregation and discrimination at the turn of the century was not unique to Cleveland—the trend was evident throughout the United States.[8] But it had a special poignancy to blacks in the Forest City because the new conditions contrasted so sharply with the integrationist tradition of the metropolis. Exclusion from restaurants and hotels became commonplace, and soon the Cleveland YMCA and YWCA barred blacks.[9] In the city's hospitals, white physicians and administrators were united in opposing the admission of black doctors and nurses to staff positions. In 1915, Women's Hospital began admitting black patients only on Saturday. "What does this mean?" one black woman asked incredulously. "Are we to arrange to get sick on Saturday only or is it possible that we are to be exempted from privileges enjoyed by every other nation or nationality?" Soon most city hospitals were segregating blacks in separate wards.[10]

If integrated facilities were declining by the early 1900s, much the same could be said for the economic opportunities that African Americans had enjoyed in Cleveland in the mid-nineteenth century. Between 1870 and 1915, Cleveland emerged as a major industrial center, but blacks had little opportunity to enter industrial occupations. Except for the most menial positions, jobs in the booming mills and foundries along the Cuyahoga River were filled by foreign-born whites, not native-born Americans of dark skin. The prejudice of corporate employers was often matched by the trade unions. The older skilled craft associations in the city—such as the carpenters' and brickmasons' unions—remained integrated, largely because black workers had been accepted into these unions during an earlier period. But the new unions of the American Federation of Labor—such as the pipefitters, paperhangers, or electricians—usually excluded blacks.[11] An African American, James Thompson, who came to Cleveland when his parents migrated from Kentucky in 1901, described in an interview what it was like to be a black electrician around the time of World War I:

Q: What was it like working as an independent operator?

A: I had the unions to worry with, but . . . we had them on old work because the unions didn't allow their men to work on old houses [except] from September till about Easter. It was too hot [during the sum-

mer]. [But] I'd go up in the hottest attic there is [on the] Fourth of July if I got paid for it. What did I care—I could use the money.
Q: You couldn't join the union?
A: No.
Q: Why?
A: Because my face was black. That's the only reason.[12]

In the face of such experiences, the number of blacks in the skilled trades declined sharply, from 32 percent of the male work force in 1870 to 11 percent in 1910. As opportunities for work in skilled or semiskilled jobs faded, more young blacks began to drift into the service occupations. The proportion of black men in this category increased from 15 percent in 1870 to 30 percent forty years later.[13] Not surprisingly, these changes were accompanied by a decline in property ownership in the black community from 28 percent in 1870 to 11 percent in 1910. It is no coincidence that this decline very closely parallels that in skilled work. At the turn of the century, the white homeownership rate was three times that for blacks.[14]

Industrialization created a need for white-collar workers and managers to run the new corporations coming into being. But in the clerical occupations blacks suffered grievous discrimination. As Harry C. Smith observed in 1916, blacks employed by the Cleveland city government were restricted to "spittoon cleaning, garbage [hunting], street-cleaning, truck driving, and other jobs of that kind." They had little chance to rise to better positions. Significantly, it was only in the post office—a federally controlled enterprise—that black Clevelanders made any substantial breakthrough in clerical employment before 1930.[15]

Largely because of increasing discrimination against black men, an increasing number of black women found it necessary to obtain work outside the home. In 1900, black women were twice as likely to be wage earners as were immigrant women. Many white women worked while they were in their teens or early twenties, then quit their jobs to devote full time to raising a family. Many black women found it impossible to compartmentalize their lives so neatly. Overwhelmingly, black women worked as domestics. Employment of women in the new department stores was restricted to whites, mostly native-born. When a Euclid Avenue department store hired two black saleswomen in 1919 and placed them conspicuously at the front of the store, it was an item worthy of mention in the black press.[16]

Excluded and victimized, black Clevelanders were often forced back on their own resources. One result was that their group activity was increasingly focused in institutions created by and for themselves. The growth of the black church was the clearest indicator of this self-reliance. Racial antagonism and the dispersal of many old-stock whites to the new suburban areas led to a sharp decline in the number of Negroes attending integrated churches. Between 1865 and 1890, blacks organized three new churches: Shiloh Baptist, Cory Methodist Episcopal, and St. James African Methodist Episcopal (AME). The period of greatest expansion came in the quarter-century after 1890, however, when seven new Baptist churches (Antioch,

Emmanuel, Gethsemane, Sterling, Avery, Mt. Haven, and Triedstone), one AME congregation (Harris), one AME Zion church (St. Paul's), one Colored Methodist Episcopal church (Lane Memorial), and one Episcopal church (St. Andrew's) were founded. Many congregations grew rapidly.

To some degree, the churches reflected the growth of class divisions within the black community. There were two recognizable elite religious institutions: Mt. Zion Congregational and St. Andrew's Episcopal. The emergence of the latter was one indication of a division in the black middle class between an older, often light-skinned group, whose occupations involved contact with whites, and a newer group of businessmen, politicians, and professionals, whose economic base was in the emerging ghetto. St. Andrew's was more of a social church than its rival, and much of its membership was originally made up of old elite families; Mt. Zion was larger and more inclusive. There were sharp differentiations among the Baptist and AME congregations also.

Fraternal orders were also an important focus of group activity among blacks. Although a few elite Negroes had been admitted to white lodges during the Reconstruction era, most lodges were segregated. Fraternal orders were popular among whites, of course, but they were more significant to the black community (and remained so for a longer period). At a time when many insurance companies refused to grant policies to blacks, the lodges provided some minimal benefits to their members. Furthermore, because the Y's and amusement parks excluded blacks (or, like Euclid Beach Park and Luna Park, restricted their participation to certain "Jim Crow" days), the lodges offered one of the few outlets for recreation and socializing outside of those made available by the churches.[17]

With the exception of the churches and lodges, Cleveland's black community developed few formal institutions until 1915. Unlike Philadelphia and Chicago, the city's black population was not large enough to support its own hospital, and a movement to establish a Negro branch of the YMCA failed in 1911, partly because the integrationist old elite of the black community opposed such a separate facility but also because there was inadequate funding for it.[18] In 1896, largely as a result of a concerted effort by black clubwomen, the Cleveland Home for Aged Colored People was established. Housed in a modest renovated house on Central Avenue, the home had considerable financial difficulties during its early years and was able to care for only a handful of the indigent elderly.

The only major secular institution for blacks established during the prewar era was the Phillis Wheatley Association, a residential, job-training, and recreation center for black girls who had come north on their own or were separated from their families for some other reason. Though strongly opposed by Harry C. Smith, George Myers, and other members of the old elite, the association was formed in 1913. During 1916, 170 girls lived for varying periods of time at Phillis Wheatley, and many more used its facilities. The institution was hardly an example of black self-sufficiency. Its founder, Jane Edna Hunter, decided early that it was better to rely on white financial support than to suffer the problems that had plagued the Home for Aged Colored People. As a result, the board of trustees came to be controlled by a group of upper-class white women whose awareness of the difficulties faced by homeless black girls was, at best, minimal. Nevertheless, Phillis Wheatley met a need in the black community, and in the years ahead it would help to buffer some of the disrupting effects of black migration to the city.[19]

Black politics during the prewar period reflected the changing status of blacks in the metropolis. In the late nineteenth century, several Cleveland Negroes held elective office, most of them serving in the state legislature. The most prominent of these, John Patterson Green, was elected justice of the peace in 1873, then won election to the state legislature in 1881 and 1889. In 1891, he became the first—and only—northern Negro to be elected to the state senate, where he served for a single term. Although barbershop proprietor George Myers never held public office, he was probably the most politically influential Negro in the city because of his friendship with Senator Marcus A. Hanna. Myers was often responsible for getting low-level patronage jobs for black politicians in Cleveland.[20]

These office seekers were able to win elections because they represented various factions within the Republican party. To some extent, their election over Democratic opponents signified the level of racial liberalism among Cleveland's white voters because blacks never made up anywhere near a majority of their voting districts. These black politicians would not even have won a place on the ballot, however, unless the white politicians who controlled the party nominating conventions had selected them. Between 1890 and 1915, two changes occurred that would eventually transform black politics. First, increasing race prejudice made black candidates less appealing to white voters, although whites might have preferred to support black Republicans over white Democrats in strongly Republican districts. The introduction of the direct primary in 1907 allowed white voters to exercise their prejudices in the Republican primary, which often effectively prevented blacks from getting on the ballot in the November election. Reacting to these circumstances, a new group of black politicians turned to building a secure political base within the emerging Central Avenue ghetto, and their first success would be at the local level rather than the state level.

The man who judged the shifting political winds most accurately was Thomas W. Fleming, who at the age of eighteen migrated to Cleveland in 1892 and immediately became active in Republican politics. At the turn of the century Fleming broke with the established black Republican leadership and set out to build his own organization. In 1903, he organized the Twelfth Ward Republican Club to "combine and solidify the Afro-American voters" living there and three years later founded the Attucks Republican Club, a citywide organization of black voters that Fleming placed at the service of the Republican machine of Cleveland. Between 1903 and 1907, Fleming tried unsuccessfully to gain election to the City Council. Democratic ascendancy during that period (Tom L. Johnson served as mayor from 1901 to 1909) was partly responsible for his failure. In 1909, however, with the aid of Republican boss Maurice Maschke and an enlarged black electorate behind him, Fleming became the city's first black councilman. After losing two subsequent elections, Fleming was again victorious in 1915 from the newly redrawn eleventh ward, and he served on the council until 1929.[21] Fleming's power was partly based on his control of the meager amount of patronage allotted his followers by the Maschke machine.

Fleming, who supported the Phillis Wheatley Association, was a strong believer in all-Negro institutions, and he viewed his own career as a model of what black unity could achieve. Yet his election to the City Council in 1909 and 1915 was by no means the clear-cut victory for the principle of racial solidarity that Fleming later portrayed it as being. In 1909, he was elected to an at-large seat spread over several wards. He needed many white votes to win and would not have gotten them without the strong support of the white Republican machine. In politics as in other aspects of community life, the prospects for black Clevelanders on the eve of World War I were tenuous and uncertain.

In some ways, the period between 1915 and 1930 represented a continuation of the trends of the preceding decades; in other ways, it was a time of improvement for blacks—albeit improvement circumscribed and limited in many ways. Progress in the face of adversity was the keynote of black Cleveland in the 1920s.

With the exception of Detroit, no northern city was more affected by the Great Migration of blacks northward in 1916-19 than was Cleveland. The city's black population quadrupled between 1910 and 1920, then doubled again in the 1920s as the migration resumed at a slower pace. By 1930, there were seventy-two thousand Negroes in the city. There were both "push" and "pull" factors involved in this movement of people. Black southerners' discontent with rigid segregation and disfranchisement, as well as a growing distaste for farming among younger blacks, impelled many to leave the South. But it is unlikely that the movement northward would have been as large as it was had there not been economic incentives. The sharp decline of immigration from Europe after 1914 (a result of the war) created both a need and an opportunity for black labor in northern industries. The *Cleveland Advocate,* a black newspaper, captured the drama of the great folk migration that resulted from these circumstances. "There is no mistaking what is going on," the paper editorialized in 1917. "It is a regular exodus. . . . People are leaving their homes and everything about them, under cover of night, as though they were going on a day's journey—leaving forever."[22]

These newcomers entered a somewhat different environment from their predecessors who arrived at the turn of the century. The interviewee Thompson related that when he came with his family to Cleveland in 1901, the city "seemed like a foreign country—everybody was speaking Jewish [Yiddish] or Italian or whatever. The neighborhoods that colored people lived in were the same neighborhoods that the people [immigrants] who came [over lived in]." By the end of the 1920s, this situation had changed considerably. The Italians and, especially, the Jews had left the Civil War district in large numbers, regrouping in enclaves in more outlying sections or dispersing throughout the city. The black community expanded by filling in areas contiguous to the earlier center of black settlement along Central and Scovill. By 1930, the section bounded by Euclid Avenue to the north and Woodland to the south was predominantly black as far east as East 55th Street, with many neighborhoods for the first time entirely segregated. The prewar boundary of East 55th Street could no longer contain the burgeoning black population, however, so there was also a dramatic expansion of the black ghetto eastward.

The development of the ghetto was not accidental. Blacks were able to move eastward gradually because the whites living there had reached an economic stage at which they were ready to move to better neighborhoods. But blacks encountered sharp, sometimes violent resistance from the working-class ethnic groups living to the south and southwest, as well as from the predominantly native white middle- and upper-class residents north of Euclid. When blacks attempted to integrate the facilities at Woodland Hills Park, slightly to the southeast of the expanding ghetto, the white immigrants from the surrounding neighborhoods reacted with hostility. Throughout the 1920s the park was a smoldering racial trouble spot.[23]

When Dr. Charles Garvin, one of the city's most prominent African Americans, built a home on Wade Park Avenue close to the border of Cleveland Heights, he discovered how difficult it was for even a well-to-do member of the race to move out of the ghetto. Whites threatened and harassed the workmen building the home. Once Garvin and his family had occupied their new home, whites dynamited the house twice. The first bomb only shattered a window, but the second did considerable damage to part of the house. During July 1926, the Garvins needed an armed guard outside their home to protect against threats made on their lives. By March 1927, Garvin's refusal to sell his home had broken the back of white resistance, and he was allowed to live in peace thereafter. Nevertheless, the traumatic experience he and his family went through must have given many blacks second thoughts about moving into white sections of the city.[24] The Garvin incident was one indication that racial discrimination was reaching new levels of intensity in the postwar period; another was the popularity of the racist motion picture *The Birth of a Nation,* which opened in Cleveland in 1917.[25]

Municipal government paid little attention to the needs of the expanding black population. In the Civil War area west of East 55th Street, recreational facilities were scarce, garbage removal irregular, and the streetcars notorious for poor service and shoddy conditions. Blacks could without contradiction say that they received both too little and too much attention from the police. City Hall made no effort to clean up the gambling and prostitution rackets on lower Central, and the number of officers assigned to black areas was inadequate. When police did enter the ghetto to make an arrest, however, they were often unnecessarily brutal. Part of the problem was the lack of black police. Incredibly, there were only a dozen black officers on the force in 1930.[26]

Discrimination in public accommodations went largely unchecked. Restaurants overcharged blacks or refused them service altogether, some even placing "white only" signs in the window. Some of the posher establishments admitted light-skinned

Negroes but excluded those of a darker hue.

The most insidious change occurred in the public school system, where a subtle process of discrimination began to take hold. Although black teachers remained integrated in the system, black students no longer were. By 1930, almost 90 percent of all black junior high school students attended four schools, while six out of ten black high school students went to a single institution, Central High. This trend was not entirely the result of the expansion of all-black neighborhoods. In 1933, black parents complained that black children on the East Side were often forced to attend Central rather than schools nearer their homes; conversely, it was charged that white students within the Central High district were allowed to transfer to other schools. This policy of selective transfers would continue for several decades, working hardships on students and intensifying the trend toward segregation in the public schools.[27]

When the student body of some schools became predominantly black in the 1920s and 1930s, their curricula often shifted from an emphasis on liberal arts to stressing skills of a more mundane nature. At Kennard Junior High School, which had become 60 percent black by 1930, administrators dropped foreign languages, reduced the number of electives, and placed more emphasis on "sewing, cooking, manual training, foundry work, and sheet metal [work]." In 1933, the local NAACP discovered that over half the tenth grade students at Central High were getting no training in mathematics and that such standard electives as languages, bookkeeping, and stenography had been dropped from the curriculum. These changes undoubtedly lowered the expectations of black students and oriented them, at an early age, toward lower-paying, less prestigious occupations. Once a powerful force for equality, the public schools by the 1930s had become yet another example of racial injustice.[28]

In spite of increasing segregation and discrimination in Cleveland, tens of thousands of migrants decided to make their home in the city. They were drawn to Cleveland—as they were to other northern centers—by the lure of steady employment. Most of the job openings were in unskilled factory labor, but blacks made significant gains in semi-skilled and skilled factory work as well. The wartime labor shortage broke the color barrier in Cleveland's heavy industries.

The rapid growth of the city's black population created opportunities for some Negroes in business and the professions. "For the first time in the history of the city," the *Cleveland Advocate* proclaimed in 1917, "The average business and professional man is making real money. He is able to meet his obligations and to lay something aside for the proverbial 'rainy day.'"[29] Between 1910 and 1930, the number of black businesses increased faster than the black population. Most of these enterprises were small, ghetto-based retail stores along Central, Woodland, or Cedar avenues. Black businesses tended to be underfinanced; unable to compete with the larger white firms and chain stores, they relied almost exclusively on the ghetto trade for their patronage.[30]

Nevertheless, some black businessmen succeeded. The tightening housing market for blacks was a boon to black real estate dealers. In 1917, a group of blacks headed by Thomas Fleming set up the Cleveland Realty, Housing, and Investment Company, and within a year they owned every apartment building on East 40th Street between Central and Scovill.[31] Alonzo Wright, who started out as a parking attendant, was befriended by a Standard Oil executive who helped him obtain the first Standard service station franchise in a black neighborhood. By the early 1930s, he had acquired six more service stations in the expanding ghetto.[32] The city's burgeoning black population also gave encouragement to black journalists. At one point in the 1920s four black weeklies were being published in Cleveland: the *Gazette,* the *Call,* the *Post,* and the *Herald.* The black population was not large enough to support so many papers, however. By 1928 the *Herald* had folded, and the two remaining competitors of the *Gazette* wisely merged to form the *Call and Post.* The *Call and Post* soon surpassed its older rival and during the 1930s became the leading black newspaper in Cleveland.[33]

The black employment picture in the postwar era was bleak. Black women, working primarily as laundresses, charwomen, and domestics, were mired at the bottom of the occupational ladder.[34] Another glaring problem was the continuing discrimination against blacks in clerical jobs. Throughout the 1920s, giant companies such as Bell Telephone and the East Ohio Gas Company refused to hire blacks "in anything but the humblest positions," and there were too few clerical jobs in black businesses to provide much employment.[35] Finally, most of the conservative American Federation of Labor unions excluded blacks, and they were aided and abetted by school administrators in the technical high schools.

Nevertheless, the economic structure of the black community was generally improving after 1915, especially for the majority of blacks in the city who had migrated from the rural South. Steady employment at unskilled or semiskilled labor in a Cleveland factory was preferable to sharecropping or tenant farming in Georgia or Alabama. As John Hope Franklin has noted, for southern agriculturalists, "the depression had already begun" in the 1920s. In coming north, black peasants did not always avoid poverty, but they at least escaped economic serfdom.[36]

Black migrants were now working alongside whites in the city's mills and foundries; yet interracial contact outside of the workplace remained minimal. The intensification of racism and growth of the ghetto in the 1920s ensured that situation. Much of black life in the Central-Woodland area thus became self-contained, and the internal development of the community assumed a new importance, as evidenced in the dynamic growth of black religious institutions in the wake of the Great Migration. In 1915, there were 17 black churches in Cleveland; by 1933, over 140. The migrants brought their own unique style of African American religion with them. Many of the new churches were storefront congregations of the Holiness and Spiritualist sects and the poorer Baptists. By the early 1920s, lower Central and Woodland were dotted with these institutions. The ministers of these churches, many of whom had no formal training, offered an informal, emotional service that appealed to many of the southern migrants. The continuity of religious experience offered by the new churches helped to ease the adjustment of black peasants to urban society. Some of the new religious institutions preserved the congregations of southern communities almost intact.

The Great Migration also led to an expansion of older black churches. As the black population moved eastward, it engulfed neighborhoods where white congregations had erected churches many years before. As a result, it usually proved unnecessary for growing black congregations to construct new churches. Usually they were able to purchase the buildings of white congregations that were anxious to sell. The growth of black religious activity during and after the war was primarily a lower- and lower-middle-class phenomenon.

By the end of the 1920s, the Central-Woodland area was stratified by class along an east-west axis. For the most part, neighborhoods became progressively higher status as one moved eastward and, to the limited extent possible for blacks, northward. Lower Central-Woodland to East 40th Street, approximately, was the oldest and most impoverished section of the African American community. This district held aging tenements, homes that had been carved up into "kitchenette" apartments, and deteriorating lodging houses. Many poor blacks, black attorney Charles Chesnutt observed, "live in dilapidated, rack-rented shacks, sometimes a whole family in one or two rooms, as a rule paying higher rents than white tenants for the same space."[37] Lower Central contained the highest illiteracy rates and lowest percentage of homeownership of any black district in the city.[38] Violence was endemic along Lower Central, especially during 1917–20, when the housing shortage was at its worst. Brawls were common among the Italians and blacks who mingled in this section,[39] but the most vicious incidents occurred between blacks and the Greeks who, through their control over the waiters' union, were eliminating blacks from jobs in leading hotels and restaurants.[40]

As one moved east, such conditions became less common: illiteracy rates dropped, the quality of shelter improved, and there was less violence and less crime. The stable working class and middle class had begun to advance beyond East 55th. There were many more single-family dwellings in this part of the black community, and the areas to the north of Central, especially, were pleasant residential districts.

Although conditions in much of the Central-Woodland district were far from ideal, it would be a mistake to assess the quality of black life in completely—or even mostly—negative terms. A case in point is the black family, which over the years has been the subject of much scrutiny and theorizing because of its supposed "matriarchal" tendencies. In Cleveland, a half-century of rapid urbanization, which one historian has hypothesized as the originating cause of the black matrifocal family, did not result in any appreciable increase in female-headed households.[41] In 1870, 85 percent of the black households in the city had been headed by two parents; in 1930 the figure was almost 83 percent—a decline of insignificant proportions. Furthermore, black fathers were absent only marginally more than immigrant or native white fathers in Cleveland. In 1930, both parents were present in 85 percent of the families of native whites of native parents; 86 percent of families of native whites of foreign or mixed parentage; and 88 percent of families of the foreign-born.[42] Despite the disrupting effects of migration and discrimination, black families were usually able to stay together in Cleveland.

This does not mean that there were no differences at all between white and black families. The housing shortage in the black community, combined with the need of many blacks to supplement their income, led many more black than white families to take in lodgers. In 1930, only slightly more than 10 percent of native white or foreign-born households had at least one lodger, whereas among black families 31 percent had one lodger and 16 percent had two or more.[43] Taking one or more persons into the household made the family pattern of some black families more complex than that of whites, but the result was not necessarily "pathological." The presence of an extra person in the house may actually have helped in the socialization of black children. Accepting lodgers was not an instance of disorganization in the family but rather was a creative adaptation to difficult circumstances.

Cleveland's black leadership responded in diverse ways to the growth of the ghetto and the hardening of racial lines that occurred after 1915. To the old integrationist elite, the new segregation was a disaster, one that sometimes struck close to home.

As they lost influence, a new elite group, led by City Councilman Fleming, businessman Herbert Chauncey, and Jane Edna Hunter, gained power. This new group of black businessmen and politicians were not overly bothered by segregation because they often relied on black patronage for their livelihoods. Although not much is known about the social thought of these individuals (they were much less articulate than their predecessors), it is clear that they did not favor protest or agitation for civil rights. They accepted separate black institutions and the development of a "group economy" as a means to racial advancement. The new elite gained ascendancy during the decade after 1915.

By the middle of the 1920s, however, a younger group of black leaders was beginning to question the complacency of Fleming and the business elite of the black community. For the most part professionals, these "New Negro" leaders tried to transcend the factionalism that had divided black leaders in the past. They believed in race pride and solidarity, but not at the expense of equal rights for the black citizens of Cleveland.[44]

Among the most important of the New Negro leaders was Harry E. Davis, a native Clevelander who attended Hiram College and Western Reserve University Law School. He was elected to the Ohio House of Representatives in 1920 and served there until 1928, when he stepped down to become the first Negro member of the city's Civil Service Commission. Another New Negro leader was Chester K. Gillespie, like Davis a northern-educated lawyer. Gillespie was active in politics but unsuccessful in his efforts to win election to the state legislature in the early

1920s. He built up his law practice and became known as Cleveland's leading civil rights attorney, bringing more suits against discriminatory restaurants, theaters, and amusement parks than any other lawyer in the city. Because of the racism of the time, these suits were not always successful, but Gillespie's activities helped keep the door of equality at the least partway ajar.[45]

Slightly older than Davis or Gillespie but of the same mentality was Dr. Charles Garvin, the prominent black physician who had endured mob harassment and bombings so that he could maintain his residency in a suburban section of the city. Like many New Negroes, Garvin was interested in black history; he researched the history of African medicine, in the process discovering that Africans had made a considerable unacknowledged contribution to the development of medical techniques.[46] Garvin also founded the Cleveland Medical Reading Club, a forum where black doctors could meet and discuss the latest advances in medicine. (At the time, the American Medical Association excluded Negroes.)[47]

The postwar era brought changes to the institutions, as well as the leadership, of Cleveland's black community. The huge influx of migrants caused problems of adjustment that the black churches were only partly able to deal with. The first secular organization that helped alleviate some of these problems was the Negro Welfare Association (NWA), an affiliate of the National Urban League founded at the end of 1917. The NWA conducted a wide range of activities. It published reports on conditions in the ghetto, helped migrants find housing, and investigated excessively high rents. In 1919, it leased a large house on Central to lodge returning black soldiers temporarily.[48]

The chief purpose of the NWA, however, was economic. The organization was successful in helping newcomers find employment, and it made a special effort to assist African Americans seeking skilled jobs. The NWA was basically a conservative organization, however, closely tied to the white industrialists who served alongside blacks on the board of trustees. These connections made it easier for blacks to get jobs through the NWA, but they also limited the ability of the organization to protest discrimination in company hiring or promotion practices.[49]

The Phillis Wheatley Association responded quickly to the crisis of the Great Migration and was immeasurably helpful to unattached black women new to the city, who were easy prey for unscrupulous men. The association also protected them from victimization by employment agencies.[50] Furthermore, it provided badly needed recreational facilities for black women. Nevertheless, most of the girls who graduated from Phillis Wheatley before 1930 became servants of one kind or another—jobs that did not threaten the white stereotype of blacks as menial workers. Phillis Wheatley grew rapidly because of white financial support, but with that support came a considerable degree of control by the board of trustees, which throughout the 1920s was dominated by white society women.[51]

Two institutions that followed a different pattern, with more independent black participation, were Karamu House and the National Association for the Advancement of Colored People. Karamu House (originally called the Playhouse Settlement) was founded in 1915 by two white graduates of Oberlin College, Russell and Rowena Jelliffe. Located at 38th and Central, Karamu's original purpose was to allow impoverished young people of both races an opportunity for artistic and dramatic expression. The Jelliffes established classes in arts and crafts, set up a theater program, and in the 1920s added a sports program and summer camp.[52] The settlement was always integrated, but as time passed it was used primarily by blacks. During the 1920s, the social center drew support from both blacks and racially liberal whites, and it became a source of pride to the black community. The creation of Karamu Theater illustrated a new interest in black folk culture; the name Karamu, given to the settlement's first permanent auditorium in 1927, derived from a Swahili word meaning "place of joyful meeting." Black theatrical groups staged a number of plays dealing with black folk culture. Karamu also helped establish the African Art Sponsors, a group that helped establish an African Art Collection at the Cleveland Museum of Art.[53]

The activities of the Cleveland NAACP also revealed an increasingly independent attitude on the part of some black Clevelanders. Established in 1914, the Cleveland branch grew slowly at first, but the prosperity of the postwar years led to greater participation; by 1922, the branch had sixteen hundred members. By the middle of the decade, it was both controlled and largely financed by blacks.[54]

The Cleveland NAACP was very much a New Negro organization. Though militant, the local branch stressed the need for flexibility and cooperation among black groups. The NAACP fought discrimination in many areas. In one typical year, 1924, the local branch brought five suits against discriminatory restaurants (winning only two); successfully ended discriminatory treatment of blacks at the Loew's Ohio Theater and the Brookside swimming pool; intervened with the manager of the Higbee department store to end its policy of refusing to allow black women to try on articles of clothing; and got the Erie Railroad to drop the idea of constructing separate toilet facilities for blacks and whites at its stop on East 55th Street.[55]

At the end of the 1920s, the new, aggressive leadership that headed the NAACP began to gain practical political power. The conviction of Thomas Fleming on bribery charges in 1929 helped clear the way for others,[56] but changes had been in the making for several years. As the black population expanded, it gradually engulfed the seventeenth and eighteenth wards, enabling two new black councilmen, Claybourne George and E. J. Gregg, to join Fleming in 1927. Both of the newcomers had run as "independent Republicans." Because of their dissatisfaction with the local party apparatus and poor treatment of blacks, they had spent the two previous years building their own political organizations outside of the regular party caucuses.

This was only the beginning of the augmentation of black political power at the local level. In 1929, Mary B. Martin became the first Negro to gain a seat on the city Board of Education.[57] Representing the balance of power on the twenty-five-member City Council, the three black councilmen moved quickly to flex their political muscle. All three had run for election promising to fight the discriminatory policies of City Hospital, which had long excluded black interns and doctors, kept black women out of the nurses' training program, and segregated patients by race. The city administration now yielded. Within a year and a half there were blacks in the internship and nurses' training programs, and the hospital's policy of segregating patients by race also came to an end.

Despite segregation and discrimination—or, perhaps, because of it—the black community of Cleveland was more united at the end of the 1920s than ever before.

Notes

1. See Eugene W. Burgess, "Residential Segregation in American Cities," *Annals of the American Academy of Political and Social Science* 140 (1928): 105, 100.

2. For a typical example of the failure to recognize the importance of the pre–World War I black migration, see Irving Kristol, "The Negro Today is Like the Immigrant of Yesterday," in *Nation of Nations: The Ethnic Experience and the Racial Crisis,* ed. Peter I. Rose (New York: Random House, 1972), 197–210.

3. James Freeman Clarke, "Condition of the Free Colored People of the United States," *Christian Examiner,* 5th ser., 4 (1859): 255; *Cleveland Leader,* March 31, 1869; Allan Peskin, ed., *North into Freedom: The Autobiography of John Malvin, Free Negro* (1966; reprint, Kent, Ohio: Kent State University Press, 1988), 72n. Data on black occupations are from Thomas Goliber, "Cuyahoga Blacks: A Social and Demographic Study, 1850–1880" (M.A. thesis, Kent State University, 1972), 64–96; data on Irish occupations are from U.S. Bureau of the Census, *Ninth Census of the United States, 1870* (Washington, D.C., 1872), 784.

4. Goliber, "Cuyahoga Blacks," 53, 60; William Ganson Rose, *Cleveland: The Making of a City* (1950; reprint, Kent, Ohio: Kent State University Press, 1990), 218, 235. Works Projects Administration, "The Peoples of Cleveland" (1942), 185, 195, manuscript in Cleveland Public Library, Sociology Division.

5. Goliber, "Cuyahoga Blacks," 22–34, 98–101.

6. An excellent discussion of the impact of the industrialization process on segregation in the city, using Chicago as a case study, is Sam B. Warner, *The Urban Wilderness: A History of the American City* (New York: Harper and Row, 1972), chap. 4. It is unfortunate that the rest of Warner's book did not follow the method of this and the preceding chapter.

7. Howard W. Green, comp., *Population Characteristics by Census Tracts, Cleveland, 1930* (Cleveland: Plain Dealer Publishing, 1931), 231–32, gives data for 1910. Green was director of the census in Cleveland.

8. See, for example, Rayford W. Logan, *The Betrayal of the Negro: From Rutherford B. Hayes to Woodrow Wilson* (New York: Collier Books, 1965).

9. Numerous examples of exclusion of blacks from restaurants and theaters during the 1900–1915 period appear in the city's black newspapers; see the *Journal* and the *Gazette,* February 4, 1911, and February 14, 1914; and Helen M. Chesnutt, ed., *Charles Waddell Chesnutt: Pioneer of the Color Line* (Chapel Hill: University of North Carolina Press, 1955), 261.

10. Chesnutt, *Chesnutt,* 238; Jane Edna Hunter, *A Nickel and a Prayer* (N.p.: Kani Publishing, 1940), 73; *Cleveland Advocate,* July 24, 1915, November, 11, 1916.

11. Frank U. Quillin, *The Color Line in Ohio* (Ann Arbor: University of Michigan Press, 1913), 155–56. The exclusion of blacks from certain trades is evident from the data in U.S. Census Bureau, *Thirteenth Census of the United States, 1910* (Washington, D.C.: GPO, 1913), 4:548–50.

12. James Thompson interview, undated, conducted by Thomas Campbell (manuscript), p. 6. Courtesy of Thomas Campbell.

13. Data from U.S. Census Bureau, *Thirteenth Census,* 4:548–50.

14. U.S. Bureau of the Census, *Negro Population in the United States, 1790–1915* (Washington, D.C.: GPO, 1918), 473.

15. Mary White Ovington, *Half a Man: The Status of the Negro in New York* (New York: Longmans, Green, 1911), 86; *Cleveland Gazette,* April 1, 1916.

16. U.S. Bureau of the Census, *Statistics of Women at Work, 1900* (Washington, D.C., 1907), 48–50; *Cleveland Gazette,* February 1, 1919.

17. Lodge notices appear in the black press. See also Harry E. Davis, *A History of Freemasonry among Negroes* (Cleveland: Prince Hall Society, 1946), 178–79, and Edward N. Palmer, "Negro Secret Societies," *Social Forces* 20 (1944): 177.

18. *Cleveland Plain Dealer,* February 1, 1911; *Cleveland Gazette,* February 14, 1914. A black YMCA, on Cedar Avenue, did not come into existence until 1923.

19. *Cleveland Gazette,* January 17, 1914; Hunter, *A Nickel and a Prayer,* esp. 99–100, on early white dominance of the association; also *Cleveland Gazette,* May 14, 1927. See also Adrienne Lash Jones, *Jane Edna Hunter: A Case Study of Black Leadership, 1905–1950* (New York: Carlson, 1989).

20. The careers of these black politicians are analyzed in detail in Kenneth L. Kusmer, *A Ghetto Takes Shape: Black Cleveland, 1870–1930* (Urbana: University of Illinois Press, 1976), 116–40; see also Green's autobiography, *Fact Stranger Than Fiction* (Cleveland: Riehl Publishing, 1920).

21. Thomas Fleming, "My Rise and Persecution" (1932), 10–100, manuscript autobiography, Western Reserve Historical Society, Cleveland, Ohio: *Cleveland Journal,* May 3, 1903, November 9, 1907, November 6, 1909.

22. *Cleveland Advocate,* April 28, 1917.

23. On Woodland Hills, see George Myers to Frank S. Harmon, August 23, 1923, and August 25, 1927, Myers Papers, Ohio State Historical Society, Columbus; Cleveland NAACP branch, "Statement of Activities . . . for the Year ending Dec. 31 (1927)," Branch Files, Container G157, NAACP Archives, Library of Congress, Washington, D.C.

24. Harry E. Davis to Walter White, February 5, 1926; Mabel Clark to James Weldon Johnson, July 12, 1926; Johnson to Clark, July 13, 1926; Davis to Johnson, July 15, 1926; Johnson to Davis, August 13, 1926; Clark to Johnson, March 24, 1927, Branch Files, Container G157, NAACP Archives.

25. *Cleveland Plain Dealer,* April 8, 1917; *Cleveland Leader,* April 18, 1917; *Cleveland Gazette,* April 14, 21, May 12, 1917.

26. On police in the ghetto, see *Cleveland Gazette,* November 24, 1917, March 2, 1918, October 11, 1919, June 12, 1920. For some time during the 1920s, black prisoners were segregated in the county jail. This policy ended in 1927. See ibid., October 30, 1926, April 30, 1927.

27. Alonzo G. Grace, "The Effect of Negro Migration on the Cleveland Public School System" (Ph.D. diss., Western Reserve University, 1932), 20–23; author's interview with Russell and Rowena Jelliffe, September 1, 1971.

28. Grace, "Effect of Negro Migration," 84–86; Willard C. Richan, *Racial Isolation in the Cleveland Public Schools* (Cleveland: Case Western Reserve University Press, 1967), 33–36.

29. *Cleveland Advocate,* January 13, 1917.

30. U.S. Census Bureau, published data on occupations for 1910 and 1930; U.S. Bureau of the Census, *Negroes in the United States, 1920–1932* (Washington, D.C.: GPO, 1935), 522, contains the 1929 survey.

31. *Cleveland Advocate,* March 31, April 21, December 8, 1917; *Cleveland Gazette,* April 28, 1917, September 7, 1918.

32. Charles W. Chesnutt, "The Negro in Cleveland," *The Clevelander* 5 (November 1930): 3–4, 24–26, 4; author's interview with Dr. William P. Saunders, August 6, 1972.

33. Author's interview with Norman McGee (one of the publishers of the *Post*), September 3, 1971; brief biography and newspaper clipping on Ormand Forte (editor of the *Herald* and its predecessor, the *Advocate*), in Western Reserve Historical Society collections.

34. See Kusmer, *Ghetto Takes Shape,* table 27, p. 287. The note on p. 286 explains the table.

35. Chesnutt, "The Negro in Cleveland," 4.

36. John Hope Franklin, *From Slavery to Freedom,* 3d ed. (New York: Knopf, 1967), 495. A classic study of conditions in one southern state in the 1920s and 1930s is Arthur F. Raper, *Preface to Peasantry: A Tale of Two Black Belt Counties* (Chapel Hill: University of North Carolina Press, 1936).

37. Chesnutt, "The Negro in Cleveland," 3; Langston Hughes, *The Big Sea* (New York: Hill and Wang, 1940), 27.

38. Data on socioeconomic status of Negroes by census tracts from Green, comp., *Population Characteristics by Census Tracts,* 58–60, 160–62.

39. See, for example, *Cleveland Gazette,* June 16, 30, 1917, August 14, 1920.

40. Ibid., November 3, 1917, September 21, 28, 1918.

41. See Theodore Hershberg et al., "A Tale of Three Cities," in *Philadelphia: Work, Space, Family, and Group Experience in the 19th Century,* ed. Theodore Hershberg (New York: Oxford University Press, 1981), 384–86. Another scholar who even more strongly identifies the black urban experience with a Frazierian "City of Destruction" thesis is Elizabeth Pleck, *Black Migration and Poverty: Boston, 1865–1900* (New York: Academic Press, 1979), 11, 202–3. Even if Pleck's analyses were without methodological faults, I do not believe the breakdown of the black family occurred in the industrial centers of the Midwest to the degree that it did in the South or the older eastern cities.

42. U.S. Bureau of the Census, *Fifteenth Census of the United States, 1930, Population* (Washington, D.C.: GPO, 1932), 6:1027, for comparative family data by ethnic and racial group.

43. Ibid., 1025.

44. For general comments on the development of the New Negro mentality in the 1920s, see August Meier, *Negro Thought in America, 1880–1915* (Ann Arbor: University of Michigan Press,1963), 256–78.

45. Clippings, 1921–28, in Scrapbook 1, Chester K. Gillespie Papers, Western Reserve Historical Society; Julian Krawcheck, "Society Barred Negroes," *Cleveland Press,* May 30, 1963.

46. "The Influence of African Culture on Modern Civilization," "Medicine in Ancient Egypt," and other essays in Charles H. Garvin Papers, Western Reserve Historical Society; Russell Davis, *Memorable Negroes in Cleveland's Past* (Cleveland: Western Reserve Historical Society, 1969), 57.

47. Charles H. Garvin, "The Cleveland Medical Reading Club," manuscript in Garvin Papers.

48. *Cleveland Gazette,* December 22, 1917, March 1, April 5, 1919; *National Urban League Annual Report, 1917–19* (New York: National Urban League, 1918), 5, 7; Annual Reports, May–August 1918, 1919–20, 1922, of the Negro Welfare Association, Cleveland Urban League Papers, Western Reserve Historical Society.

49. See assessment of the organization's generally conservative thrust in Kusmer, *Ghetto Takes Shape,* 255–57.

50. An excellent article on the problems of migrant women is Darlene Clark Hine, "Black Migration to the Urban Midwest: The Gender Dimension," in *The Great Migration in Historical Perspective,* ed. Joe Trotter (Bloomington: University of Indiana Press, 1991), 127–46.

51. *Cleveland Gazette,* March 10, 1928; author's confidential interview with contemporary of Jane Hunter, n.d.

52. *Cleveland Gazette,* July 3, 1915; Arna Bontemps and Jack Conroy, *Anyplace But Here* (New York: Hill and Wang, 1966), 278–86; Katrine M. Baxley, "The House the Jelliffes Built," *Oberlin Alumni Magazine* 62 (April 1966): 18–22; John Selby, *Beyond Civil Rights* (Cleveland: World Publishing, 1966), 11–47.

53. Selby, *Beyond Civil Rights,* 55–60, 82–83, 100–104; and from author's extensive interview with Russell and Rowena Jelliffe, September 1, 1971.

54. F. E. Young to May Childs Nerney, January 25, 1914, Container C 416, NAACP Archives; "Report of A. W. Hunton, October 6 to November 8, 1922," Container C65, ibid.

55. Claybourne George to Walter White, April 21, 1924; George to Robert Bagnall, June 10, 1924; "NAACP Has Lunch Room Proprietor Fined $50 for Discrimination in Cleveland," press release, June 13, 1924; *Annual Report of the Cleveland Branch . . . 1924* (N.p., 1924), 1–2, all in NAACP Archives.

56. R. O. Huus and D. I. Cline, "Election Fraud and Councilmanic Scandals Stir Cleveland," *National Civic Review* 18 (1929): 289–94.

57. *Cleveland Gazette,* November 9, 1928, February 23, November 9, 16, 1929; Davis, *Memorable Negroes,* 47.

Cleveland: The Evolution of Black Political Power

William E. Nelson, Jr.

Black Control of Local Government

THE UPSURGE in the election to public office of "new breed" black politicians has been most effective in the promotion of the social and economic interests of upwardly mobile, elite sectors of the black community.

Relying heavily on their appointment powers and the existence of local affirmative action mandates, black mayors of major American cities have significantly expanded the representation of members of the black middle class in public sector employment. One major study of this process notes that though the rate of increase in total black municipal employment in cities with black mayors has been important, the rate of increase in the number of blacks in top civil service administrative and professional positions has been especially dramatic.

Apparently, black mayors have skillfully used the powers of their office and their broader political influence to promote the recruitment of members of the black middle class into major positions in local government. Detroit mayor Coleman Young appointed blacks to 51 percent of the city's department head positions; under Young, they also filled 41 percent of the top positions on municipal boards and commissions.

Strict enforcement of affirmative action mandates and residency requirements by black mayors has resulted in a significant penetration by blacks in lower echelons of municipal bureaucracies as well. Thus, over the decade from 1973 through 1983, black representation on the police forces in black mayoral cities such as Detroit, Newark, and Atlanta increased dramatically. In Detroit, the increase was sixfold; in Newark and Atlanta it was threefold.[1]

Economic benefits flowing to the black middle class have not been limited to public sector jobs. Black mayors have also substantially increased contracting and

Originally published in *The New Black Politics: The Search for Political Power,* ed. Michael B. Preston, Lenneal J. Henderson, Jr., and Paul Puryear (Longman, 1982). Reprinted with permission.

purchasing opportunities in local government for black business firms. In Detroit, the proportion of city business flowing to minority business firms increased from 3 percent in 1973 to 20 percent in 1977.[2] As mayor of Cleveland, Carl Stokes not only channeled city contracts to existing black businesses but was responsible for the establishment of several successful black firms whose access to the resources of local government has yielded lucrative benefits.

Although black mayors have been modestly successful in increasing access to public resources by members of the black middle class, they have been unsuccessful in significantly altering the social and economic position of the black community as a whole. Unemployment and poverty in black mayoral cities remain among the highest in the nation. Black governance of major American cities has not only failed to stem the tide of urban decay but has precipitated policies of central city disinvestment by state and federal governments, as well as private corporate interests.[3] These patterns have had a devastating effect on the economic position of black citizens dependent upon public assistance, heavily concentrated in cities governed by black mayors.

A close examination of patterns of decision making in black-controlled cities suggests that the new black politics has not led to a substantial alteration in the flow of major economic benefits at the local level. Elected on reform platforms that promised profound changes in the policy-making process, black mayors have almost uniformly embraced corporate-centered strategies that have virtually precluded the redistribution of major benefits to broad segments of the black community. In practical terms this has meant that in Detroit, Mayor Coleman Young abandoned the anticorporate philosophy he held before his election in 1973 in favor of policies that offer tax breaks and social investment subsidies to the business sector while reducing social consumption benefits to inner-city neighborhoods.[4] Liberal tax abatement policies in Detroit to attract corporate investment and promote downtown development have allowed the same corporate interests that dominated the budgetary process before the election of Mayor Young to maintain their premier influence; at the same time, municipal revenues flowing into the black community have been reduced.

These issues and problems underscore the difficulties inherent in the effort to use the electoral process as a new base of power for the black community. Questions relating to the impact and effectiveness of black governance have occupied center stage in Cleveland's political process since the election of the city's first black mayor, Carl B. Stokes.

The Rise and Fall of the Stokes Machine

Carl Stokes was swept into the mayor's office in Cleveland in 1967 on the back of a massive grass-roots mobilization of the black vote. Stokes viewed the outcome of the 1967 mayoral contest not as a personal victory but as a mandate fundamentally to alter the subordinate social, economic, and political posture of the black community. A native of Cleveland, Carl Stokes had been an active participant in the militant struggle for social justice waged in the city by civil rights activists in the 1960s. He represented a new breed of politician, consumed with visions of racial progress and committed to the proposition that creative social change could be achieved through the direct involvement of black administrators in local public policy making.

As an experienced politician, Stokes clearly understood that he could not realize the social and economic goals of his administration without the creation of an enduring base of power in the black community. He viewed his election as the first black mayor of Cleveland as only the first stage in the campaign to forge a position of permanent power and influence for the community in the Cleveland political system. The second stage would have to entail the creation of a stable political organization capable of mobilizing broad-scale support for the implementation of the social reform agenda put forward in both the public and private sectors by his administration. During Stokes's first two-year term, efforts were made to lay the foundation for such an organization through the unification of black Democratic politicians under the banner of a separate black caucus. Shortly after his reelection in 1969, a formal decision was made to establish a new organization called the Twenty-first District Democratic Caucus.[5]

The Twenty-first District Democratic Caucus represented a determined effort on the part of Carl Stokes and his supporters to expand the arena of effective black political influence within the Democratic party. Members of the caucus found, however, that the leaders of the Cuyahoga County Democratic party were not receptive to the notion of the exercise of influence over party policy by a separate black caucus led by Carl Stokes. The caucus's demands for input into the selection of party candidates for public office were flatly rejected. In the wake of this rejection by the regular party, members of the caucus decided to withdraw en masse from the party and establish their own independent political organization.

The decision by the black caucus to withdraw from the local Democratic party established the political context for the formation of one of the most powerful political machines in the country. Operating as a nonpartisan political instrument, the Twenty-first District Caucus began to take on the character of a formal third party. Rules and procedures of the organization called for the screening of candidates, the endorsement of candidates across party lines, and the fielding of an independent slate of candidates for public office. With the power of both black ward committeemen and black city councilmen under one central command, the caucus exercised firm control over the black vote in the city, county, and congressional elections in the Twenty-first District. In several key elections held between 1969 and 1971, the caucus demonstrated its strength as a crucial political force in local elections. Although severely restricted in experience and organizational resources, the caucus was able not only to elect its own candidates to public office but to mobilize critical black support behind both Democratic and Republican candidates for public office.

The consolidation of political power in the office of the mayor, undergirded by the electoral strength of an independent black-controlled political machine, dramatically altered power relations between black and white communities in Cleveland. The existence of a cohesive political power base extending beyond the office of mayor opened the door to the prospect that black political control would become institutionalized in Cleveland. Through shrewd bargaining and careful political organizing, leaders of the caucus would be in a position to wring major concessions from both of the regular political parties.

Central to plans for institutionalizing black control in Cleveland was continued black representation in the mayor's office and the maintenance of a cohesive, independent political organization in the black community. Prospects for achieving these objectives were seriously weakened by Stokes's announcement that he would not seek a third term in the 1971 mayoral contest. Efforts by the black community to maintain control over the mayor's office were negated by the defeat of Arnold Pinkney, one of Stokes's chief lieutenants, for the mayorship in 1971. A number of black politicians began to succumb to pressure to return to the fold of the Democratic party, which offered patronage to keep their ward organizations alive. Unity within the caucus was further undermined by conflict among its three key leaders, Arnold Pinkney, Councilman George Forbes, and Congressman Louis Stokes, over internal organizational procedures and the distribution of political benefits. Pinkney and Forbes broke all formal ties with the caucus; their departure was followed by a mass exodus of black elected officials from the caucus back into the fold of the regular Democratic organization.[6]

Ascendancy of the Forbes Machine

The decade of the 1970s witnessed a sharp transformation in the character and structure of black politics in Cleveland. During the Stokes era the fundamental goal of black politics was the redistribution of power in ways that would allow blacks to control their own destinies and share equally in the rewards of city government. The return of black leadership to the Democratic party fold after Stokes's departure changed the fundamental goal of black politics from community uplift to self-aggrandizement. Within the confines of the Democratic party the sense of common purpose that united black political forces across geographic, political, and class boundaries rapidly began to dissipate. Black political leaders ceased to champion programs of social reform and community redevelopment, instead embracing more pragmatic programs that would enhance their access to high levels of material benefits. This style of politics continued to grow in magnitude and influence in the decade of the 1970s; in the 1980s the basic pillars of traditional machine politics remained firmly in place.

Without dispute, the most powerful black politician in Cleveland (some say the most powerful politician of the 1980s) was George Forbes, president of the Cleveland City Council. Forbes emerged as the acknowledged boss of Cleveland's black political machine.

Forbes's political career began in 1963 with his election to the city council one year after graduating from Cleveland's John Marshall College of Law. Throughout most of the Stokes era, Forbes remained in the background as a loyal and faithful supporter of the mayor. In the aftermath of the decision by Stokes to retire from Cleveland politics and move to New York City, Forbes surfaced as one of the chief participants in the negotiations designed to resolve differences between the Twenty-first District Caucus and the Cuyahoga County Democratic party. Under the initial terms of the agreement reached by the caucus and party leaders, Forbes was to be named cochair of the county party organization. Before this agreement could be sealed, however, Congressman Louis Stokes stepped forward, laid claim to the position, and served in this capacity for more than a year. In exchange for his agreement to step aside, party officials promised to support Forbes in a bid to become president of the Cleveland City Council. Eventually Forbes was not only successful in his quest for the council presidency but assumed the dual role of county party cochair in 1974.

As county party cochair, Forbes was able to amass an incredible amount of personal power. His party position gave him immediate and direct access to party patronage, a resource he used liberally to create a network of influence and support throughout city and county governments.

It was in his role as president of the City Council, however, that Forbes assembled the political contacts and formal power required to become boss of the new Cleveland machine. The foundation of his power base was his ability to collect "IOUs" by determining the distribution of public and private patronage to members of the City Council. A skilled administrator and politician, he parlayed his control over committee assignments and budgets into almost dictatorial control over the council.[7]

Through the manipulation of both external and internal resources, Forbes was able to silence most of his critics on the City Council. For example, Fanny Lewis entered the council in 1979 as an outspoken critic of Forbes. Eventually, she was compelled to solicit his support for her effort to build a major federally subsidized housing project in the Hough area called Lexington Village.

After becoming president in 1973, the political position of George Forbes was seriously challenged in the council in only two instances. In June 1980, a group of white council persons led by ninth ward councilwoman Barbara Pringle filed petitions to place on the election ballot a proposal to have the council president elected by citywide vote rather than by members of the council itself.[8] The ballot issue failed by a wide margin. A more serious threat to Forbes's power erupted in November 1981, when black councilman Lonnie Burten announced that he would run against Forbes for council president. Burten received the backing of ten of twenty-one members, including two black councilmen. The Burten revolt was broken when community pressure compelled one of the two black councilmen supporting Burten to renounce his support.

Forbes built his base of political influence not only on his ability to exercise control over the council but also on his extensive political ties with members of the business community. These ties were first firmly forged during the administration of Mayor Ralph J. Perk. At an early point in his career as council president, Forbes teamed up with Mayor Perk to push through the City Council a redevelopment package designed to provide extensive incentives and benefits to the business community. The centerpiece of this redevelopment package was tax abatement, a policy that exempted major national corporations sponsoring construction projects in the downtown area from the payment of local revenue.[9] Forbes's participation in these efforts established for him a solid reputation as a friend of business interests. This reputation continued into the Kucinich administration when Forbes played a major role in blocking efforts by Kucinich to implement urban populism by taking away tax incentives from major corporations. Forbes's relationship with the corporate sector was mutually beneficial for both parties.

Black ministers have been major recipients of public funds passed down through City Council. Some respondents suggested a one-to-one relationship between the support of black ministers for black machine politics and their role as recipients of public funds to support their ongoing community-related activities and church operating expenses.

Black churches are part of a broader institutional web that locks vital elements of the black community into the dynamics of black machine politics in Cleveland. In the final analysis, most major interest groups in the black community, including community associations and black businesses, must look to some facet of city government for fiscal and political support. The point should be underscored in this regard that over time George Forbes extended the reach of his influence into high levels of city government beyond the City Council. According to some observers, Forbes's influence in the Voinovich administration was so great that he usurped a good deal of the mayor's decision-making authority.

George Forbes was able to cultivate strong rank-and-file black support for his role as boss of city politics by using the power of his office to write affirmative action requirements into city legislation and speaking out strongly against discrimination in key areas such as law enforcement and housing. Thus in March 1983, Forbes announced that he was taking steps to bring airlines operating at Cleveland's Hopkins International Airport into compliance with the city's equal employment opportunity goals. One newspaper quoted Forbes as saying, "One of the requirements for doing business in this city is that you have to have blacks working for you."[10]

Despite the allure of his image as a militant black activist, the general thrust of Forbes's political leadership was toward forging strong links between the black community and the Democratic party and concentrating material benefits in the hands of party activists and their clients. In this sense, black politics in Cleveland during the Forbes era came full circle, from a politics of independence and community uplift, to a politics of subordination and self-aggrandizement. Clearly, the vision of a cohesive black political movement designed to assuage black grievances and establish a permanent base for community control in the public and private sectors practically disappeared from the political landscape. It was replaced with a focus on individual benefits and the concentration of power in the hands of a small political elite.

That the ascendancy of the Forbes machine did not produce a corresponding increase in benefits for the black community is suggested by the small percentage of blacks holding key positions in the Voinovich administration, the extraordinarily high level of unemployment in the black community, and the continuing emphasis on Cleveland's urban redevelopment program on downtown development rather than the social and economic rehabilitation of central city neighborhoods.[11] Indeed, to the extent that the new machine in Cleveland was wedded to old machine politics, it operated as a crucial obstacle to the transference of major benefits from the public sector and private institutions to the black community.

The Dissipation of Black Political Mobilization

Carl Stokes's success in elevating black political influence in Cleveland to new levels of authority was primarily because of the strong political mobilization of the black community as an independent force in local politics. This political mobilization was characterized by strong black-led civil rights protests, a major upsurge in black voter registration, and cohesive black voting in local elections. In the 1980s, black politics in Cleveland was marked by the dissipation of black political mobilization. With the passing of the black power era under Carl Stokes, blacks in Cleveland lost a great deal of confidence in their ability to influence public policy through protest action. The result was the virtual demise of the civil rights movement as an instrument of power in the black community.

The demise of black protest activity was accompanied by a decline in the effectiveness of political organizations in the black community. Worthy of special note was the continuing weakness of the Twenty-first District Caucus as an instrument of political power in Cleveland elections. Although the caucus continued to screen candidates and to make endorsements, there was little evidence that its endorsements carried significant weight in elections.

The political power of the caucus was undermined by its lack of patronage, the absence of a substantial war chest to finance campaigns, and the dual membership of most of its members in the caucus and the Democratic party. Its most important electoral role involved grass-roots campaign activities on behalf of its chairman, Congressman Louis Stokes.

Thus, in the post-Stokes era there existed in Cleveland no viable, independently organized caucus of black politicians. The most logical group to form such an organization, black council members, were politically tied to the Forbes machine by patronage benefits and a single-minded concentration on the building of successful electoral organizations in their wards. At no time did these individuals meet to plan a community agenda or even a common legislative agenda.

At the community level, traditionally strong organizations such as the St. Clair–Superior Coalition and the Buckeye-Woodland Community Congress were bordering on the brink of dissolution because of a significant loss of government funding. The most serious danger was the loss of permanent staff, without which these groups could not serve as effective vehicles for political mobilization. The neighborhood movement in the black community has historically been slow to emerge because of the transient character of black residents. When new organizations have evolved, city councilmen have frequently viewed them as rivals to existing ward clubs.

In the 1980s, the black community not only witnessed the atrophy of effective black political organization but the disintegration of its political leadership structure as well. With the exception of George Forbes, the cadre of political leaders that led the black community to majestic heights of power in the 1960s virtually disappeared from effective roles in Cleveland politics.

Carl Stokes was viewed as the only potential rival to Forbes. Arnold Pinkney's political influence declined in the wake of his absence from the electoral process for several years and his conviction on conflict of interest charges in conjunction with his service as a member of the Cleveland–Cuyahoga County Port Authority.[12] Because of his location in Washington, Congressman Louis Stokes was unable to build a base of power in local politics.

Constituency work by a U.S. congressman in Cleveland simply could not yield the host of political benefits equivalent to those emanating from the entrenched position Forbes held inside the Democratic and Republican camps. At the councilmanic level, Forbes attempted to eliminate one potential rival for power by negotiating the appointment of councilman Michael White to a vacant seat in the Ohio Senate in Columbus.[13] Another major rival, Lonnie Burten, died of a heart attack. Virgil Brown, the first black politician to be elected to a countywide office, was burdened with the handicap of being a Republican in a Democratically controlled city.

Thus the responsibility for black political mobilization resided totally in the organizational and leadership hands of George Forbes and the Forbes machine. The Forbes machine, however, showed no inclination to engage in the broad-scale electoral mobilization of the black community characteristic of the Stokes years.

The absence of organized voter mobilization campaigns in the black community resulted in a significant decline in black political participation. As Table 1 clearly shows, while the number of registered black voters between 1965 and 1985 greatly increased, the number of blacks participating in elections declined significantly.

Table 1
Selective Summary of Cleveland's Mayoral General Elections in Black Wards, 1965–1985

	1965	*1967*	*1975*	*1979*	*1985*
Registered voters	103,123	99,885	102,380	107,919	151,920
Turnout (W)	76,377	73,093	75,253	58,570	53,720
Turnout (%)	74.1	80.4	73.5	47.69	36.77

Source: Joseph P. McCormick, "The Continuing Significance of Race: Racial Change and Electoral Politics in Cleveland, Ohio. 1961–1977" (unpublished paper, Department of Political Science, Howard University, Washington, D.C., 1979); Larry Brisker, "An Election Analysis of the General Election, November 5, 1985, Cleveland, Ohio" (unpublished report, Pollmet, Inc., Cleveland, Ohio, Cuyahoga County Board of Elections, 1985).

The point should be underscored that although registration in black wards in the 1985 mayoral election was higher than registration in white wards (151,920 to 149,915), 65,703 voters turned out in white wards, while 53,720 voters turned out in black wards.[14] Clearly, a major facet of the black electoral problem in Cleveland during these years was turnout.

Although pockets of political strength in the black community persisted, the most salient feature of black political life citywide was the absence of effective black political leadership and organization. Extremely important in this regard was the failure of the Forbes machine to engage in across-the-board political mobilization. Like traditional political machines, the Forbes machine concentrated on delivering the vote only for organization candidates; it also resisted the temptation to activate more voters than those required to win elections. Completely removed from the political scene was the intensive grass-roots political campaigning that succeeded in driving unprecedented numbers of blacks to the polls in the Stokes era. It was replaced by a listless, issueless style of political campaigning that discouraged broad-scale participation by the black masses in the electoral process.

The centralization of political authority in the black community produced neither political unity nor enhanced countywide power. Young, independent candidates faced a maelstrom of political opposition in the black community in their bid for public office. One such candidate in 1985 was compelled to build her campaign on the back of volunteers from the Black Women's Leadership Caucus and a few courageous black ministers. Members of the black political establishment refused to embrace her campaign until the last minute, when it was clear that she had an excellent chance of victory. The absence of a citywide organization to map strategies, groom candidates, and deliver votes seriously undermined the impact of the black community as a center of power in the electoral process.

The 1985 General Election

The continuing political weakness of the black community was vividly revealed in the 1985 general election for mayor. In a city where blacks represent more than 50 percent of the registered vote, the black community was unable to mount serious opposition to the reelection of a white Republican mayor, George Voinovich. One reason for the lack of black opposition to Voinovich was that during his term of office, Voinovich had gone out of his way to court black support. Voinovich's public stand in behalf of the desegregation of the Cleveland Police Department was especially important in forging his image as a friend of the black community. Most critically, Voinovich was strongly supported by black political leaders, who in turn discouraged the emergence of serious opposition to the mayor's reelection.

George Forbes announced to the Cleveland community that he thought George Voinovich was doing a pretty good job and did not see why any opposition was necessary. According to one Cleveland respondent, when Forbes talks like that in public, he is using sign language, a code to his troops to sit this one out.[15]

Voinovich's close political ties to the leadership structure of the black community translated into astonishing electoral strength in the black community. Table 2 reports the outcome of the 1985 general election in the black community. Voinovich received 84.12 percent of the vote in black wards (1 through 10). His opponent, Gary Kucinich, received only 15.88 percent of the black vote. The percentage of Voinovich's vote in the black community was much higher than the percentage of the vote he received in the white community. In the white wards (11 through 21) Voinovich received 61.48 percent of the vote to 37.52 percent for Kucinich. Despite a lower turnout in the black community, Voinovich received 42,953 black votes to 39,716 white votes. Thus in the 1985 general election the black community was a major base of power for Voinovich. In a city where very few black Republicans reside, Voinovich's tremendous electoral appeal in the black community provided additional evidence of the near absence of organizational forces to mobilize black political resources behind a social and economic agenda developed and controlled by blacks.

Triumph of the New Insurgents

In the 1990s the winds of change have continued to swirl across the landscape of Cleveland politics. Critical insight into the character and direction of this change was vividly illuminated by the outcome of the 1989 mayoral election. When the final votes were counted, State Senator Michael White emerged as the first Cleveland mayor of African American descent in two decades.

The White mayoral victory was emblematic of a dramatic shift in political power from old guard politicians to a new generation of political insurgents.[16] Few signs of this political transformation, which began to take root during the era of the Forbes

Table 2
Summary of 1985 Cleveland Mayoral General Election in Black Wards

City wards	Registered voters	Voters	Percent voter turnout	Gary Kucinich	Percent vote Kucinich	George Voinovich	Percent vote Voinovich	Total
1	17,304	7,639	44.15	1,183	16.21	6,113	83.79	7,296
2	14,846	5,277	35.54	948	18.78	4,099	81.22	5,047
3	17,168	6,978	40.65	944	14.25	5,681	85.75	6,625
4	15,518	5,271	26.84	800	15.90	4,233	84.10	5,033
5	14,358	4,165	33.35	700	17.96	3,198	82.04	3,898
6	14,732	4,789	32.77	661	14.53	3,888	85.47	4,549
7	15,740	4,828	37.29	635	13.97	3,910	86.03	4,545
8	15,389	5,870	31.70	725	13.12	4,801	86.88	5,526
9	14,248	4,878	28.25	581	12.61	4,027	87.39	4,608
10	12,617	4,025	57.13	823	21.51	3,003	78.49	3,826
TOTALS	151,920	53,720		8,000		42,953		50,953

Source: Larry Brisker, "An Election Anaylsis of the General Election, November 5, 1985, Cleveland, Ohio" (unpublished report, Pollmet, Inc., Cleveland, Ohio, Cuyahoga County Board of Elections, 1985).

machine, were evident in January 1989, when Michael White declared his candidacy for mayor. In the early stages of the primary campaign, White was not considered to be a leading contender for the mayor's office.[17]

Given his legendary role as a major power broker in Cleveland politics, George Forbes was generally viewed as the most likely black politician to recapture city hall for the black community in the 1989 mayoral race. Initial estimates of Forbes's chances of succeeding outgoing mayor George Voinovich did not take into account, however, a number of critical factors. First, Forbes's electoral appeal in a citywide election was untested. His previous election victories as a candidate had been limited to noncompetitive campaigns in his councilmanic district. Second, though Forbes enjoyed considerable popular support in the black community, his reputation in the white community was sullied by his image as an intractable racial militant with an explosive temper. Black insurgents, unhappy with Forbes's political legacy, would argue with much credibility that as the resource base of the Forbes machine expanded, the abysmal economic plight of the black underclass grew progressively worse.

Michael White emerged in 1989 as a leader of the new insurgents. Once a devoted protégé of George Forbes, White became, during his years on Cleveland City Council and in the Ohio Senate, a vocal and effective critic of the Forbes machine and what he considered to be its outmoded style of patronage politics. Defying the predictions of political pundits, White quickly moved out of the shadows of George Forbes in the mayoral primary. White assembled an energetic campaign staff and launched a highly organized and vigorous citywide campaign.[18]

White's articulation of a new direction for Cleveland encompassed a conciliatory stand on issues of race relations and social interaction designed to assuage fears by whites that the election of a black mayor would intensify racial turmoil and conflict. In the West Side white community, White promised as mayor to work assiduously to diminish racial polarization and to address social and economic issues of concern to all citizens of Cleveland. White's message of racial conciliation began to generate positive reactions in these communities. An editorial endorsement by the *Cleveland Plain Dealer* applauding White as a new leader who would heal the wounds of racial division enhanced his political credibility and helped to build a base of solid support among potential white voters.[19]

The outcome of the primary race reflected White's escalating momentum. While George Forbes won the primary with 38 percent of the vote, Michael White came in second with 25 percent. White's showing in the primary represented an astounding personal victory. He had managed to obtain a place in the general election by polling one-third of the vote in black wards and 20 to 25 percent of the vote in white wards.

In the general election Michael White captured 56 percent of the vote to George Forbes's 44 percent. With two black candidates in the race, the balance of power in the election resided in West Side white wards. Michael White campaigned vigorously on the West Side advancing an agenda of "new leadership" that would remove Cleveland from the doldrums of economic inertia, racial conflict, and social despair. The outcome of the 1989 mayoral contest produced significant consequences for the structuring of power and brokering of political and economic interests in Cleveland. Michael White's campaign not only placed new leadership in City Hall but simultaneously swept into the City Council a new leadership corps composed of insurgents allied with White—several of whom were elected for the first time in 1989—and individuals regarded as Forbes loyalists but who were not a part of the machine's inner circle. The new council president was Jay Westbrook, a white councilman from the West Side who had formally identified with White during the campaign. Westbrook's appointment led to the ascension to key leadership positions of young white council members who had never before enjoyed positions of leadership or influence.

The White Administration: Challenges and Directions

Clearly in the 1990s, the coordination and control of black political interests in Cleveland has shifted from old-guard black politicians to Michael White and his political allies. The key issue is whether or not the current shift in political leadership portends a major shift in policy direction. On this issue the verdict is mixed. During his tenure as mayor, Michael White has given strong signals that he intends to move the social agenda from a focus on race-based issues to one that stresses multiethnic approaches to problems of concern to broad sectors of the Cleveland population.

In keeping with this philosophy, White has made downtown corporate development a cornerstone of his administration. White has accepted the challenge of building a downtown corporate base to combat the economic hardships produced by the loss of major manufacturing industries in Cleveland over several decades. Plans for downtown development have incorporated strong support for the construction of the Rock 'n Roll Hall of Fame and an expansion and refurbishing of facilities at Cleveland's Hopkins Airport. The crown jewel in the White administration's economic revitalization program is the Gateway Project, an ambitious $344-million redevelopment program that delivered a new baseball stadium for the Cleveland Indians, a new basketball arena for the Cleveland Cavaliers, and a major facelift to sites adjacent to these projects in the downtown area. Viewing the Gateway Project as a critical test of the ability of his administration to deliver on promises to the corporate community and stimulate employment and economic growth, White led the fight to obtain a $400,000 per-year tax limitation for the project from the Ohio legislature. To blunt criticism of tax abatements for corporate interests, White proposed that $240,000 of the $400,000 tax payment go to the Cleveland school system, and the establishment of a $1 million pool from which the school system would get another $360,000 a year.

Although the Gateway Project has involved cooperative arrangements between city, county, and state officials and private institutions, much of the political capital emanating from the completion of the project has been harvested by the White administration.

> Michael White is above all things a politician and all politicians like to see money moving. Because when money is moving things happen. A lot of money was moving for Gateway and he was the principal person for Gateway. Without him there would be no Gateway. We have to move into areas where there is some activity that will generate decent dollars. Gateway was thought by the larger community to be one of those areas. It would put a brand new face on downtown. The people who run Tower City needed a new front door. This presents a magnificent new entree into downtown. It would bring people into Tower City Center and every new person represents a potential customer. Mike was on TV constantly with that and that set him up as a person whose greater goal was the community.[20]

There are some who question whether the commitment to downtown development represents a new agenda or the reintroduction of the policy priorities of previous administrations. Mayor White has attempted to stress the point that he supports a policy of balanced growth. In this regard he has sought to reassure grass-roots citizens that he is committed to promoting policies of neighborhood as well as downtown revitalization. During the first four years of his administration, the number one community priority of Mayor White has been school reform. Emphasizing that a great city must have a superior public school system, White has sought to promote school reform in several ways. First, he attempted to influence policies of the Cleveland School Board by endorsing four of his political allies for seats on the school board for the November 1991 elections. In a remarkable display of political power and acumen, all four of the candidates won their races, giving him influence with a majority of the seven-member board.[21] Second, White played an instrumental role in the appointment of Sammie Campbell Parrish as superintendent of Cleveland Public Schools. Parrish was apparently the mayor's personal choice for the job. Upon assuming office she developed a program called Vision Twenty-one, designed to implement a range of programs compatible with the reform objectives articulated by the mayor's office. Third, White has initiated a weekly mayor's forum on public education. Coordinated by mayoral appointee Larry Robinson, this forum is intended to bring together individuals from broad sectors of the community—business, labor, education, community organizations—to discuss educational issues and work on solutions to key educational problems. Among the accomplishments of the mayor's forum has been the raising of public awareness about educational issues, the mobilization of community support for the end of busing, and transmission to the public of vital information concerning the financial status of the school system in preparation for a school levy vote during the 1993–94 academic year.[22] Fourth,White has appointed Chris Carmody as liaison between the Mayor's Office and the Board of Education.

The White administration's approach to community issues has also focused on the goal of neighborhood revitalization. To achieve this goal, White has encouraged the involvement of community organizations in the rehabilitation of declining neighborhoods through the construction of private housing. Funding from community development block grants has gone to community groups such as the Mt. Pleasant Community Council to spearhead the effort to expand the stock of private family housing in inner-city neighborhoods. Community housing initiatives have been buttressed by efforts to stimulate economic growth in inner-city neighborhoods. The chief product of this effort has been the formation of the Minority Business Council, an organization designed to bring minority businesses and contractors together to coordinate efforts to obtain major city contracts. In recognition of his pioneering achievements in the area of minority business development, White received the Freedom Fund Award from the Cleveland Branch of the NAACP.

The success White has enjoyed in promoting policies of balanced growth has yielded rich political dividends. White ran for a second four-year term as mayor without substantial opposition and won the election. Early plans by Cleveland School Board member James Carney to challenge White for reelection disappeared in the face of realities that a run against White would be extremely expensive and would probably not produce favorable results. During his first four years as mayor,

White forged a powerful political coalition that is, by all estimates, unbeatable. A key component of this coalition is the business community, which contributed more than one million dollars to White's campaign war chest. His enthusiastic support for an aggressive downtown development strategy has made him extremely popular in business circles. In this regard, one newspaper reported, "His 40th birthday party at a downtown hotel resembled a well-attended Chamber of Commerce meeting."[23]

White has also effectively polished and promoted his image as a champion of the "people's" causes. In the black community he has expanded the dedicated cadre that worked for his election in 1989 into a formidable communitywide organization. The secret of his success is embedded not only in the school and neighborhood development policies he has embraced, but in his skills as orator and communicator.

> Mike is a master of the media. He has a formidable personality. He has an excellent public image; he has excellent public skills. He uses those tools that modern communicators use, mainly the television set. He has mastered those things you have to master to be a politician. Mike is an excellent public speaker. He is very forthwith and forthright in presenting his views to the public. People trust him. They take his word for things.[24]

A pervasive image as an articulate urban crusader has made Mike White the unrivaled political personality in Cleveland politics. Few remnants of the Forbes machine remain, with most of Forbes's lieutenants who are still politically active choosing to jump on the White bandwagon. Michael White's mayoral power has extended to the City Council where council president Jay Westbrook has consistently delivered votes in support of the mayor's major legislative programs. Because of his success in Cleveland, White is being promoted by the Black Elected Democrats of Ohio (BEDO) as a prospective candidate for statewide office.[25]

While much was accomplished during the first four years of the White administration, a host of serious problems remain. In the face of mounting crime and violence, White was not able to deliver on his campaign promise to increase the ranks of Cleveland police to two thousand by the end of his first term. Like other major American cities, Cleveland is experiencing a financial crisis that militates against the allocation of funds for the hiring of increased numbers of fire and safety personnel. Demands by Cleveland fire and safety unions for increased benefits for their members have served to aggravate and magnify the task of creating and maintaining public service bureaucracies to fight the growing menace of urban crime. In addition, problems relating to the restructuring of the city's infrastructure, air and water pollution, health, and poverty continue to mount in a city where the outmigration of middle-class citizens has greatly reduced available resources to combat them.

The lingering question is whether the new black leadership in Cleveland has the skill, the resource base, and the vision to build the kind of mass-based political movement required to effectively address both long and short range social and economic problems in the city. The realization of this goal will require the combining of administrative competence with organizational mobilization capable of transforming power relations from a concentration on elite benefits to a permanent focus on the needs, interests, and aspirations of ordinary citizens.

The Unfinished Agenda

The state of black politics in Cleveland must be viewed with apprehension; after two decades of struggle, the black community remains caught up in a web of traditional politics. One does not sense, even from the new insurgents, a commitment to a politics of independence and system transformation. Notably absent from the structure of Cleveland black politics is a cohesive black caucus reminiscent of the one used so effectively by Carl Stokes to promote black social, economic, and political development. Black community groups remain relatively inactive and ineffective. The political alliance between the White administration and Cleveland's white community is, at best, fragile. Institutionalized black control will require the maintenance of multiracial alliances, the building of a permanent organizational structure to mobilize collective black political action in the electoral arena and the policy process, and the effective penetration of arenas of private power and wealth by black elites and the black masses.

The need to establish and implement progressive policy objectives and build effective political alliances constitutes the unfinished agenda of the new black politics. Since Cleveland is a dynamic city and politics is a process of learning and growth, there remains room for optimism that in the years ahead the progressive face of black politics in the city will not only emerge but become paramount.

Notes

1. Peter K. Eisinger, "Black Mayors and the Politics of Racial Economic Advancement," in *Readings in Urban Politics*, ed. Harland Hahn and Charles Levine, 2d ed. (New York: Longman, 1984), 251.

2. Richard Child Hill, "Crisis in the Motor City: The Politics of Economic Development in Detroit," in *Restructuring the City*, ed. Susan S. Fainstein et al. (New York: Longman, 1983), 108.

3. James Curtis Smith, "Big City Black Mayors: Redefining the Dilemmas of Governance" (paper prepared for the annual meeting of the National Conference of Black Political Scientists, Chicago, Ill., 1984), 28.

4. Hill, "Crisis," 109–13; Betty Woody, *Managing Crisis Cities: The New Black Leadership and the Politics of Resource Allocation* (Westport, Conn.: Greenwood Press, 1982), 27–28.

5. For a more detailed discussion of the formation of the Twenty-first District Democratic Caucus, see William E. Nelson, Jr., "Cleveland: The Rise and Fall of the New Black Politics," in *The New Black*

Politics: The Search for Political Powers, ed. Michael B. Preston, Lenneal J. Henderson, Jr., and Paul L. Puryear (New York: Longman, 1982), 188.

6. On the conflict involving Stokes, Forbes, and Pinkney, see ibid., 195–200.

7. Todd Swanstrom, *The Crisis of Growth Politics: Cleveland, Kucinich, and the Challenge of Urban Populism* (Philadelphia: Temple University Press, 1985), 112.

8. "Forbes Enemies File Petition to Elect Council Leadership," *Call and Post,* June 21, 1980.

9. Swanstrom, *Growth Politics,* 112.

10. "Forbes Puts Airlines into EEO Compliance," *Call and Post,* March 1982.

11. Swanstrom, *Growth Politics,* 246–52.

12. Interview, Fall 1985, Cleveland. This study is based on a series of confidential interviews with political activists in Cleveland conducted by the author in the Fall of 1985 and Summer of 1993.

13. Bart Greer, "Passing the Reins of Power," *Renaissance Magazine,* February 1991, 18–19.

14. Saundra C. Ardrey, "Cleveland and the Politics of Resurgence: The Search for Effective Political Control," in *Dilemmas of Black Politics: Issues of Leadership and Strategy,* ed. Georgia A. Persons (New York: HarperCollins, 1993), 116.

15. Interview, Fall 1985, Cleveland.

16. "White Defied Conventional Wisdom," *Cleveland Plain Dealer,* August 22, 1992.

17. Interview, Summer 1993, Cleveland.

18. "White King of Political Hill in '91," *Cleveland Plain Dealer,* January 5, 1992.

19. Interview, Fall 1993, Cleveland.

20. "White King of Political Hill."

21. Interview, Fall 1992, Cleveland.

22. "White King of Political Hill."

23. Interview, Fall 1992, Cleveland.

24. See "For Mike White, the Future is Now—or Maybe, Later," *Call and Post* (Columbus Edition), August 26, 1993.

25. Ibid.

Open Housing in Metropolitan Cleveland

W. Dennis Keating

MORE THAN two decades after the Kerner Commission warned of two societies—one black and one white—and after the passage of the federal fair housing law, Cleveland, Ohio, continued to have one of the most segregated housing markets in the United States. In 1990, 47 percent of the city's population and 25 percent of Cuyahoga County's population was black. Based on 1980 census data, Cleveland and its suburbs ranked among the nation's most segregated central cities and metropolitan regions. On a scale of housing segregation in which a score of 100 represents total segregation, Cleveland rated 87.5 in 1980, compared to 90.8 in 1970. Chicago remained the worst-segregated large city, with scores of 91.9 in 1970 and 87.8 in 1980. Among midwestern cities generally, the segregation index average score dropped from 87 in 1970 to 78 in 1980.[1]

In Cleveland, twenty-two of thirty-five neighborhoods were racially "isolated" in 1986, just as they were in 1968. Although Cleveland was one of the first cities to establish a Community Relations Board to deal with racial problems, it was only decades later that the City Council enacted a controversial fair housing ordinance in 1988. In testimony before Congress in 1987, the civil rights activist Jordan Band recounted examples of increasing racially motivated confrontations and violence in Cleveland. In addition to a racially segregated private housing market, most of the city's public housing is segregated and most of Cleveland's suburbs have rejected public housing.

Most of the efforts to encourage racial integration in housing have taken place in Cleveland's suburbs. In 1990, about 13 percent of the population in the suburban communities of Cuyahoga County was black, but a majority of suburbs had a black population of less than 2 percent. This was still an increase over 1980. The leading agency promoting racial diversity in housing is the Cuyahoga Plan, a regional nonprofit fair housing agency established in 1974 and funded by Cuyahoga County, several suburban cities, and local foundations. According to the Cuyahoga Plan, if black families lived in suburbs they could afford and were randomly dispersed, no Cuyahoga County suburb would have had a black population of less than 11 percent in 1980. Its conclusion was that racial discrimination, not economics, largely explains Cleveland's segregated housing patterns.[2]

The metropolitan housing market, like that of the city of Cleveland is split between east and west. Most of the urban and suburban black population lives to the east of the Cuyahoga River, which divides the area. Most black suburbanization has been in the eastern suburbs. Two suburbs—East Cleveland and Warrensville Heights—went through a rapid racial transition in the late 1960s and early 1970s and have both largely resegregated, with black populations of 94 and 89 percent respectively in 1990.

In contrast, two older eastern suburbs have integrated and maintained their racial diversity. Shaker Heights, renowned as one of America's first planned suburbs, originally excluded blacks and other minorities through restrictive covenants, as did many American suburbs. As blacks began to move to Shaker Heights in the 1950s and 1960s after restrictive covenants were ruled illegal, there was white resistance. Neighborhood and civic leaders encouraged peaceful integration, however, which led to several city ordinances designed to outlaw discriminatory housing practices and to promote stable racial diversity. Shaker Heights established its own municipal housing office in 1967 to work with prospective home buyers and renters and cooperative realtors and to market Shaker Heights as an integrated community.[3] The black population of Shaker Heights in 1990 was approximately 31 percent. Although Shaker Heights is considered an affluent suburb with expensive housing stock, there is access for those with moderate income. To expand this access, Shaker Heights in 1986 created the Fund for the Future of Shaker Heights supported by local foundations and designed to encourage residential integration by providing below-market mortgage loans to home buyers, black and white, willing to make pro-integrative moves within the city. During its first four years, the fund made more than one hundred loans.

Neighboring Cleveland Heights has a similar history. Racial transition began in the early 1970s. When problems arose, concerned residents, civic groups, and churches formed the Heights Community Congress in 1972. The congress became the catalyst in persuading the city in 1976 to adopt comprehensive fair housing policies similar to those of Shaker Heights to promote and maintain stable racial diversity. The black population of Cleveland Heights in 1990 was approximately 37 percent.

In the remainder of the eastern part of Cuyahoga County, only four cities had a black population of more than 10 percent in 1990. The western communities in the county are much more racially segregated; in 1990, most had less than 2 percent black population.

The best-known example of segregated housing in Cleveland's West Side is the city of Parma, Cleveland's largest suburb with a 1990 population of eighty-eight thousand, fewer than 1 percent of which was nonwhite. Parma was sued in 1973 by the U.S. Department of Justice and found guilty in 1980 of violating federal fair housing laws in several respects. It has since been subject to a remedial court order. In the absence of racial litigation, other segregated western Cleveland suburbs have not voluntarily initiated fair housing programs.[4]

The same is generally true of the eastern suburbs. Fearing that it would be increasingly difficult to maintain integration in only a few suburban communities, the cities of Shaker Heights, Cleveland Heights, and University Heights and their school boards joined together in 1984 to form the Eastern Suburban Council for Open Communities (ESCOC). Its purpose was to encourage prospective black home buyers and renters to consider the predominantly white housing markets of Hillcrest. Hillcrest consists of six eastern suburban communities which immediately border the three ESCOC cities to the north. ESCOC received financial support from local foundations and has worked with sympathetic neighborhood groups and realtors. Its unique voluntary regional approach induced many blacks to look for housing in Hillcrest, and many have bought houses or rented apartments there. ESCOC had to overcome such obstacles as the 1983 firebombing of a black family's house in Lyndhurst and the refusal of city officials in such cities as South Euclid to join ESCOC and publicly support its activities. ESCOC disbanded in 1990 after internal disagreements over its future directions.

In the past, there have been efforts to institute metropolitan government in Cleveland, but they have failed. Efforts to persuade the suburbs to enter into cooperative agreements with the Cuyahoga Metropolitan Housing Authority to decentralize public housing within Cuyahoga County have also generally failed.[5] The regional planning agency, Northeast Ohio Areawide Coordinating Agency, has no viable regional fair-share plan for subsidized housing.

In this vacuum, the Metropolitan Strategy Group (MSG) has emerged as a major lobbying force for fair housing in Cleveland's suburbs. It consists of all those agencies and organizations involved in promoting open, fair housing. Its chair, Charles Bromley, also served as president of National Neighbors, a major national organization promoting interracial neighborhoods.

The MSG has lobbied municipal, county, state, and federal governments to promote neighborhood integration and fair housing and serves as a clearinghouse for activists in both areas. Perhaps its most notable success was the creation in 1986 by the Ohio Housing Finance Agency (OHFA) of a Pro-Integrative Bonus Program. This "set-aside" allowed fair housing and other agencies to offer below-market mortgages to eligible first-time home buyers willing to make pro-integrative moves into racially imbalanced neighborhoods. This experimental program was created in the wake of protests by MSG that the state's mortgage revenue bond program was reinforcing rather than changing segregated residential patterns in metropolitan Cleveland. After an interval of two years and MSG intervention, OHFA renewed the program in 1988. Ohio's state government has not taken an active role in addressing such controversial issues, leaving responsibility at the local level. Although MSG's members have supported the strengthening of the federal Fair Housing Act enacted in 1988, there was little hope of federal leadership for open housing during the 1980s.

What has been accomplished in Cleveland's suburbs since 1970? If the sole criterion of change is the segregation index, there has been little progress. Cleveland and most of its suburbs remain heavily segregated. Some residential racial patterns have changed, and many suburbs now have either a very small minority population (still generally under 5 percent), but only two of Cleveland's fifty-nine suburbs have a minority population proportionally about the same as that of the county—Cleveland Heights and Shaker Heights. Although there has been no resegregation as occurred earlier in East Cleveland and Warrensville Heights, those eastern suburbs with a growing minority population have usually not initiated voluntary pro-integrative policies. Meanwhile, there continue to be an alarming number of violent incidents involving race, both within the city and in the suburbs. In the absence of concerted, intensive, and protracted efforts by public officials and community leaders at all levels of government, it is difficult to be optimistic about dramatic changes that will alter Cleveland's basic patterns of residential racial segregation, either within the central city or the surrounding suburbs.

The situation, however, is not totally bleak. Cleveland Heights (since the 1970s) and Shaker Heights (since the 1960s) have maintained their status as voluntarily pro-integrative maintenance communities with support from citizens and the municipal governments. The creation of ESCOC and its innovative approach was a promising step toward expanding the housing choices of blacks seeking suburban housing and possibly inducing other suburban governments to consider initiating pro-integrative policies before a crisis necessitates their action. The existence of the MSG and its advocacy for regional housing integration programs like OHFA's Pro-Integrative Mortgage Bonus program and the activities of the Cuyahoga Plan in both investigating and documenting racial discrimination in housing and working with suburban communities to promote open housing give hope that there is a constituency for open housing policies.

In Parma, there has been some progress, although the pace has been slow. The city successfully appealed the appointment of a special overseer to audit implementation of the federal court order. Therefore, a local fair housing committee and an oversight committee did not begin their work until 1983. Since then, the city has applied for and received community development block grant funding from HUD, part of which has paid for programs mandated by the court order. Parma established its own housing agency and has attracted minority tenants with Section 8 vouchers. In 1987, Parma's first subsidized housing project, a sixty-unit Section 8 project, was completed. In 1988, a long-delayed advertising program was launched—with the involvement of the Cuyahoga Plan—to attract minority home buyers. A new Parma city administration has been more supportive in its efforts to promote fair housing than its predecessor, as evidenced by the passage in June 1988 of a municipal fair housing ordinance before any of Parma's neighboring suburbs adopted similar fair housing policies.

The Cuyahoga Plan's audits have confirmed that racial discrimination still affects the choices of blacks seeking to purchase homes and rent apartments in Cleveland's suburbs. A comparative study was conducted of housing search patterns and attitudes on housing integration in Cleveland's suburbs.[6] A sample of more than four hundred home buyers in twelve Cleveland suburbs who purchased houses in 1985 was surveyed in 1986, and almost half responded to a follow-up survey in 1987.

This study revealed that these home buyers primarily chose their houses and neighborhoods for conventional reasons (e.g., renters who wanted to own). Racial patterns were not the primary reason for their moves or their selection of a house. Attitudes on racial integration in housing varied considerably; most respondents already lived in Greater Cleveland, and about 40 percent purchased a house in a suburb where they already lived. Those who preferred to live in a racially integrated neighborhood were more likely to choose Cleveland Heights and Shaker Heights and to use these housing offices to locate their homes. In contrast, the highest rate of preference for living in all-white or predominantly white neighborhoods was found among Parma home buyers, all of whom were white in this sample from 1985. Attitudes in the Hillcrest communities were less polar. Almost all black home buyers favored racially integrated neighborhoods.

When asked if they favored government intervention to promote racially mixed neighborhoods and open housing, the most support came from home buyers in the communities with voluntary integration management programs—Cleveland Heights and Shaker Heights. The lowest levels of support came from Parma, where only 23 percent favored such government intervention. White support for open housing went from 50 percent in Parma to 85 percent in Cleveland Heights.These attitudinal findings suggest that those suburbs with overt and well-known pro-integration management housing policies will attract whites who generally favor such policies. In fact, Cleveland Heights and Shaker Heights aggressively seek to attract these prospective home buyers, whereas the communities without fair housing policies do not attract as many. The case of Parma suggests that court-ordered mandatory fair housing policies do not necessarily change the opinions of many residents on open housing.

National opinion surveys since the 1960s have shown that gradually a majority of Americans have come to favor open and fair housing legislation and policies.[7] Cleveland, despite its still heavily segregated housing market, is no exception.

A 1991 survey by the Citizens League of Greater Cleveland confirmed this. A majority of Clevelanders (72 percent) said that they wanted racially mixed neighborhoods; only 18 percent disagreed. Blacks (82 percent) were more supportive than whites (68 percent). This majority opinion has increased each year from the beginning of this survey, 1988, when 66 percent responded positively to this question. Opposition to racially mixed neighborhoods remained higher in the suburbs than in the city of Cleveland. Blacks were more likely to move into racially mixed neighborhoods and less likely to leave when racial patterns change than were whites. The Citizens League Research Institute report concluded that "neighborhood integration is seen as an important societal goal but it is unlikely to occur without vigorous efforts by the community's leadership."[8]

These data reveal that although a majority of whites, homeowners and renters alike, are much more tolerant of blacks than was true two decades ago, most whites do not move in search of racially integrated neighborhoods. Local efforts to promote racially integrated living patterns, which are our stated national goal, must actively seek to educate and attract prospective homeowners and renters. Because so few suburbs have undertaken such activities voluntarily, it is essential that regional organizations like ESCOC, the Cuyahoga Plan, and the MSG exist and receive public and private financial support and, just as important, the cooperation of all cities within metropolitan areas. Mere enforcement of existing fair housing laws has not significantly changed basic patterns of racial segregation in housing, even though white support for integrated housing has risen. Much more comprehensive programs, including pro-integrative housing incentives, are essential. If such programs exist in only a few suburbs, then Cleveland's pattern of most suburbs remaining segregated seems very likely to continue.[9]

Notes

1. Douglas S. Massey and Nancy A. Denton, "Trends in the Residential Segregation of Blacks, Hispanics, and Asians, 1970–1980." *American Sociological Review* 52 (1987): 802–25.

2. Cuyahoga Plan, *A Report on Population and Race* (Cleveland: Cuyahoga Plan of Ohio, 1983).

3. Stephen J. Alfred and Charles R. Marcoux, "Impact of a Community Association on Integrated Suburban Housing Patterns," *Cleveland State University Law Review* 19 (1970): 90–99.

4. Phillip J. Cooper, *Hard Judicial Choices: Federal District Court Judges and State and Local Officials* (New York: Oxford University Press, 1988); Cuyahoga Plan, *Municipal Approaches to Fair Housing* (Cleveland: Cuyahoga Plan of Ohio, 1989).

5. Norman Krumholz, "Twenty Years after Kerner: The Cleveland Case," *Journal of Urban Affairs* 12 (1990): 285–97.

6. W. Dennis Keating, William J. Pammer, and Linda S. Smith, *A Comparative Study of Three Models of Racial Integration in Housing in Cleveland* (Cleveland: College of Urban Affairs, Cleveland State University, 1987).

7. Howard Schuman, Charlotte Steeh, and Lawrence Bobo, *Racial Attitudes in America: Trends and Interpretations* (Cambridge, Mass.: Harvard University Press, 1985).

8. Citizens League Research Institute, *Race Relations in Greater Cleveland: A Report on the Attitudes, Opinions, and Experiences of Greater Clevelanders* (Cleveland: Citizens League Research Institute, 1991).

9. W. Dennis Keating, *The Suburban Racial Dilemma: Housing and Neighborhoods* (Philadelphia: Temple University Press, 1994).

Part 8

URBAN REDEVELOPMENT

Policy, Planning, & Prospects

Introduction

THIS SECTION addresses alternative approaches to Cleveland's redevelopment. According to conventional wisdom, older cities like Cleveland are disadvantaged competitors for urban investment. Their serious handicaps, it is said, include congestion, relatively expensive land, dilapidated housing, antiquated neighborhoods, and a variety of social problems.

Government leaders and private institutions have generally accepted this analysis and have formulated plans and policies designed to reverse the flight from the city of middle-class families and industry. In the 1950s and 1960s, slum clearance through the urban renewal program was used as a means of restoring the central business district and building market-rate housing. Cleveland's urban renewal program was among the boldest in the nation, but it was riddled with problems.

In the 1960s, a variety of new federal programs such as Model Cities sought to cope with problems of social control in the ghettos. By the 1970s and 1980s, the emphasis had shifted to economic development. Most of these programs, called public-private partnerships, were supported by a growth coalition of interest groups that benefited from the programs: city politicians, real estate and development interests, newspapers, corporations, and construction trade unions.

Planning and programs focused on the needs of Cleveland's downtown, causing some participants in the redevelopment process to feel that the neighborhoods and their residents were being neglected. These planners and neighborhood advocates argued that concerns for downtown should be overshadowed by a concern for people rather than property, and especially for poor people and others who were disfranchised. They spoke in favor of here-and-now solutions rather than those in a distant future and for direct participation by those affected rather than by faraway experts. The authors of many of the essays in this section share this common political perspective—a concern not only for the city of Cleveland as an institution but for the residents of Cleveland's neighborhoods.

Norman Krumholz begins with a discussion of the period from 1969 to 1979, when he was Cleveland's city planning director. During that period, the planners chose to side with the poor and working-class residents of the city's neighborhoods. They selected as their overriding objective the goal "more choices for those who have few." Krumholz recounts cases in which he and his staff tried to serve goals of equity and fairness rather than mere development. He also points to the many difficulties and dilemmas inherent in such professional planning practice.

Richard Shatten, former executive director of Cleveland Tomorrow, describes the creation of that organization. It is made up of the fifty chief executive officers of Cleveland's largest corporations—arguably the most powerful decision makers in the city. He argues that corporate leaders had largely withdrawn from public affairs until the ill-starred administration of Mayor Dennis J. Kucinich. Then they realized that their leadership—in concert with enlightened political leaders—was essential to maintain Cleveland as a good place to do business. How they organized Cleveland Tomorrow, chose their goals and objectives, and moved toward implementation are the subjects of this chapter.

Housing and neighborhood revitalization are the focus of the essay by Christopher Warren, a former community organizer and director of a neighborhood-based nonprofit development corporation, who, in 1990, was named Cleveland's director of community development. Warren describes an insider's view of the struggle to provide neighborhood stabilization and housing that can be afforded by Cleveland's low- and moderate-income families.

Keating, Krumholz, and Metzger analyze the public-private partnerships formed in Cleveland in the decade of the 1980s. While public-private partnerships assumed generally equal distributions of resources and benefits, the authors suggest that the time, attention, and resources applied to downtown projects have overwhelmed the relatively little attention paid to Cleveland's neighborhood-based programs. This article reflects the view that public-private partnerships may be a new format for an old and pervasive imbalance of power that systematically disadvantages urban neighborhoods and their people.

Phillip Clay, in the final essay, points to the historical imbalance in Cleveland and other cities between the haves and the have-nots. Blacks and other minorities in Cleveland, he argues, demand access to the benefits of the system, and others who have controlled that access must give way. Clay argues that much more important than a "fair share" of the benefits of government is the need to reweave the "social fabric" in many neighborhoods so that calm and reasoned discourse and civility may return.

Government, Equity, Redistribution, and the Practice of Urban Planning

Norman Krumholz

In 1969 I joined the administration of Carl B. Stokes, the first black mayor of any American city with over five hundred thousand in population. As director of the Cleveland City Planning Commission, I was intent on producing a new general land use, transportation, and public facilities plan for the city. An earlier plan under the direction of John T. Howard, later a professor at the Massachusetts Institute of Technology, had been published twenty years before, and a new plan seemed in order. After a few short months of studying the city and its people, however, it became obvious to me and my staff that this traditional planning exercise would be irrelevant.

Like most other older industrial cities in the Northeast and Midwest, Cleveland had been experiencing population loss, plant closings, rising unemployment, and poverty for many years. Between 1950 and 1980 the population dropped from 914,000 to 570,000; in the 1960s alone, the city lost 50 percent of its white population and 28 percent of its families with incomes over the SMSA median. In the face of a rapidly inflating national economy, Cleveland's property tax base had been shrinking. Much of the city's public and private physical plant—now from seventy-five to one hundred years old—was approaching obsolescence. Public service costs were high and rising while the quality of public services appeared to be falling. Disinvestment and abandonment of factories, homes, and other property were well under way in many parts of the city; census tracts that had reported 3,000 residents in 1960 counted 300 to 400 in 1970.

It seemed to me and a small cadre of new planners that Cleveland did not need an elaborate new plan and regulations for controlling growth; the city was not growing, it was declining in almost every respect. What Cleveland clearly needed, we thought, was a way to deal with its obvious problems: personal and municipal poverty, unemployment, bad housing and rotting neighborhoods, lack of personal mobility, and the many destructive effects of racial segregation and discrimination. None of these problems could be addressed with a new general land use plan, an urban design scheme, or a new zoning ordinance.

We could have ignored this insight and plunged forward with an updated version of Cleveland's 1949 land use plan. No one would have criticized us; after all, that was what the city charter said we should do. Instead, we began the first halting steps toward a new role for the city planning agency—one worthy of our training and resources. Our approach, we decided, would be based on one overriding goal: that, in a context of limited resources, we must place first priority on the task of promoting more choices for those Cleveland residents who had few, if any, choices. We were not aiming at more choices for all, but more choices for those who had few.

The planning agency's role would be to offer information, criticism, and policy guidance to the city, its people, and its decision makers consistent with this framework—one that emphasized greater equity. In effect, we had chosen to reject the unitary concept of the public interest; we had chosen sides in favor of the poor. But we felt and argued that our goal was not utopian, not radical, not altruistic or benevolent. It was a familiar goal, rooted in the egalitarian ideals of our birth and growth as a nation and in our Judeo-Christian religious traditions as well. It was, ultimately, a just goal, one that promoted a society in which equity was at least as important as efficiency. We called this concept "equity planning." The concept helped us generate a work program, a method of analysis, and a means of picking issues and allocating the personnel of the planning agency for the entire ten years I served as director. The style was open, proactive, and interventionist, and the focus was on the specific needs of the people of the city, with particular emphasis on those city residents who had the least and needed the most.

Putting goal statements down on paper—in memos, reports, speeches, or even journal articles or book chapters—is relatively simple; it is much more difficult to move from statement to reality. What did we actually do to implement our goal? Three examples of our work in Cleveland will make clear how our goal shaped our practice. Although these three cases took place in Cleveland during the 1970s, urban planners and others will recognize some variation of these same themes in their own cities today.

Case 1: Downtown Commercial Development

In the mid-1970s, a real estate developer approached the city with plans to build a $350 million commercial complex in downtown called Tower City. When the legislation reached the City Planning Commission (CPC), we found that the city was being asked to waive important rights it had to the project site, improve the Public Square immediately adjacent to the site at a cost upwards of $25 million, agree to contribute to the site about $15 million in capital improvements (which we did not believe were the city's responsibility), and agree to give the developer property tax abatements for twenty years. In return, the developer offered to build two new office buildings.

It seemed to us as we reviewed the proposal that the proper purpose of new development was to provide permanent new jobs for city residents—especially the unemployed—and net tax increases to the public treasury, not to simply trade old bricks for new at startling public cost. So we called in the developer and proposed a deal: in exchange for our support for the project, the developer would agree to pay for his own site improvements, forgo tax abatements, and provide a percentage of all the new jobs to city residents, giving the city's job training office the first crack at any new job openings. (Planners will recognize this as an early and rudimentary form of what is now known as "linkage," as practiced in Boston, San Francisco, and other cities.) The developer refused our terms, and the CPC, on the recommendation of its staff at a well-publicized meeting, turned down the Tower City project. We emphasized that we were not antidevelopment but merely opposed to development that imposed unfair burdens on the city with no assurance of new offsetting tax revenues or permanent jobs for city residents. Nonetheless, our rejection of the development was highly controversial. The CPC's rejection was ultimately overridden by the City Council by a thirty-one to two vote, but partially because of the widespread public discussion on the issues raised by the CPC the project was not begun for more than a decade.

Case 2: Public Transit

Most city planners define urban transportation problems in terms of auto access, parking, or available highway capacity to meet peak demand. Our goal of providing more choices to those who had few led us to define the city's key transportation problem in a different way, as one of improving the mobility of the transit-dependent population—the old, sick, and poor who lack regular access to an automobile and depend exclusively on public transit to get around the metropolitan area. Such transit-dependent persons made up about one-third of all Cleveland households in 1970. We used the following rationale: Most of us who have a car enjoy more mobility than anyone else in history. But our national choice for an automotive society has raised fares, weakened transit service, and curtailed the mobility of those who must depend on public transit. These transit-dependent individuals were therefore entitled to compensatory considerations. So we became advocates for improved public transit service. At the same time, we were not across-the-board transit enthusiasts; we carefully tailored our support to include only services that would benefit the transit-dependent, such as reduced fares, improved levels of service on buses, and innovations such as door-to-door dial-a-bus service for the poor, elderly, and handicapped. With the support of neighborhood-based and senior coalitions (some of which we had helped energize), we opposed proposals by the transit bureaucracy and the business community to build new, expensive fixed-rail transit systems, including a proposed elevated downtown people mover. On analysis, we had concluded that these radially oriented rail systems provided little service to the transit-dependent but would only provide more access to downtown, more subsidies to relatively affluent long-distance riders, and more deficits for the regional transit agency which it might well try to cure by reducing service or raising fares on the bus fleet that carried 87 percent of all riders. We argued our priorities in the five years we served as lead negotiators for Mayors Stokes and Perk in the negotiations that led to the establishment of the Greater Cleveland Regional Transit Authority (RTA). During these protracted negotiations, our position dismayed the transit bureaucrats and angered some of Cleveland's civic leaders, but ultimately we achieved many of our goals with respect to the needs of the transit-dependent population. The final deal provided no support for new rail systems but did provide that a twenty-five-cent fare would be maintained for at least three years; that senior citizens and the handicapped would ride free during nonpeak periods (twenty hours daily) and pay only half-fare at peak; that service frequencies and route coverage within the city would be improved; and that Community Responsive Transit, a supplementary dial-a-ride or prescheduled service, would be initiated.

Today, the twenty-five-cent fare is gone, but door-to-door services for the elderly and handicapped are a regular part of RTA's program, and general bus service has been very much improved in the city.

Case 3: Lakefront Development

Cleveland has three lakefront parks. In the glory days of Cleveland's growth, they were pristine—the pride of the city. People from all over the Midwest came to Cleveland to vacation in these parks. By 1970, though, the glory of our lakefront parks was a thing of the past. They were filthy, dangerous, vandalized, and unused. In 1973, the city was hit by a devastating storm that battered the parks, tore up the remaining facilities, and left them in shambles. Clearly, the city was not going to be able to repair or maintain them. Working closely with the city's parks department, my staff evolved the notion that the parks should be considered a regional, rather than a city, resource, and that a broader funding base than the city should be found to maintain them. During the City Council's hearings on the decline of these parks, the parks director and I suggested just that: that they be leased to another entity—the state of Ohio or the metroparks system—that had the money and the will to restore and maintain them.

Three weeks later, the City Council passed just such a resolution, proposing to lease the three parks to the state of Ohio's Department of Natural Resources. The council then sent the resolution on to the administration for review. The parks director and I went to see then, mayor Perk, urging him to support the bill. "Do it," we said, "do it." But he clearly had reservations. He had taken much criticism the year before for "selling" the city's sewer system to a regional authority. His critics said he could not manage the city so he was giving away its assets, and he was afraid of a repeat of the same scenario. The council was Democratic and so was the governor at the time, so our Republican mayor worried about being attacked by political foes for running an incompetent "giveaway" administration. He decided to disapprove the resolution, and it died.

But although the 1973 legislation died, there was no stopping the long, cold slide of deterioration in Cleveland's lakefront parks. By 1976 their condition was scandalous. Garbage was being dumped openly in two of the parks, and the public was outraged. The media, the business establishment anxious to promote the city, citizens at large—everyone was aware of their condition. The Cleveland Foundation surveyed the parks and published a critical report. With another election coming up, Mayor Perk looked for a way out. To me, the solution was obvious, and when the subject came up at a cabinet meeting, I suggested we lease them to the state of Ohio. "Do it," I said, "do it." Only this time, the Republican mayor would provide the leadership and his old friend, the recently elected Republican governor of Ohio, would ensure a smooth and successful outcome. I offered myself as lead negotiator and assured the mayor that if things fell apart, he could blame everything on his planners. The mayor, who had rejected this exact idea three years before, embraced it this time. Within a year, we had drafted and executed a ninety-nine year lease with the state, had gotten $7 million for essential capital improvements in the first year, and had turned over the three lakefront parks to the Ohio Department of Natural Resources.

By 1990, the state had spent over $36 million on beaches, fishing piers, bathhouses, roads, erosion control devices, and other capital improvements, plus another $11 million for operating and maintenance expenses. Six million people visited these renovated parks in 1988; they were the most popular parks in Ohio.

Lessons

These three examples are, I believe, representative of many of the cases in which my staff and I were involved during my ten-year tenure as planning director in Cleveland. What do they tell us that might be of value to other practicing planners or students who might be interested in equity planning?

First, the cases make clear that equity planning can be done. Such planning can produce benefits for the poor and working-class residents of the city; and planners can do it and survive, indeed, prosper. For ten years, under three administrations that could not possibly have been more different—one led by a black, liberal Democrat (Carl B. Stokes), one led by a white, ethnic, conservative Republican (Ralph J. Perk), and one led by a nominal Democrat and self-described urban populist (Dennis J. Kucinich)—we consistently worked the equity side of the street and did so in a visible, open, interventionist way. Although we were frequently involved in conflict and controversy with powerful public and private players, we were not punished, chastised, or dismissed. Instead, we found we could form coalitions with former adversaries on certain issues, and the planning agency acquired greater influence, prestige, resources, staff, and success with the passage of time.

A corollary of the Cleveland experience is also important: equity planning is a good way for planners to attack the basic underlying problems of our urban areas. In this regard, it is much more effective than traditional urban planning. What now passes for planning and for economic development in many cities is a simple variation of "trickle-down" ideology, in which planners do not so much plan as help "package" development proposals made by others. It follows this model: shovel the public subsidies in at the top, and net tax increases and jobs for the unemployed will (supposedly) come out at the bottom. This is the model that gave us the Poletown project in Detroit and any number of downtown buildings in cities everywhere. Unfortunately, "trickle-down" planning does not work. All it does is raise the rate of return on private investment and get the public to underwrite the risk of new development. To produce tangible benefits for the poor and unemployed, well-funded programs in education, training, and job development and placement must be specifically directed toward the disadvantaged. Most of the support for such programs must come from a concerned federal government, but equity planning at the local level is one way to help.

Next, the Cleveland experience suggests that successful equity planning practice depends on the committed and cooperative efforts of many people, not just the planning director. Indeed, very little is explained by the isolated activities of the director. The deal we achieved with the creation of the new state lakefront parks mandated cooperation among the mayor, City Council, the state General Assembly, and the governor. These were the big players, and their agreement was ultimately essential, but the outcomes would have been far different except for the efforts of a committed city planning staff and our allies at the city parks department and the Cleveland Foundation that kept raising the issues, restating good ideas that may have been forgotten, and pointing out the equity-related implications of certain actions for the city's future. The same is true for our success in the transit negotiations in which the support of neighborhood-based and senior advocates was crucial. Success in cases like these and many other planning issues is not an individual achievement but the general accomplishment of many.

This is not to deny that my personality or the personalities of my key staff members was irrelevant; quite the contrary. But the personalities of many, many actors in the city are relevant to the quality and character of the coalitions and working relationships the planning staff can nurture and build as it works. In every city, every day, planners across the country have opportunities to pursue a professionally effective, politically astute, progressive planning practice. If planners want to work toward more equitable outcomes, the opportunities are everywhere.

One of the reasons interested planners can work on an equity agenda is because planners have a certain freedom to define their functions broadly. Planners do not follow rigorous procedures as do such line agencies as police, fire, or waste collectors. To an extent, planners are free to define their own agendas. My staff, for example, at one time or another was working on highways and public transit, public versus private electric power, neighborhood revitalization and housing, regionalization, changing state law on the ownership of tax-delinquent private property, and negotiating leases on Cleveland's port, stadium, and waterfront parks. The reason we were able to involve ourselves in such diverse functions had little to do with the definition of planning in the Cleveland city charter; it had to do with our interest in these areas because of their equity implications and because no one else in local government was involved in them.

Few people in local government understand just what it is that city planners are supposed to do (that confusion may extend to the academy as well). Beyond the narrowly defined powers and responsibilities mandated to planners by their city charters, the scope of the planning function is not specified by law nor is it uniform from city to city by practice. Because of this, city planners have considerable freedom to define their own roles and responsibilities and their relationships with the public at large and with political decision makers.

They must, of course, be visible to these decision makers. The mayor and other powerful players will not instinctively turn to their planners in search of wisdom. Neither law, custom, nor their own political instincts will suggest that they do so. Mayors Stokes, Perk, and Kucinich did not naturally turn to their planners; we went to them. Nor, contrary to the expectations of many planners, will political decision makers spell everything out for their planners. Politicians have refined to a high art the practice of saying nothing on an issue until they are confident of the extent of political support. They assiduously avoid stating clear goals or objectives. As a result, planners themselves must expect to define problems, look for equity angles, and shape directions.

To an extent, the ball is in the planners' court. If they want to be effectively used, they must seize the initiative, develop the work programs and equity-based analyses that are relevant to political decision making, bring their work to the attention of decision makers, and convince them of its worth. By broadening their definition of the planning function and taking a more equity-oriented activist posture, city planners can protect public resources, negotiate for public benefits, and save valuable city assets.

Tips on How to Do It

Planners interested in introducing more equity in their work must operate on two levels of engagement. At the first level, reasonable discharge of professional responsibilities requires that planners understand the ramifications of proposals made by themselves or by others which come before their planning commissions for review and approval. They must be responsible to the goal of equity in their analyses of these proposals. They must ask whether the clear benefits of these proposed programs go to those most in need or to those least in need and ask whether those who are called upon to pay for these programs are those most able to pay or those least able to pay. Then they must make the results of these analyses and the equity questions they raise available to the planning commission, the media, the public at large, and local decision makers. Simply raising the question of the impact of these programs on the city's poor and working class is an extremely useful function. This is surely a proper function of planning agencies; it may be castigated as divisive or negative (and sometimes will be), but it can never be wrong.

The second level of engagement requires considerable technical competence in economics and cost-benefit analysis as well as a good deal of political finesse. Once planners understand that certain proposals lead away from equitable outcomes, they must design alternatives in which the benefits go to those in need, and those most able to pay do, in fact, pay most of the costs. Then they should use their institutional role in the community to argue for these programs. In this model, the equity planner's function is not to seek consensus—that is a politician's job—but to articulate the interests at stake and the probable results of alternative choices on the city's future, and to advocate decisions consistent with the interests of those city residents who have few choices.

It is extremely important to make information public and to make one's analyses, one's self, and one's agency visible and vocal. One of the most important weapons we had in Cleveland against lucrative deal making was publicity, the value of being publicly seen, of being put up for public view. This, I believe, is precisely what a public-serving planning agency should do—be proactive, anticipate problems and opportunities, generate research and analysis, and get the information to public representatives and to the public at large.

The best way to get information to the public is not through a planning report but through the news media. As I learned from John T. Mauro, my boss in Pittsburgh during the 1960s, it is important for planners to establish good, respectful relations with the press and TV people. Be friendly and open with them; do not try to mislead them. Write your own press releases for distribution—especially on controversial actions. Take the time to make sure the reporters understand the reasons for your decisions. Try to make the reporters like and respect you; they can make the planning agency look good or terrible.

An important part of public visibility may be viewed as petty and mundane, but I believe it is important. It has to do with how one speaks and dresses. In Cleveland, our public posture was to present ourselves in a cordial but professional way, without compromising the facts of a case or our integrity. We wanted to be seen as apolitical, neutral, but competent advisers. We found that a good way to do this was to wear conservative suits, ties, and button-down shirts. It also helped to avoid taboo words and concepts. Some words and concepts in our society are so weighted down with negative meaning that they can keep otherwise reasonable ideas from ever being discussed. Consider the fate of "central economic planning" or "socialized medicine." Controversial ideas can reach the table if couched in acceptable language. An example is our 1971 proposal to condemn and expropriate Cleveland's investor-owned electric utility, CEI, in favor of expanding the city-owned municipal light plant. This is the New York City equivalent to condemning Con Edison. I could have made the proposal to the CPC while wearing striped bell-bottomed pants and a tie-dyed T-shirt, much in vogue at the time. I might have said: "We propose to expand public power by smashing the greed of the private sector. All power to the people!" That would have been indiscreet. Instead, wearing a dark flannel suit, cordovan oxfords, and a white, button-down shirt with a paisley tie, I described it as "a sound business venture" and "a good deal for the city," one that "would lower electric costs" and "make Cleveland a more attractive location for new investment." I think the low-keyed presentation helped capture some support and perhaps helped preserve Cleveland's municipal light system.

A planner can publicly advance equity interests most effectively if he or she takes care to pose the issues in a sober, faintly skeptical, professional way while looking businesslike. Planners should avoid being seen as ideological or political; they should be professional, but they should also focus attention on the equity aspects that are inherently a part of many of the local issues that come before them. The job of equity planners is not to usher in national social movements but to try, bit by bit, to improve conditions in their cities for their needy residents while also trying to support broader progressive movements.

Two other elements needed by would-be equity planners are time and persistence. To be accorded a place at the public bargaining table, planners like other players must be prepared to invest time and energy in developing a position and earning the respect of others. The transit case in Cleveland evolved over a period of five years; the state lakefront park concept has been evolving since 1976. Other cases demand the same commitment. If my staff and I had not participated in those issues over the long pull, it is doubtful we would have been able to influence the outcome. So some considerable commitment of time is needed. Persistence is also invaluable. In the lakefront park case, the same mayor accepted the exact proposal he had rejected three years earlier. So don't be afraid to bring up again and again good ideas that have been shot down before. Nobody else in local government is likely to perform this important function.

Concluding Points

First, equity planning works. It is clear from the Cleveland experience that a planning practice that focuses on equity considerations can be accomplished and can provide important benefits to the poor and near poor of a city. It is unlikely that traditional urban planning approaches can accomplish as much for the poor and working classes.

Second, opportunities to do equity planning exist every day in every city in America. Opportunities to pursue a professionally effective, politically astute, progressive planning practice need only be seized. They may not be proclaimed as loudly as they were in Cleveland, but they can be expressed in the many analyses and recommendations made by a planning staff every day. Indeed, there is a growing evidence from many cities that such equity-oriented efforts are under way. Consider Mayor Ray Flynn's Boston and the linkage work of Peter Dreier and the Boston Redevelopment Agency (BRA); Rob Mier's job development work in Mayor Harold Washington's Chicago; Rick Cohen negotiating low-income set-asides in the new housing developments in Jersey City, and the lessons of citizen participation and neighborhood-based development in Denver, Santa Monica, Berkeley, and other cities. Planners need not blow trumpets and rally the troops as much as they need to raise equity issues, be visible and public, be professional, be persistent, and educate their political superiors and the public at large.

Finally, practicing equity planning may be less ideological than practical. Sadly, the problems addressed by equity planning are not going away. In many cities, the number of poor and near poor is growing to the point that they make up a substantial portion of the population. More and more black and Hispanic mayors will be elected from that population. There will be differences among these minority mayors just as there are differences among white mayors; Coleman Young is not like Harold Washington any more than Tom Bradley is like Carl Stokes. Some minority mayors may not mandate equity planning any more than their white predecessors, but they will want to do more for their constituents. In cities with black or white progressive mayors, planners anxious to explore their own models of redistributive justice might use the Cleveland experience of the 1970s as a good place to start.

Cleveland Tomorrow: A Practicing Model of New Roles and Processes for Corporate Leadership in Cities

Richard A. Shatten

The Context of Urban Change

For most of America's history, city governments have been at the center of urban change so that the practice of governance and the ways government could be used were the definitive features of what we called development. Public entrepreneurs such as Robert Moses created public authorities, which, in turn, created public infrastructure. Urban political bosses such as Richard Daley manipulated political organizations in the service of city development, and private developers like Cleveland's Van Sweringens built on the government foundation.

By the 1960s, issues of income redistribution and racial equality were at the center of urban politics in many cities, including Cleveland, and this politics was translated into urban development through the practices of urban renewal. But urban renewal seemed to contain as many problems as it sought to resolve and, by the 1970s, much of this great wave of our urban history had calcified into the now familiar refrain of suburban sprawl, urban development, plant closings, the underclass, stagnant economies, and moribund institutions. St. Louis, Youngstown, and parts of America's great cities, including New York and Los Angeles, became subjects of news reports asking the question, Can these places ever be renewed?

The same question was certainly relevant to Cleveland. It was no different from any other mature city in its struggle to cope with urban change. Through the 1960s and the 1970s, Cleveland experienced a series of false starts as it sought to develop a response to the rising maelstrom of problems.

One of these starts, in the wake of the Hough riots and the election of Carl Stokes, the first black mayor of a major city, was a program called Cleveland Now. Although organized by the city's corporate elite, the program was a failure from its inception. Although it was a coalition of powerful and well-meaning local residents, Cleveland Now could never break with the old government-based mode of urban development, tying its solutions to city problems to City Hall, thus lacking an independent voice. When the administration of the city changed and a new mayor took over City Hall, Cleveland Now was disbanded. Its demise brought a host of proposals for the physical redevelopment of the city: hotels were announced with fanfare but never built, ambitious new developments on the lakefront were promised and then forgotten, and a new jetport was designed for the middle of Lake Erie.

Urban Change: Cleveland

Other than the occasional success of an individual entrepreneur, the larger business community of Cleveland remained largely invisible or played traditional roles throughout this entire period. Public action by business in Cleveland, as in most cities, typically took three forms. First, every community had a Chamber of Commerce pursuing community improvement, member services, and private sector advocacy. Second, each city usually had some lawyers, businessmen, and bankers pursuing so-called "downtown interests." Third, communities organized occasional ad hoc coalitions to accomplish a specific goal: they raised money for a new museum or developed legislation to build a new highway or bridge and then disbanded and disappeared.

The structure of the business community of Cleveland closely resembled the three-part organization described above. As the economy of the city went into almost total eclipse in the 1970s, the local Chamber of Commerce, "downtown business interests," and certain ad hoc groups mobilized in an attempt to create an economic development response similar to those being offered by most other cities in the country. They set out to search for new firms and, through a package of training grants, loans, and other inducements, entice them to move to Cleveland. They bragged that the city possessed a "good business climate" defined, in typical fashion, as low taxes and nonunion labor. Very few firms paid much attention to this approach, inasmuch as every city seemed to have its own version of the same model. By the end of the 1970s, the economy of Cleveland was still in a state of development crisis and the businesses were still unresponsive to the crisis.

Economic Development and Cleveland Tomorrow

In the 1980s the situation had changed and Cleveland had become a recognized example of how to organize the private sector in the service of urban development. The main unit of corporate organization is a group called Cleveland Tomorrow, which pioneered new practices of economic development, creating a new role for corporations to build on existing institutions and bring weight and energy to the community agenda. *Fortune* magazine recognized this phenomenon in March 1989 in an extraordinary story entitled "How Business Bosses Saved a Sick City." The article gave Cleveland Tomorrow credit, indeed too much credit, for the tide of recovery that swept the city during the 1980s. The article concluded:

> Listening to Clevelanders' earnest talk about how they are turning their town around, and looking at what they've accomplished, is an impressive, oddly moving experience—and not just because it's exhilarating to see people take their fate in their hands instead of complaining about irresistible, impersonal forces. Beyond that, you can't help thinking that *this* is what community is all about. Doubtless it sounds comic to speak of Clevelanders in the same breath as Athenians, but isn't this at least a little like what the Greeks meant by the civic ideal—the public life in which people achieve their fullest humanity?

This was pretty heady stuff. But *Fortune*'s prose underscored Clevelanders' recognition that something very different was taking place in their city.

Cleveland Tomorrow

INITIATION AND DEVELOPMENT

By the early 1980s urban development was at a standstill in Cleveland and intervention by the local business community was largely ineffective. In early 1980, a group of chief executive officers (CEOs) came together, gravely concerned about the fate of the community. At first they met in the traditional ad hoc manner, seeing themselves as a short-term corporate alliance bound together for the purpose of identifying a solution to a problem, getting it done, and then going away. The initial group of eight looked very much like the traditional downtown interest group inasmuch as it included the head of a major downtown law firm closely connected to the power structure, the publisher of the daily newspaper, several other CEOs, and the head of the Federal Reserve Bank.

They recommended the formation of Cleveland Tomorrow to help launch six programs.[1] Most of the founding members assumed that Cleveland Tomorrow would disappear after launching the six initiatives. They also expected that, as in the past, their recommendations would focus on changing government structure so that City Hall could exert its dominant role and implement what they had launched.

But the Cleveland Tomorrow organization that emerged shifted the emphasis of business leadership from the traditional model to a very different approach to private sector intervention. In the early 1980s Cleveland's city government was in a precarious position at the very least. The city had suffered through the first bond default of any major American city since the Great Depression, and the new political order brought to power in the wake of the city's crisis could not initially be counted on to spearhead urban recovery. The traditional development model of letting government do it would no longer work. If the private sector really wanted to effect change it would have to do it itself.

Economic power had to be organized in a new way and for the long haul—no ad hoc or temporary organization would suffice. Cleveland Tomorrow expanded to include thirty-seven members, and later, fifty. Each corporate member had to generate at least $300 million in revenue a year. Individual participation in Cleveland Tomorrow was not offered to those who represented these fiscal resources but to those who controlled the economic resources of a corporation—namely the CEOs. Cleveland Tomorrow defined corporate citizenship and participation in the development of the city in new and previously untapped levels of commitment. It was a permanent development organization run not by politicians, but by the very highest levels of the private urban economy. Coming together in a new setting, these CEOs would identify priorities, initiate action, and repeat the process as long as it was necessary. Their programs were private sector-based—venture capital funds, university research centers, and labor relations councils.

HOW IT WORKS

The fifty members of Cleveland Tomorrow meet as a full board to make binding decisions. The organization is governed by an officer group of five that meets monthly for a three-hour dinner with staff. Cleveland Tomorrow was very deliberate about the way it chose to work. A host of seemingly mundane rules were developed to ensure an effective organization. First and foremost, membership is limited to chief executive officers—the top person in an organization who can take action on behalf of that organization. The board meets six times a year. A board member may not send a substitute. If a board member misses a meeting, a staff member later briefs him on what happened. Staff rarely meets alone with elected officials. These rules ensure a comprehensive commitment to assure the active ownership of the organization by its members.

Cleveland Tomorrow does not take on a project until after a member has reviewed it and become involved in its governance. For example, in 1985 the Playhouse Square Foundation asked Cleveland Tomorrow for assistance in raising $4 million to help rehabilitate a seven-thousand-seat complex of old vaudeville theaters. The proposal was referred to a committee, which studied Playhouse Square for a year. The committee decided that the Playhouse Square proposal was sound but suggested that rather than the $4 million requested, $13 million would be needed, plus an operating subsidy. The results of the committee's study and recommendations for funding the Playhouse Square proposal were then presented to the board of Cleveland Tomorrow. The board voted to adopt Playhouse Square as a priority and to make financial commitments to its development. Within twelve weeks every member of Cleveland Tomorrow had signed a pledge card to the capital campaign that led to the April 1988 opening of the complete Playhouse Square complex.

A member must study the plan and make a recommendation to the board, and the board has to adopt the recommendation. It formally recommends support of a project or funding only after two reviews at a trustees' meeting and direct input from every member. The board is the decision-making body—there is no executive committee. For example, Cleveland Tomorrow made a commitment to Cleveland's inner harbor, a partnership of the state, city, foundations, and companies to establish open space on Cleveland's lakefront. The process leading to this commitment included a meeting at which half of the board voted to act, individual meetings with staff members and those who did not attend board meetings, makeup meetings for others, and a second reading of the action at a subsequent board meeting. The process caused fifty people to pay attention, to know that the group was going to make a commitment.

LEADERSHIP

Cleveland Tomorrow is based on the premise that an informed community leadership, oriented to action, can effect community improvement. Cleveland Tomorrow would not exist were it not for E. Mandell de Windt, chairman of Eaton Corporation. When it was decided to replace the original eight-member ad hoc group with a permanent organization, de Windt called thirty-six people on the phone and said, "You're joining." If a CEO asked why, he was told, "Because this is the right thing to do and I want you to do it." Who could turn down the CEO of Eaton Corporation, former chairman of the National Business Council, former chairman of many national organizations?

A committed membership can accomplish its objectives. Cleveland Tomorrow passed two direct tests of its members' commitment to the organization. First, attendance at meetings held virtually constant at 55 percent over its first eight years, each member attending about half of the meetings. Second, the members pay their dues on time and at the requested level, contributing about $740,000 each year to operate the organization. The involvement and participation of these CEOs is vital because they represent the true energy and power of the organization. These corporate leaders have the knowledge and ability to direct and represent the organization throughout the community. If they were not involved, the organization would quickly degenerate into just another volunteer board hiring staff to do a job.

AN INFORMED AGENDA

Since its formation, Cleveland Tomorrow has spent over $2.8 million on studies designed to increase understanding of the Cleveland economy. These studies were funded by foundations and corporations. They have not only helped identify issues that needed addressing but have also helped the organization understand the issues with enough detail to map complete courses of action.

In the 1980 study that led to the formation of Cleveland Tomorrow, researchers interviewed two hundred opinion leaders in Cleveland and around the country to determine what urban revitalization strategies worked and what strategies didn't. The result was a list of possible ways to turn Cleveland around. Items on that list represented conflicting points of view: whether to move toward metropolitan government or toward decentralized government; whether to clear vacant land in the city and reuse it or to undertake housing rehabilitation and historic preservation. Some of the problems Cleveland faced were the demands of organized labor, bad management, the public schools, crime, a port that is not open year-round, and a lack of good hotel space downtown.

The key to Cleveland Tomorrow's early success was the artful filtering of this universe into a clear policy direction. The corporate membership agreed to the following: (1) Cleveland had lost its competitive position in the world economy, (2) manufacturing was declining relative to the nation, and (3) corporations were not replacing those jobs with new companies. Further, the corporate members agreed to promote labor-management cooperation and new company formation based on the research and technology in the region's universities, hospitals, and federal labs. This linkage of problems and action gave Cleveland Tomorrow focus. Two years later, the organization did another study, adding physical development to the problem-solving agenda. A philosophy and point of view about how the organization could contribute to downtown and neighborhood revitalization was formulated. In 1988, Cleveland Tomorrow released a study entitled *Cleveland Tomorrow: Building on a New Foundation,* based on the work done over the previous six years. The report featured an overview of recent economic trends, identified the challenges to the region, and presented Cleveland Tomorrow's response.

Each of the studies undertaken has enabled corporate Cleveland to be effective through its knowledge, not just its perceived power. The research has provided a basis for expert testimony, enabled the leadership and staff to be credible in relations with other organizations, and established Cleveland Tomorrow as a solid community resource that can be mobilized to face important issues.

The importance of knowledge and power, rather than just power, is evident from the experience of a sister organization in Pittsburgh, the Allegheny Conference. One of the problems in Pittsburgh at the time the conference was formed, in 1946, was air pollution. Because of the heavy smoke from coal furnaces and coal locomotives, the state of Pennsylvania ruled that homeowners must replace their furnaces and the railroads must convert to diesel locomotives. The railroad industry lobbied against the ruling in Harrisburg until the corporate leaders of Pittsburgh confronted them. The representatives of steel and other industries, which were large purchasers of space on the trains, convinced the railroads to cease their opposition to the clean air measures. According to the members of the Allegheny Conference, that was the last time they ever used power. They have continued to be perceived as powerful, but their real power comes from being a good resource to government. Much of the physical development in Pittsburgh has been done through studies paid for or overseen by private sector organizations and implemented by government.

Cleveland Tomorrow is effective because it is well financed, well staffed, well informed, and well organized so that it can marshal these resources to act quickly and properly "seat" an issue in the community. Its commitment to high-quality research and its powerful membership help attract top staff and strong financial support. Together these resources can be successfully applied to civic initiatives that require public investment, corporate participation, and foundation support.

Finances

Part of Cleveland Tomorrow's ability to get issues addressed quickly comes from a dues structure that raises sufficient funds both to support the core organization and to provide modest grants to get new organizations and programs started. Cleveland Tomorrow has a dues policy that is geared to making all members, regardless of size or corporate fiscal base, reasonably equal partners. Based on the size of their corporations, members contribute $7,000, $15,000, or $30,000. A share of the dues supports modest grants for programmatic initiatives that leverage larger amounts of money from the membership and from foundations. As a result, Cleveland Tomorrow is always leveraging its resources to stimulate the development process. Through 1991, $4 million of dues had supported a program resulting in over $700 million of funds invested in Cleveland Tomorrow priorities.

The nature of the membership and the ability of the CEOs to make final decisions affecting the organization and their corporate participation in it enable the organization to raise money quickly for particular issues—in amounts and with impacts that few other organizations in the Cleveland area possess. One example of this is the way corporations, through Cleveland Tomorrow, pledged support to the Playhouse Square development.

Staff

Staff is the other important resource that enables Cleveland Tomorrow to act effectively. Staff members play a central role in the organization. They must operate in a way that helps the corporate leadership to act productively in a complex, fast-moving, and often volatile urban arena. The members must always be in a position to act persuasively and, at times, very quickly. Staff thus must have the skills to work directly with a community elite responsible for making public and private decisions with broad impact on the city. Staff must be skilled at running a volunteer organization and be accustomed to acting through leadership rather than as independent operators. Staff must also enjoy a sophisticated yet broad-ranging, analytical orientation so they can filter information in a manner that enables leaders to make choices.

Perhaps the best way to characterize the staff at Cleveland Tomorrow is that the organization attracts those who tend to straddle professions. The best staff are those who combine training and professional experience in business, philanthropy, and public policy. Each dimension is important to serving the diverse constituents of Cleveland Tomorrow's community leadership and programs.

Research

Effective research must be done in close cooperation between leaders and staff. Staff and leaders agree together to undertake studies. Before initiating a study, a member of the board participates with staff on a study committee. The combined effort of board members, staff, and researchers makes for a consistently more informed and involved process.

PARTNERSHIP

Partnership is the core principle that guides the implementation of projects. At the base of everything Cleveland Tomorrow does is an acute awareness of the limitations of corporate participation in urban life. Corporate organizations cannot be all things to all people, and there are many things they should not do. This philosophy has led to a variety of operating principles that have helped Cleveland Tomorrow advance. First, it does not operate programs inside its own organization. The staff totals three professionals and three secretaries. Instead, Cleveland Tomorrow identifies areas of importance and then finds a partner. For example, if the problem is labor relations, it joins with the Work in Northeast Ohio Council (WINOC), with a membership comprised of half organized labor and half management. In turn, WINOC has joined with Cleveland State University to tap its expertise. If the problem is low-income housing, Cleveland Tomorrow joins with neighborhood-based organizations and a national expert in low-income housing.

Working through partnerships has several advantages. First, board composition can be tailored to the particular needs of the problem. If, for example, Cleveland Tomorrow is starting a venture capital fund, it can create a board with expertise in venture capital, not just large-scale corporate management. Second, the membership does not have to be involved in the financial or administrative day-to-day activities of the organization. The members need only hear reports on progress from the one CEO designated to participate on a priority project. In addition, Cleveland Tomorrow does not have to run the initiative and instead can focus on critical policy issues. Cleveland Tomorrow can then continue to focus on urban development and the new organization or partner can focus on the operations and the program. Third, if Cleveland Tomorrow operates a program, it has to hire a vice-president to run it. If the program is independent, it can hire a president. Cleveland

Tomorrow can dramatically improve the quality of the staff working on the projects by giving up a little ownership. Perhaps more important, the staff has direct and unambiguous responsibility for accomplishing the objectives set forth by the member leadership.

An alternative approach would be to build a set of programs through a single operating organization. Such an approach preserves control, but it requires staff to focus on internal management rather than external relationships. Further, the program operators tend to be employees working for other staff. This is markedly different from the decentralized approach in which staff work directly for the member leadership.

Its role as a partner reflects Cleveland Tomorrow's true position in the community. If it oversteps its bounds, it fails. For example, for much of 1987 and 1988, Cleveland Tomorrow tried to be the convener of the effort to develop a new Cleveland baseball stadium—a much more ambitious undertaking than just being a partner. Cleveland Tomorrow was not able to get the job done. The members learned that this was a public project that required private sector support—not the other way around. When the organization let the public sector take the lead and assumed a supportive role, the outcome for the stadium project became more optimistic.

In any Cleveland Tomorrow partnership, a formal process establishes it as an affiliated program that includes the vote of the board of trustees. Affiliated programs agree that a member of Cleveland Tomorrow's board becomes a principal in their organizations and that staff from Cleveland Tomorrow can participate in the affiliate's board meetings. This leads to strong board-to-board relationships and strong staff relationships. Cleveland Tomorrow staff do not serve on any boards. That duty is reserved for the members.

Another important set of external relations is with elected officials and leaders of key community institutions. Cleveland Tomorrow consciously establishes and nurtures these relationships. The members routinely invite public officials, university presidents, and state department directors to meet with their board or special committees without any preformed agenda. The purpose of these meetings is to build mutual understanding and identify common ground. This has been especially important at the state level—the source of over half of the financial resources for the priority programs of Cleveland Tomorrow.

Lessons from Cleveland

Offering general lessons from one organization in a particular city is a risky venture. Myron Magnet of *Fortune* magazine suggested that the one word that characterized successful communities was *partnership*. Although Cleveland is still a community with conflicts, it no longer experiences the bitter adversarial relationships of the past. This is a dramatic change in the character of urban development. Rather than downtown versus neighborhoods, the common rhetoric across the city is how to get more development in the neighborhoods and, at the same time, maintain the impressive record of downtown growth and development. Cleveland Tomorrow subscribes to and attempts to foster this politics and rhetoric of development across all segments of the community. It has been successful in doing this by practicing the following principles:

AN INFORMED AGENDA

Communities that pursue an informed agenda are more likely to succeed over the long run. The greatest challenge facing community leaders is choosing from the array of options presented to them on an almost daily basis. Cleveland Tomorrow learned how to build an organization focused on action with a process of choice that filtered the mass of information confronting community leaders.

Every community has exceptional talent in its public and private sectors. In many places, that leadership is unable to marshal itself around a common agenda, choosing instead to divide its efforts over a modest set of efforts that may or may not affect fundamental issues. Cleveland Tomorrow has learned that providing the leadership with clear, well-researched options is fundamental to mobilizing the leadership and gaining the right level of consensus and action. Without good information, leaders are likely to retreat to long-held positions and less likely to stake out new alliances, much less new action.

Cleveland Tomorrow's reliance on research enhances staff support and leadership involvement, thereby stimulating the leadership to make high-quality choices. Those choices can be sustained over a long period of time—sufficient time to show results.

PROCESS MATTERS

Organizations work best when they are attentive to how they operate and when they choose to frame and reframe what they do. Cleveland Tomorrow was created with the intent of succeeding. It developed rules that reinforce its orientation toward CEO involvement and action. The rules are important and ground much of what is done. Cleveland Tomorrow does not get stuck in the rules. Instead, it stays focused on getting things done and designing processes that work. The rules and process are the tools that enable Cleveland Tomorrow selectively to mobilize the power of its corporate members, giving them a better way to represent their economic base in community debate and decisions.

PARTNERSHIPS ARE NOT PABLUM

The references that are made to the importance of public-private partnerships in facilitating the economic development process might lead one to conclude that they are simply the next civic innovation to become popular in America. Cleveland Tomorrow learned that partnerships of *any* kind are far easier to talk about than they are to make work effectively. It is very hard to design a workable partnership, but the result is worth the effort. Partnerships are just about the best way to get things done.

A partnership requires that the participants loosen control to achieve an objective. They require historic adversaries or strangers to trust each other. Effective partnerships are based on thoughtful consideration of what each party brings to the table. Cleveland Tomorrow partnerships are not merely the letterheads of impressive community leaders. They are designed to bring together the tools necessary to meet an objective. People bring money, expertise, relationships, and vision to a partnership.

For all this to happen, the partnership requires confidence by each party that they can all work together and succeed, and that the consequences of failure can also be shared. This sense of individual and collective confidence makes everything easier. People take risks, make a little extra effort, and put in a bit more time when they are optimistic about their future. A good self-image restores a city's, as well as an organization's, ability to behave with a sense of community.

Cities that think they can get things done probably do. Cleveland Tomorrow is proud to have contributed to Cleveland's sense that it can set ambitious goals, dream great dreams, and see results. Now it is up to the machinery of urban partnership to continue to keep the community on track.

Note

1. These programs included a manufacturing research institute, a labor-management cooperation program, an industrial competitiveness project, and a business advocacy project.

Postpopulist Public-Private Partnerships

W. Dennis Keating, Norman Krumholz, & John Metzger

CLEVELAND HAS been cited as an outstanding example of the use of public-private partnerships to promote urban revitalization in the 1980s. As a midwestern Rust Belt city with a declining population, continuing losses of manufacturing employment, and strong racial divisions, Cleveland has faced very serious economic and social problems since World War II. In 1978, during the populist mayor Dennis Kucinich's brief administration (1977–79), Cleveland became the first major American city since the Depression to default on its fiscal obligations. More recently, however, Cleveland has been hailed as a "comeback" city.[1]

Under the leadership of Republican mayor George Voinovich (1979–89) and his successor, Democrat Michael White, the city relied heavily on the private sector (corporate and philanthropic) for leadership and financial support for urban redevelopment programs. Representatives of these interests have played a leading and, at times, decisive role in determining public policy. This has resulted in the initiation of major redevelopment projects, privately controlled and often publicly subsidized. The city's major focus has been on the redevelopment of its downtown, or central business district. This approach is similar to that of the city's urban renewal policies of the late 1950s and 1960s. Massive land clearance projects were aimed at the private commercial redevelopment of downtown Cleveland. Both eras of public-private partnerships assumed benevolent operation of the "trickle-down" theory of urban economic growth, which predicts that private downtown development will create jobs and increase the tax base, indirectly benefiting the rest of the city.

In this essay, we will argue that the emphasis on public-private partnerships during the administrations of Mayors George Voinovich (elected Ohio's governor in 1990) and Michael White resulted in an unbalanced development strategy for Cleveland. Downtown development completely overshadowed the redevelopment of the city's neighborhoods. Although neighborhood-based development groups

Originally published as "Cleveland: Post-Populist Public-Private Partnerships" in *Unequal Partnerships: The Political Economy of Urban Redevelopment in Postwar America,* ed. Gregory D. Squires.

received assistance from the city and from private corporations and foundations, this assistance did not nearly equal that provided for major downtown development projects. The political influence of neighborhood nonprofit development groups is weak relative to that of their for-profit counterparts, which exert much more influence at City Hall.

The Decline of Cleveland's Economy, Downtown, and Neighborhoods

Public-private partnerships are hardly an innovation in Cleveland. Like most U.S. cities, Cleveland embarked on a major post–World War II urban renewal program, which was supported by the city's corporate leadership.

The vehicle they used to promote Cleveland's urban renewal program was the nonprofit development foundation. The first of these foundations, the Cleveland Development Foundation, was created in 1954. It helped the city's Urban Renewal Department prepare plans and programs for early Title I projects, including the St. Vincent's and Gladstone projects. In 1960, a second development foundation called the University Circle Development Foundation (later University Circle, Inc.) was established. Its purpose was to protect the medical, cultural, and educational institutions of the University Circle area, which were threatened by an enveloping black ghetto. Foundation consultants produced the University-Euclid renewal plan, which was then executed by the city.

Cleveland's urban renewal program was similar to those of most U.S. cities; it was run by a coalition of business and political leaders. The costs were not equally shared; they fell most heavily on the minority poor. Moreover, the city admittedly cut back on police, fire, and other services in designated urban renewal areas. In many projects, housing for poor blacks was demolished and replaced by institutional and commercial development. An estimated 1,780 poor and black families were displaced from the St. Vincent's project alone; no replacement housing was constructed, nor was relocation assistance provided. Instead, a hospital and community college were built on the cleared land.

Two qualities distinguish Cleveland's urban renewal efforts from those of most other cities, however. First, the city's program was controlled by the City Council, not by an autonomous urban renewal authority. This meant a slow process as council members from Cleveland's thirty-three wards negotiated or disputed the elements of various plans. The slow pace of redevelopment is exemplified by the Erieview urban renewal project, Cleveland's key downtown redevelopment project. Although this $45 million project is rated a success by most observers, some parcels that were cleared in the early 1960s remained vacant in 1991.

Second, Cleveland's program was wildly ambitious. It was assumed that if land were assembled in large parcels, titles cleared, and costs written down, a market would exist for a vast amount of land in the city. As a result, the city designated 6,060 acres of land (one-eighth of all land in the entire city) for clearance. Unfortunately, urban renewal promoters were to be disappointed. The market proved unable to absorb even a fraction of that amount and, in 1967, the federal government suspended the city from further urban renewal assistance until it could better implement its program.

Cleveland found that urban renewal did not revive its downtown or stem the tide of suburbanization. Instead, the city experienced a steady loss of population and employment and an erosion of its tax base—what has been termed a "growth crisis."[2]

The recent growth of downtown corporate and financial service employment and the creation of a new entertainment district in the formerly industrial Flats have not yet changed the overall economic picture in Cleveland. Like most other older, industrial cities in the Northeast and Midwest, Cleveland has experienced population loss, waves of manufacturing plant closings, rising unemployment and poverty, and the growing deterioration of an aging housing stock. Cleveland's population decreased by 177,081 during the 1970s, a drop of 24 percent, and dropped another 68,200 during the 1980s to 505,000 in 1990. The city projects continued population decline through the year 2000, with the loss ranging from 42,000 to 101,000, depending on various factors. Cleveland's traditional economic base of manufacturing industries has eroded significantly since World War II. Manufacturing employment in the city declined by 59 percent between 1947 and 1982. Service industry employment, nearly one-third of which is located downtown, has picked up some of the slack, although these new jobs have either been in highly skilled business and professional-technical services or in low-paying personal and support services.[3] Since 1980, Cleveland's poverty rate has increased by more than one-third; as of July 1990, it was 39.7 percent. More than 72 percent of the population of three black neighborhoods on the East Side are poor.[4] In 1990, Cleveland had the worst black unemployment rate among the nation's big cities—20.7 percent.[5]

Growing poverty rates, combined with deteriorating housing conditions, have created a housing crisis in many Cleveland neighborhoods. An "exterior conditions" survey by the Cuyahoga County Regional Planning Commission in 1984–85 identified twenty-four thousand substandard one- to four-unit structures in Cleveland, representing 19 percent of the total stock. The city's Department of Community Development estimates that nearly one-third of the housing stock is substandard if interior conditions are also considered. Much of the city's public housing is substandard, and several thousand units are vacant despite long waiting lists. The estimated cost of repair is over $140 million.

Much of the Cuyahoga Metropolitan Housing Authority housing is close to downtown and close to or within the boundaries of several public-private partnerships. These partnerships, which include the Mid-Town Corridor, the St. Vincent's Quadrangle, the Warehouse District, and the Ohio City Redevelopment Association, are often considered models. The city's successful application to be named an All-American City by the National Civic League featured the work of the Mid-Town Corridor. But the partnerships do not include public housing tenants on their boards or committees and they tend to ignore the needs of tenants and the housing authority's physical facility needs in their planning; so has the city. In a typical case, the city spent $3.5 million for sidewalks, street trees, lighting, and infrastructure in the Warehouse District in the hope of attracting a new, upscale population to live in mostly vacant downtown warehouse lofts. But the city has not addressed the substantial capital improvement needs of the eight hundred families now living in the authority's Lakeview Terrace, west of the Warehouse District. Similarly, the St. Vincent's Quadrangle and Mid-Town Corridor partnerships virtually ignore the forty-eight hundred housing authority units located near their boundaries.

Cleveland's public-private partnerships have not adequately addressed such problems as the decline of manufacturing, the increase of poverty, and racism, which cloud the prospects for future redevelopment.

Cleveland's Power Structure

To understand the basis for the creation and use of public-private partnerships in Cleveland, it is necessary to understand the city's power structure and its interest and role in redevelopment. The power structure of Cleveland's banks, utilities, and industrial corporations has been and is a tightly knit business establishment whose activities have long been chronicled by historians. From about 1870 to the turn of the century, Cleveland was one of the most powerful industrial cities in the world. Cleveland industrialists such as Mark Hanna, Charles Brush, and John D. Rockefeller were figures of international importance.

Close business and banking relationships are reinforced by a pattern of social relationships. Almost all Cleveland banks and corporations have memberships at the exclusive Union Club, almost all are members of the Cleveland Growth Association, and almost all are members of the same country clubs. Their officers lead civic committees and occupy chairs on the distribution committees of Cleveland's large philanthropic foundations, whose grants and contributions to the city and to the city's nonprofit corporations help set the public agenda. Their leadership in large public projects is often decisive.

Cleveland's power structure can exercise crucial influence regarding the outcome of important problems, such as the city's financial default in 1978. Indeed, default was brought on by the power structure after Mayor Dennis Kucinich refused to sell the Municipal Light Plant to its private competitor. Any discussion of the power structure in Cleveland would be incomplete without mention of the new players in the game and their agendas. The older banking and industrial elite generally favors conservative growth politics in which the city government is expected to play a passive role, merely providing basic services and keeping taxes low. Since the 1950s, however, a new group of service sector business elites has emerged and has shaped public policies in favor of their substantial investments in the city's downtown. This group, made up of developers, property owners, and businessmen, favors liberal growth policies in which the city government is expected to play an active role in facilitation and providing subsidies (such as urban development action grants, or UDAGs, and tax inducements) to further downtown development. Urban renewal, convention center and hotel development, entertainment attractions, modernization of infrastructure, and higher taxes to support better public services are all part of this growth coalition's agenda. This group now dominates the development program of the city of Cleveland and the Cleveland Growth Association.

Another significant change has been the change of corporate leadership resulting from the takeover of Cleveland corporations by non-Cleveland and multinational groups (e.g., the 1987 takeover of Standard Oil of Ohio by British Petroleum and the 1989 sale of Higbee's, Cleveland's only major downtown department store, to a national chain).

The Cleveland Growth Association is Cleveland's renamed Chamber of Commerce. It functions as a civic booster (especially for the downtown); a promoter of development, tourism, and business subsidies; and a powerful representative of local business interests. In 1990 it had a budget of $5.1 million and a staff of eighty-five. The association has been an enthusiastic supporter of the public-private partnerships concept. One of the most important recent examples of the association's role in such partnerships is its underwriting of much of the cost of the Voinovich administration's Civic Vision land use plan.

Cleveland Tomorrow, founded in 1982, is composed of the chief executive officers of fifty of Cleveland's major corporations. It has played a leading role in decision making on major policy issues affecting the city. It too has underwritten part of the Civic Vision planning process. In addition, Cleveland Tomorrow has helped create programs to foster and encourage business development, restore Playhouse Square, a historic seven-thousand-seat theater district, and administer grants and other funds for neighborhood-based development through a new organization named Neighborhood Progress, Inc. (NPI). NPI is now the key agency controlling funding to Cleveland's neighborhood-based community development corporations (CDCs).

Cleveland's two major foundations play a critical role in civic decision making. In 1993, the Cleveland Foundation had assets of $750 million and distributed over $30 million in grants and another $2.6 million in program-related investments. Its Distribution Committee is composed of leading corporate and civic leaders and was headed in 1991 by former corporate CEO John J. Dwyer. The foundation has been an active participant in virtually all major development decisions in Cleveland. It has provided substantial financial support for such projects as Playhouse Square, lakefront development, and the city's Civic Vision land use plan. The Cleveland Foundation also has provided support for Cleveland's neighborhood organizations. From 1981 to 1990, it provided $2.8 million to individual CDCs. It has also supported the Center for Neighborhood Development at Cleveland State University, an organization that provides technical assistance, training, and research support for CDCs. From the Center's creation in 1979 through 1990, the Cleveland Foundation provided $580,000 in support. The foundation has provided substantial support to the Cleveland Housing Network and the Cleveland Neighborhood Development Corporation. The former is a coalition of thirteen CDCs involved in housing; the latter is a citywide coalition of CDCs involved in commercial development. In 1987, the Cleveland Foundation announced that it would allocate $5 million for neighborhood development during the next several years, and it has provided those funds through NPI.

The Cleveland Foundation's grant making has its critics. It was criticized by the National Committee for Responsive Philanthropy for not giving more support to Cleveland's disadvantaged, giving only $5.5 million to the disadvantaged out of total grants of $22.2 million in 1988.[6]

The Gund Foundation has joined the Cleveland Foundation in most of these ventures. In 1993 the Gund Foundation had assets of $430 million and made grants totaling $15 million.

The third major source of funding for CDCs has been BP America, formerly the Standard Oil Company of Ohio. In 1990, its Social Investment Fund contributed $270,000 to Cleveland CDCs, $250,000 to the Enterprise Foundation for support of CDCs, and additional funding to national organizations involved in neighborhood development.

The philanthropic contributions of these three local funders have been supplemented by those of two national funders: the Local Initiatives Support Corporation and the Enterprise Foundation.

A Downtown-Corporate Redevelopment Strategy

Cleveland's revitalization strategy has not been detailed in any written plan or program, although a new general land use plan called the Civic Vision was developed in the second half of the 1980s. Like the plans of many other central cities, Cleveland's general plan was very outdated. The city's previous general land use plan had been formulated in 1949. It reflected the expectation that Cleveland would continue to grow, even though the city's postwar population decline was well under way. In 1974, however, the City Planning Commission did adopt a social policy plan that addressed the city's economic and social inequities.[7]

In November 1984, Mayor Voinovich announced that the city would develop the Civic Vision plan.[8] Priority was given to the downtown plan, financed by the foundations, the Greater Cleveland Growth Association, Cleveland Tomorrow, and the office building association. There was no delay in decisions concerning the award of UDAG grants and major development projects while the new general plan was being developed (although after the fanfare of the mayor's announcement in a City Club speech, development of the plan proceeded slowly).

The planning process was guided by the local business and civic leaders on the Downtown Plan Steering Committee. In addition to the downtown plan, Civic Vision included a citywide plan to provide a comprehensive and coordinated approach to land use, zoning, expenditure of the city capital budget, and the use of community development block grant funds. The chairman of the Citywide Plan Steering Committee was director of the Cleveland Housing Network and was appointed the city's director of community development in 1990. The Downtown Plan was published in 1988; the Citywide Plan was not published until 1991.

The Downtown Plan is a traditional land use and development plan. It avoids any discussion of affordable housing, linking downtown's growth to the welfare of city residents in neighborhoods, Cleveland's 40 percent poverty rate, or the serious problem of homelessness.[9] Nor were these issues addressed in the Citywide Plan.

Although support has been given to neighborhood development groups, the city's main emphasis has been to encourage private development, primarily in the downtown area, and to provide all available subsidies—local, state, and federal. Private developers have largely determined land use decisions.

Specific project development efforts now being made delineate the outlines of Cleveland's primary strategy—the redevelopment or maintenance of five areas: downtown, the riverfront and Flats, a commercial-institutional corridor on the East Side, a university-cultural center, and housing and neighborhoods. With the exception of the last areas, virtually all the focus is on areas to the east of the Cuyahoga River.

Downtown is said to be the financial, administrative, and entertainment center of metropolitan Cleveland. The largest share of the city's resources and administrative energies is targeted at this area. New development plans for downtown include office, commercial, and entertainment facilities emphasizing a rehabilitated Playhouse Square, the largest theater restoration project in the United States. Planned facilities also include a commercial-recreational project on the lakefront modeled after Baltimore's Inner Harbor and possible redevelopment of the city-owned stadium and lakefront airport; a new stadium for the Cleveland Indians and a new arena for the basketball Cavaliers; a new Rock 'n Roll Hall of Fame; and Tower City, an expanded office-hotel-retailing center integrated with the area's rapid transit system. New hotels are to be built in the vicinity of the refurbished Convention Center to allow Cleveland to compete aggressively for regional and national convention business. New high-rise market-rate housing is to have high priority in downtown to provide a somewhat permanent population, as well as a market for restaurants and entertainment facilities.

The Flats area along the Cuyahoga River is to be developed as a restaurant-bar-entertainment complex that will take advantage of its proximity to the waterfront. It is to draw its market from downtown and the entire region. The city hopes to develop upper-income housing in the Flats if possible, supplemented by selected redevelopment of commercial and recreational activities compatible with riverfront uses.

The Euclid Corridor, or Dual-Hub Corridor, runs from Public Square in the heart of downtown through Playhouse Square to University Circle, the metropolitan area's center of cultural, university, and medical services. City planning efforts here include the acquisition, clearance, and preparation of sites for new industrial or commercial investment. The Dual-Hub Corridor is proposed as the location of a $700 million to $1 billion light rail transit system that will tie downtown to University Circle.

University Circle, the eastern end of the corridor, is the home of the city's art and history museums, Case Western Reserve University, the Cleveland Orchestra, and several large medical complexes, including the Cleveland Clinic, the city's largest employer. Plans for this area include the addition of new market-rate housing and the expansion of these institutions.

Planning objectives for Cleveland's housing and neighborhoods include housing rehabilitation, new construction where possible, and promotion of neighborhood revitalization throughout the city. The activities of the city's many neighborhood-based, nonprofit housing development corporations are to be assisted by CDBG funds, state funds, and contributions from local and national foundations. Local corporations are also involved in neighborhood-based development by providing financial and staff support for some of the neighborhood corporations.

Overall, in Cleveland as in most large U.S. cities, the driving force shaping the city's investment policies and development plans is a downtown-corporate strategy. The city is to be transformed primarily into a corporate headquarters center, with banking, legal, and professional support services. Although Cleveland is known throughout the world for its heavy industry and manufacture of durable goods, no emphasis is being placed in reindustrialization. Instead, the efforts are being directed toward developing commercial office buildings, hotels, and recreational and retail activities centered in the downtown area. The active participants in developing this blueprint are downtown developers, bankers, corporate executives, the political establishment, the media, and the private foundations.

Financing Public-Private Partnerships: Urban Development Action Grants and Tax Abatements

The key financial mechanism for implementing public-private partnerships in Cleveland during this era was the urban development action grant (UDAG) program until it was terminated by the Reagan administration in 1987. Mayor George Voinovich's status as a leading Republican big-city mayor and his aggressive lobbying efforts enabled Cleveland to enjoy a windfall of UDAG money after the election of Ronald Reagan in 1980. Cleveland's share of the UDAG program far exceeded that of other Ohio cities; in 1985 the city was ranked fourth nationally in grant dollars obtained—behind New York, Detroit, and Baltimore. Between 1981 and 1988, Cleveland was awarded forty UDAGs totalling $103,308,548. According

Table 1
Distribution of UDAG Projects in Cleveland, 1981–1988

Location	Project Type				
	Commercial/ office	*Industrial*	*Housing*	*Health/ institutional*	*Total*
Downtown[a]	16	0	0	1	17
University Circle	2	0	1	1	4
Neighborhoods	6	0	3	3	12
Other areas[b]	0	6	0	1	7
TOTAL	24	6	4	6	40

Source: City of Cleveland, Department of Economic Development.
[a] Includes central business district, Playhouse Square, Warehouse District, and the Flats.
[b] Includes industrial and institutional areas outside of downtown, University Circle, and the city's residential neighborhoods.

to city data, this has made possible "the leveraging of $672.9 million to private investment and allowed Cleveland to retain 3,973 jobs and to create a projected 7,875 jobs," of which only 1,096 had been created through 1988.[10]

Tables 1 and 2 show the distribution of UDAG projects and dollars in Cleveland from 1981 to 1988 by geographic location and project type. The most common UDAG in Cleveland was for downtown commercial-office projects. The sixteen UDAGs in this category have accounted for 70 percent of the program's dollars in Cleveland since 1981. In contrast, only four UDAGs were awarded for housing projects.

The largest and best-known recipient of UDAG money in Cleveland has been the Tower City Center project. First announced in 1974, it includes renovation of the Terminal Tower building (now the second largest downtown structure and the historic centerpiece of Cleveland's Public Square) and redevelopment of the adjoining real estate for construction of a multi-use retail, office, and hotel complex at an announced cost of $279 million. Since 1980, Tower City has been awarded five UDAGs totaling $31.5 million for bridge, street, and public transit repairs; retail development; and conversion of the old central post office facility to commercial and office space. The project also received $54 million in additional subsidies from the Federal Urban Mass Transit Administration, the Ohio Department of Transportation, and the Greater Cleveland Regional Transit Authority. Tower City benefited from state-subsidized improvement of the adjacent Public Square at a cost of $12 million.

The redevelopment of Tower City Center began in 1987 and was completed in 1990. It is expected to be the anchor for the rebuilding of Cleveland's downtown retail market. But Tower City now faces competition from the newly completed

Table 2
Distribution of UDAG Dollars in Cleveland, 1981–1988

Location	*Commercial/office*	*Industrial*	*Housing*	*Health/institutional*
Downtown[a]	$72,221,495	$0	$0	$351,750
University Circle	$1,350,000	$0	$5,500,000	$1,200,000
Neighborhoods	$10,047,493	$0	$4,606,000	$2,276,810
Other areas[b]	$0	$4,300,000	$0	$1,455,000
Total	$83,618,988	$4,300,000	$10,106,000	$5,283,560

Source: City of Cleveland, Department of Economic Development.
[a] Includes central business district, Playhouse Square, Warehouse District, and the Flats.
[b] Includes industrial and institutional areas outside of downtown, University Circle, and the city's residential neighborhoods.

Galleria, a large, modern retail facility built by the Jacobs brothers with the benefit of a $3.5 million UDAG on the old Erieview urban renewal site near the lakefront. Whether the heavily subsidized Tower City can compete and coexist with the Galleria and other proposed new downtown commercial developments remains uncertain because retail square footage in downtown has been falling for decades. By mid-1993, it appeared that retail vacancies were increasing in other parts of downtown.

The Jacobs brothers announced in 1988 the development of two new office towers and two new hotels adjacent to Public Square and the mall, estimated to cost $250 million. They received a $10 million UDAG to assist in restoration of the historic Society Bank building, which is part of the project. The Society Bank project was completed in 1992. The other project was stalled by the overbuilding of the Cleveland office market. It may proceed by 1996. Both Jacobs brothers (together they bought the Cleveland Indians baseball franchise in 1986) were multimillionaires.[11] A son is developing several projects in the Flats, including the powerhouse restoration project, which received a $4 million UDAG in 1988. The Tower City grants and the Galleria UDAG indicate that subsidizing upscale retail development that attracts upper-income suburban consumers to Cleveland's downtown continues to be the linchpin of the city's public-private partnership development strategy.

The Voinovich administration was considerably less aggressive in initiating public-private partnerships that used UDAGs for low- and moderate-income housing projects sponsored by CDCs. Only two UDAGs, both used for the Lexington Village housing project, were obtained for this purpose. Lexington Village was developed in 1985–87 on twelve acres of land in Hough (a low-income black neighborhood that had been devastated by riots in the late 1960s) by the Famicos Foundation, a local nonprofit housing rehabilitation organization, and by McCormack, Baron and Associates, a private developer. Phase I, a $13.7 million project financed with a $2.6 million UDAG, $3.5 million of city subsidies, and $3 million of foundation money, resulted in construction of 183 low- and moderate-income town-house apartments, all of which have been leased. Phase II is a $7.1 million project with a $1.4 million UDAG that added 94 housing units to the existing development in 1990. Tower City's $86 million in direct subsidies dwarfs the $10 million committed to Lexington Village.

The city has used UDAG repayments to capitalize a small-business revolving loan fund, which as of August 1987 had awarded eight loans totaling $626,000 and committed an additional $1.1 million for thirteen more loans. This fund has also been used to help small businesses relocate away from the site of the new stadium and arena. Unlike other cities, however, Cleveland did not use UDAG repayments to fund housing rehabilitation programs operated by CDCs.[12]

Tax abatements for residential development projects were revived by the Voinovich administration in 1986 and have been continued and broadened by his successor, Mayor Michael White. Tax abatements had been abandoned as a development incentive policy during the late 1970s, after public outcry over the tax breaks granted to several downtown development projects helped elect Dennis Kucinich as mayor on an antiabatement platform. The revival of tax abatements in the mid-1980s occasioned little controversy.

Most of the abatements granted were for market-rate projects such as the Euclid–Mayfield Triangle apartments in University Circle and the new residential development in the Warehouse District bordering downtown. The White administration has also begun to use tax abatements to support low- and moderate-income housing in the neighborhoods, as well as market-rate housing development.

In April 1991 the city passed legislation without debate, declaring all of Cleveland, except downtown, a Community Reinvestment Area in which full tax abatement is allowed for up to fifteen years on residential construction and conversion. A council subcommittee worked on legislation to exempt commercial development as well. Tax abatements can also be granted in all of Cleveland's industrial areas. Here new investments are eligible for a tangible personal property abatement for ten years. Tangible personal property includes machinery, equipment, leasehold improvements, and inventory.

In 1986 the LTV Steel Corporation received the first abatement granted under this program for a $37 million investment in its hot and cold strip mill. The city's abatement applies to $19 million of this investment because half of the mill is located in adjoining Cuyahoga Heights. The value of this abatement is estimated at $3.6 million over ten years.

In March 1988, the Jacobs brothers and Forest City Enterprises both asked for 100 percent twenty-year tax abatements worth an estimated $225 million, in addition to the UDAGs received, to further subsidize the building of the downtown projects discussed earlier. The city supported their requests and thus provoked a public debate over the necessity for this subsidy, the absence of conditions limiting the abatements, and the substantial loss of revenue to Cleveland's beleaguered public schools, which would give up 60 percent of the foregone restrictions (later renounced). The city rejected any linkage between these tax abatements and requests that the developers invest in neighborhood projects. The current stated policy is to disallow tax abatements for downtown projects unless they include a hotel. But the city granted tax abatements to the new stadium, arena, and Rock 'n Roll Hall of Fame. This position, in 1991, was being challenged by the Cleveland Board of Education, which will be the major governmental loser from these tax abatements.

Although it has provided financial incentives such as UDAGs, tax abatements, industrial revenue bonds, and tax increment financing, the city has largely left development planning to the private sector. Individual and corporate developers such as Forest City Enterprises, the Jacobs brothers, civic groups such as the Playhouse Square Foundation, the stadium and arena committee, and the North Coast Development Corporation have controlled downtown development planning. In 1988, Cleveland Tomorrow proposed the creation of a citywide development corporation to promote large-scale development projects everywhere in the city. This development corporation had not yet emerged in 1993.

Community Development Corporations: Cleveland's Junior Partners

The CDCs play a secondary role in the city's development strategy. Unlike their private sector counterparts, they are heavily dependent on subsidies for both their operations and their projects. Because of general cutbacks in the federal community development block grant program, the level of city support for CDCs is a critical issue.

Table 3 reveals the decline of Cleveland's total CDBG allocation since 1981 (except for 1991–92) and the low proportion of funding for nonprofit housing. The city's CDBG allocation decreased 35 percent between Years VII (1981–82) and XIII (1987–88). Although the number of nonprofit housing groups funded by the CDBG grew from five to eighteen in that period, their portion of the total CDBG dollar pie shrank by $1 million in these years. In 1987, the city used CDBG money to create a new program, the Neighborhood Development Impact Grant, which in two funding rounds targeted $1.3 million for real estate development and commercial improvement projects sponsored by nonprofit CDCs. In 1989, the city funded the Home Ownership Made Easy program for middle-class buyers. It also has supported numerous CDCs involved in commercial development. In 1991–92, Cleveland's CDBG allocation went up, but the number of nonprofits had risen to twenty-four and the percentage of CDBG funds allocated for their use was under 4 percent.

When neighborhood interests were concerned, the private philanthropic foundations took the lead in providing financial assistance. Cleveland Tomorrow also began to express interest in neighborhood redevelopment. In 1987 it helped create Neighborhood Progress, Inc., which now administers most of the funding for

Table 3
CDBG Allocation and Nonprofit Housing Groups in Cleveland, 1981–1988

CDBG	*Year*	*Total CDBG allocation*	*No. of nonprofit housing groups funded*	*Amount of nonprofit housing funding*	*Nonprofit housing as % of CDBG*
VII	1981–82	$37,626,000	5	$1,711,000	4.5
VII	1982–83	$33,116,084	12	$2,013,000	6.1
IX	1983–84	$31,403,000	12	$1,800,000	5.7
X	1984–85	$29,139,000	11	$1,225,000	4.2
XI	1985–86	$28,816,000	15	$1,250,000	4.3
XII	1986–87	$24,471,000	14	$ 914,500	3.7
XIII	1987–88	$24,569,000	18	$1,005,500	4.1

Source: City of Cleveland, Department of Community Development.

Cleveland's CDCs. Foundation financial support contributed to the survival and expansion of the network of CDCs in Cleveland and the growth of citywide umbrella organizations like the Cleveland Housing Network. In 1979, the foundations financed creation of the Center for Neighborhood Development at Cleveland State University. The city, of course, also contributed key financial support in the form of CDBG allocations to the CDCs and their projects. Allied and individual CDCs sought the support of both.

In general, the CDCs developed their own priorities and projects. The projects were almost all devoted to low- and moderate-income rehabilitated housing. With the emergence of NPI as the key local intermediary, emphasis shifted toward new housing to be sold to families with higher incomes. The funders are influencing the direction of neighborhood development to the extent that they make their funding priorities known through NPI. Mayor White has also placed emphasis on his goal of the annual construction of a thousand new homes, rather than on rehabilitated units. Until 1987, the funders were not asked to fund large-scale neighborhood projects. The exception was Lexington Village in Hough. Investment in this project pales, however, in comparison with the investment being made in the development downtown and around the Cleveland Clinic and University Circle. For the most part, CDCs were involved only in small development projects; therefore, most CDCs remained small in their budget, staff, and project development.

With fewer subsidies available to attract private developers to inner-city rehabilitation and the city's public housing agency beset by problems, CDCs have emerged as important actors in low-and moderate-income housing and commercial development. Nonprofit CDCs have influenced the housing situation in several ways. First, nonprofit developers have weatherized and rehabilitated thousands of housing units for low- and moderate-income persons. As of July 1991, the Cleveland Housing Network and its member groups had rehabilitated 700 units of low-income housing under a lease-purchase program in which vacant homes are acquired and rehabilitated at low cost and subsequently leased, with an option to purchase, to low-income families. Another 175 units (some for low-income families) were underway in 1991. Three CDCs in Cleveland are producing an average of 25 renovated homes per year in the conventional market. In addition, four CDCs have renovated 165 units of multifamily rental housing in seven buildings scattered across the city.

Second, nonprofit CDCs have generated additional public and private housing investment. Through 1990, the Cleveland Housing Network had invested $6.5 million of government money and $5.6 million of bank and foundation funds in its housing rehabilitation projects. The CDCs have used CDBG funds in rehabilitation programs that leverage seven to ten dollars in private funds for every CDBG dollar.

Third, nonprofit developers have influenced the creation of innovative public policies for solution of specific housing problems. In response to a growing arson rate, three housing advocacy groups formed the Cleveland Anti-Arson Coalition in 1981. The coalition worked with city officials and Cleveland State University to develop an Arson Early Warning System that contributed to lower arson rates in the neighborhoods. The Union-Miles Development Corporation worked with the Center for Neighborhood Development to develop new state receivership enabling legislation that was passed in 1984 as a remedy to the problem of vacant abandoned property.

Finally, nonprofit CDCs have worked with banks, foundations, and state and local government to leverage resources and create new public and private institutions that support low- and moderate-income housing development. For example, the New York–based Local Initiatives Support Corporation has matched the contributions of Cleveland corporations and foundations to create a $3.1 million neighborhood development loan and grant fund, of which $2.4 million has been invested in more than forty Cleveland community development projects since 1981. The Enterprise Foundation, likewise, has created a $2.1 million loan and grant fund and has given $250,000 in technical assistance for CDCs providing low- and moderate-income housing. The CDCs have worked closely with the Ameritrust Development Bank to finance housing and commercial development projects. The CDCs have also worked with the Ohio Department of Development and the Ohio Housing Finance Agency to create state-funded programs that support low- and moderate-income community development. They led the successful 1990 fight for a change in the Ohio constitution to allow the state and the city to provide additional financial assistance to lower-income housing developments.

The Politics of Revitalization

Economic and racial divisions have pervaded Cleveland's postwar politics. Carl Stokes, the first black mayor of a major U.S. city, was elected in 1967 in the wake of the 1966 Hough race riot. When a conservative Republican mayor succeeded Stokes, community activism had not yet peaked. During the 1970s there was a surge of neighborhood organizing in Cleveland, aided by the Commission on Catholic Community Action and focusing on such issues as redlining, disinvestment, and tax abatements. This movement and the political organizing of the Ohio Public Interest Campaign in turn provided the basis for the 1977 victory of Dennis Kucinich, campaigning on a populist platform.[13] The turbulence associated with Kucinich's brief reign as mayor, his adamant opposition to tax abatements for corporate developers, and his support for the municipal power company eventually united corporate and business opposition and led to his defeat in 1979 (he had narrowly survived a 1978 recall election) and the election of conservative Republican Voinovich. Voinovich served until 1989 and was succeeded by black Democrat Michael White. White was elected on a pro-neighborhood platform but has continued to place primary emphasis on downtown projects, while broadening the granting of tax inducements.

Cleveland's power structure, unlike those of some other major U.S. cities, has not always presented a united front on development issues. In recent years, there was considerable disagreement over whether a proposed new stadium and a Rock 'n Roll Hall of Fame should be sited on the lakefront, where other competing development had been planned, or elsewhere in the downtown area. A proposal to finance a domed stadium out of property taxes was defeated in 1984. Another proposal to build an open stadium for the Indians and an arena for the Cavaliers was successful in 1990. A similar rift has occurred over whether the city's lakefront airport should be replaced by housing and commercial development. The mayor and City Council, civic and business interests, and the *Cleveland Plain Dealer*, the city's only major newspaper, have long bemoaned the lack of downtown hotel space sufficient to attract convention and tourist business. But they have been unable to attract developers. In fact, when a powerful Democrat leader and hotel owner did not receive city support for a tunnel to connect the renovated, city-owned convention center with one of his downtown hotels, he threatened to withdraw from the city's convention bureau and to sell his hotels as sites for future office development. He carried out his threat in 1985. Thus, in some circumstances when there have been competing economic interests and conflicting views among the local civic elite and developers, it has proved difficult to develop a consensus and put together a public-private partnership that can efficiently accomplish downtown development goals.

By the early 1990s, there was relatively little active community organizing in Cleveland. Only a few community organizations were left that had a broad membership base. Consequently, the CDCs, many of which had been created by parent community advocacy organizations, had emerged as the major vehicle representing neighborhood interest in Cleveland's redevelopment process. Funding was not available for community organizing or organizers; it was available for development. The Commission on Catholic Community Action, which played a critical role in galvanizing Cleveland's neighborhoods in the 1970s, no longer acted as a catalyst for community organizing.

In the 1970s, the neighborhood groups did not involve themselves in partisan politics, as evidenced by their refusal to back Dennis Kucinich against those campaigning for his recall in 1978, despite his administration's support of neighborhood development. The CDCs remained politically quiescent during the 1980s. Dependent on the largess of the city in awarding CDBG funds as well as on private foundations and, to a lesser extent, on corporate investments, CDCs could not easily afford to antagonize their funders by taking contrary positions on controversial public issues.

In the 1989 general election, however, some important CDC leaders backed liberal candidate Michael White over his opponent, entrenched City Council president and power broker George Forbes. After White's upset victory, Christopher Warren, a longtime neighborhood advocate and former director of a neighborhood CDC and the Cleveland Housing Network, became director of the city's Community Development Department. To a limited extent, Cleveland had joined such cities as Boston, Chicago, and San Francisco where neighborhood groups backed and helped elect progressive reform candidates for mayor.[14]

White's election did not result in a turn to the left or to an increase in neighborhood clout. Although his predecessor, George Voinovich, was a conservative Republican, White retained many of his officials and policies. Mayor White has not attempted to rally a neighborhood constituency in support of citywide issues. He has been in the forefront of such downtown projects as the new tax-supported baseball stadium, basketball arena, and Rock 'n Roll Hall of Fame. His highest priority for transit improvement is not improved mobility for Cleveland's transit-dependent population but the proposed Dual Hub transit line, which would offer them little improved service.

Nor has Cleveland attempted to implement a downtown neighborhood linkage policy such as emerged in Boston, Chicago, and San Francisco.[15] Instead, unconditional tax inducements are being granted for virtually all new development. There was no opposition from the CDCs to the subsidizing of market-rate and luxury housing. Rather, as junior partners in development, the CDCs sought tax abatements for their own projects as well. The opposition to tax abatement for downtown commercial development in 1988 did not involve the CDCs. Nor have they pressed for a larger share of city revenues.

The CDCs' lack of clout was reflected in the pattern of awarding of UDAGs. Under Mayor Voinovich, Cleveland did very well. Most UDAG recipients were commercial and industrial and were located in the central business district. The only major neighborhood UDAG was the Lexington Village project. Unlike many other cities, Cleveland made no special provision for seeking and supporting UDAG awards to neighborhood groups. CDCs did not press for UDAG payback funds to go into neighborhood investment or housing trust funds. Instead, the city reserved the right to determine the future use of these funds, and they were mostly for small business. Although some neighborhood groups sought UDAG payback funds, their use had not yet become a major public issue.

What neighborhood-based CDCs gained during the Voinovich and White administrations is credibility; they earned respect locally and nationally for their accomplishments. White's Community Development Department has continued CDBG allocations to support CDCs, although the level of support continues to be low. A competent neighborhood activist is now Cleveland's community development director. The Civic Vision planning process has included neighborhoods, and the mayor did select neighborhood representatives to chair and sit on the Steering Committee. This could be viewed as an effort to gain credibility for this process in the neighborhoods; however, it does show that Cleveland's neighborhoods cannot easily be ignored.

Conclusion

All of this support for neighborhoods from the public and private (corporate and philanthropic) sectors suggests that public-private partnerships in Cleveland have been a resounding success. This is not the case, however. First, despite these well-intentioned efforts over a ten-year period (1980–90), the many problems facing Cleveland's poor neighborhoods were not alleviated by public-private partnerships. Poverty, unemployment, crime, substandard housing, racial tension, and physical blight increased and persist in too many of the city's neighborhoods. This is in part simply a reflection of the reduction of federal urban aid by the Reagan and Bush administrations, the inability of a state government with limited resources to make up for this loss of federal aid, and the unwillingness of Cleveland's more affluent suburban neighbors to share their tax base with an impoverished city.

Second, although these factors have been important constraints, it is also true that only a fraction of available public and private resources has been directed to neighborhood development. Much more investment, both public and private, went into downtown development than has gone into neighborhood reinvestment.

Third, and perhaps most important, this allocation choice reflects the lack of political power of the CDCs. They have received as much as has been deemed possible by Cleveland's power structure. No one suggests that this is adequate to deal with neighborhood problems, but it does reflect the primary emphasis on downtown development. Cleveland is a typical example of the creation of public-private partnerships whose main focus is downtown development—an indication of the continued dominance of the trickle-down theory of economic development. Although Cleveland's revitalization does not approach that of many other cities, there is little evidence to suggest that trickle down will have any more effect in Cleveland's poor neighborhoods than in those of other cities. A much more progressive public interventionist policy to promote redistribution programs at the municipal level would be required to extend the benefits of central business district growth more equitably to Cleveland's poor and working-class neighborhoods. Redistributionist policies could include such policies as conditioning public subsidies on the creation of jobs for poorer city residents; encouraging more neighborhood-based projects and using UDAG paybacks from major downtown projects to support neighborhood development; maintaining emphasis on low- and moderate-income housing rather than higher-priced, less affordable housing; implementing a city-linked deposit policy (adopted in 1988) to generate more lender investment in neighborhood projects; and requiring concessions from private developers benefiting from public subsidies like tax abatements downtown to assist neighborhood development or guarantee jobs for city residents.

This redistribution can happen only under a different leadership representing low- and moderate-income neighborhood interests—one that is better able to implement programs to deal with the issues raised under Kucinich that his brief administration could not effectively translate into viable policies. Kucinich's inability to heal racial divisions and his antagonization of his neighborhood constituency appear to have set back the development of a progressive neighborhood-based political movement in Cleveland.

If CDCs are to make a more noticeable impact on urban revitalization, all levels of government and the private sector will have to commit much greater resources than they have in the past. Cleveland's limited commitment to CDCs does not differ from the commitment made by other cities. In addition to a more equitable policy at the local level, there must be greatly increased federal support for neighborhood-based housing and economic development programs if urban problems are to be addressed seriously.

Notes

1. "Fatter City: Cleveland Makes a Comeback," *Time,* December 29, 1980, pp. 116–17; E. H. Methvin, "Cleveland Comes Back," *Reader's Digest,* March 1983, pp. 109–13.

2. Todd Swanstrom, *The Crisis of Growth Politics* (Philadelphia: Temple University Press, 1985).

3. Thomas Bier, "Population and Housing Projections," Report to the Cleveland Planning Commission, Civic Vision Program, 1987; Cambridge Systematics, Inc., "City of Cleveland Retail Market Study," Report to the Cleveland Planning Commission, Civic Vision Program, 1987; Michael Fogarty, "Cleveland: Economic Analysis and Projections," Report to the Cleveland Planning Commission, Civic Vision Program, 1987.

4. *Poverty Indicators and Trends, 1980–1987: Cuyahoga County* (Cleveland: Council for Economic Opportunities in Greater Cleveland, 1987).

5. *Cleveland Plain Dealer,* May 19, 1991.

6. *The Cleveland Foundation and the Disadvantaged: Top-Down Solutions for the Toughest Problems* (Washington, D.C.: National Committee for Responsive Philanthropy, 1991).

7. Norman Krumholz, Janice Cogger, and John Linner, "The Cleveland Policy Planning Report," *Journal of the American Institute of Planners* 41, no. 5 (September 1975): 298–319.

8. "Cleveland Takes on Everything," *Planning* 54, no. 5 (May 1988): 2–6.

9. W. Dennis Keating and Norman Krumholz, "Downtown Plans of the 1980s: The Case for More Equity in the 1990s," *Journal of the American Planning Association* 57 (1991): 136–52.

10. Unpublished data, City of Cleveland, Department of Economic Development, 1988.

11. "The 400 Richest People in America," *Forbes*, October 1987, pp. 142–347.

12. Unpublished data, City of Cleveland, Department of Economic Development, 1988.

13. Todd Swanstrom, *Crisis of Growth Politics;* Pierre Clavel, *The Progressive City* (New Brunswick, N.J.: Rutgers University Press, 1986).

14. Chester Hartman, *The Transformation of San Francisco* (Totowa, N.J.: Rowman and Allanheld, 1984); Gregory D. Squires, Larry Bennett, Kathleen McCourt, and Phillip Nyden, *Chicago: Race, Class, and the Response to Urban Decline* (Philadelphia: Temple University Press, 1987).

15. W. Dennis Keating, "Linking Downtown Development to Broader Community Goals: An Analysis of Linkage Policies in Three Cities," *Journal of the American Planning Association* 52 (1986): 133–41.

Housing: New Lessons, New Models

Christopher Warren

I RECALL A meeting that took place in the winter of 1978 at Merrick House, a community center in the near West Side Tremont area of Cleveland. Six residents had gathered around a table to discuss what could be done about abandoned homes and arson in their neighborhood. Wilma, seventy-eight years old and a longtime resident of the community, was the first to bring it up: "Why don't we just buy that bombed-out house on Starkweather before the city tears it down?" Jack, another member, countered by throwing two dollars on the table and asking, "OK, how much more do we need?"

Two years later, this group, Tremont West Development Corporation (TWDC), had raised $25,000 from small grants, pancake breakfasts, and aluminum can recycling. This money saved the home on Starkweather. In the years since, ten other nonprofit neighborhood-based groups have joined the TWDC. Together they constitute the Cleveland Housing Network (CHN). The CHN has saved more than six hundred homes like the one on Starkweather and by 1990 was prepared to rehabilitate and develop over one hundred additional homes every year. The idea initiated by Wilma and Jack has become a forceful program for change in housing policy in Cleveland.

I have been part of this process since the earliest days in Tremont, and it is from the vantage point of my experience in the process that I would like to discuss the growth and development of CHN as a model for community housing policy. More particularly, I will discuss, challenge, criticize, and, in the process, attempt to shed some light on the role of nonprofit community-based organizations doing housing development in the older, low-income neighborhoods of Cleveland.

My Role as a Community Organizer

For almost my entire professional life, I have been a community organizer. I certainly did not start out to be, nor do I consider myself now, a professional housing policy specialist. During the 1970s, I worked with several groups—the Welfare Rights Organization, the *Plain Press* (a community newspaper), and the TWDC—all organizations working for change at the neighborhood level. But for all our work, the condition of housing in Cleveland continued its decline and the need for better-quality housing remained unabated as well. Our inability to get these needs met directly through community organizing finally led us, as the story of Wilma and Jack suggests, to become developers ourselves—or developers of last resort. As a result, by 1980 I had ceased being a community organizer, and I had become the director of TWDC, a small, nonprofit producer of rehabilitated housing.

I have learned since that my career path is similar to those of many others in this field, in Cleveland and across the country. Upon reflection, this should not be surprising because there was no place that formally trained people to do community-based nonprofit development. Housing development had always been either pure real estate and marketing or public housing. Those of us new to this area in the late 1970s almost all came from an organizing background. Because my experience is more the rule than the exception, it may be evidence of how people react to possibilities for change in cities generally resistant to change.

CHN: Developer of Last Resort

We faced at every turn (and continue to confront) conflicting demands, goals, and interests. These might be more aptly termed the "rules of the game" in the everyday political world of housing development. Simply put, they are the following: the physical and human demands of development are compromised by the drive for political power; the immediate and compelling needs of low-income people clash with the broader, diverse interests of the full community; and the interests and resources of much-needed private investment in development conflicts with the absolute need for public support.

I introduce these conflict-filled rules because every undertaking of the CHN has involved a reconciliation of these competing demands within a real world of finite resources, mixed loyalties, and hard economic conditions. The community development process is mediated by the broader citywide conditions of political power, competing community needs, and private profit.

The Famicos Model

In 1950, the Hough neighborhood was home to a population of generally middle-class whites. Ten years later, in a shattering model of residential turnover driven by racial fears, Hough had become a black, lower-class slum. In July 1966, the Hough riots erupted leaving four dead, thirty injured, and over 250 fires in its wake. One census tract, shown below, shows the dynamic racial change from 1950 to 1960.

Hough Census Tract 1124

	1950	*1960*
Total units	3,014	2,921
Vacancy rate	2.6	6.0
Median contract rent (as percent of county median)	98	107
Percent overcrowded	11.1	32.7
Population	9,157	11,785
Percent black	1.6	91.3
Median income of families and unrelated individuals (1957–59 constant dollars)	3,781	3,652
As percent of county median income	90.4	61.9

Source: U.S. Census, 1960, 1970

Responding to this crisis, in 1967, a Roman Catholic nun named Sister Henrietta of the Sisters of Charity moved to Hough to help residents with their basic needs in the face of extreme poverty and deprivation. Three years later, she organized the Famicos Foundation, a nonprofit, community-based housing group to provide decent, affordable housing for low-income families. Sister Henrietta was joined by many volunteers, including Bob Wolf, a retired corporate executive who has been president and chief fund-raiser for Famicos for many years. During the early 1970s, Wolf and others evolved the Famicos model, a low-cost, no frills approach to homeownership for the poor.

The Famicos model was a lease-purchase program containing the following elements:

1. Vacant, abandoned, and often condemned homes were purchased by a nonprofit organization at the lowest price possible.
2. The nonprofit organization employed for-profit contractors and volunteers, including the lease-purchaser, to repair the home to code standards.
3. The nonprofit organization borrowed low-interest, fifteen-year funds from public or private sources to pay for the acquisition and rehabilitation.
4. Once rehabilitated, the home was rented to a low-income household for an amount sufficient for the nonprofit to amortize its debt over fifteen years and pay for normal operating expenses (taxes, insurance, maintenance).
5. The rent was applied to the debt and the renter was granted an option to purchase the property for the principal balance of the debt. The option was exercisable as early as the fifth year and as late as the fifteenth year.
6. During the lease term, the nonprofit organization helped the lease-purchaser acquire the skills necessary to manage the rigors of homeownership.

From 1970 to 1977, Famicos bought approximately eighty vacant homes in the Hough and St. Clair–Superior neighborhoods on Cleveland's East Side. It rehabilitated and sold those homes on a lease-purchase basis to families with annual incomes of $11,000 or less. Disciplined family selection, home repair training for families, and rehabilitation that emphasized safety and durability were the hallmarks of the Famicos approach.

During the late 1970s, Famicos's success attracted the attention of five nonprofit community-based organizations, similar to TWDC, that had mobilized residents to fight against housing abandonment, arson, and disinvestment. Famicos Foundation provided these groups with financial and technical help to start the lease-purchase program in their own neighborhoods. In addition to TWDC, groups in the St. Clair–Superior, Glenville, Broadway, and Near West Side neighborhoods undertook rehabilitation of single-family houses for the first time.

I can vouch for the appeal the Famicos model had for neighborhood organizations desperate to do something positive about abandoned and dangerous properties. In 1976, in the Tremont area alone, the city tore down seventy-five single-family homes. One especially unscrupulous slumlord had been convicted for intentionally setting fires to dozens of properties he owned and collecting lucrative insurance proceeds. Vacant, abandoned homes became a symbol of all that was wrong in depressed neighborhoods. Few issues attracted as much concern or caused such terror. Those living near an abandoned building worried about blighting influences on property values and insurance premiums, and almost everyone experienced a morbid sense of loss the day the bulldozers arrived.

Most appalling was the fact that the city of Cleveland was spending millions of dollars to tear down structurally sound, highly livable housing. This housing, through the lease-purchase contracts, could be made affordable for people living nearby who were paying more than half their income for incredibly inadequate housing.

Neighborhood Response: The Network

In Cleveland neighborhoods, the abandoned home became Public Enemy No. 1, and community organizations responded aggressively. Special arson investigations were demanded from the city and federal law enforcement agencies. Residents established volunteer house watch systems and pressured building inspectors to get tough with slumlords. Local lenders, through the Community Reinvestment Act, were challenged to make mortgage financing available for responsible buyers. Demands for a "housing court," specializing in abating code violations and encouraging rehabilitation, drew many organizations together in a legislative campaign.

Unfortunately, these victories only touched the surface. The slumlords may have had to pay a fine or—in rare cases—go to jail, but the vacant houses remained vacant. Use of the Community Reinvestment Act enacted some concessionary lending from banks, but few borrowers lined up for the benefits.

The Famicos model offered some hope: it gave neighborhood groups a definite, practical, and tangible solution to a problem. The model offered a way to take control of wasted real estate and meet the needs of residents. As Wilma had suggested, "Why don't we just buy the house?"

The lease-purchase arrangement was a good tool for meeting the housing needs of low-income families. Then, as today, most low-income housing was rented on a month-to-month basis. Written leases were unheard of. The Famicos model not only provided safe, secure, and affordable single-family housing, but it also gave tenants long-term guarantees and a financial stake in their residence.

In 1981 the five neighborhood organizations and Famicos formalized their working relationships by creating the Cleveland Housing Network. The network represented the convergence of three goals: the production of reasonable homeownership opportunities for poor families, the preservation of the current housing stock, and, therefore, the stabilization of neighborhoods. What was started by Famicos as essentially a philanthropic effort in Hough was transformed into a multi-neighborhood redevelopment coalition. The three purposes of CHN were reflected in its mission statement: "CHN is organized to stabilize neighborhoods by saving existing housing and creating affordable home ownership opportunities and to promote neighborhood controlled development."

Network Structure and Operations

As an association of six autonomous organizations, CHN's role was to pool and share financial, construction, and management resources for the lease-purchase and other programs. Rather than competing for the same resources, the six organizations believed that CHN, representing their mutual interests, could capture enough public and private funds for the common program. In addition, the network centralized development and financial functions, creating economies of scale that benefited all groups.

The history of shared experience among the neighborhood groups and Famicos made possible a well-understood division of labor between CHN and its member groups. CHN was responsible for raising both working and permanent capital, providing construction supervision, handling legal and financial transactions, coordinating property management, and soliciting core operating support for member groups. The member groups retained the responsibility for property selection, rehabilitation design, contractor bidding, volunteer labor, lease-purchaser selection, and the day-to-day management of the properties.

Direct control of CHN by the member groups was ensured by a board of trustees composed of a representative from each of the groups and five independent trustees elected by the group representatives.

Capital support for the program first came from low-interest, city of Cleveland community development block grant (CDBG) loans. In 1981, the city lent CHN $400,000 on the following terms:

1. CHN would use the funds to acquire and restore single-family homes.
2. The funds would not be secured by a mortgage.
3. Repayment of the loan would be made from the time the property was occupied, at an interest rate of 5 percent, amortized over fifteen years.
4. Repayment of the funds would be made to a revolving account managed by CHN and used for future investment in CHN housing.
5. The city would retain the right to recover its principal at the end of fifteen years, to the extent funds existed in the revolving account.

The city's assistance amounted to a capital grant for the lease-purchase program. With acquisition plus rehabilitation costs averaging $18,000 per house, the city's low-cost, soft loan was essential for CHN to maintain rents at levels affordable to low-income families (between $100 and $225 a month).

CHN relied extensively on CDBG funds until 1985. Annual allocations enabled CHN to rehabilitate over 150 homes. CHN also used its citywide coverage to negotiate and administer a city-funded weatherization program. About 3,000 homes in many Cleveland neighborhoods were weatherized by CHN member groups from 1981 through 1985.

New Partners

As CHN's capacity to produce new housing grew—three new neighborhood organizations joined the network by 1985—the availability of CDBG funds dropped sharply because of federal cutbacks. To meet the challenge of producing more low-income lease-purchase housing with less public resource, CHN turned to the Enterprise Foundation to find new sources of low-cost capital.

The Enterprise Foundation is the brainchild of James W. Rouse, the multimillionaire real estate developer who developed Baltimore's Inner Harbor and other festival markets in many cities. After stepping down as chief executive officer of the Rouse Company in 1979, Rouse established the Enterprise Foundation to focus on the housing needs of the very poorest families. In 1986, this national intermediary foundation came to Cleveland to provide loans, grants, and technical assistance to neighborhood-based nonprofit agencies. It works very closely with the Cleveland Housing Network.

A new financing model called the Cleveland Housing Partnership (CHP) was created. The partnership was an outgrowth of work between CHN and the Enterprise Foundation to make up for the shortfall in CDBG funds by using tax credits for low-income housing investment under the federal tax code. With Enterprise,

BP America, and Cleveland Tomorrow leading the way, a multimillion-dollar equity fund was established to invest in low-income housing provided by CHN. After the syndicated tax credits are exhausted in fifteen years, the partnership will sell the individual housing units to tenant families.

The CHP model has three components. First, the CHN lease-purchase program was adapted to provide access to corporate investments through equity syndication. Working with BP America and Cleveland Tomorrow, it obtained an initial equity commitment of $2.1 million from Cleveland corporations. CHN learned how to provide corporate investors with a competitive rate of return in the form of federal income tax benefits—no small task for a scattered-site development program. Second, below–market-rate mortgage loans were secured from commercial lenders by using low-cost, linked deposits solicited from benevolent organizations. Third, the city of Cleveland provided rental rehabilitation and weatherization funds to supplement diminished CDBG support.

The two new players in the partnership were charter members in Cleveland's corporate community. BP America was formerly Standard Oil of Ohio (SOHIO). Its national headquarters is in Cleveland, where it has become one of the major funders of nonprofit housing activities. Cleveland Tomorrow is an organization made up of fifty CEOs of the largest corporations in the Cleveland area. It provides funding and direction for projects it considers high priority, including neighborhood development.

The CHP financing mechanism enabled CHN to fund restoration of 284 homes for lease-purchasers from 1986 through 1989. Therefore, in just eight years almost 500 homes had been restored and returned to a permanent place in the city's housing stock. Although the three goals of the CHN were not fully met, it was clear that Cleveland had at last arrived at a process that was beginning to bring restored housing, ownership, and stability to distressed neighborhoods of the city.

In 1988, the success of the CHP program led to the formation of a two-tiered equity investment fund called the Cleveland Housing Partnership Equity Fund. Through the fund, Cleveland corporations have committed $4 million a year to be invested in low-income housing development by CHN and other Cleveland developers.

This equity infusion has helped CHN to meet additional goals. The equity investments were sufficient for CHN to recover a portion of its operating expenses in the form of development fees, thus reducing its reliance on short-term operating grants. The corporate investors made a reasonable return on their equity, thus creating a positive incentive to reinvest their earnings in subsequent projects. The success of the program spawned new government housing initiatives. Three new state funding programs have been created to encourage nonprofit housing development similar to CHN's program.

The partnership approach, with its ability to attract previously inaccessible sources of capital, has been used by various CHN member groups to acquire, rehabilitate, and manage multifamily rental properties. In 1988 and 1989, 170 multifamily units in eight buildings were rehabilitated through three partnerships of this kind. The addition of apartment buildings to the nonprofit development agenda sharply raised the production of affordable housing units. Diversification has had its costs, however, as the nonprofits struggle to learn the intricacies of commercial real estate financing and adjust to the role of landlord, a decidedly foreign station in life for Cleveland community organizations.

Although the scattered-site lease-purchase and multi-unit rental housing developments have been successful, the tax syndicate financing process used to develop them is extremely complicated. An example is the complexities faced by a fifty-three-property, eighty-unit development completed in 1989. A limited partnership called Cleveland Housing Network Limited Partnership VI (CHNLP VI) was formed. The CHNLP VI owns the properties and syndicated tax benefits for investors. As a subsidiary of CHN, Network Restoration, Inc. (NRI), became the managing general partner with a 1 percent interest in CHNLP VI. As managing general partner, NRI has sole responsibility for the day-to-day operations of CHNLP VI. A for-profit subsidiary of the Enterprise Social Investment Corporation, the Enterprise Community Housing Organization (ECHO), serves as a special limited partner, with a 0.01 percent interest in CHNLP VI. ECHO's responsibilities are to advise the general partner on the payment of any partnership expenditures; to select a successor general partner in the event of the removal of the general partner; and to approve accountants and counsel for the partnership. Cleveland Housing Partnership Equity Fund (CHPEF) is the sole limited partner with a 98.99 percent interest. CHPEF is an investment fund created by twenty-six major Cleveland corporations. The eighty units were acquired and repaired during 1989 by CHN's member organizations. Construction financing was provided by the city of Cleveland and the Enterprise Foundation. The rehabilitated homes are now rented to low-income households (below 60 percent of the area's median income) at rents no more than $180 per month. Most families qualify for and receive Section 8 rent subsidies linked with the project's participation in the city's Rental Rehabilitation Program. The rent subsidies are for five years.

CHNLP VI financed the project in the following ways. The limited partner invested $910,080, with payments staged over a five-year period. An investor note collateralized an equity bridge loan provided by the State Development Loan Program of the Ohio Housing Finance Agency (OHFA). The limited partner's return on investment will be in the form of federal income tax credits. The tax credits are awarded on a competitive basis by the OHFA. The project also received a $350,000 first mortgage from Society National Bank, payable at the rate of 6.5 percent and amortized over fifteen years. The rate was based on the maximum debt service the project could pay and still produce affordable rents for low-income households. Society Bank's commitment required CHN to raise $300,000 in below-market linked deposits from benevolent institutions. The condition was met by deposits from the following sources:

Depositor	*Amount*	*Rate, Term*
Catholic Charities	$75,000	5%, 10 years
Neighborhood Progress, Inc.	$70,000	2%, 10 years
Community Development Finance Fund	$75,000	5%, 10 years
(two deposits)	$70,000	2%, 10 years
St. Paul's Episcopal Church	$10,000	3%, 5 years

Additional debt financing was provided through two loans made by CHN to the partnership. CHN Loan I (from rental rehabilitation funds) was in the amount of $400,000. Those funds were lent at 8 percent, with interest only paid annually and the principal amount due at the end of fifteen years. During Years 1 to 5 (the period Section 8 rent subsidies are in force), 6 percent interest will be paid and 2 percent deferred; in Years 6 to 15, 2 percent interest will be paid and 6 percent deferred. CHN Loan II was in the amount of $419,008. These funds were lent at a rate of 2 percent, interest only paid annually and the principal amount due at the end of fifteen years. Sources were the city of Cleveland's CDBG program and the state of Ohio's Residential Housing/Energy Conservation Program.

Repayment of the principal in Year 15 will enable CHN to acquire the properties for the outstanding debt. Tax benefits to the limited partners will be exhausted at the same time. The project also used weatherization grants totaling $139,000 from the city of Cleveland, through the Home Weatherization Assistance Program.

In sum, financing the project involved one conventional bank loan; five separate linked deposits from four sources; two secondary mortgage loans made by the city to CHN and subsequently to the partnership; one weatherization grant made by the city; and two interim loans, one by the city and one by the Enterprise Foundation. Fourteen applications to eight sources were made, negotiated, and closed to raise $2.2 million for the project.

Despite the complexities, the partnership model has become an ongoing and almost routine approach to low-income housing development in the neighborhoods served by CHN. In 1990 CHN expected to develop an additional 100 to 110 single-family and 50 to 60 multifamily units.

New Issues and Directions

CHN's results have not been achieved without troubling side effects. In fact, our successes have spawned new problems. One of them has been rapid growth. The production of units of housing quadrupled between 1986 and 1989, straining the limited human resources of the CHN. It takes a great deal of time to involve community leaders in decision making, to keep everyone informed about sophisticated financing, and to connect community organizing activities with development strategies. Member organizations with staffs of one or two people cannot fulfill these tasks efficiently and at the same time develop fifteen to twenty new properties and manage an existing portfolio. There are not enough hours in the day, and staff capabilities are consistently overtaxed.[1]

Our successes have also led us in new directions. In 1988, for example, CHN and other nonprofits formed the Housing Development Coalition to channel the energies of nonprofit housing groups into efforts for change in public policies. Assuring that neighborhood interests would be represented in private funding efforts such as Neighborhood Progress, Inc., has been a principal concern of the coalition. The coalition was also an instrumental force in the successful campaign to declare housing a public purpose by amendment to the Ohio constitution—an amendment adopted by Ohio voters in November 1990.

Expansion of the low-income lease-purchase program has caused most groups to reassess their housing goals. We have come to realize that neighborhood stability will not be reached if the sole result of our work is low-income housing. In March 1989 CHN started the Homeward Program to acquire, rehabilitate, and sell single-family homes to qualified home buyers, regardless of income, on a conventional basis. A working capital fund was created by short-term loans and grants from foundations, and set-aside of mortgage revenue bonds were made by the state to assist buyers. Although the Homeward Program has grown slowly—245 houses had been completed by spring 1993—it promises to be an important instrument for neighborhood housing development.

In the same spirit, five groups are planning to build single-family homes for conventional sale. More than one hundred new homes are on the drawing boards of these groups.

The ultimate success of the lease-purchase program hinges on the ability of lessees to become economically self-sufficient. The option to purchase has marginal value to families for whom the basic costs of homeownership are prohibitive. Recognizing this dilemma, CHN started a Family Development Program to help lease-purchasers become employed and maximize their family income. Counselors apply a methodology perfected by the Ohio Center for Family Development. Since the program began in 1989, intensive counseling has helped more than sixty lease-purchasers obtain gainful employment.

Pride in the record of CHN must be tempered by acknowledgment that private investment in low-income housing has not been possible without public funding, and not enough public funding is available to meet neighborhood needs. Private investments in the program rely heavily on several forms of subsidies: tax credits, linked deposits, and substantial government-backed secondary mortgage loans. The Center on Budget and Policy Priorities cited in its 1989 report on the housing crisis in Cleveland that 55 percent of all poor renter households spend at least 70 percent of their income on housing and 86 percent of poor renter households spend at least 30 percent of their income for housing, more than the proportion considered affordable by the federal government. Moreover, the financing model created by the CHN is not easily replicated by other developers. A simple fact remains: the amount of money poor people can afford is not enough to support the cost of decent housing. The success of the CHN must not be permitted to justify further erosion of public support for low-income housing. The CHN approach, which dictates that neighborhood organizations should control neighborhood development, does not replace public funding; it gives it the proper direction.

CHN must build and expand on its experiences. One hundred housing units a year is not a goal, it is a beginning. Low-income families must take part in the economic revival of our city and must share in the rewards of this rebirth. Low-income housing cannot be isolated from thriving communities.

Phillip Clay, Cleveland State University's 1987–88 Albert A. Levin Professor of Urban Studies and Public Service, wrote about the heralded economic growth of cities such as Boston and Atlanta: "Such a trend contributes to the creation of two cities: an 'economic city' of great wealth and growth and a 'residential city' of poverty. . . . In transformed cities, housing becomes less affordable, income differences more extreme, and mobility . . . more difficult."[2]

The Cleveland Housing Network is committed to a future that closes the distances between the haves and the have-nots and transforms decaying neighborhoods into healthy places to live and raise families. CHN's approach, which eschews the monolithic solutions of government in favor of community-devised and controlled programs, offers solid hope for Cleveland neighborhoods.

Notes

1. Keith P. Rasey, W. Dennis Keating, and Philip Star, "Management of Neighborhood Development: Community Development Corporations," in Richard Bingham et al., *Managing Local Government: Public Administration in Practice* (Newbury Park, Calif.: Sage, 1991).

2. Phillip L. Clay, *Transforming Cleveland's Future: Issues and Strategies for a Heartland City* (Cleveland: Levin College of Urban Affairs, Cleveland State University, 1988).

Transforming Cleveland: Housing, Population, Neighborhoods, and the Future

Phillip L. Clay

IN THE 1980s analysts and lay observers perceived major cities like Cleveland to be dying: population decline, deteriorating offices and housing, loss of urban fiscal base, and other problems fueled this perception.[1] A myriad of questions abounded: Should the poor move to the suburbs? Could urban neighborhoods be saved? Should housing be built downtown? And perhaps most ominous, could the city still exist as a major economic unit?

By most accounts these questions were real. Some major firms, including Fortune 500 companies, remained downtown, but many were setting up shop outside the central city, expanding to other cities (and countries), or caught up in the corporate restructuring that made corporate growth and regional economic well-being less correlated. Neighborhood confidence and investment lagged, and institutional disinvestment mounted. Cities like Cleveland became increasingly divided along racial lines. Federal dollars to reverse urban decline proved insufficient or ineffective.

As cities languished, suburban communities held their own or expanded their size and influence. Some took on features of cities, including regional malls, office and industrial parks, conference and sports facilities, and hotels.[2]

The funeral dirges for cities were premature. The decade of the 1980s was a good one for cities. Although they continued to experience familiar problems of earlier years, cities showed increasing resilience and sometimes dynamism. Now, even the most pessimistic national forecasts expect cities to survive, although different and smaller than their pre-1950 versions.[3] This essay explores this transformation as the new urban dynamic. First, I outline urban transformation within a national context and then explore housing and issues of population decline as particular areas for transformation opportunities in Cleveland.

The National Experience

Transformation as used here is the process by which change—led by economic revitalization—reshapes the central city. Transformation is associated with economic reinvestment, a reduced rate of decline in population or households, growth in jobs led by business services, increased retail activity, and new investment in middle-income or luxury housing and residential amenities. A variety of service and infrastructure changes aim at establishing a sense of place and increasing the viability and magnetism of the city as a region's center. The point here is that cities have been transformed: office development, downtown malls, new parks and street design, and new infrastructure have all combined to bring people back as consumers and residents. There has been substantial growth in housing and housing investment, as well as in services and facilities to address middle-class needs. Condominium developments and gentrification are two visible examples of transformation. The traditional and widespread phenomenon of "filtering down" has been joined by "filtering up" and upgrading.[4]

The transformation of the cities has not occurred at the expense of suburban expansion. Suburbs have continued to outpace central cities on all the major indicators—office construction, job growth, and housing development. It has become clear, however, that central cities and suburbs are more interdependent than previously thought.[5] Additional office space in the core increases demand for suburban back office space. Growth of manufacturing and distribution in the suburbs increases the need for business services in the suburbs and for advanced business services that cluster at the city's core.

During the 1980s, transformation was largely a big city phenomenon, occurring in New York, Boston, San Francisco, Washington, Los Angeles, Atlanta, Pittsburgh, and Chicago, among others.[6] Denver, Seattle, and Houston experienced transformation but also suffered sharp setbacks as they adjusted to shifting regional economies.[7]

During most of the 1980s, because of the limited gains in Cleveland transformation was marginal to this group. The recession that started in 1990 demonstrated that the social economies of *all* cities were delicate and that transformation, even in the strong cities, had not produced a recession-proof new structure. In fact, some problems such as declining fiscal bases, racial strife, crime and drugs, and congestion appear intractable. There has been a deeper entrenchment of the urban underclass, whose fortunes seem unrelated to shifts in local trends or national cycles.[8]

Even in "transformed" cities, the urban crisis has not lessened, but class divisions have sharpened substantially. A growing number of people in cities are doing very well. Cities have been able to build upon what the middle class and investors bring to the table. They have been much less successful in helping the poor out of poverty and ending the vestiges of segregation.

Cleveland's Experience during the 1980s: Marginal Transformation

Transformation in Cleveland was dramatic, but it appeared partially to reverse the city's long slide into decline since the 1950s. The city recovered slowly from recession in the 1980s, showing new building and reinvestment in the central city office areas, new development on the long-neglected lakefront and Cuyahoga River, expansion in the theater district, and further expansion of the medical facilities. New downtown retail malls and the entertainment district defied pessimists. The most dramatic shifts, however, were in attitude. Once characterized by low civic esteem and divided purpose, key players in the city appeared committed in the 1980s to forging major private investment and public expenditure decisions.

For all this, there has been no dramatic improvement in the housing and neighborhood development in the city. The suburbs continue to grow and the city continues to lose population, unable to maintain its sagging housing market. The twin challenge of transforming the housing and managing the population loss is the subject of the remainder of this article.

Housing

It is estimated that Cleveland by the year 2005 will have fewer than 420,000 residents, over 60 percent of them black, Hispanic, or other minorities. The number of occupied housing units will have dropped from 218,297 in 1980 to 175,347 at the turn of the century, with a 600 percent increase in vacant units, or 65,286. There is no reason to believe that, if things continue as they are now, Cleveland will experience the modest growth in downtown residential population that other major cities experienced in the 1980s.[9]

The housing market dynamics vary significantly among neighborhoods in Cleveland, between the city and its suburbs, and among suburbs. Some issues in the marketplace and between the market and public policy include the following: maintenance of the existing stock; demand for older central city housing; the future of older suburbs; targets of opportunity for new construction in various markets, including downtown; rehabilitation versus new construction; future of public housing; relationship between economic development and housing; and the role of nonresidential structures in meeting future housing demand. Trends in these areas shape housing's contribution to transformation and are touched on below.

More than any other public policy, the city is a major actor in housing dynamics. The powers of zoning, taxation, building regulation, land use, and land disposition and control or influence on subsidy programs are all important in shaping housing outcomes. The challenge is to shape a city plan that attempts to orchestrate the market.

My discussion of housing policy in Cleveland focuses on two main policy areas: conservation and maintenance of the existing inventory of housing, and strategic roles for new construction. These are bases for transformation in the housing sector that preserves existing viable housing and finds strategic niches for new development.

HOUSING CONSERVATION AND PRESERVATION

In contrast to the 1960s and 1970s, when demolition was more common, housing conservation has become a major emphasis in urban housing policy. Reclaiming older housing is perceived as critical to meeting the nation's housing needs in a cost-effective manner.[10]

In the 1960s and 1970s, Cleveland demolished thousands of units of old housing. Today, vacant lots stand alongside abandoned structures, dramatic evidence of the city's dwindling housing stock. The city must stop the decline, especially in its limited multiunit inventory. But policy makers cannot expect that owners on their own will make investment without some assurance that their initiative will be supported by the market and by public policy.

Residential investment is more complex for investors who hold multifamily properties. Tax reform and the urgency of the bottom line make it necessary to intervene more strategically by offering both "carrots" (access to rehabilitation funds, tenant subsidies, and public commitment to a neighborhood strategy) and "sticks" (code enforcement that is selective and sensitive). When public actions such as these are pursued in the context of a coordinated neighborhood policy that places neighborhood development inside the "envelope" of economic development, the power of policy can be far greater than the uneven and nonstrategic efforts of the past. The Federal Housing Act of 1990 offers some useful incentives and programs for homeownership, rehabilitation, neighborhood development, and planning.

Preservation of public and federally assisted housing is also important. The fate of this housing is largely in the hands of the federal government and the mandates of the 1990 Housing Act. If funding is available, the critical feature in Cleveland will be the capacity of the nonprofit and public sectors to take on the task of preserving these buildings with new capital improvements and management.[11]

New leadership is trying to invigorate public housing in Cleveland and offers the promise that this low-income housing will be preserved and modernized. Because Cleveland has one of the ten largest public housing authorities in the country and projects are concentrated in several parts of the city, the opportunity to restructure and revitalize the public housing operation is an excellent chance to make a major contribution to the visual environment and to the lives of thousands of poor tenants.

The low cost of private housing in Cleveland does not reduce the need for an active housing policy, new production, or even the continuation of deep subsidy. Low cost is often used as an argument that Cleveland needs little support for housing development. Low housing costs are not evidence of a lack of problems but, in a perverse sense, strong evidence that a real problem exists. Low cost may mean that investors have little income with which to maintain existing housing at a reasonable level. The lack of income discourages investment. The lack of investment reduces quality and then demand. The end game begins. Home sellers need appreciating prices to maintain housing, earn a return on their investment, and be able to afford to upgrade to the new or better housing. New market construction cannot be done in the city if the gap between the prices and rents of the plentiful stock of old housing and the rents or prices of unassisted new construction is great.

Finally, if values are stagnant or declining, as they are in most sections of the city, the tax base does not grow in real terms except with higher rates.[12] The result is a paralyzed city housing market in which the major activity is in suburbs or in special parts of the city where location and other features support investment. The goal of local housing strategy has to be to strengthen the housing market (which in practical terms means neighborhoods).

NEW PRODUCTION

Despite stagnant demand in a city and the significant level of building in the suburbs, there are a variety of reasons why, under specific circumstances, new construction can occur in the city. With the passing of the baby boom, there will be less pressure for new housing generally and more accommodation of nonfamily households, including upgraders. This means that adult households are looking for interesting and stimulating environments, including downtown housing. Presently, such housing development is not taking place in Cleveland. It will take a major leap of faith to get such investment going, especially in the wake of regional economic realities.[13] New housing construction will have to find a place in one of the following market niches in a transformed city: (1) low- and moderate-income families in new neighborhoods selected for extensive investment; (2) family and nonfamily housing in new or expanding activity centers such as the medical area or the theater district; (3) luxury housing for executives and professionals in high amenity locations; (4) low-income infill on vacant lots as part of a scattered-site public housing program; (5) housing to promote mixed-income living in the city; and (6) housing for special populations (e.g., the homeless and the elderly).

In all of these instances, the case for new housing would be place-specific, that is, the various housing programs will work in some areas but not in others. In most cases, there needs to be a public subsidy to make the housing affordable to the poor or make its price attractive for the nonpoor.

DEALING WITH SHRINKAGE

As Cleveland's population decreases, a major issue will be how neighborhoods reconfigure when their populations decline. There is no reason to expect that each area in the city will decline at an equal rate. Rates of decline will reflect demographic change, market factors, housing condition, and impacts from unknown events.[14] Cleveland once had more than 914,000 people. The population has declined steadily. By the year 2000, perhaps less than half that number will still be in the city.

If nothing is done to influence the pattern of land use, a destabilizing series of contractions will further weaken the entire housing market in the city. Many residents who can leave will, new buyers will be scarce, and the haphazard pattern of market contraction will drain neighborhood confidence in all but the strongest areas in the city.

Increasingly, buyers of investment properties, when they appear, will be those who deal in "distressed property." The purchase may appear propitious, but the end game will seal the sad fate of the neighborhood.[15]

Very poor renters will be especially hard hit because they are personally not in a position to make a decision in the market other than whether to move in an attempt to cope. They have few choices to escape the city. As in urban renewal, some will make successive moves. In a collapsing market they become pieces on a giant chess board—always just ahead of the health official who condemns the property or just ahead of the bulldozer.

The aim here is not to suggest what pattern of land use, housing, and physical development should be followed to address shrinkage. The information on which to base such a decision is not available. More important, those patterns are part of a decision that should be made in a community planning process that involves each neighborhood in the choices for itself that contribute to a plan for the city. Once made, the plan indicates how housing, infrastructure, land use, and investment decisions can be made so that they provide the greatest number of options for residents to live in enhanced communities in the city. It would outline how neighborhood fragments connect and how residential uses relate to other uses. The plan would also indicate how decisions about choices are made so that shrinkage is transformative, that is, all residents have positive choices about where to live. The environment for investment is reinforced, if not subsidized, by public action. Having fewer people is not accepted as a death sentence but as a challenge to reconfiguring on behalf of those who stay.

No city has ever been explicit about plans for transformative shrinkage. Cleveland would be the first city to articulate such a policy, even though many other cities act (or react) deliberately to reflect a smaller population—a kind of "triage" by default.

The process suggested here—not triage but a process to generate appropriate transformative interventions to help all residents—will be extremely controversial because any serious neighborhood assessment process can only result in good news for some areas (i.e., opportunities and resources for reinvestment) and pain for others (i.e., consolidation of services, demolition rather than rehabilitation, and relocation).

The choice for the city is whether it creates a process that is widely accepted in the communities and involves the residents in making these hard choices, or whether the city and its residents prefer that the "hidden hand" of the market (and those who manipulate it) make the decisions. In a city with a soft housing market, the hidden hand is likely to be clumsy and indelicate, if not perverse.

If a comprehensive plan for addressing shrinkage is developed for the city and each of its communities, it will constitute a firm basis on which to make critical decisions, not just in housing development but in schools and infrastructure, public services, and economic development. Stakeholders in the affected neighborhoods (hospitals, universities, and the like) can be called on and planning can proceed on a new and transformed basis. Residents should never be excluded, but participation need not be limited to them. Involving all stakeholders also provides a clear basis on which to build a community commercial, industrial, or institutional development strategy.

Sensible planning cannot proceed without making hard choices and sending clear signals about how limited public resources, public planning, and regulation will relate to private initiatives and how the public and private sectors can work together to raise the quality of community life, even as the city shrinks.

These choices cannot be made without including residents of the neighborhood in the process, which should be framed positively with the primary purpose of being a decent environment for every Cleveland family that can be maintained for the future. The reweaving of the social fabric of communities must also be part of the process.

Finally, given the demographic and income characteristics of the city, many Cleveland neighborhoods are certain to remain or become low-income areas. Strong working-class areas on the West Side, as well as the East Side, might also be at risk of decline. Low-income areas tend not to be stable over time. Because of disinvestment and physical decline, as well as social problems, they deteriorate and become more crisis-ridden.

A goal of neighborhood transformation is to create stable low-income areas. In such places, the speculation and disinvestment forces are held at bay; public subsidies to repair viable properties are provided; codes are enforced; the social fabric is strengthened; social agencies and community organizations are empowered; and self-help is encouraged. The actors in all these cases are both neighborhood residents and the public and private sectors.

A Final Note on Cleveland Suburbs

The future of Cleveland neighborhoods and suburbs is tied more closely than it might first appear. The future of some older working-class suburbs mirrors that of city neighborhoods. They will have a moderate to deep decline in population. When this occurs, they will in some cases draw on the city for replacement households. Sometimes, these households will be available and will move, assuming the city of Cleveland does not become more attractive. In other cases, replacement households will not be available. Those relying on young middle-class white families (or ones that are not attractive to black families) will have a quickly declining pool on which to draw.

To some degree, Cleveland is in direct competition with these suburban communities for those in the city who can afford to upgrade their housing. The extent to which Cleveland can shore up its neighborhoods and provide hope that conditions will improve will determine its success in this competition.

Other suburbs of Cleveland—older middle- and upper-middle class areas—have been areas to which the black middle class has moved. Unless the city can do more to increase the confidence of the black middle class, including improvement in the schools, the more the city will lose blacks to these suburban areas. These places also will have a shrinking pool of white families and must rely on attracting larger shares of those moving to the region.

Newer suburban areas compete with the city in a different way. They attract middle-class people out of the city and other suburbs. The extent to which Cleveland follows the national trends toward new mixed-use nodes in the suburbs, where housing, office, and commercial space create small "new towns," will determine how serious this competition will become for the city, not just loss of population from the city but also the loss of jobs and retail and other benefits associated with the concentration of these uses in the central city.

The conclusion is simple. The city and its leaders should commence to plan for the city's physical future in a way that takes into account its competitive possibilities. Although prospects for Cleveland are brighter than before, the challenge to accomplish over the decade what Indianapolis and Pittsburgh achieved, for example, is still great. The possibility exists. The city's spirit seems ready. The precedent is there. Hope and possibility are powerful ingredients for transformation.

Notes

1. Katherine Bradbury, Anthony Downs, and Kenneth Small, *Urban Decline and the Future of American Cities* (Washington, D.C.: Brookings Institution, 1982).

2. Christopher B. Leinberger and Charles Lockwood, "How Business Is Shaping America," *Atlantic Monthly* 258 (October 1986): 43.

3. Bradbury, Downs, and Small, *Urban Decline.*

4. Dennis E. Gale, *Neighborhood Revitalization and the Post-Industrial City* (Lexington, Mass.: Lexington Books, 1984) and *Resettlement and Incumbent Upgrading in American Neighborhoods* (Lexington, Mass.: Lexington Books, 1979).

5. Documentation on the structure and function of the giant integrated megalopolis goes back almost three decades. See Jean Gottmann, *Megalopolis: The Urbanized Northeastern Seaboard of the United States* (New York: Twentieth Century Fund, 1961).

6. The recession that started in 1990 dampened development and revitalization efforts.

7. Clarence N. Stone and Heywood T. Saunders, eds., *The Politics of Urban Development* (Lawrence: University of Kansas Press, 1987); Susan Fainstein et al., *Restructuring the City: The Political Economy of Urban Redevelopment* (New York: Longman, 1983); Joe R. Feagin, "Sunbelt Metropolis and Development of Capital: Houston in the Era of Late Capitalism," in *Sunbelt/Snowbelt: Urban Development and Regional*

Restructuring, ed. Larry Sawyers and William K. Tabb (New York: Oxford University Press, 1984), 99–127; Commission on the Year 2000, *New York Ascendant: The Report of the Commission on the Year 2000* (New York: State of New York, 1987).

8. The character and special policy challenges of the underclass are presented in William J. Wilson, *The Truly Disadvantaged: The Inner City, The Underclass and Public Policy* (Chicago: University of Chicago Press, 1987).

9. Reinvestment is not meant to suggest net growth, only that the residential population and other features did increase (or in some cities, the rate of decline shrank significantly). There may be dramatic increases in some areas of the city that are more than offset by decline in other areas. See City of Cleveland, *Civic Vision: Population Projection* (Cleveland: City of Cleveland Planning Commission, 1989).

10. William Apgar, "The Changing Utilization of the Housing Inventory: Past Trends and Future Prospects" (Cambridge Joint Center for Urban Studies, Working paper, 83-1, 1983).

11. The act sets up nonprofits as the preferred owners of properties that change hands.

12. When the tax base does not increase (in real terms), services decline and the cost burden falls on those who do not need the most costly services (older white owners who, for example, do not have children in school), while those who need the service have too few resources to afford to pay the higher prices that are required. Although state aid may help solve this problem and was plentiful in the 1980s, states are now having a hard time balancing their books and are giving less aid to local communities.

13. New housing production in downtown never caught on in Cleveland during the 1970s and this has no doubt reinforced doubt about its viability. It is important to note that this housing preceded the more recent reinvestment in the city.

14. Some areas will have this experience because of aging and the arrival of no new households. This will be slow and, in the short run, is manageable. Others will face massive out-migration. In the latter case, population decrease will be rapid and self-aggravating.

15. "Distressed properties" are those that cannot be operated profitably and still provide reasonable services while paying taxes and meeting other obligations. Not even the exclusion of tax benefits makes such property a good investment. The owners of such property are willing to collect rents and slowly withdraw services such that after a while the property will have to be abandoned, but not before the owners have "milked" it of all possible cash, including insurance proceeds if there is a fire.

Contributors

ROLDO BARTIMOLE has been writing and producing a biweekly newsletter, "Point of View," on Cleveland politics, business, and media since leaving the *Wall Street Journal* in 1968. He has been reporting for thirty-three years, including two tours at the *Cleveland Plain Dealer* in the 1960s. In 1991, through the Shafeek Nader Trust for Community Interest in Washington, D.C., he was awarded the Second Annual Joe A. Calloway Award for Civic Courage "in recognition of his independent, compassionate, fact-based journalism, his stamina and personal courage to pursue his civic calling, and his authentic reporting in an era of conglomerate, homogenized, predigested journalism."

THOMAS E. BIER is Director of the Housing Policy Research Program in the Maxine Goodman Levin College of Urban Affairs at Cleveland State University. He has specialized in housing and demographic studies of the Cleveland region for over fifteen years. He holds a Ph.D. in organizational behavior from Case Western Reserve University.

MITTIE OLION CHANDLER is an associate professor in the Maxine Goodman Levin College of Urban Affairs at Cleveland State University. She earned a Ph.D. in political science and a master's degree in urban planning from Wayne State University after attending undergraduate college at Michigan State University. Her research has focused on low-income housing, public housing policy, fair housing, and urban politics. Chandler's book, *Urban Homesteading: Programs and Policies,* was published in 1988. Her articles have appeared in *Policy Studies Review, Journal of Planning Education and Research,* and *Journal of Planning Literature.*

JULIAN CHOW is an assistant professor at the School of Social Welfare, State University of New York at Albany. His research interests have been on urban poverty issues specifically focusing on neighborhood and community change. Specializing in community analysis, he is particularly interested in applying geographic information systems (GIS) to studying urban demographics and improving the human service delivery system.

PHILLIP L. CLAY is Professor of City Planning at MIT, where he teaches courses on housing, urban demographics, and community development. From 1980 to 1984 he served as assistant director of the MIT-Harvard Joint Center of Urban Studies. He is the author of *Neighborhood Renewal* (1979) and the coauthor, with Robert Hollister, of *Neighborhood Planning and Politics* (1983). In addition, he has written numerous articles, reports, and monographs. He has served on a variety of national and local committees, task forces, and other policy groups and has presented congressional testimony on issues of national housing policy.

CLAUDIA J. COULTON is a professor at the Mandel School of Applied Social Sciences, Case Western Reserve University. On the faculty since 1978, she currently serves as Co-Director of the Center for Urban Poverty and Social Change and teaches in the areas of statistics and research design. In the past, Coulton chaired the doctoral program (1983–88) and the health specialization program (1979–83) at the school. Over the past decade, she has directed numerous research projects related to the provision of health and mental health services, the problems of the elderly and the chronically ill, and the concentration and persistence of urban poverty. She has published over fifty scientific papers on these studies in social welfare, health, and aging literature. She has served on commissions, task forces, and editorial boards related to these subjects.

EDWARD W. HILL is Professor of Urban Studies and Public Administration at the Maxine Goodman Levin College of Urban Affairs at Cleveland State University. He has written on economic development finance, public education policy, planning ethics, and regional labor markets. He coauthored a book on bank reform with Roger Vaughan, *Banking on the Brink: The Troubled Future of American Finance* (1992). He is also coeditor of *Financing Economic Development* (1990), *The Metropolis in Black and White: Place, Power, and Polarization* (1992), and in 1996 a comparative international volume, *Global Perspectives on Economic Development Finance*. Dr. Hill is editor of *Economic Development Quarterly* and a member of the editorial board of the *Journal of Planning Education and Research*. He earned his doctorate in urban and regional planning and economics from MIT.

FREDERIC C. HOWE was a Progressive reformer who remained politically active from the Progressive Era into the New Deal. He was a strong ally of Progressive Cleveland mayor Tom L. Johnson and wrote extensively on national, social, and economic issues.

W. DENNIS KEATING is a professor and the Associate Dean for the Maxine Goodman Levin College of Urban Affairs at Cleveland State University. He has also been Director of the Urban Planning, Design, and Development Program at the college. He has published widely in the areas of housing policy and law, urban and neighborhood development, and urban planning. His most recent book was *The Suburban Racial Dilemma: Housing and Neighborhoods* (1994).

NORMAN KRUMHOLZ is a professor in the Maxine Goodman Levin College of Urban Affairs at Cleveland State University. He previously served as a planning practitioner in Buffalo, Pittsburgh, and Cleveland, serving as Cleveland planning director from 1969–79. He is a past president of the American Planning Association (1987) and received the APA award for Distinguished Leadership (1990). He is the author of numerous articles and book chapters on planning practice, ethics, and theory. His most recent book (with Pierre Clavel) is *Reinventing Cities: Equity Planners Tell Their Stories* (1994).

KENNETH L. KUSMER, a native Clevelander, attended Oberlin College and received his Ph.D. from the University of Chicago. Currently Professor of History at Temple University, he has also taught at the University of Pennsylvania and in 1987–88 held the position of the Fulbright Distinguished Professor at the University of Göttingen in the Federal Republic of Germany. In addition to his book, *A Ghetto Takes Shape: Black Cleveland, 1870–1930* (1976), he has published numerous articles on African American ethnic and social history.

MYRON MAGNET is a member of the board of editors of *Fortune* magazine and a fellow of the Manhattan Institute for Policy Research. He holds both a B.A. and a Ph.D. from Columbia University and a B.A. and an M.A. from the University of Cambridge. He has taught at Middlebury College and at Columbia. In addition to over fifty feature stories in *Fortune* and articles in numerous other publications, he is the author of *Dickens and the Social Order* (1985).

JOHN T. METZGER is a president's fellow in the Ph.D. program in urban planning at Columbia University and research associate with the Real Estate Development Research Center. He has a master's degree in urban planning and policy from the University of Illinois at Chicago and has published articles and book chapters on local economic development, community reinvestment, and urban planning. He was formerly on the staff of the Center for Neighborhood Development at Cleveland State University.

EDWARD M. MIGGINS received a B.A. from Fairfield University in 1966, a Ph.D. from Case Western Reserve University in 1975, and a National Endowment for the Humanities (NEH) Fellowship at Columbia University in 1979. He has been employed at Cuyahoga Community College since 1972 and is currently a professor of history and urban studies and director of the Greater Cleveland Oral History and Community Studies Center at the college. Among other publications, he has edited and helped write *The Birth of Modern Cleveland: 1865–1930* (1988), *A Guide to Studying Neighborhoods and Resources on Cleveland* (1984), and *Responding to the Challenge: Cuyahoga Community College, 1963–1988* (1989). He is currently producing an oral history play on aging and *Communities of Memory: Oral History, Ethnic Folklore and Multicultural Education.*

CAROL POH MILLER is a historical consultant in Cleveland. She has written extensively on Cleveland history and architecture, for which she received the Public Education and Awareness Award from the Ohio Historical Society in 1988. She is coauthor of *Cleveland: A Concise History, 1796–1990* (1990) and a contributor to *The Encyclopedia of Cleveland History* (1987). Her articles and reviews have appeared in *Inland Architect, Technology and Culture,* the *Cleveland Plain Dealer,* and other publications. A native of New Jersey, Miller holds a B.A. in American Studies from Douglass College of Rutgers University and an M.A. in American Studies from The George Washington University.

WILLIAM E. NELSON, JR., is a research professor of Black Studies, Professor of Political Science, and Director of the Center for Research and Public Policy at the Ohio State University. Nelson received his Ph.D. in political science from the University of Illinois in 1971. He is the former president of the National Conference of Black Political Scientists and former chair of the National Council for Black Studies. In 1990 he served as a visiting Fulbright Scholar at the University of Liverpool, England. He is the coauthor of *Electing Black Mayors: Political Action in the Black Community* (1977), and a number of other academic studies in the areas of race and ethnic politics and urban policy.

DAVID C. PERRY is Professor of Planning and Design at the State University of New York at Buffalo. A holder of the Albert A. Levin Chair of Urban Studies and Public Service at Cleveland State University, Perry is the author or coauthor of several books, including

Police in the Metropolis (1975), *Violence as Politics* (1973), *The Rise of the Sunbelt Cities* (1977), *Managing Local Government* (1991), and *Building the Public City* (1994). Perry's articles have appeared in many books and scholarly journals, and he has written for the *Nation* and the *New York Times.* He was awarded the Levin Chair for his continuing work on the personal and public papers of legendary city builder Robert Moses.

RICHARD A. SHATTEN is Executive Director of the Mandel Philanthropic Program. He was Executive Director of Cleveland Tomorrow, a committee of fifty chief executive officers pursuing a variety of programs to strengthen the region's economic vitality. Before joining Cleveland Tomorrow, Shatten was an associate with McKinsey and Company, an international management consulting firm. A native Clevelander, Shatten received a Bachelor of Arts in government from Harvard College and Master of Business Administration from Harvard Business School.

TODD SWANSTROM is an associate professor of political science at the Rockefeller College of Public Affairs and Policy at the State University of New York at Albany. After working for the city of Cleveland as a city planner, he published *The Crisis of Growth Politics: Cleveland, Kucinich, and the Challenge of Urban Populism* (1985). In 1994 he coauthored, with Dennis Judd, *City Politics: Private Power and Public Policy,* a comprehensive text on urban politics in the United States. He also coauthored, with Bruce Mirott and Raymond Seidelman, an introductory theme text in American politics entitled *The Democratic Debate* (1995).

CHRISTOPHER WARREN was selected in 1990 by Cleveland's new mayor, Michael R. White, to be the city's Director of Community Development. In this cabinet-level position, Warren is responsible for the city's housing, neighborhood development, and code enforcement programs. Warren draws on twenty years of experience as a community organizer and housing-development professional in Cleveland neighborhoods. During the 1970s he worked as a community organizer for the Welfare Rights Organization and Merrick House. He was the first executive director of Tremont West Development Corporation and served this community development organization from 1980 to 1985, when he was hired to head the Cleveland Housing Network. Warren is a graduate of Hiram College.

ROBERT A. WHEELER is Associate Professor of History, First College, Cleveland State University. He received his B.A. in history from Rutgers University in 1964 and his combined Ph.D. from Brown University in 1972. Since that time he has taught at Cleveland State. He has written extensively on northeastern Ohio including recent articles on "Land and Community in Rural Nineteenth Century America: Clairdon Township, 1810–1870, The Literature of the Western Reserve." He is author of ". . . Pleasantly Situated on the West Side . . ." (1980), is coauthor (with Carol Poh Miller) of *Cleveland: A Concise History,* and is currently working on a social history of the Western Reserve before the Civil War.

CHRISTOPHER WYE is the director of the Performance and Assessment Program of the National Academy of Public Administration in Washington, D.C. He has published a number of articles on the black experience in Cleveland and a book, *Midwest Ghetto: Patterns of Negro Life and Thought in Cleveland, Ohio 1929–1945* (1973).

Bibliography

Abbot, Virginia Clark. *The History of Woman Suffrage and the League of Women Voters in Cuyahoga County, 1911–1915*. Cleveland: William Feather Co., 1949.

Abbott, David T. "CEI Plotted For Years to Ruin Muny Light, Mayor Tells City Club," *Cleveland Plain Dealer,* February 17, 1979, p. 10A.

Adams, Terry K., and Greg J. Duncan. *The Persistence of Urban Poverty and Its Demographic and Behavioral Correlates.* Ann Arbor: University of Michigan, 1988.

Advisory Commission on Intergovernmental Relations. *State-Local Taxation and Industrial Location.* Washington, D.C.: Advisory Commission on Intergovernmental Relations, 1967.

Advisory Group. *Report to the Mayor on the Linkage Between Downtown Development and Neighborhood Housing.* Boston, Mass.: Advisory Group, 1983.

Akers, William J. *Cleveland Schools in the Nineteenth Century.* Cleveland: W. M. Bayne, 1901.

Albrandt, Roger S. *Neighborhoods, People, and Community.* New York: Plenum Press, 1984.

Alburn, Wilfred H., and Miriam R. Alburn. *This Cleveland of Ours.* Vols. 1–4. Chicago: S. J. Clarke, 1933.

Alesci, Frank. *It Is Never Too Late: A True Life Story of an Immigrant.* Cleveland: St. Francis Publishing House, 1963.

Alfred, Stephen J., and Charles R. Marcoux. "Impact of a Community Association on Integrated Suburban Housing Patterns." *Cleveland State University Law Review* 19 (1970): 90–99.

Alsop, Roger. "Bankers in Cleveland Are Clearly Jubilant City Has New Mayor." *Wall Street Journal,* December 8, 1979.

American Institute of Architects, Cleveland Chapter. *Cleveland Architecture, 1796–1958.* New York: Reinhold, 1958.

Angel, William, and David Perry. "The Politics of Efficiency: A Paper on the Political Economy of the American City." Austin, Tex., 1978. Unpublished.

"Anger, Doubt Follow Housing Plan," *Cleveland Plain Dealer,* June 3, 1973, 4A.

Ardussi, Steve. "Newton D. Baker and Cleveland's Struggle for Home Rule." Ph.D. dissertation, Princeton University, 1970.

Armstrong, Foster, Richard Klein, and Cara Armstrong. *A Guide to Cleveland's Sacred Landmarks.* Kent, Ohio: Kent State University Press, 1992.

Auletta, Ken. *The Streets Were Paved with Gold.* New York: Random House, 1975.

Austin, Arthur. *Complex Litigation Confronts the Jury System: A Case Study.* Frederick, Md.: University Publications of America, 1984.

Avery, Elroy, and M. McKendree. *A History of Cleveland and Its Environs: The Heart of New Connecticut.* 3 vols. New York: Lewis, 1918.

Avery, Robert B., and Thomas M. Buynak. "Mortgage Redlining: Some New Evidence." *Federal Reserve Bank of Cleveland, Economic Review* (1981): 18–32.

Bane, Mary J., and David T. Ellwood. "Slipping Into and Out of Poverty: The Dynamics of Spells." *Journal of Human Resources* 21 (1986): 1–23.

Barker, Roger G., and Herbert F. Wright. *Midwest and Its Children: The Psychological Ecology of an American Town.* New York: Harper & Row, 1955.

Barnekov, Timothy, Robin Boyle, and Daniel Rich. *Privatism and Urban Policy in Britain and the United States.* Oxford: Oxford University Press, 1989.

Bartimole, Roldo. "Ameritrust." *Point of View* 13 (1981): 1–4.

———. "Tired City." *Point of View* 17 (1984): 1–4.

Barton, Josef J. *Peasants and Strangers: Italians, Rumanians, and Slovaks in an American City, 1890–1950.* Cambridge, Mass.: Harvard University Press, 1975.

Bay Village Historical Society. *Bay Village: A Way of Life.* Bay Village, Ohio: Bay Village Historical Society, 1974.

Beauregard, Robert A. *Economic Restructuring and Political Response.* Newbury Park, Calif.: Sage, 1989.

Beck, John H. "Is Cleveland Another New York?" *Urban Affairs Quarterly* 18 (1982): 207–16.

Becker, Bob. "Voters Give Support to City Light System." *Cleveland Plain Dealer,* November 7, 1990, p. 1A.

Beer, Thomas. *Hanna.* New York: Knopf, 1929.

Behnke, Dickson, and Tkach. *Cleveland Lakefront State Park: A Positive Statement for Cleveland's Lakefront.* Cleveland: Behnke, Dickson, and Tkach, 1979.

Berkman, Ronald, and Todd Swanstrom. "A Tale of Two Cities." *The Nation,* March 24, 1979, 297–99.

Bier, Thomas, Edric Weld, Mark Hoffman, and Ivan Maric. *Housing Supply and Demand: Cleveland Metropolitan Area, 1950–2005.* Cleveland: The Urban Center, Maxine Goodman Levin College of Urban Affairs, Cleveland State University, 1988.

Bing, Lucia J. *Social Work in Greater Cleveland: How Public and Private Agencies Are Serving Human Needs.* Cleveland: Welfare Foundation of Cleveland, 1938.

Bingham, Richard D., et al. *Managing Local Government: Public Administration in Practice.* Newbury Park, Calif: Sage, 1991.

Bingham, Richard D., and Randall W. Eberts. *Economic Restructuring of the American Midwest.* Boston: Kluwer, 1990.

Block, Fred. "The Ruling Class Does Not Rule." *Socialist Revolution* 33 (1977): 6–28.

Bluestone, Barry. "Economic Crises and the Law of Uneven Development." *Politics and Society* 3 (1972): 65–82.

Bluestone, Barry, and Bennett Harrison. *The Deindustrialization of America.* New York: Basic Books, 1982.

Boast, Thomas H. "A Political Economy of Urban Capital Finance in the United States." Ph.D. dissertation, Cornell University, 1977.

Bond, Bob. *Focus on Neighborhoods: A History of Responses by Cleveland Settlement Housing and Neighborhood Centers to Changing Human Needs.* Cleveland: Greater Cleveland Neighborhood Centers Association, 1990.

Bonutti, Karl. *Selected Ethnic Communities in Cleveland: A Socio-Economic Study.* Cleveland: Cleveland State University, 1974.

Borchert, James. *Lakewood: The First Hundred Years.* Norfolk and Virginia Beach: Donning, 1989.

Bourne, Henry E. *The Church of the Covenant: The First Hundred Years.* Cleveland, 1945.

Bradbury, Katharine L., Anthony Downs, and Kenneth A. Small. "Alternatives for One Declining Area: Cleveland, Ohio." In *Urban Decline and the Future of American Cities,* 237–57. Washington, D.C.: Brookings Institution, 1982.

———. *Futures for a Declining City: Simulations for the Cleveland Area.* New York: Academic Press, 1981.

Breckenfeld, Gurney. "Refilling the Metropolitan Doughnut." In *The Rise of the Sunbelt Cities,* edited by David C. Perry and Alfred J. Watkins. Beverly Hills, Calif.: Sage, 1977.

Breckenridge, Tom. "Centerior, Sued by Shareholders, to Enact Reforms." *Cleveland Plain Dealer,* January 13, 1990, p. 2B.

Brenkus, Mildred. *My People: A Brief Look at People, Problems, and Personalities among Clevelanders Living in Poverty.* Cleveland: Inner City Protestant Parish, 1967.

Bridges, Benjamin, Jr. "State and Local Inducements for Industry: Part 2." In *Locational Analysis for Manufacturing,* edited by Gerald Karaska and David Bramhall. Cambridge, Mass.: MIT Press, 1969.

Brooks, C. H. "Infant Mortality in SMSAs Before Medicaid: Test of a Causal Model." *Health Services Research* 13, no. 3 (1978): 3–15.

Browarek, Matthew F. *A Heritage of Books: A Selected Bibliography of Books and Related Materials on Cleveland to Be Found at the Cleveland Public Library.* Cleveland: Cleveland Public Library, 1984.

Brown, Kent L. *Medicine in Cleveland and Cuyahoga County, 1810–1976.* Cleveland: Academy of Medicine, 1977.

Campbell, Thomas F. "Cleveland: The Struggle for Stability." In *Snowbelt Cities,* edited by Richard M. Bernard, 109–36. Bloomington: Indiana University Press, 1990.

———. *Daniel E. Morgan, 1877–1949: The Good Citizen in Politics.* Cleveland: Western Reserve University Press, 1966.

———. *Freedom's Forum: The City Club.* Cleveland: City Club, 1963.

———. "Municipal Ownership." In *The Encyclopedia of Cleveland History,* edited by David D. Van Tassel and John J. Grabowski, 699–703. Bloomington: Indiana University Press, 1987.

Campbell, Thomas F., and Edward M. Miggins, eds. *The Birth of Modern Cleveland, 1865–1930.* Cleveland: Western Reserve Historical Society, 1988.

Case School of Applied Science. *Cuyahoga Miracle: Technology and Evolution of the Cuyahoga Valley during the Last One Hundred Years.* Cleveland: Case School of Applied Science, 1937.

Center for Regional Economic Issues. *Cleveland Economic Analysis and Projections.* Cleveland: Center for Regional Economic Issues, Weatherhead School of Management, Case Western Reserve University, 1987.

Chandler, Mittie Olion, Virginia O. Benson, and Richard Klein. "The Impact of Public Housing Location on Urban Residential Property Values." *Real Estate Issues* 18 (Spring–Summer 1992): 2.

Chandler, Mittie Olion, W. Dennis Keating, and Phil Star. "Lakeview Terrace (Cleveland): from Landmark Public Housing to Tenant Management and an Uncertain Future," 1989. Unpublished.

Chapman, Edmund H. *Cleveland, Village to Metropolis: A Case Study of Problems of Urban Development in Nineteenth Century America.* Cleveland: Western Reserve Historical Society and the Press of Western Reserve University, 1964.

Chatterjee, Pranab. *Local Leadership in Black Communities: Organizational and Electoral Developments in Cleveland in the Nineteen-Sixties.* Cleveland: Case Western Reserve University, 1975.

Chesnutt, Helen M. *Charles Waddell Chesnutt: Pioneer of the Color Line.* Chapel Hill: University of North Carolina Press, 1952.

Christiansen, Harry. *Trolley Trails through Greater Cleveland and Northern Ohio.* Vols. 1–2. Cleveland: Western Reserve Historical Society, 1975.

Chudacoff, Howard P. *The Evolution of American Urban Society.* Englewood Cliffs, N.J.: Prentice-Hall, 1975.

Citizens League of Greater Cleveland. "Cleveland Named All-American City by National Municipal League," *News Bureau Cleveland,* March 12, 1982.

———. *Seventy-Five Years of Doing Good: The Story of the Citizens League, 1896–1969.* Cleveland: Citizens League of Cleveland, 1971.

Citizens League Research Institute. *Race Relations in Greater Cleveland: A Report on the Attitudes, Opinions, and Experiences of Greater Clevelanders.* Cleveland: Citizens League Research Institute, 1991.

City of Cleveland. *Prospectus for Public Power System Improvement Bonds.* Cleveland: City of Cleveland, 1987.

City of Cleveland v. *CEI,* 37 Ohio St. 3d 50, 524 N.E. 2d 441 (1988).

Civic Vision: Citywide and Downtown Plans. Cleveland: Cleveland City Planning Department, 1988, 1992.

Clark, Gary R. "CEI Fighting MUNY Legislation, Mayor Charges." *Cleveland Plain Dealer,* February 26, 1982, p. 20B.

———. "Good Deal, Bad Deal? How CEI-City Pact Failed at Last Minute." *Cleveland Plain Dealer,* August 12, 1984, pp. 1A, 26–27A.

Clay, Phillip. *Transforming Cleveland's Future: Issues and Strategies for a Heartland City.* Cleveland: Cleveland State University, 1988.

Cleaveland, Moses, Papers. MS. 3233, Western Reserve Historical Society, Cleveland.

Cleveland Americanization Committee. *Americanization in Cleveland.* Cleveland: Cleveland Americanization Committee, 1920.

Cleveland Centennial Commission. *Official Report of the Centennial Celebration of the Founding of the City of Cleveland and the Settlement of the Western Reserve.* Cleveland: Cleveland Printing and Publishing Co., 1896.

Cleveland: The Greater Cleveland Fact Book. Cleveland: Greater Cleveland Growth Association, 1993.

Cleveland Public Library. History Department. Clipping files.

Cleveland Urban League. *The Negro in Cleveland, 1950–1963.* Cleveland: Cleveland Urban League, 1964.

Coates, William G. *A History of Cuyahoga County and the City of Cleveland.* Chicago: American Historical Society, 1924.

Comer, Lucretia Garfield. *Strands from the Weaving: The Life of Harry A. Garfield.* New York: Vantage Press, 1959.

Concord v. *Boston Edison Co.,* 111 S. Ct. 1337 (1991).

Condon, George. *Cleveland: The Best Kept Secret*. New York: Doubleday, 1967.

———. *Cleveland: Prodigy of the Western Reserve*. Tulsa, Oklahoma: Continental Heritage Press, 1979.

———. *Yesterday's Cleveland*. Miami, Fla.: E. A. Seeman, 1976.

Congregation Tifereth Israel. *The Temple, 1850–1950*. Cleveland: The Temple, 1950.

Cooper, Phillip J. *Hard Judicial Choices: Federal District Court Judges and State and Local Officials*. New York: Oxford University Press, 1988.

Coulton, Claudia J., and Shanta Pandey. *"Geographic Concentration of Poverty and Risk to Children in Urban Neighborhoods."* American Behavioral Scientist 35, no. 3 (1992): 238–57.

Cramer, Clarence H. *Case Western Reserve: A History of the University, 1826–1976*. Boston: Little, Brown, 1976.

———. *Newton D. Baker: A Biography*. Cleveland: World, 1961.

———. *Open Shelves and Open Minds: A History of the Cleveland Public Library*. Cleveland: Case Western Reserve University, 1972.

Crane, Jonathan. "The Epidemic Theory of Ghettos and Neighborhood Effects on Dropping Out and Teenage Childbearing." *American Journal of Sociology* 96, no. 5 (1991): 1226–59.

Crissey, Forrest. *Theodore E. Burton, American Statesman*. Cleveland: World, 1956.

Croly, Herbert. *Marcus Alonzo Hanna, His Life and Work*. New York: Macmillan, 1919.

Cuyahoga Plan. *A Report on Population and Race*. Cleveland: Cuyahoga Plan of Ohio, 1983.

Davis, Allen R. *Spearheads for Reform: The Social Settlements and the Progressive Movement, 1890–1914*. New York: Oxford University Press, 1967.

Davis, Russell H. *Black Americans in Cleveland from George B. Peake to Carl B. Stokes, 1796–1969*. Washington, D.C.: Associated Publishers, 1972.

———. *Memorable Negroes in Cleveland's Past*. Cleveland: Western Reserve Historical Society, 1969.

Daye, Charles E., et al. *Housing and Community Development*. Durham, N.C.: Carolina Academic Press, 1989.

Dear, Michael, and Allen J. Scott, eds. *Urbanization and Urban Planning in Capitalist Society*. New York: Methuen, 1981.

Downs, Anthony. *Inside Bureaucracy*. Boston: Little, Brown, 1967.

Downtown Cleveland Planning Reports, 1959–1986: An Annotated Bibliography. Cleveland: Cleveland City Planning Commission, 1986.

Due, John F. "Studies of State-Local Tax Influences in Location of Industry." *National Tax Journal* 14 (1961): 163–73.

Duncan, G., and S. Hoffman. *Teenage Underclass Behavior and Subsequent Poverty: Have the Rules Changed?* Newark: University of Delaware, Department of Economics, 1990.

Dunfee, Charles D. "Harold H. Burton, Mayor of Cleveland: The WPA Program, 1935–1937." Ph.D. dissertation, Case Western Reserve University, 1975.

Durham, Frank. *Government in Greater Cleveland*. Cleveland: H. Allen, 1963.

Eberts, Randall. *Common Bonds, Divergent Paths: An Economic Perspective of Four Cities*. Cleveland: Federal Reserve Bank of Cleveland, 1988.

Elkin, Stephen L. *City and Regime in the American Republic*. Chicago: University of Chicago Press, 1987.

Ellis, William D. *The Cuyahoga*. New York: Holt, Rinehart, and Winston, 1966.

———. *Early Settlers of Cleveland*. Cleveland: Cleveland State University, 1976.

Ellwood, David. "The Spatial Mismatch Hypothesis: Are Teenage Jobs Missing in the Ghetto?"

In *The Black Youth Unemployment Crisis,* edited by R. Freeman and H. Holzer, 147–85. Chicago: University of Chicago Press, 1986.

Ellwood, David T., and Larry H. Summers. "Poverty in America: Is Welfare the Answer or the Problem?" In *Fighting Poverty: What Works and What Doesn't?,* edited by S. H. Danziger and D. H. Weinberg, 78–105. Cambridge, Mass.: Harvard University Press, 1986.

Fainstein, Susan S., and Norman I. Fainstein. "Federal Policy and Spacial Inequality." In *Revitalizing the Northeast,* edited by G. Sternleib and J. W. Hughes. New Brunswick, N.J.: Center for Urban Policy Research, 1978.

Ferroni, Charles D. *The Italians in Cleveland: A Study in Assimilation.* New York: Arno Press, 1980.

Flats Oxbow Association. *Flats Oxbow Long-Range Development Plan.* Cleveland: Flats Oxbow Association, 1986.

Fogarty, Michael S. "Civic Vision Employment Projections Revisited." *REI Review* (Spring 1989): 29–31.

Fordyce, Wellington. "Nationality Groups in Cleveland Politics." *Ohio State Archaeological and Historical Quarterly* 46 (1937): 109–27.

Freilich, Ellen S. "Cleveland Plain Dealer's Pressured by Reporters, Prints a Story It Stifled." *Columbia Journalism Review* 18 (May–June 1979): 49–57.

Friedman, Lawrence M. *Government and Slum Housing.* Chicago: Rand McNally, 1968.

The Gamut Looks at Cleveland. Cleveland: Cleveland State University, 1986.

Garfinkle, Irwin, and Sara McLanahan. *The Effects of the Child Support Provisions of the Family Support Act of 1988 on Child Well-Being.* IRP Discussion Papers. Madison: University of Wisconsin, Institute for Research on Poverty, 1990.

———. *Single Mothers and Their Children: A New American Dilemma.* Washington, D.C.: Urban Institute, 1986.

Garofalo, Gasper A., and Chul S. Park. "The Location of Manufacturing in CALE." *REI Review* (Fall 1988): 14–23.

Gartner, Lloyd P. *History of the Jews of Cleveland.* Cleveland: Western Reserve Historical Society and the Jewish Theological Seminary of America, 1978.

Geronimus, Arline T. "On Teenage Childbearing and Neonatal Mortality in the United States." *Population and Development Review* 13, no. 2 (1987): 245–79.

Glaab, Charles N., and A. Theodore Brown. *A History of Urban America.* New York: Macmillan, 1976.

Glazer, Nathan, and Daniel Patrick Moynihan. *Beyond the Melting Pot: The Negroes, Puerto Ricans, Jews, Italians, and Irish of New York City.* Cambridge, Mass.: MIT Press, 1976.

Gleisser, Marcus. *The World of Cyrus Eaton.* New York: A. S. Barnes, 1965.

Goebelt, Margaret S. *Fairview Park in Historical Review.* Cleveland: J. S. Swift, 1978.

Gold, Herbert. *Family: A Novel in the Form of a Memoir.* New York: Arbor House, 1981.

Gormley, William. *The Politics of Public Utility Regulation.* Pittsburgh: University of Pittsburgh Press, 1983.

Governance: Improving the Effectiveness of Special Purpose Governments in Greater Cleveland. Cleveland: Governmental Research Institute, 1989.

Grabowski, John J. *Sports in Cleveland: An Illustrated History.* Bloomington: Indiana University Press, 1992.

Grabowski, John J., and Walter C. Leedy. *The Terminal Tower, Tower City Center: A Historical Perspective.* Cleveland: Western Reserve Historical Society, 1990.

Green, Constance McLaughlin. *American Cities in the Growth of the Nation*. New York: J. DeGraff, 1957.

Green, David E. *The City and Its People . . . A Brief Statement of the Character and Distribution of the Population of Cleveland*. Cleveland: Federated Churches of Cleveland, 1917.

Green, Howard W. *Relation of the "Central Area" to the Entire City*. Vols. 1–3. Cleveland: Cleveland Health Council, 1944.

Griffin, Burt W. *Cities within a City: On Changing Cleveland's Government*. Cleveland: Cleveland State University, 1981.

Gurwitz, Aaron, and Thomas Kingsley. *The Cleveland Metropolitan Economy*. Cleveland: Cleveland Foundation, 1982.

Haberman, Ian S. *The Van Sweringens of Cleveland*. Cleveland: Western Reserve Historical Society, 1979.

Hadden, Jeffrey K., Louis H. Masotti, and Victor Thiessen. "Making of Negro Mayors—Cleveland and Gary." In *Big City Mayors: The Crisis in Urban Politics*, edited by Leonard I. Ruchelman, 122–41. Bloomington: Indiana University Press, 1969.

Halprin, Lawrence. *A Concept for Cleveland: Strategy for Downtown*. Cleveland: Greater Cleveland Growth Association, 1974.

Harris, Mary E., and Ruth M. Robinson. *The Proud Heritage of Cleveland Heights*. Cleveland: H. Allen, 1961.

Hatcher, Harlan H. *A Century of Iron Men: The Cleveland Cliffs Iron Company*. Indianapolis: Bobbs-Merrill, 1950.

———. *The Western Reserve: The Story of New Connecticut in Ohio*. 1949. Reprint, with a Foreword by George W. Knepper, Kent, Ohio: The Kent State University Press, 1991.

Hatcher, Harlan H., and Frank Durham. *Giant from the Wilderness: The Story of a City and Its Industries*. Cleveland: World, 1955.

Havighurst, Walter. *Vein of Iron, the Pickands, Mather Story*. Cleveland: World, 1978.

Hays, Allen R. *The Federal Government and Urban Housing*. Albany: State University of New York Press, 1985.

Hellman, Richard. *Government Competition in the Electric Utility Industry: A Theoretical and Empirical Study*. New York: Praeger, 1972.

Hendry, Charles C. *Between Spires and Stacks*. Cleveland: Welfare Federation of Cleveland, 1936.

Herrick, Clay. *Cleveland Landmarks*. Cleveland: Cleveland Landmarks Commission, 1986.

Herson, Lawrence J. R., and John M. Bolland. *The Urban Web: Politics, Policy, and Theory*. Chicago: Nelson-Hall, 1990.

Hill, Edward W. "Restructured Cleveland: Manufacturing Matters, Services Are Strengthening, Earnings Erode." In *The Economic Restructuring of the American Midwest*, edited by Richard D. Bingham and Randall W. Eberts, 103–40. Boston: Kluwer, 1990.

Hill, Edward, and Thomas Bier. "Economic Restructuring: Earnings, Occupations and Housing Values in Cleveland." *Economic Development Quarterly* 3 (1989): 123–43.

Hill, Edward W., and Heidi M. Rock. *Education as an Economic Development Resource*. Cleveland: Cleveland State University, College of Urban Affairs, 1989.

Hiram House Social Settlement. *Pioneering on Social Frontiers, 1896–1936*. Cleveland: Hiram House, 1937.

Hobbs, Michael A. "Utility Admits Role in Anti-Issue 5 Campaign." *Cleveland Plain Dealer*, November 3, 1990, pp. 1B, 8B.

Hoffman, Mark. *Population and Household Projections: Cleveland Metropolitan Area, 1985–2020.* Cleveland: Cleveland State University, 1988.

Hoffman, Naphtali. "The Process of Economic Development in Cleveland, 1825–1920." Ph.D. dissertation, Case Western Reserve University, 1981.

Hogan, Dennis P., and Evelyn M. Kitagawa. "The Impact of Social Status, Family Structure, and Neighborhood on the Fertility of Black Adolescents." *American Journal of Sociology* 90 (January 1985): 825–55.

Holley, Mark. "Cleveland Zapped by Top Power Bill," *Cleveland Plain Dealer,* July 27, 1991, p. 5B.

Holzworth, Walter F. *Men of Grit and Greatness: A Historical Account of Middleburg Township, Berea, Brook Park, and Middleburg Heights.* Berea, Ohio: Walter F. Holzworth, 1970.

Howard, Nathaniel R. *The First Hundred Years: A History of the Union Club in Cleveland.* Cleveland: Union Club, 1972.

———. *Trust for All Time: The Story of the Cleveland Foundation and the Community Trust Movement.* Cleveland: Cleveland Foundation, 1963.

Howe, Frederic C. *Confessions of a Reformer.* 1925. Reprint, Kent Ohio: The Kent State University Press, 1988.

———. *The Modern City and Its Problems.* New York: Charles Scribner's Sons, 1915.

Hughes, Mark A. *Misspeaking Truth to Power: A Geographical Perspective on the "Underclass" Fallacy.* Princeton: Princeton University, 1989.

Humphrey, Nancy, and George E. Peterson. *The Greater Cleveland Community Capital Investment Strategy.* Washington, D.C.: Urban Institute, 1983.

Humphrey, Nancy, George E. Peterson, and Peter Wilson. *The Future of Cleveland's Capital Plant.* Washington, D.C.: Urban Institute, 1979.

Husselman, Roy. *Cleveland's Municipal Light Plant Still Pesters Power Trust.* Chicago: Public Ownership League of America, 1931.

Hynes, Michael J. *History of the Diocese of Cleveland.* Cleveland: Diocese of Cleveland, 1953.

"The Illuminating Company, A Cleveland Radical Research Group." *The Cleveland Papers.* Cleveland: Privately printed, 1970.

Izant, Grace G. *John D. Rockefeller: The Cleveland Years.* Cleveland: Western Reserve Historical Society, 1972.

Jedick, Peter. *Cleveland: Where the East Coast Meets the Midwest.* Cleveland: Peter Jedick, 1980.

Jeffries, Leo W. *Ethnic Communities in Cleveland: An Exploratory Study of Ethnics and Mass Communication in Cleveland.* Cleveland: Cleveland State University, 1978.

Jeffries, Leo W., Jean Dobos, and Jae-won Lee. *Public Perception of the Quality of Life: A Dynamic Model for Interdisciplinary Research.* Cleveland: Cleveland State University, Department of Communications, 1989.

Jirran, Raymond J. "Cleveland and the Negro Following World War Two." Ph.D. dissertation, Kent State University, 1972.

Johannesen, Eric. *Cleveland Architecture, 1876–1976.* Cleveland: Western Reserve Historical Society, 1979.

———. *From Town to Tower.* Cleveland: Western Reserve Historical Society, 1983.

Johnson, Tom L. *My Story.* 1911. Reprint, Kent, Ohio: Kent State University Press, 1993.

Jollie, Rose Marie. *A Brief History of Cleveland and the Central National Bank of Cleveland.* Cleveland: Central National Bank, 1965.

Jones, Bryan. *Governing Urban America.* Boston: Little, Brown, 1983.

Joskow, Paul L. and Richard Schmalansee. *Markets for Power: An Analysis of Electric Utility Deregulation.* Cambridge, Mass.: MIT Press, 1983.

Judd, Dennis R. *The Politics of American Cities: Private Power and Public Policy.* Boston: Little, Brown, 1979.

Kasarda, John D. "Urban Industrial Transition and the Underclass." *Annals of the American Academy of Political and Social Science* 501 (1989): 26–47.

Keating, W. Dennis. *The Suburban Racial Dilemma: Housing and Neighborhoods.* Philadelphia: Temple University Press, 1994.

Keating, W. Dennis, William J. Palmer, and Linda S. Smith. *A Comparative Study of Three Models of Racial Integration in Housing in Cleveland.* Cleveland: Levin College of Urban Affairs, Cleveland State University, 1987.

Kellman, Barry, and Nicholas J. Marino. "City of Cleveland v. CEI: A Case Study in Attempts to Monopolize by Regulated Utilities." *Cleveland State Law Review* 30 (1981): 5–39.

Kenealy, Edward J. *The Cleveland Municipal Light Plant.* Cleveland: Penton Press, 1935.

Kennedy, James H. *A History of the City of Cleveland, Its Settlements, Rise and Progress, 1796–1896.* Vols. 1–2. Cleveland: Imperial Press, 1897.

Kingsley, Thomas. *Cleveland Regional Trends: Responses to the Business Cycle.* Cleveland: Cleveland Foundation, 1982.

Kitchel, Bob. "Cleveland's Future Public Housing Projects Struggle to a Standstill in Council," *Cleveland Press,* August 18, 1970, A3.

———. "New Public Housing Will Be Scattered in the City," *Cleveland Press,* May 11, 1971, p. A1.

Krumholz, Norman. "Recovery: An Alternative View." In *Roads to Recovery,* edited by Paul Porter and David Sweet, 173–90. New Brunswick, N.J.: Rutgers University Press, 1984.

———. "A Retrospective View of Equity Planning." *Journal of the American Planning Association* 48 (1982): 163–74.

———. "Twenty Years After Kerner: The Cleveland Case." *Journal of Urban Affairs* 12 (1990): 285–97.

Krumholz, Norman, Janice Cogger, and John Linner. "The Cleveland Policy Planning Report." *Journal of the American Planning Association* 41 (1975): 298–304.

Krumholz, Norman, and John Forester. *Making Equity Planning Work: Leadership in the Public Sector.* Philadelphia: Temple University Press, 1990.

Kusmer, Kenneth L. *A Ghetto Takes Shape: Black Cleveland, 1870–1930.* Urbana: University of Illinois Press, 1976.

Lackritz, Mark E. "The Hough Riots of 1966." M.A. thesis, Princeton University, 1968.

LaRiccia, Michael. "The Viability of Public Housing in Cleveland's Central Area," 1988. Unpublished.

Lawless, James. "Completion of Perry Unit 2 Studied," *Cleveland Plain Dealer,* September 10, 1989, p. 10B.

Lawrence, Ann T. *Cleveland's Flats: The Incredible City under the Hill.* Cleveland: History Associates, 1979.

Leech, Margaret. *In the Days of McKinley.* New York: Harper & Brothers, 1959.

Leedy, Walter. "Cleveland's Terminal Tower—The Van Sweringens' Afterthought." *Gamut* 8 (1983): 3–26.

Levy, Donald. *A Report on the Location of Ethnic Groups in Greater Cleveland.* Cleveland: Cleveland State University, 1972.

Lieberson, Stanley. *A Piece of the Pie: Black and White Immigrants Since 1880.* Los Angeles: University of California Press, 1980.

Lorenz, Carl. *Tom L. Johnson: Mayor of Cleveland.* New York: A. S. Barnes, 1911.

Lupold, Harry F., and Gladys Haddad. *Ohio's Western Reserve: A Regional Reader.* Kent, Ohio: Kent State University Press, 1988.

Luttner, Steven. "Council to Get Plan for Muny Lease Monday," *Cleveland Plain Dealer,* December 14, 1984, pp. 1A, 18A.

Lynch, Maxine. "Public Housing Finds Support in Suburbs," *Cleveland Plain Dealer,* December 23, 1985, p. 16A.

McGunagle, Fred. "Tax Bite Starts Tomorrow; Muny to Woo CEI Customers," *Cleveland Press,* February 28, 1979, p. 1.

Maher, Richard L. "Cleveland: Study of Political Paradoxes." In *Our Fair City,* edited by R. S. Allen, 123–47. New York: Vanguard Press, 1947.

Malvin, John. *North into Freedom: The Autobiography of John Malvin, Free Negro, 1795–1880.* 1966. Reprint, Kent, Ohio: The Kent State University Press, 1988.

Margulis, Harry, and Alex R. Staneff. "Neighborhood Revitalization: An Examination of Housing Rehabilitation Strategies in Cleveland, Ohio." *Eastlake Geographer* 20 (1985): 43–57.

Marschall, Dan, ed. *Battle of Cleveland: Public Interest Challenges Corporate Power.* Washington, D.C.: Conference on Alternative State and Local Policies, 1979.

Masotti, Louis H. *Shoot-Out in Cleveland: Black Militants and the Police, July 23, 1968.* New York: Bantam, 1969.

Massey, Douglas S. *American Apartheid: Segregation and the Making of the Underclass.* Chicago: Population Research Center, University of Chicago, 1989.

Massey, Douglas S., and Nancy Denton. "Suburbanization and Segregation in U.S. Metropolitan Areas." *American Journal of Sociology* 94 (1988): 592–626.

Mier, Robert, Joan Fitzgerald, and Lewis A. Randolph. *African-American Elected Officials and the Future of Progressive Political Movements.* Chicago: School of Urban Planning and Policy, Center for Urban Economic Development, University of Illinois at Chicago, 1991.

Miggins, Edward, ed. *A Guide to Studying Neighborhoods and Resources on Cleveland.* Cleveland: Cleveland Public Library, 1984.

Miggins, Edward, and Mary Morgenthaler. "The Ethnic Mosaic: The Settlement of Cleveland by the New Immigrants and Migrants." In *The Birth of Modern Cleveland, 1865–1930,* edited by Thomas Campbell and Edward Miggins, 104–40. Cleveland: Western Reserve Historical Society and Associated University Presses, 1988.

Miller, Carol Poh, and Robert Wheeler. *Cleveland: A Concise History, 1796–1990.* Bloomington: Indiana University Press, 1990.

Miller, Herbert A. *The School and the Immigrant.* Philadelphia: William F. Fell, 1916.

Mollenkopf, John. *The Contested City.* Princeton: Princeton University Press, 1983.

Molyneaux, David G., and Sue Sackman. *75 Years: An Informal History of Shaker Heights.* Shaker Heights, Ohio: Shaker Heights Public Library, 1987.

Neff, James. *Mobbed Up: Jackie Presser's High Wire Life in the Teamsters, the Mafia, and the FBI.* New York: Atlantic Monthly Press, 1989.

Nelson, William E., and Philip J. Meranto. "Cleveland and Gary: The Ingredients of Successful Mobilization." In *Electing Black Mayors: Political Action in the Black Community*, 67–165. Columbus: Ohio State University Press, 1977.

Northern Ohio Data and Information Service. *Cleveland Area Atlas*. Vol. 1: *Census Tracts in Cuyahoga County*. Cleveland: Cleveland State University, 1988.

Norton, James A. *The Metro Experience*. Cleveland: Press of the Western Reserve University, 1963.

Office of Technology Assessment. *Electric Power Wheeling and Dealing: Technological Considerations for Increasing Competition*. Washington, D.C.: Superintendent of Documents, U.S. Government Printing Office, 1989.

Ohio Public Interest Campaign. *Electric Rates and the "Level Playing Field": A Comparison of 500 KWH Electric Bills Charged by Investor-Owned and Municipally-Owned Utilities in Ohio*. Columbus: Ohio Public Interest Campaign, 1989.

———. *Rate Abatements*. Columbus: Ohio Public Interest Campaign, 1979.

Old Brooklyn: A Historic Narrative and Projection for the 1980s. Kent, Ohio: Commercial Press, 1979.

O'Malley, Michael. "Brookpark's Moth Drawn to Municipal Power Light," *Cleveland Plain Dealer*, June 13, 1991, pp. 1A, 5A.

———. "Brookpark O.K.'s a City Power System," *Cleveland Plain Dealer*, November 6, 1991, pp. 1B, 3B.

———. "Power Plan Generates Legal Threat: CEI Would Seek $75 Million if City Sets Up Own System," *Cleveland Plain Dealer*, August 29, 1991, pp. 1B, 3B.

———. "Study Says Residents Can Save 30% if City Builds Power System," *Cleveland Plain Dealer*, August 21, 1991, pp. 1B, 4B.

Orth, Samuel P. *A History of Cleveland, Ohio*. 3 vols. Chicago: S. J. Clarke, 1910.

Pap, Michael. *Ethnic Communities of Cleveland*. Cleveland: John Carroll University, 1973.

Perry, David, and Lawrence Keller. "Public Administration at the Local Level: Definition, Theory, and Context." In *Managing Local Government: Public Administration in Practice*, edited by Richard Bingham et al., 3–30. Newbury Park, Calif.: Sage, 1991.

Perry, David C., and Alfred J. Watkins. *The Rise of the Sunbelt Cities*. Beverly Hills: Sage, 1977.

Petersen, Gene B., Laura H. Sharp, and Thomas F. Drury. *Southern Newcomers to Northern Cities: Work and Social Adjustment in Cleveland*. New York: Praeger, 1977.

Peterson, Paul. *City Limits*. Chicago: University of Chicago Press, 1981.

Phipps, Peter. "Kucinich Goes to Big Screen at City Club to Sell His Stand." *Cleveland Press*, February 17, 1979, p. 6.

Piercy, Caroline. *The Valley of God's Pleasure: The Saga of the North Union Community Which Became Shaker Heights*. New York: Stratford House, 1951.

Pogue, Richard. *The Cleveland Foundation at Seventy-Five: An Evolving Community Resource*. New York: The Newcomen Society of the United States, 1989.

Porter, Philip. *Cleveland: Confused City on a Seesaw*. Columbus: Ohio State University Press, 1976.

Post, Charles A. *Doan's Corners and the City Four Miles West*. Cleveland: Caxton, 1930.

Primeaux, Walter J., Jr. "Competition between Electric Utilities." In *Electric Power Deregulation and the Public Interest*, edited by John C. Moorhouse, 395–423. San Francisco: Pacific Research Institute for Public Policy, 1986.

———. *Direct Electric Utility Competition: The Natural Monopoly Myth.* New York: Praeger, 1986.

"Public Power Costs Less." *Public Power* 26 (January–February 1991): 16.

Rasey, Keith P., W. Dennis Keating, and Philip Star. "Management of Neighborhood Development: Community Development Corporations." In *Managing Local Government: Public Administration in Practice,* edited by Richard Bingham et al., 214–36 Newbury Park, Calif.: Sage, 1991.

Rawlings, Charles. *Suburbanization of the Negro Population.* Cleveland: Cleveland Church Federation, 1963.

Reiner, Vic. "Cleveland Public Power Expanding." *Public Power* 22 (May–June 1987): 10–16.

Roberts, Les. *Full Cleveland.* New York: St. Martin's Press, 1989.

Robinson, Cervin. *Cervin Robinson/Cleveland, Ohio: An Exhibition of 100 Photographs Commissioned by the Cleveland Museum of Art.* Cleveland: Cleveland Museum of Art in cooperation with Indiana University Press, 1989.

Rogers, David. *The Management of Big Cities: Interest Groups and Social Change Strategies.* Beverly Hills: Sage, 1971.

Rose, William Ganson. *Cleveland: The Making of a City.* 1963. Reprint, Kent, Ohio: The Kent State University Press, 1990.

Rubenstein, Judah. *Estimating Cleveland's Jewish Population.* Cleveland: Jewish Community Federation, 1980.

Rudolph, Richard, and Scott Ridley. *Power Struggle: The Hundred Year War Over Electricity.* New York: Harper and Row, 1986.

Runyan, Timothy J. "Redeveloping Cleveland's Lakefront." *Gamut* 21 (1987): 74–79.

Sabath, Donald. "Stokes Led Public Housing Spree," *Plain Dealer,* February 29, 1972, p. 5A.

Sabol, John. "Suburban Mayors Cool to Public Housing," *Cleveland Press,* June 17, 1970, p. F12.

Sacks, Seymour. *Financing Government in a Metropolitan Area: The Cleveland Experience.* Glencoe, Ill.: Free Press of Glencoe, 1961.

Salling, Mark, and Robert Van Der Velde. *Demographic and Housing Characteristics of Migrants and Non-migrants in the Cleveland SMSA.* Cleveland: NODIS, the Urban Center, Maxine Goodman Levin College of Urban Affairs, Cleveland State University, 1985.

Savas, Emanuel S. *Privatization: The Key to Better Government.* Chatham, N.J.: Chatham House, 1987.

Scheiber, Harry N. *Ohio Canal Era: A Case Study of Government and the Economy, 1820–1861.* Athens: Ohio University Press, 1969.

Schuman, Howard, Charlotte Steeh, and Lawrence Bobo. *Racial Attitudes in America: Trends and Interpretations.* Cambridge, Mass.: Harvard University Press, 1985.

Sego, Michael A., ed. *Politics in the Making: Greater Cleveland.* Cleveland: Cuyahoga Community College, 1967.

Semer, Milton P., et al. "A Review of Federal Subsidized Housing Programs." In *Housing in the Seventies,* 82–144. Washington, D.C.: U.S. Department of Housing and Urban Development, 1976.

Shaw, Archer H. *The Plain Dealer: One Hundred Years in Cleveland.* New York: Knopf, 1942.

Snavley, Charles. *A History of City Government in Cleveland, Ohio.* Westerville, Ohio, 1902.

Soja, Edward W. *Postmodern Geographies: The Reassertion of Space in Critical Social Theory.* London: Verso, 1989.

Squire, Richard J. *Historical Guide to Greater Cleveland*. Bedford, Ohio: Lincoln Press, 1964.

Stainer, Harry. "Consumers' Counsel Assails Utility Profits." *Cleveland Plain Dealer*, August 10, 1989, pp. 1C, 6C.

State, ex rel. Schulman v. *Tegreene*, 55 Ohio St. 2d 22, 377 N.E. 2d, 1988.

Stecher, Robert M. *City Hospital, 1889–1960: A Page from the History of Cleveland Metropolitan General Hospital*. Cleveland: Medical Library Association, 1963.

Stokes, Carl B. *Promises of Power: A Political Autobiography*. New York: Simon and Schuster, 1973.

Storper, Michael, and Richard Walker. *The Capitalist Imperative: Territory, Technology, and Industrial Growth*. Oxford: Basil Blackwell, 1989.

Sussman, Marvin B., and R. Clyde White. *Hough, Cleveland, Ohio: A Study of Social Life and Change*. Cleveland: Press of Western Reserve University, 1959.

Swanstrom, Todd. *The Crisis of Growth Politics: Cleveland, Kucinich, and the Challenge of Urban Populism*. Philadelphia: Temple University Press, 1985.

Sweet, David, and Kathryn W. Hexter. *Public Utilities: Rights and Responsibilities*. New York: Praeger, 1987.

Taylor, Henry. "Social Transformation Theory, African Americans, and the Rise of Buffalo's Post Industrial City." *Buffalo Law Review* 39 (Spring 1991): 569–606.

Thompson, Al. "Muny Vote Called a Rebuke to CEI," *Cleveland Press*, February 28, 1979, p. 10.

Tittle, Diana. *Rebuilding Cleveland*. Columbus: Ohio State University Press, 1992.

Toman, Jim. *Cleveland's Changing Skyline*. Cleveland: Cleveland Landmark Press, 1984.

Townes, W. "Light Rate to be Cut if Issue Wins," *Cleveland Press*, December 20, 1938, pp. 1, 14.

U.S. Bureau of the Census. Census of Population. Washington, D.C.: U.S. Government Printing Office.

U.S. Works Progress Administration in Ohio. "Annals of Cleveland, 1818–1935: A Digest and Index of the Newspaper Record of Events and Opinions." Multigraphed by the Cleveland WPA Project 16823. Cleveland, Ohio, 1938.

Van Tassel, David D., and John J. Grabowski, eds. *The Encyclopedia of Cleveland History*. Bloomington: Indiana University Press, 1987.

Vincent, Sidney Z. *Merging Traditions: Jewish Life in Cleveland, A Contemporary Narrative, 1945–1975. A Pictorial Ohio Record, 1839–1975*. Cleveland: Western Reserve Historical Society, 1978.

Wacquant, Lois J. D., and William J. Wilson. "The Cost of Racial and Class Exclusion in the Inner City." *Annals of the American Academy of Political and Social Science* 501 (1989): 8–26.

Warner, Sam Bass. *The Private City: Philadelphia in Three Periods of Its Growth*. Philadelphia: University of Pennsylvania Press, 1968.

Weiner, Ronald. "The New Industrial Metropolis: 1860–1929." In *The Encyclopedia of Cleveland History*, edited by David Van Tassel and John J. Grabowski, xxix–xliii. Bloomington: Indiana University Press, 1987.

Western Reserve Historical Society. *Original Plan of the Town and Village of Cleveland, Ohio, October 1, 1796*.

Wheeler, Robert A. "*. . . Pleasantly Situated on the West Side . . . .*" Cleveland: Western Reserve Historical Society, 1980.

Whelan, Ned. *Cleveland: Shaping the Vision; a Contemporary Portrait.* Chatsworth, Calif.: Windsor Publications, 1989.

Whittlesey, Charles. *Early History of Cleveland, Ohio.* Cleveland: Fairbanks, Benedict & Co., 1867.

Wilson, William J. *The Truly Disadvantaged: The Inner City, the Underclass, and Public Policy.* Chicago: University of Chicago Press, 1987.

Wise, P. H., and A. Meyers. "Poverty and Child Health." *The Pediatric Clinics of North America* 35 (1988): 1169–86.

Wright, Howell. *Cleveland's Municipal Electric Light Plant or Municipal Government in the Electric Light and Power Business.* Chicago: Utilities Publication Company, 1930.

Index

CLEVELAND
A Metropolitan Reader
was composed in 10/13 Linotype-Hell Palatino
on a Gateway 2000 PC using PageMaker 5.0 for Windows
at The Kent State University Press;
imaged to film from application files,
printed by sheet-fed offset on 60-pound Domtar acid-free stock,
notch adhesive bound with paper covers
printed in two colors on 12-point C1S stock
and finished with film lamination
by Braun-Brumfield, Inc.;
designed by Will Underwood;
and published by
The Kent State University Press
KENT, OHIO 44242

4.0 × 3.0 = 12
4.0 × 3.0 = 12
3.0 × 4.0 = 12
3.0 × 4.0 = 12

48 ÷ 14 = 3.42
4.00
÷ 2
3.71